ANALECTA

OR

MATERIALS

FOR A

HISTORY OF REMARKABLE PROVIDENCES;

MOSTLY RELATING TO

SCOTCH MINISTERS AND CHRISTIANS.

BY

THE REV. ROBERT WODROW,

MINISTER OF THE GOSPEL AT EASTWOOD.

VOLUME FOURTH.

PRINTED FOR THE MAITLAND CLUB.

M.DCCC.XLIII.

THE MAITLAND CLUB,

APRIL, M.DCCC.XLIII.

THE RIGHT HONOURABLE

THE EARL OF GLASGOW,

𝔓𝔯𝔢𝔰𝔦𝔡𝔢𝔫𝔱.

HIS ROYAL HIGHNESS THE DUKE OF SUSSEX.

HIS GRACE THE DUKE OF ARGYLL.

JOHN BAIN, ESQ.

DAVID BALFOUR, ESQ.

SIR DAVID HUNTER BLAIR, BART.

BERIAH BOTFIELD, ESQ., M.P.

SIR THOMAS MAKDOUGALL BRISBANE, BART., G.C.B.

HIS GRACE THE DUKE OF BUCCLEUCH AND QUEENS-
BERRY.

10 JAMES BOGLE, ESQ.

WALTER BUCHANAN, ESQ.

THE MOST NOBLE THE MARQUESS OF BUTE.

ALEXANDER CAMPBELL, ESQ.

SIR ARCHIBALD CAMPBELL, BART.

THE HONOURABLE HENRY COCKBURN, LORD COCKBURN.

JAMES T. GIBSON-CRAIG, ESQ.

THE MAITLAND CLUB.

WILLIAM CRAWFURD, ESQ.

JAMES DENNISTOUN, ESQ.

JAMES DOBIE, ESQ.

20 RICHARD DUNCAN, ESQ., [TREASURER.]

WILLIAM JAMES DUNCAN, ESQ.

JAMES DUNLOP, ESQ.

JAMES EWING, ESQ., LL.D.

JOSEPH WALTER KING EYTON, ESQ.

WILLIAM FLEMING, D.D.

WILLIAM MALCOLM FLEMING, ESQ.

JOHN FULLARTON, ESQ.

JOHN GRAHAM GILBERT, ESQ.

JOHN GORDON, ESQ.

30 JOHN BLACK GRACIE, ESQ.

THE RIGHT HONOURABLE THOMAS GRENVILLE.

JAMES HAMILTON, ESQ.

LAURENCE HILL, ESQ., LL.B.

GEORGE HOUSTOUN, ESQ.

JAMES HUNTER, ESQ.

THE HONOURABLE JAMES IVORY, LORD IVORY.

JOHN CLARK KENNEDY, ESQ.

JOHN KERR, ESQ.

ROBERT ALEXANDER KIDSTON, ESQ.

40 GEORGE RITCHIE KINLOCH, ESQ.

JOHN GARDINER KINNEAR, ESQ.

JOHN LEADBETTER, ESQ.

MATTHEW LEISHMAN, D.D.

JOHN GIBSON LOCKHART, ESQ., LL.D.

REV. LAURENCE LOCKHART.

THE MAITLAND CLUB.

WILLIAM LOCKHART, ESQ., M.P.
JAMES LUCAS, ESQ.
ALEXANDER MACDONALD, ESQ.
THE VERY REV. DUNCAN MACFARLAN, D.D., [VICE-PRE-
    SIDENT.]
50 ANDREW MACGEORGE, ESQ.
ALEXANDER MACGRIGOR, ESQ.
GEORGE MACINTOSH, ESQ.
JOHN WHITEFOORD MACKENZIE, ESQ.
ROBERT MACLACHLAN, ESQ.
ARCHIBALD MACLELLAN, ESQ.
ALEXANDER MACNEILL, ESQ.
JAMES MAIDMENT, ESQ.
THOMAS MAITLAND, ESQ.
JOHN MAXWELL, ESQ.
60 WELLWOOD MAXWELL, ESQ.
WILLIAM MEIKLEHAM, ESQ.
WILLIAM HENRY MILLER, ESQ.
ROBERT MONTEITH, ESQ.
JAMES PATRICK MUIRHEAD, ESQ.
WILLIAM MURE, ESQ.
WILLIAM SMITH NEIL, ESQ.
ALEXANDER OSWALD, ESQ.
JOHN MACMICHAN PAGAN, ESQ., M.D.
WILLIAM PATRICK, ESQ.
70 HENRY PAUL, ESQ.
EDWARD PIPER, ESQ.
ROBERT PITCAIRN, ESQ.
JAMES CORBETT PORTERFIELD, ESQ.

THE MAITLAND CLUB.

HAMILTON PYPER, ESQ.

THE QUÆSTOR OF THE LIBRARY OF THE UNIVERSITY OF GLASGOW.

PHILIP ANSTRUTHER RAMSAY, ESQ.

JAMES CAMPBELL REDDIE, ESQ.

JOHN RICHARDSON, ESQ., LL.B.

THOMAS RISK, ESQ.

80 WILLIAM ROBERTSON, ESQ.

ROBERT RODGER, ESQ.

ANDREW RUTHERFURD, ESQ., M.P.

JAMES SMITH, ESQ.

JOHN SMITH, ESQ., LL.D., [SECRETARY.]

WILLIAM SMITH, ESQ.

WILLIAM SMYTHE, ESQ.

MOSES STEVEN, ESQ.

DUNCAN STEWART, ESQ.

ARCHIBALD SWINTON, ESQ.

90 SYLVESTER DOUGLAS STIRLING, ESQ.

WILLIAM STIRLING, ESQ.

WILLIAM STIRLING, ESQ., YR.

JOHN STRANG, ESQ.

THOMAS THOMSON, ESQ.

WILLIAM B. D. D. TURNBULL, ESQ.

DAWSON TURNER, ESQ.

ADAM URQUHART, ESQ.

PATRICK WARNER, ESQ.

PREFATORY NOTICE.

THE ANALECTA, now presented to the MAITLAND CLUB, through the munificence of the EARL OF GLASGOW, are the private *memoranda*, or rough notes, of the Rev. ROBERT WODROW, who was Minister of the parish of Eastwood, in the county of Renfrew, and is well known as the author of the " History of the Sufferings of the Church of Scotland, from the Restoration to the Revolution." His father, James Wodrow, was installed Professor of Divinity in the University of Glasgow, on the 9th of March 1692, and continued to discharge the duties of that important and honourable office till the period of his death, on the 25th of September 1707. The great-grandfather of the Professor was Patrick Wodrow, who, previous to the Reformation, was Vicar of Eaglesham, in the neighbourhood of Glasgow, but who, subsequently, abandoned the pale of the Church of Rome.*

* Life of Professor Wodrow, written by his son, and published, from the original MS., by the late Rev. Dr Campbell of Edinburgh, pp. 6, 115, 118, 182. Edin. 1828.

Robert Wodrow was born at Glasgow, in the year 1679. It is uncertain, as he informs us himself, in what month of that year this event took place; but when alluding to it, in his Life of his father, he mentions an occurrence which happened at the time, and which, as connected with the history of the family, and with the violent persecution which was then carried on throughout the country, may be supposed to have made a deep impression on his mind, from his earliest years, and tended to call forth the strong sympathy evinced by him in the fiery trials of his unhappy countrymen. His father was, at this period, denounced, like many others, as a field preacher, and obliged, on that account, to remain in concealment. His mother, believing herself to be dying, had expressed a wish to see her husband, that she might take a final leave of him. A notice to this effect was conveyed to old Wodrow. Accordingly, as soon as the evening was sufficiently advanced to warrant the hope that he might not be observed, he went to his own house, after having disguised his person in the best way he was able. On passing " the guard-house in the Trongate," however, he was unfortunately recognized. A party immediately followed to apprehend him. After searching all the other rooms of the house, they were only restrained by delicacy from entering the apartment in which Mrs Wodrow was, and to which Mr Wodrow had, on his arrival, immediately proceeded.

The officer who commanded the party left the house for

about an hour ; but, before doing so, he caused every door and window to be carefully guarded. At this critical juncture, Dr Davidson, a medical gentleman, made his appearance, who brought along with him " a man-servant, with a lantern carrying before him, it being now night ; and the soldiers allowed him to go in, with his servant, when he told them his errand." Dr Davidson had been sent for on Mrs Wodrow's account. The family must, in such circumstances, have been in a state of extreme excitement and alarm. The reader may conceive their feelings, when he is told, that during this anxious interval the future chronicler of the Sufferings of the Scottish Church first saw the light. The next thing to be considered was, how to provide for the safety of his father :

" A method offered to the Doctor," says Robert Wodrow himself, " which proved effectual, through God's goodness, for his escape ; and he proposed that my father should change coats with his servant—a pretty large man—and put on his bonnet, and briskly take up the lantern, and go out before his new master, with all the assurance he was master of. The thing took ; and the soldiers having seen the Doctor come in, just now, with a servant, when he went off, let him pass without observing the matter. In a quarter of an hour or thereby, the captain returned, and searched the whole house, and my mother's room, with the greatest care, so that they stugged with their swords the very bed my mother was lying on, jealousing he might be concealed there. My mother was now easy, do as they would, and told them, with much cheerfulness, the bird was flown, and they needed give themselves no further trouble, for he was out of their hands, and not in that house. At length they gave over, being convinced she told them the truth."*

* Life of Professor Wodrow, pp. 61-64.

In the year 1695, Robert Wodrow entered upon the study of theology, under the superintendence of his father, in the University of Glasgow; and for two successive years, during the College recess, he acted as domestic tutor in the family of his relative, Sir John Maxwell of Pollock, one of the Senators of the College of Justice. He was then appointed Librarian to the University. This office was filled by him for six years.[*] After undergoing the requisite trials in the Presbytery of Paisley, he became a licentiate of the Church, in March 1703. On the 28th of October, in the same year, he was ordained Minister of Eastwood, having succeeded, as pastor of that parish, the Rev. Matthew Crawford, a pious and laborious clergyman, who left behind him, in two folio volumes, a MS. History of the Church of Scotland,[†] which is still unpublished, though it is now in the Library of the Church.

---

[*] Life of Professor Wodrow, p. 116.

[†] Crawford's History of Renfrewshire, p. 35. Paisley, 1818. " After King James' death, Mr Crawford is very short, till the 1637; and from thence, to the lamentable division 1650, he gives a very distinct and large account of matters, which I heartily wish had been long since published." (Original Letter of Robert Wodrow, in Dr Burns' edition of Wodrow's History, Vol. I. p. xx.) The Synod of Glasgow and Ayr, as appears from the following extract from their Minutes, of date 7th October 1701, had resolved, at a very early period, to take steps for the publication of Crawford's History :—" The Synod recommends to the Principall of Glasgow, the Professor, [James Wodrow,] Mrs James and David Brown, Mr Patrick Simpsone, Mr Robert Mure, and Mr John Orr, and John Alexander of Blackhouse, Ruleing Elder, To meet att Glasgow the first tuesday of November, and consider upon most proper expedients for getting Mr Matthew Crawford's historie accurately printed, and afterward to appoint their own dyets."

Natural history seems to have engaged a considerable share of the attention of Wodrow, both before and after his induction at Eastwood. Mr George Crawford, author of the Peerage of Scotland, describes him as his " very worthy friend," and " a gentleman well seen in the curious natural products of the country."* And, in a letter addressed to Mr Edward Lhuyd, keeper of the Ashmolean Museum at Oxford, and dated Eastwood, August 26, 1709, Wodrow says—" My lot is, by Providence, cast in the parish of Eastwood, and my house within a quarter of a mile from the Aldhouse Bourn, where you and I were a lithoscoping."†

His Correspondence, which is now in course of publication by the Wodrow Society, shows the high estimation in which he was held by many of the most distinguished men of his day. It likewise furnishes abundant proof of the extraordinary activity of his mind; of the interest which he took in every subject connected with science or general literature; and of the zeal and fidelity with which he devoted himself to the discharge of the more immediate duties of his sacred profession.

In his " History of the Early Part of the Reign of James the Second," Charles James Fox bears honourable testimony

* Crawford's History of Renfrewshire, *ut supra*, first published in 1710.
† Wodrow Correspondence, Vol. I. p. 33.

to the character of Wodrow as an historian. He mentions an interesting anecdote of the unfortunate Earl of Argyle, and then refers to Wodrow, as vouching for the truth of it, " whose veracity," he adds, " is above suspicion."* Elsewhere he says— " To recite all the instances of cruelty which occurred," at this period, in Scotland, " would be endless; but it may be necessary to remark, that no historical facts are better ascertained than the accounts of them to be found in Wodrow. In every instance where there has been an opportunity of comparing these accounts with the records, and other authentic muniments, they appear to be quite correct."†

The present volumes contain the materials for a Work, which the Author appears to have contemplated from an early period of his life. He received the first hint of it from his father, who, not long before his death, lamented to him that no particular account had been given, by any one, of the " remarkable providences and appearances in this Church." He, therefore, " advised me," says Wodrow, " in my youth to set down what I happened to hear from good hands, and well attested, of this kind. Which advice I have, in part, followed."‡ Much of the information collected in this way was afterwards embodied by him in his manuscript " Collections upon the Lives of the Re-

---

* P. 208.   † Pp. 131, 132.   ‡ Life of Professor Wodrow, p. 4.

formers and most Eminent Ministers of the Church of Scotland," which are now in the Library of the University of Glasgow, and from which some selections were published by the Maitland Club in 1834.

The future historian, so far, at least, as he may be desirous to illustrate the ecclesiastical affairs of Scotland, will be greatly aided in his researches by the light which, in different parts of the Analecta, is thrown upon the characters and actions of many eminent men, and the causes of events. It extends over a most important period in the history of Scotland, commencing in 1701, and terminating in 1731. In what is stated by the Author, under the date of January 1728,[*] an apology will be found for defects of style, mistakes, repetitions, or the consequence that may seem to be attached to matters of little moment or trifling interest. He says there, that he does not pledge himself for the truth of many things which he has mentioned; that he gives them simply on the authority of his informers; and that they were written down at the time he heard them, principally with a view to aid his own memory, or for the use of his children. This will even go far to vindicate him from the charge of excessive credulity, to which it will be imagined he has, on various occasions, subjected himself.

[*] Vol. III. p. 470.

There can be no doubt, however, that Wodrow believed in the prevalence of witchcraft in his day, and in the reality of spectral appearances. This may be discovered even in his History; but he can hardly be said to have been, in this respect, a greater slave to his superstitious notions than many of those who, in that age, and in both parts of the island, were most distinguished by their rank or their learning. In the year 1685, a book was published by George Sinclair, Professor of Philosophy in the University of Glasgow, having for its title, " Satan's Invisible World Discovered, or a Choice Collection of Relations anent Devils, Spirits, Witches, and Apparitions." In the Preface, the Author speaks of those whose " thick and plumbeous capacities cannot conceive" the strange things which he relates; and he pronounces King James' Dialogues on *Dæmonologie* to be " a piece as far beyond all other men's writings, as himself was beyond all princes in his time." The first Relation which Professor Sinclair gives in his book, is the case of Sir George Maxwell of Pollock. It was supposed that his death was caused by the diabolical arts of five witches and a wizard, all of whom, after a solemn trial at Paisley, were found guilty, and, with the exception of one of them, who obtained a respite, on account of her youth, condemned to be burned. The particulars of this trial, along with a minute account of the machinations and judicial confessions of the supposed culprits, are gravely detailed in a letter which was sent to Professor Sinclair, and which was written by the Lord Justice-Clerk, who was the son of Sir George Maxwell, and the friend and patron of Robert Wodrow.

Sir George Mackenzie of Rosehaugh, King's Advocate in the reigns of Charles II. and of his successor, has a long chapter on witchcraft in his " Laws and Customs of Scotland in Matters Criminal." Besides discussing various other equally important points, Sir George descants on " the devil's mark," which is given, he says, as some allege, " by a nip in any part of the body ;" adding, with scrupulous accuracy, to prevent all mistakes, that " it is blue"! Others, moreover, he tells us, affirm that this mark " is sometimes like the impression of a hare's foot, or the foot of a rat or spider." He is equally learned upon the mode in which witches " raise storms in the air," and " torment mankind by making images of clay or wax !"*

It is clear, that Lord Fountainhall was not in the humour, any more than Sir George Mackenzie, " that noble wit of Scotland," as Dryden was pleased to style him, to treat with disrespect the insane pretensions of certain old women, or to run any risk of offending them. For we find, in a work of his, the following passage :—" Of the presumption, minarum præceden-

* Pp. 91, 100, 103. Edin. 1678.

tium et damni secuti, see the criminal lawyers, requiring they be, malæ famæ, and such, qui minas exequi soliti sunt; and the foresaid præsumption of damnum minas subsequens takes mainly place in malefices committed by witches."*

Many of the Covenanters, it is well known, were firmly persuaded that Archbishop Sharp had a familiar, whom he was accustomed to consult. But Dr Hickes, who was afterwards Dean of Worcester, took his revenge by charging Major Weir with sorcery. In his Ravillac Redivivus,† he tells a story of the said Major getting access to the house of a gentlewoman in Edinburgh, nobody knew how; assuring his friend to whom he writes, that when the lady screamed, the Major " immediately disappeared," though " the windows and doors were all close shut." Hickes makes " little doubt but his coachman to the fiery coach conveyed him in and out, through the chimney, or, perhaps, by the door, which the cursed familiar might open and shut again."

In the year 1720, Lord Torphichen was led to believe that his third son, Patrick, was bewitched. He, therefore, caused his tormentors to be seized. The minister of the parish, as

* Lord Fountainhall's Historical Observes of Memorable Occurrents in Church and State, from October 1680, to April 1686, p. 25. Edin. 1840. Printed by the Bannatyne Club.   † Pp. 67, 68.

well as others, caught the infection. A fast was proclaimed, and a sermon was preached on the occasion, which was afterwards published, by the desire of Lord Torphichen.*

Dr Hutchinson was of opinion that the Church of England and its clergy had comparatively little to answer for in giving countenance to the prejudices of the common people regarding witchcraft. This, perhaps, may be true. Nevertheless, he admits, that, in the famous trial of Jane Wenham of Walkern, in Hertfordshire, in the year 1712, some of the English clergy, "though otherwise men of no ill character, were so weak as to try charms, and give way to scratching, and promote the prosecution."† And when speaking of the rapidity with which supposed witches multiplied in some parts of England, Dr Samuel Johnson quotes the saying of Bishop Hall, that he knew a village in Lancashire, where their number was greater than that of the houses.‡

It is melancholy to think that the masculine mind of such a man as Sir Matthew Hale, Lord Chief-Justice of England, was not proof against the prevalent frenzy. A trial took place at Bury St Edmunds, in Suffolk, in the year 1664, at which he presided. The accused were two women, whose names were

* Law's Mem. Pref. Not. p. civ.
† Historical Essay concerning Witchcraft; see Dedication. London. 1720.
‡ Johnson's Works—Observations on the Tragedy of Macbeth, vol. ii. p. 64. Lond. 1816.

Amy Duny and Rose Cullender. No fewer than thirteen different indictments were laid against them. Sir Thomas Brown of Norwich, the famous physician, was in court, and having heard the evidence, was called upon for his opinion. When thus interrogated, he declared it to be his firm conviction, " that the fits were natural, but heightened, by the devil co-operating with the malice of the witches, at whose instance he did the villanies." Such a strong and unequivocal declaration as this could not fail to influence the minds of the jury. The two unfortunate women, therefore, were found guilty, and immediately ordered for execution, although the Lord Chief-Justice, who, during the whole trial, was in a state of the utmost perplexity, had declined even to sum up the evidence, praying only, " that the great God of heaven would direct their hearts in that weighty matter."*

It was not, indeed, till near the middle of the last century, that a bill was brought into the House of Commons, which was afterwards passed into a law, repealing the former statutes against witchcraft, and declaring, that no prosecution shall for the future be carried on against any persons for conjuration, witchcraft, sorcery, or enchantment.†

---

* Hutchinson's Hist. Ess. concerning Witchcraft, pp. 139-157.

† 9th George II. c. 5. Judge Blackstone, when quoting this Act, very cautiously remarks, that " the ridiculous stories that are generally told, and the many impostors and delusions that have been discovered in all ages, are enough to demolish all faith in such a dubious crime, *if the contrary evidence were not also extremely strong.*"—(*Commentaries on the Laws of England*, vol. iv. p. 61.)

We do not say, however, that with the abrogation of the ancient laws against witchcraft, all belief has vanished from among us in the exercise of preternatural power, by crazed beldams or others. The disgraceful scenes that were enacted near Boughton, in East Kent, in the year 1838, by the *soi-disant* Sir William Courtenay and his fanatical followers, forbid us to cherish any such idea. After the death of their leader, the peasantry of Kent expressed their confident expectation that he would come to life again on the third, or on the seventh day. Nor is it, we find, among the uninformed portion of the community only that such superstitious fancies are still continuing to linger, and to exert an unhappy influence. We have a proof of this, in what an English nobleman, the Earl of Shrewsbury, has recently written regarding " the Holy Virgins of the Tyrol." His Lordship finds no difficulty in believing that " blood flows upward ;" that the sheets upon which the Addolorata reposes, " and upon which so much blood flows every week, from so many wounds, are not stained with the least drop ;" that though the sheets of her bed " have never been changed for five years, they are still [1839] perfectly clean ;" and that " a person lived without food for twenty years in perfect health and strength."*

* See " A Letter from the Earl of Shrewsbury to Ambrose Lisle Philips, Esq., descriptive of the Estatica of Caldaro, and the Addolorata of Capriana, being a second edition, revised and enlarged ; to which is added the Relation of Three successive Visits to the Estatica of Monte Sansavino, in May 1842." Lond. C. Dolman, 61, Bond St.

But, perhaps, a still more remarkable instance of superstitious credulity, taking into consideration the character or avowed principles of the person, is that of the late Lord Byron. That celebrated nobleman, unhappily for himself and for others, made light of the prophecies of Scripture, and did not admit the reality of the miracles wrought by our Saviour ; yet, with strange perversity and inconsistency, as we learn from his biographers, did he, down to the close of his life, attach importance to the predictions of a *spaewife*. He was, likewise, it would appear, a believer in *wraiths*. " It was about this time," says his biographer, Mr Thomas Moore, " that Mr Cowel, paying a visit to Lord Byron at Genoa, was told by him, that some friends of Mr Shelley, sitting together one evening, had seen that gentleman, distinctly, as they thought, walk into a little wood at Lerici, when at the same moment, as they afterwards discovered, he was far away in quite a different direction. ' This,' added Lord Byron, *in a low, awe-struck tone of voice,* ' was but ten days before poor Shelley died.' "*

Such extraordinary aberrations of the human mind, when displayed by persons who might have been expected, from their education, or talents, or station in society, to be raised above the influence of vulgar prejudices, can hardly be contemplated by any one without pain, and without a feeling of personal hu-

* Works of Lord Byron, edited by Thomas Moore, Esq., vol. v. p. 365. Lond. 1832.

miliation. They are adverted to, however, simply for the purpose of guarding honest Wodrow from unthinking ridicule, by showing that an instinctive love of the marvellous, or a tendency to superstition, is not the exclusive characteristic of any particular class or order of men.

In the " Memorabilia of the City of Glasgow, selected from the Minute Books of the Burgh," there is the following entry : " 10 January 1712. Call subscribed to Mr Robert Woddrow, minister of Eastwood, to be minister of the South Quarter." This invitation to Wodrow to accept the pastoral charge of one of the churches of Glasgow was honourable to him, as proceeding from those who were necessarily well acquainted with his professional qualifications, and the assiduous and faithful manner in which he laboured to promote the highest interests of the parishioners of Eastwood. It does not appear, however, to have been sought for by himself, or even wished. Lord Pollock was likewise averse to his leaving Eastwood. Although the Provost and Magistrates, therefore, appealed against the decision of the Synod, who, by a majority, declared it was not expedient to translate Wodrow to Glasgow, contrary to his own inclinations, the appeal, in consequence of the personal interference of Lord Pollock,* was afterwards abandoned.

The people of Stirling were likewise desirous to secure to

* Wodrow Correspondence, vol. i. pp. 287, 288.

themselves the benefit of his ministerial services. He was earnestly solicited to undertake the cure of their souls in 1717, and likewise in 1726. But he was too strongly attached to his flock to consent to leave them. He died in his fifty-fifth year, on the 21st of March 1734.

The numerous unpublished MSS. which he left behind him, have justly earned for him the name of the indefatigable Wodrow. A large portion of these, including the Analecta, were, in the year 1828, safely lodged in the Library of the Faculty of Advocates, through the active and zealous agency of his able biographer, the Rev. Dr Burns of Paisley. The account which Dr Burns has given, in a letter to the writer, of the discovery of what he justly considered to be a valuable literary treasure, is this:—

" It was in 1825, when residing for a short time in the parish of Stevenston, my attention was called to the probable existence of important MSS. belonging to the Collections made by Wodrow, and still in the possession of the friends and descendants of that most indefatigable collector of the records of our Church. The perusal of his biographical account of his father, Professor James Wodrow of Glasgow, since published under the superintendence of Principal Lee, stimulated my inquiries. With the valuable aid of Miss Wodrow, granddaughter of the historian, who had a good many MSS. in her own possession, and who gave me useful hints as to the probable resting-places of others, I succeeded, partly by domiciliary visits to garrets, and other repositories, where these exuviæ had remained for a series of years undisturbed, and partly by correspondence with surviving relatives of the historian, in unkennelling from the dust of years some four-score volumes of various sizes, and almost all in excellent preservation.

Of these, one half comprises chiefly Lectures, Sermons, Homilies, and other compositions of a similar class, by the father of the historian, the historian himself, his brother Alexander, several of the worthies of the Covenanting age, and many of the Theological Students under Professor Wodrow, from 1690 to 1707. Several of these volumes are in my possession ; others remain where I found them, and a considerable number belong to Miss Wodrow at Saltcoats. These MSS., however interesting in other respects, were not considered of sufficient importance or value to attract the attention of the Curators of the Advocates' Library. I shall assuredly do all I can to obtain for them a place on the shelves of the ' Library of the Church of Scotland.'

" Of the remaining forty volumes, which were transferred by me in June 1828, (with consent of parties,) to the repositories of the Advocates' Library, the larger part consists of copies of Wodrow's Letters *to* his correspondents, and the letters *from* these correspondents, in their original form. Of the first of these classes, one volume is still wanting to complete the set. Of the second class, the series is complete. Selections from both of these collections are at present in the process of printing by the Wodrow Society, under the inspection of a most competent Editor, Professor M'Crie.

" Of the other volumes, several are of a miscellaneous description ; and six embrace the Analecta. Wodrow's object, in these Analecta, seems to have been to put down the various incidents in his life, with remarks on matters and things in general; thus forming, in some sort, the materials of autobiography. From a man whose observant eye allowed nothing to pass unnoticed, a singularly varied melange was thus to be expected."

In the year 1839, the Rev. David Landsborough, the present worthy incumbent of the parish of Stevenston, and the successor of the Rev. Dr James Wodrow, the youngest son of the historian, was fortunate enough to rescue from obscurity, in the Island of Cumbrae, a small MS. volume, which has obtained the name of Wodrow's Diary. The eldest son of Robert Wodrow, after resigning his parochial charge, resided some time in the Little Cumbrae, and died there. In this way, the Diary came into the possession of the late parochial schoolmaster, whose widow gave it to one of the elders of the parish, from whom Mr Landsborough received it. It was soon afterwards deposited, by Mr Landsborough, in the hands of Robert Wodrow, Esq., the great-grandson of the historian, who has kindly favoured the writer with the use of it.

The handwriting is evidently that of the author of the Analecta. An additional proof of the authenticity of this interesting little volume, were this necessary, might be pointed out in the following "Memorandum," which is written upon the first page :—" That ye Transaction between Mr John Simson, and Mr Rob'. Wodrow, as to ye Library, was wt ys expresse proviso, yt ye Sellary should be equally divided betwixt them. In testimony of our mutuall agrement to ys, we have subscribed wt our hands, at glasgow, the twenty and eight day of July, jai. vi. nynty and eight years.   "J. S.
                                                   " R. W."

The book is of the 18mo size, but closely written, and bound in vellum. In addition to the Diary, which extends to sixty-three pages, it contains a catalogue of the books acquired by the author previous to the month of July 1703. These must have formed a valuable private collection. They are arranged under different heads, viz. Divinity, Philosophy, Philology, Sacred and Profane History, and Miscellany Books.

The first entry in the Diary is dated April 3, 1697, when Wodrow could not be more than nineteen years of age; and the last is under February 26, 1701. The various matters which are recorded, are indicative of the same ardent and inquisitive mind for which the Author was distinguished in the course of his subsequent life. They comprehend some simple chemical experiments, observations with the microscope, cures for some common diseases, memorable interferences of Divine Providence, meteorological observations, interesting anecdotes, &c. They are not of so much value as to warrant the enlargement of the present Work, by the insertion of the whole of them. It has been thought, however, that the following extracts from the Diary may not prove uninteresting, and that they may be viewed as forming an introduction to the Analecta, not altogether inappropriate.

" *May* 17, [1697.]—That the reasons of the curats in the North ther standing out were 2 fold. 1. The divisions in the first parliament, that gave hopes to fish in muddy waters. 2dly, The examination of some of them; and the processes wer strict, and discovered them. Therfor, the rest resolved to stand together in a body, and seek help from England. But the Bishops there are of 2 factions; the one holding, that wee Churchmen should [not] at all stand out against the civil government, any wher. Of this, the two archbishops, and the greater part of the rest are, so that our Scots Commissionaries did but come little speed.

The other party are for mentening the hyararchy against all opposers; they favoured our Scots Commissioners, but, being weak themselves, did not much good."

" *June* 10.—This day the witches wer execute at Paisley, wher 2 of them solemnly protested innocency; and one of them, Easmith, [Neasmith,] impricated God's curse on us all. The first 6 dyed impenitently. But ther seemed to be odd contradictions in the case of the seventh, Marg. Lang. Shee, after prayer at the stake foot, which few or none heard, went up on the stool, and began rhetorically thus :—It's neither seemly or fit that a woman should speak in publick; but my case is extraordinary, therefore I hope I may be allowed. As to this sin of mine laid to my charge, I confesse that when I was young, after I had committed the unnaturall sin, the divil appeared to me, as a gentleman on horsback, and desired me to give up myself to his service, which 1 did, through the terror on me at that time, and the conscience I had of the great guilt of my late sin, and I durst never forsake this again for fear. But as to what was said befor the Lords at Edinburgh, that I renounced my baptism in Balgarran yeard, and entered into a new covenant with the divil, and gote the mark, this I absolutely deny. Then she prayed for Balgarran's family, that God would deliver that damsell from the power and works of the divil; then for her own family, particularly for her piouse and godly good-man. Then she prayed for the prospering of the interest of Christ, and the sending of the power with the Gospell, for strenth to the ministers. Then she fell on confessing her sins, as ignorance, foality, slighting God's offers of Christ, (but not a word of witchcraft.) This she closed with, that there was nae sin but shee was guilty of. Then she began to lament the impenitency of the rest; and said, it was sad to see so many goe carelessly to death. Then she exorted all young persons to bewar of all sin, especially scandalouse and lusfull. Then shee added, Lord, I cannot weel tell what to think of my own case. Sometimes I have fears, because of my sad sins; sometimes I desire to hope. However, I'll walk through this dark step of death by faith and dependance on Jesus Christ. After this, the 2d time shee prayed for the prosperity of the Church, and power of the Gospell, and in this shee dyed. Mr [James] Hutcheson [Minister of Killallan] told me, that at that time she spoke not as she used to do, (which was like an angell's,) before this ; yet she seemed to me to be pretty fervent."*

* There is an instance of the Privy Council of Scotland, after the Restoration, granting at one sederunt fourteen separate commissions to take trials of witches.—(*Hugo Arnot's Criminal Trials*, p. 366.) On the 19th of January 1697, a warrant was issued by the Privy Council to Lord Blantyre, Sir John Maxwell of Pollok, Sir John Shaw of Greenock, William Cunningham of Craigends, Alexander Porterfield of Duchall, and others, to examine and imprison persons suspected of witchcraft, in the case of Christian Shaw, daughter of John Shaw of Bargarran, in the parish of Erskine, and county of Renfrew. On the 9th of March, these commissioners reported, that there were not fewer than twenty-four persons accused and suspected of witchcraft, in the case which they had been appointed to investigate. A new warrant was therefore issued by the Council, appointing most of the commissioners formerly named, along with Lord Hall-craig, Mr Francis Montgomery of Giffin, Sir John Houston of that Ilk, Mr John Kin-caid of Crosbasket, Advocate, and Mr John Stewart, younger of Blackhall, Advocate, " to meet at Renfrew, Paisley, or Glasgow, to take trial of, judge, and do justice upon the foresaid persons ; and to sentence the guilty to be burned, or otherwise executed to death, as the commissioners should incline."—(*Id.* pp. 364, 365.) The part which the Synod of Glasgow and Ayr acted in this unhappy business, appears from the follow-ing Minute of their proceedings, dated Irvine, April 6, 1697 :—" The Synod being in-formed by some of the brethren of the Presbytery of Paisley, that a Commission of Jus-ticiarie, from the Privie Councill, is to sitt at Paisley, April 15th instant, for triall of those indicted for witchcraft ; and considering that it is expedient some brethren of the Synod be nominate to joine with the Presbyterie of Paisley, for advice and supervising a narrative and relation, upon occasion of a young gentlewoman, Bargarran's daughter, her being haunted and afflicted by Satan and his instruments, and for advice in other matters incident, competent to ministers, during the sitting of the said Judicatorie,— the Synod nominates the brethren following, Mr John Wilson, Moderator, Mr William Dunlop, Mr Robert Wyllie, Mr John Bannantyne, Mr Patrick Warner, Mr Alexander Orr, Mr James Browne, Mr John Ritchie, Mr John Petticrew, and Mr Thomas Lin-ning, to join with their brethren of the forementioned Presbyterie, to the effect foresaid : And also, if they find expedient, to appoint a Synodal fast upon the account foresaid, and to advertise the brethren thereof in due time." Seven of those who were brought to trial were found guilty by the jury, after remaining in deliberation for six hours, and condemned to the flames. Margaret Lang, who was one of the number, is represented to have been a person of considerable talent, and till now, to have been possessed of an un-blemished reputation. Her employment was that of an *accoucheuse.* Wodrow mentions,

"*June* 27, 1697.—This night Mrs Marion told me, that she heard Secretary Ogilvy say, that when he was in the north, he saw a man

in the course of the present Work, (vol. i. p. 364,) that he learned from the Rev. Andrew Turner, her parish minister, that before she was accused by Christian Shaw, she was " under good repute, and not the least suspected for witchcraft, or any ill, but esteemed a great Christian." She is even said to have made "harangues in her own defence, which neither divine, nor lawyer, could reasonably mend." This was looked upon, however, as one of the strongest proofs of her guilt.—(*History of the Witches of Renfrew-shire*, p. 161.) The Rev. Mr Bell, in his MS. Treatise on Witchcraft, after referring to " the business of the sorceries exercised upon the Laird of Bargarran's daughter, *anno* 1697," describes this, with a degree of bitterness, which may well be excused in the circumstances, to have been "a time, when persons of more goodness and esteem than most of their calumniators were defamed for witches."—(*Law's Memorialls*, Pref. Not. p. xciii.) As to the confessions, which Margaret Lang and her wretched associates are said to have made, a key to these is furnished by Sir George Mackenzie. He candidly declares, " *ex certissima scientia*," that the poor creatures, who, in those days, were charged with their terrible crime, were often deprived of their reason, and thus led to imagine the most ridiculous and absurd things ; and he adds, that most of them were " tortured by their keepers," and that " this usage was the ground of all their confession."—(*Laws and Customs of Scotland in Matters Criminal*, pp. 86, 87.)

Mr Neil Snodgrass, writer in Paisley, was law-agent for Margaret Lang, or some of the other accused parties. To undertake such an office in those days must have required a considerable degree of moral courage. In consequence of the part he acted, Mr Snodgrass brought upon himself some abuse, if not suspicion. He and a Mr William Reid, an apothecary in Paisley, were at variance regarding a stair and boundary-wall of a house, belonging to one or other of them. Some altercation having arisen between them on this subject, Reid told " the said Mr Neille to goe and consult his *master* anent them." A person who was present asked, who was his master? " He knowes," replied Reid, " whos actions he laitly agented. Let him consult him." This sally gave rise to an action for defamation, in connection with which the judgment which follows was pronounced :—" *Paisley*, 24 *Aprile* 1697.—The judge for interloqutor, Finds relevant the pursuer proveing, that he was late procurator or agent for the late pannells in witchcraft, and the defender thereafter, in passion, requyring him to gae consult his master anent the gevills lybelled ; which, when asked quho, he, the defender, told him whose cause he lately was procurator or agent in : Finds, that the word master cannot be ascryved to ane client one or moe, because of this speciall repugnancie, viz., that agents rather consal clients, than clients them ; lykas, clients could not be consulted in gevills ; and sua finds that the forsaid scandalous words, being proven, there that was taken. He lived solitary, in a cave, and drank water and eat raw flesh, and went just naked. He had a language, which was neither Highland nor English, or a mixture of both ; and was understood by none there. That the country people told him there wer several of them there. That the generally proposed overture for civilizing the Highlands, was by establishing schools for the English tounge, and endeavouring to make all speak it. But the Secretary thought the best way for this was to find a way to take their plades from them ; for they use them to ly in, to cary things in, for cloaths, and for what not. Soe these being taken away, they would get other utensils, and soe, by degrees, be civilized."

" *Sept.* 20, 1697.—The best way for loosing, or rather reading, write by numbers, or a key, &c., is by observing the monosillables, as I, o, a, the, this, that ; and the write may be easily solved at lenth. The best way for secrecy in such writing, is to have particular characters for the ordinary monosillables. That the present King's Advocate, in the night time, observed his first wife awaken with a cry, and weeping ; and he asked her what ailed her? O ! sayes shee, I thought my sister Scott was dead, and I saw it. They both remarked the exact time of the night, and they got nottice to-morrow, that at that exact time she dyed. The relator heard the Advocate tell this. Query. If this might not be accidental? she knowing that she was sick, and fearing her death."

" *Oct.* 8, 1697 —That P[rincipa]l C[arstaires,] he heard the K[ing,] (and two other gentlemen heard it also,) say, that he would never agree to ye establishing of any but presbitry in Scotland."

together with the witnesses present, taking and understanding by *master*, the devill, to the best of their knowledge, relevant to inferr the scandall lybelled, and punishment whereof, accordingly, for the fyak, reserving the partie lesed assythment inteir, till ane Sitting Session. (Signed) Ro. Sempill, Ball. Dept.—The pursuer offers to prove the complaint conform to the interloqutor, *per testes.* The defender's procurator protests against interloquitor for coast, skaith, and damage, and remeid in law."—(*Paisley Magazine,* m.dccc.xxxviii. Edited by the late W. Motherwell, Esq.,pp. 154, 155.)

"*Aprile* 9, 1698.—This day,*   told me that he knew his coosin, ye Lord Kincairn, fast 16 days and more, without tasting any thing ; but sometimes once in the two dayes he would have taken a glasse of water. He was first very loose in his walk, and after turned (and yet is) a strict Burignianist.†

" That Poeret's peice on Education had raised great heats in Hamburgh. That Poeret‡ lives a little from Amsterdam, in a large country house, where many come and take chambers ; and he and they live all in common, and serve one another."

"*Feb.* 25, 1699.—The foresaid person told me he was at the execution of the last witches, and with the surgeons that cut the leg of the first, where the mark was, into which the pin§ went so far, as it was said to be, through her leg. They found, and he saw it, that the   run only between the two bones in the leg, the tibia and the other, and was not through them."

"*May* 31, 1699.—This night I was with   ,¶ who told me, that the late Mr Maclaury, minister in   told him, with Mr   , that as to the second sight, he was in the highlands, about 30 miles from Inverary, in an acquaintance' house ; and at 9, [night,] sitting with him in the house, about a pite fire, in midst of converse, he started. So, the said minister asked him what ailed him ? O ! sayes

* The name is in short-hand.

† Madame Antonia Bourignion was a French lady, who published some mystical writings, and pretended to be inspired. Her opinions made some noise in Scotland, and were condemned by an Act of the Church.

‡ *Vide* vol. iii. pp. 472, 473.

§ One of the modes of detecting witches resorted to in those days, was by running pins into particular parts of the body. This operation, both in England and Scotland, was actually reduced to a trade ; the person who followed it being called a pricker. It was believed that the devil's mark, or stigma, took away all feeling from the part of the body on which it was imprinted. The business of the pricker was to find out such a mark, and to test its character, by passing a pin through it, for the purpose of ascertaining whether or not it was devoid of sensibility.—(*Scott's Letters on Demonology and Witchcraft*, p. 297 ; *Pitcairn's Criminal Trials*, vol. iii. pp. 599–602.)

¶ The names are written in short-hand, and cannot be decyphered.

he, I see such a gentleman, whom they both knew, stabbed with a dagger,* in such part, in such a place, and by such a man ; and the said gentleman is killed. The said minister asked him, how he knew it ? He said, he saw it. So he asked him, how he saw it, and how he got that power ? He said he knew not ; but said he had it ever since he was a child. The man was under a good fame, for an honest and good man. The said minister, about two dayes after, came back to Inverary, and the forsaid gentleman was, that day he came, buried, and had been killed with all the forsaid circumstances."

" *Dec.* 31, 1700.—This afternoon   told me that Mr Ray was once a fellow in on of the Universitys, and apeared much for the Covenant : and because he would not renounce it, he was afterwards put out of the University, and reduced to some straits ; on which a gentleman bestowed L.50 per annum, and a country house, upon him, in which he lived hitherto privately ; and on this stock has done all these noble things the learned world is soe much endebted to him for. Compare this with the Preface to his Wisdom of God, in the Works of Creation and Providence."

" *Feb.* 26, 1701.—This night being with Mr Alexander Edward, ane episcopall minister, weel versed in architecture, and curiouse in antiquity, that lives in Angus, he told me the Laird of Fintrime, a man that was very curiouse, and extreamly weel seen in history, and aboundantly

---

* It was said that the death of the Duke of Buckingham was predicted by a Highland soer, who exclaimed, " Pish, he will come to nothing, I see a dagger in his breast." —(*Aubrey's Miscellanies*, p. 275 ; *Law's Memorialls*, Pref. Not. p. lxiii.) So far from ridiculing the pretensions of the Highland seers, the great English moralist himself was not indisposed to give credit to them. After summing up the arguments for and against the possession of the second-sight, he says,—" To collect sufficient testimonies for the satisfaction of the public, or of ourselves, would have required more time than we could bestow. There is, against it, the seeming analogy of things confusedly seen and little understood ; and for it, the indistinct cry of national persuasion, which may be, perhaps, resolved at last into prejudice and tradition. I never could advance my curiosity to conviction, but came away at last only willing to believe."—(*Dr Johnson's Journey to the Western Islands, Works*, vol. viii. p. 305.)

credible, gave him this account of Spotswood's History. That he wrote it at King James' command, and that, after he had drawen 4 or 5 different draughts of it, he at lenth came and offered it to the King. He gave it to the Scots Secretary, the Earl of Lanerick, with orders to print it in a fine letter, and good paper. The Secretary, whether from some dissatisfaction at the author, or the Book, (my author knows not which,) laid it up in his study, and did nothing in it. The King dyed within a while, and Lanerick came down to Scotland, in Montrose' time. The Earl's Secretary and he fell out; and he ran away with severall of the Earl's papers, and the autograph of Spotswood among them, and came to Montrose, then upon the hills. The Books, through the said Secretary's unsetled condition, turned a little loose. About two years after, Montrose was banished, and all his followers ordered to depart the Kingdome, having two moneths allowed them. In this time, the said Secretary of the Earl of Lanerick came to Mr Wisheart, then minister at [North Leith,] afterwards Bishop of Edinburgh, after the Restoration, who being rabled out of his charge, went over to Holland. To this Mr Wisheart did the said Secretary give the said MSS. The Laird of Fintrime was then in Holland, and declares that the said Mr Wisheart began to transcribe the said MSS. with his own hand; and that he many times dictated to him. By the time he was half done with it, Archbishop Spotswood's friends, knowing the said copy was given to Lanerick, and now thinking it lost, printed the history from a former draught of the Archbishop's. That when the print came to Mr Wisheart, he found it considerately different from his MSS., and wanted many things his had. The said Laird sayes he never met with Bishop Wisheart, after he came home, to enquire what became of the MSS. If this MS. be now in the hands of Archdeacon Nicholson,* I most enquire.

" That there is yet at Saint Andrews Mr George Martine, that was long Comissary-clerk there, and had access to many old papers, and is very

* Afterwards Bishop of Carlisle, the Author of the English, Scotch, and Irish Historical Libraries.

well seen in them ; as likewise is curious in stones, shells, &c. That he, before the last Revolution, drew up a large History* of the Arch-bishops, Deans, &c., of St Andrews, and had it ready for the presse ; that the Revolution stoped its printing. That he has done several other considerable things in our Scots antiquitys. That he looks on him as the greatest antiquary now in Scotland."

The present Work has been printed from a copy of the Ana-lecta, which was transcribed with great care from the original MSS. in the Library of the Faculty of Advocates. The system of contraction practised by the author, and his antiquated or peculiar orthography, may have given rise to some mistakes, particularly in regard to proper names. The Members of the Club and others, it is not doubted, will make allowances for these.

An Index is appended, which, from its minuteness and accuracy, must add greatly to the value of a work of such a miscellaneous character, especially as a book of reference.

M. L.

MARCH 31, 1843.

* From a letter to James Anderson, Esq., who wrote " Collections relating to the History of Mary Queen of Scotland," and other works on Scottish affairs, we learn that this MS. History came, at a subsequent period, into the possession of Wodrow. In that letter, dated " Eastwood, Nov. 19, 1717," Wodrow says, " I'll have a copy of Mr Martin's History of St Andrews for you, as soon as may be. Any other MSS. I have you may freely command, as if they were your own."—(*Dr Burns' Hist. of Suf. of Ch. of Scot. Original Letters*, vol. i. p. xxiii.)

WODROW'S ANALECTA;

OR

MATERIALS FOR A HISTORY OF REMARKABLE PROVIDENCES.

M.DCC.XXVIII.

June.—THIS moneth I have the affecting accounts of Dr Cotton Mather's death in February last. His character, see funerall sermons on him. He and I have corresponded these twenty years. He was extremly usefull, and did much service to souls. His stile in his writtings is peculiar. He and his father keeped life in the Independent interest in New England, and I find severall of the remaining Ministers there incline to come nearer Presbiterian government, and to have Judicatorys brought to their proper weight and influence. He was a person of singular piety, and a deep concern for the generall concerns of souls.

In the close of the last moneth, Provost Peady dyed at Glasgou of a pleurisy. He was at the Assembly for his friend Mr Simson, and got cold there. He was a person of great substance, much modesty, and great firmnes. He has scarce left his equall, take him altogether, in that place ; and in their present broken, divided state, they wanted a man of his firmnes, and resolution, and piety. His death is a neu stroak to that place, and they have mett with many of late. Their losses, this last year, I am told, amount to twenty-eight thousand pound sterling ; and, indeed, it's a wonder to me hou they stand throu.

The meeting of Royall Burghs was this moneth. Party work prevails in all Societys, and there the Magistrates of Edinburgh prevail, and have hightened the tax on Glasgow, Rutherglen, and Dumbartan, for their opposition to Shaufeild; and no representations, though never so reasonable, of the losses of the Toun of Glasgou, could be heard, but a very great addition is laid on them, though under all their losses they are the most active, stirring place in Scotland. But all methods are taken by the present managers to bring them lou and bear them doun.

[*June* 26.]—Towards the end of the moneth, on the 26th, the Colledge of Glasgou had a neu squabble about the choice of the Dean of Faculty. These on the Duke of Montrose side had the plurality, and thought themselves sure; but about an hour before the election they wer surprised with a sist put in the hand of Aikenhead, Rector, and Mr J. Hamiltoun, Vice-Chancellor, from the Lords of Session, that is, Lord Milton, surreptitiously taken out in March, and never heard of till nou, discharging them to act till their election was discussed before the Lords. The sist was most informall, and of no weight in lau, and every way informall. The Rector and Vice-Chancellor, houever, stoped, and Mr Ch[arles] Murthland went over and mett with the other side, which was what carryed their point. Without him they had not been a quorum, and consequently no election; but he was peremptory, and would go, being Clerk. Mr William Wisheart was chosen Dean of Faculty, and Mr Gray protested against the choice. Mr Carmichael, Loudoun, Forbes, Anderson, and Dr Brisbane, refused to meet with the other side, and Mr J. Hamiltoun. The other side wer Principal Campbell, Mr Dunlop, Mr J. Simson, Mr R. Simson, Mr Dick, and Mr Ross. Mr Gray went in and desired Mr Murthland to withdrau. He sayed for himself, that being Clerk he behoved to be there, and did not understand Mr Grayes motion. But it's feared he was frighted with his sellaries being attacked, or some other reason of that nature prevailed; for had he withdrauen the other side could not have acted. Upon his refusal, Mr Gray protested against Mr J. Simpson, as having no right to sitt there, being suspended from all ecclesiasticall function; and against Mr Andreu Ross, as not being *compos mentis*, and consequently that the election was void and null. Houever, they went on, and chose Mr Wisheart, and [in] the afternoon deposed Mr Murthland from being Clerk. Ther seems to be litle difficulty as to the Rector, and litle of weight to be said against his election; but the Vice-Chancelor used still to be in the person of the Principall till nou, and there are feu instances of another's being chosen; and I find the Duke of Montrose is not fond to have that affair tryed, in the present state of things, when he has so litle to say at Court; because, though his right to nominat the Vice-Chancelor be unquestionable, yet his oun right as Chancelor he does not love to be touched, because, except the Earl of Hyndford and he, ther wer no Chancelors but chosen by the Colledge, and the A. B. [Archbishop] under Prelacy was Chancelor *ex officio*; and nou, that that falls to the Croun, he is unwilling to have the Croun's right in that matter canvassed. Houever, he is in no hazard, for the Colledge choiced him also.*

Mr Glass' affair, since the Assembly, is in short: The Commission conversed with him at great lenth, and gained no ground on him; houever, they inclined to favour him, if he could be reclaimed, and continoued the sentence of suspension, but appointed a Committee to converse him, and that with pouer to remove the sentence, or at least to prepare matters for it; but instead of that, as soon as he went home he preached, and broke the sentence of suspension, and resolved, it seems, to breake all squares with the Church, and set up upon his oun leggs on the Independent way. Upon this, the Committy did not meet; and I belive the Synod will depose him.

The Congress at Soisons mett this moneth, but we have litle accounts of them. Much depends on the state of the King of Spain's health; and hou far they will yeild, or hou farr Spain and France are in concert and under a secret treaty, must be left to time to discover; houever, matters seem to be in such a situation as it will be some moneths before the Congress will come to any bearing.

* This seems unintelligible. The Earl of Hyndford and the Duke of Montrose were elected by the University, and there is no trace of interferense on the part of the Crown.

Mr Walter Ross, Minister in Sutherland, tells me, that in their Presbytery, at the earnest desire of the people, they keep the Sacrament of the Supper in their vacancys. That, at their Communions there, they have vast confluences : That people come fifty miles to a Communion, and the bulk of the religious people through the country wait on them : That they are very much straitned what to do, by the vulgar notion they have in that country, that it is not laufull to take money for the entertainment of strangers from neighbouring places at such occasions ; and yet the charges to the place wher the Sacrament is is so great, that Ministers for the people's sake only have the Communion once in two years.

He tells me, old Mr Walter Denoon is still alive in their Presbitry : That he is much failed, and no wonder, for he is near one hundred years old : That the Presbitry regularly supplys him.

He adds, Mr Murdoch M'Kenzie, first Bishop of Ross after the Restoration, was a very naughty man. He was deposed and excommunicat by the Assembly at Glasgou, 1638 ; and that some of the Noblemen, upon the probation found against him, votted depose, excommunicat, and he should be hanged likewise. Sir George Monroe, Generall of the Scots forces in Ireland, was called to him about some lands, and brought charters with him. Sir George was a man well seen in Latine and charters. The Bishop looked some of them, but had not so much learning as to understand the Latin. Sir George twitted him with his ignorance. This the Bishop took so ill, that he turned his violent persecutor, and got him laid up in prison as one disaffected to the Goverment, when nothing was really to be charged on him save his bantering the Bishop.

July, 1728.—This moneth, we have the certain accompt of a presentation to Mr John M'Dermitt, Minister at Air, to Renfreu. It hath been carryed on in a very odd manner. Mr Campbell hath procured it without ever consulting either session or heretor, and all kepit dormant. The bulk of the people never heard of him. This I take to be the warst use can be made of Patronages, when Ministers have them or the mater* in their hands, and without any concert with either their fellow

* Power of filling up the Benefice.

Ministers or Session, or any concerned, press in a Minister upon a place. Thus Mr C[ampbell] was put in on Renfreu; and this way, it seems, he inclines to serve them with another, especially if ther be, as I fear ther is, a designe to serve a party by bringing in a Minister to manage Magistrates. If Ministers go on to countenance such practises, we shall soon have a corrupt Church. And this was the very method by which Prelacy was brought in to Scotland in the Sixth King James' time, by plying the Court, and making the King to interest himself in setlments, and nominating Ministers for their purposes, and thrusting them in upon Presbitrys and people.

This moneth, the Duke of Hamiltoun gave the parish of Cambuslang a peremptory answer, that he would give no other to them than Mr Finlater's son, his Minister. The people have withstood him these five or six years, and will never come in to him. The Synod have appointed Committys, and the Presbitry never calls them. I knou not a parish in the West of Scotland in such a taking as Cambuslang and Hamiltoun. Cambuslang has been, on the matter, vaccant these fourteen years; and I am told ther is not one under sixteen years who ever has been catechised; and all floues from the servants about the Duke, who have their litle brigues* to get in their freinds. Akenhead is very ill treate by the Duke; he has been usefull to the family. Promises have been made for Mr M'Culloch, the people's choice, and matters are still staved off. I really think superior Judicatorys are to blame for not calling Presbitrys to an account in matters of this nature.

This moneth, the old affair of Mr Finlater, in Hamiltoun, is, I find, broke out afresh. See it in the former volume. The witness which the Synod formerly advised the Presbitry not to take her deposition, because a single witness, and the circumstances seemed dubious, came to dye; and on her death-bed she declared her self burdened in conscience in that matter; continoued positive in asserting that she sau vile cariage betwixt Mr F[inlater] and Naismith. She sent for two or

---

* Cabala, plots. Fr. *brigue.*

three Elders, gave an ample declaration in their presence. She sent for Mr R. Hamiltoun ; but, it seems, he refused to come. Houever, this revived the scandall ; and she being under some name for piety, and going of [off] time with these declarations, hath set all the old storys abroach, and many things since. This fell in when, upon the occasion of a neu Communion, a visitation was sought, and the dissenting Elders, which are the whole but three or four, gave in a matteriall lybell against Mr Finlater ; and it being turned to a lybell by the Presbitry, upon the dissenting Elders offering to make the articles good, this moneth, I think, the Presbitry entered in the relevancy. The first article, relating to the former scandall, they found not relevant, as what the Synod had overuled formerly, and being a single witness, they thought nothing could be made of it. Severall other articles they found relevant, which, if proven, no doubt are sufficient to depose a whole Presbitry, if so [they] be guilty. He is lybelled or informed against as not having visited the parish of Hamiltoun these eighteen years and more ; for refusing to visit the sick ; for his baptizing the children of scandalous persons, in privat, without any reason or eminent hazard, and refusing privat baptisme to other eminently religiouse ; for bearing company only with the loose and profane part of the toun, and neglecting those that are seriouse. He is charged with open breach of Sabbath, by his own carnall discourse, his servants bringing in stands of watter through the streets, digging roots, [and] cutting kail ; in the Sabbath, for profanity in his family ; and, lastly, for breaking the interdictment with Naismith, the correspondence with that family and his continouing, and he himself frequently being seen go out and in. The dissenters, on the Presbitry's interloquiture, appealed to the Synod. I wish that matter may be made plain to us.

This moneth, Aikenhead and Mr Hamiltoun petitioned the Lords of Session against the suspension narrated last moneth. Mr Dundas was their Advocat ; and that case appeared very black, as opened up by him. See the papers in print. In short, the Lords almost unanimously reponed them to the exercise of their office, but referred the merites of the election of the Dean of Faculty till the next session. Their great care is to preserve the Dean of Faculty; and hou he can stand, and two of the electors fraudulently eluded of their votes, I cannot see, consistent with reason or justice.

This moneth the warm debates continou before the Lords of Session between the Old and Neu Bank. Mr Dundass appears with much boldnes for the Old Bank, and the Lords, for most part, favour it.

Agust, 1728.—This moneth, our vacancys take up all our time in Presbitry, and two of them go well on in their setlment. The Earl of D[undonald] being sensible of his mistake with my Lord P[ollock,] as to Old Kilpatrick, makes amends in Lochwinnioch, and frankly goes on with the people's inclinations to Mr Pinkarton. We have a most harmonious application for moderating a call; Mr Pinkarton gives in a very limited acceptance when the presentation came in, and a call is ordered to be moderat, wher, I hear, all went on with full smoothnes. In this I cannot but observe a present retribution. The affair of Kilpatrick is in the former volume, and the stope was on Mr P[inkerton's] part, upon a very clear footing, and nou his setlment is clear and plain to as good a benefice, and a farr more comfortable people.

Killellan hath had severall clouds at first, but they are blouen over. Mr Bruce,* a relation of the Patron, Barrochan, was presented; the Patron went in to signe a call; the heretors, elder, and people, came in. We wer difficulted at first, from the accompts of his being once a Non-subscriber; but he early left them, and since his quitting them they are most uneasy to him, and his life there is burdensome. This account we have verifyed by the most notted Ministers of our principles in Ireland, so that the Presbitry goes in frankly to the setlment, and the call is like to be harmonious.

Renfreu is like to cost us more trouble. We had the King's presentation on the 20th of this moneth, and a letter from Mr M'Dermitt, not directed to us, but Blythswood. No demands wer made to make any further steps in this matter, and we wer not very willing to take any

* Of Holywood, Ireland.

hastily. We kneu the heretors, thirteen to four, are against the setlment; and no great wonder. We expect applications on both sides
next Presbitry day; and unles that violent party nou setting up for Mr
M'Dermitt push things to great extremitys, it's not very probable they
will cary. Houever, the place is like to lye desolat for some time, and
the Councill and people in toun are indeed mostly to blame themselves,
for they stoup to all C[ampbell's] projects.

At Glasgou, this moneth, two things happen pretty singular, which
twenty or thirty years ago would have been very odd in Glasgou, the
setting up of an Episcopalian Meeting-house, and publick allowing of
Comedies.

Last moneth and this, a house was fitted up in James Corbet's land in
the Broad Closs, opposit to the Colledge, for a Meeting-house, and one
Wingat, a Nonjuror, was got from the East country, who prayes not for
the King. Northside, Richard Graham, Barrowfeild, Keir, and others,
contribute to it, and the collections go to the preacher. Some Sabbaths
they preached, and a mobb was threatned; upon which the Magistrates
sent for Wingat and threatned him. Mr A. Duncan took it up, and
B[ailey] Murdoch warned him of his danger. He was very uppish, and
said he would continou, and ther wer Ministers that had not taken the
oaths. The Bailey said ther wer none such in the toun, and if ther wer
elsewhere they prayed for the King; and said he would put a padlock
on the dore. Mr Duncan said he would take it off again. This was in
privat. He was sent for, with Wingat, to [the] Magistrates in judgment. Ther he was warned of their hazard; the acts of Parliament
wer cast up; and ther danger told them, of six moneths' imprisonment.
They wer modester before them, yet would not promise to forbear.
They are again cited before them. What the issue will be, time must
discover. They take heart from the want of a Provost, and the dis-
couragements the Magistrates meet with. A privat house would hold
them all, but they incline to make an appearance; and a Meeting-house
at Glasgou makes a great noise indeed, and strenthens their party and
interest. These two or three years there have been strong efforts used
(see former volume) to have publick Meeting-houses set up in the West

and South of Scotland, where the greatest opposition was formerly made
to Episcopacy; and this, no doubt, makes a great dash abroad, wher
things are magnifyed; and what the consequences will be to following
generations, I tremble at the thoughts.

Things are at a very lou pass; any remains of goverment we have is
in the hands of the Justices of the Peace, and Magistrates of touns.
The first mind litle or nothing, and these* at Glasgou are brou-beaten;
and the bulk of our gentry, and many young merchants, &c., at Glasgou, are disgusted: men of no principles, and like to turn Jacobite, and
the Goverment in England are for an illimited Tolleration, and screu
the principles of liberty to that pitch as, I fear, in the issue, Jacobites
and Papists get stronger footing in a litle than many are aware of. The
Lord himself interpose and prevent us, with the blessings of goodness!

Towards the close of this moneth a company of Strollers and Commedians came to Glasgou, part of A. Ashton's people at Edinburgh, to
act the Beggars' Opera. The Magistrates wer applyed to for a room,
and B[ailay] Murdoch, who is too easy, as is said, by a mistake gave a
kind of allouance of the Weighouse to act in. They acted two or three
dayes, and had very feu except the first day. After that they got not
so much as to pay their musick. Houever, the Magistrates complean
of the Ministers, that they applyed not to them before hand, to prevent
their allowance, if they kneu of it. I think they wer wrong; but considering the noise made at Edinburgh by these strollers, and the brisk
opposition made by the Magistrates of Edinburgh, they should have
considered better before they alloued them.

Sabbath after the Ministers preached against going to these Interludes
and Playes, and compleaned that they wer countenanced by those in the
goverment. This the Magistrates do not take so well, considering that
they had not spoke to themselves about it, but, as I signifyed, to one of
them. Sin and duty is to be told, and Ministers are bound to do so.
Mr Rob, of Kilsyth, preached in the beginning of September, the 5th,
and went through all that was agoing about Meeting-houses, Playes,
error, and profanes;† and spared none, as I hear.

Ther seems litle left nou to Ministers but free rebuking of sin, in

* The Magistrates.   † Profaneness.

point of doctrine ; and it may be when other things fail, **the present state of things** may lead to more freedom and plaines* this way. Indeed, thir Playes, Interludes, and Operas, are very unaccountable at this time, when the Lord seems to be calling aloud to mourning !

Towards the end of this moneth ther was a very considerable tempest of wind, which shook a great deal.† Generally a seed is shaken,‡ and in many places three seeds, and in some, they say, five seeds. A hail shour went over a great many places, which cutt the vittall in a most dreadfull manner. Besides this, ther is a great loss this year to the merchants in Glasgou in their tobaco trade. One of them tells me, that, at a modest calculation, of the forty shipps or some more, which went out of Clyde this season, there will be eighteen thousand pounds sterling of loss, which is a vast summe for the toun of Glasgou.

In the end of this moneth there hapned a violent rable§ at the Kirk of the Shotts, on Sabbath the 25th, if I be not forgot. Mr James Millar was presented to that parish. He has a pretty unanimous call, but Sir John Inglis' tennants, and a feu others, opose him ; and when he came to preach about twenty-six of them barricadoed the Church dores, took the keyes of the Church, and abused the people who offered to go in. There was a violent mob, and the Duke of Hamilton's Bailay read the proclamation against riots, and was beat, and the proclamation torn, on the Lord's day. Ther wer a good many wounded and brused on all hands. Mr Millar was in the change-house, and pressed them to all soft measures, but nothing would prevail. When they could have no access to the Church, he preached to a great number out of the change-house window. The rable very much disturbed him and the people, and gathered stones, and threatned him even in time of prayer. These disorders are for a lamentation. They are prosecuted for a riot before the Sherrif Dalserfe,‖ and some are fyned, and others are imprisoned. Alace ! we have litle or no goverment, and things are ready, if Providence prevent not, to run in confusion.

---

* Plainness.   † Of standing corn.   ‡ It is presumed the author means that one seed, and sometimes even five seeds, were shaken from each stalk of corn ; perhaps five times what was sown.
§ Riot.   ‖ Hamilton of Dalserf.

September, 1728.—I hear little this moneth, nor since the Assembly, concerning Mr Simson. He continoues making a party for himself, in Presbitrys, but generally more cautious in speaking than he has been for some time; and yet, I hear, when his scholars come to Glasgou, he talks with the same freedom with them, and with the same latitude as formerly. I hear of a conference with three, Mr B[ur]n[e]t, Mr William Brown, [and] Mr William Jamison, wherin he declared, in so many words, that in nothing he had altered his sentiments; that he continoued just what he had taught them.

The affair at Renfreu I shall not enlarge upon : it will best be seen in our Presbitry's minutes ; and its turning towards me is what makes me say the less on it, till I see the event. This moneth, the Presbitry alloued or ordered the sentiments of the people, and all concerned, to be enquired into, and report to be made. We had lauers pleading many hours before us, which I never sau in our Presbitry. Indeed, they tend rather to perplex than much to clear up this matter. I happen to be in the chair, and the affair of the Presentations being elapsed to the King, not being given in within six moneths after the vacancy, that of the Act of Parliament, which seems to prohibite · presentations to settled Ministers, and that of the acceptation, whether Mr M'Dermitt's acceptation came up to the terms of lau, wer at full lenth pled for five or six hours. We went on, and ordered the state of the parish to be brought in by one of our number,* who wer for the presentee, or† a free call.

I hear very lamentable accounts of Mr Hill, Minister at Hollywood. He has been under very great damps for two years or more. He was a man of piety and considerable parts. His case was sent into Edinburgh to the physitians ; they desired him to come in. Accordingly he went ; the physitians conversed with him, and found him under no bodily distemper, but reconed he was melancholy and damped. They endeavoured to reason him out of his damps ; he told them that he was unwilling to enter on that subject with them, because he apprehended they wer not much conversant in it. They turned all to jest, and alledged he was vapourish, &c. When he sau them this way, like to triumph in words

---

* To ascertain.   † For.

and generalls of no signification, Mr Hill, who is a man of good reading and reasoning, plucked up his spirit a litle, and told them, since they wer ready to run away with the harrous, he was willing to reason with them even on their oun principles. Accordingly, he entered a litle on his case, and the grounds of his damp,—sin, distance, uselesnes, anger, and the like; and hou reasonable it was for all men, if not mere Atheists, to be concerned about the subjects: That concern about them was neither vapour nor a bodily distemper, nor craze, and weaknes of mind. He menteaned the argument with three or four of the physitians there for some hours, and silenced them, in point of reasoning. They, at parting, told him that they wer nou convinced he was far from crazednes, or vapour; that his trouble was what lay no way within their reach, and he might return home when he pleased, for any thing they could do him service in. He continoues still under his damps, and now ouns he prayes litle or none, and will not even desire others to pray for him, but does not refuse to joyn with them when they offer to pray with him. I hear of late (Jan. 1720) that he continoues much the same, only some better. This good man is a very aufull instance to us Ministers.

I am well informed, by one present, that Mr John Welsh was at Edinburgh in the end of the 1679, or therabout. Ther had been a great intimacy between him and Mr Hamiltoun of Kinkell. He was at that time in prison at Edinburgh. Mr Hamiltoun was suffered to go out sometimes with a keeper with him in the day time, and came still at night back. One day, finding Mr Welsh in town, and desirouse to meet with him, he got rid of his keeper for a little money, and came wher Mr Welsh was. When they wer together, his wife brought the allarum that ther was a search, and that it was already in the same land they wer [in]. Mr Welsh paused for a little, and at lenth he said to Miss [Mistress] Hamiltoun, "Be not affrayed, I am assured the searchers shall not once come near us!" and so it was, they did not enter that house. This was the last time Mr Welsh was at Edinburgh, before he went to London and dyed. Mr Hamiltoun's son, a minister, has this from his mother, and tells me. He adds, that Mr Welsh's buriall was the greatest that for many years had been seen at London. That most of the Dissenters changed their text that Sabbath he was burryed, that ther congregations wer invited to the buriall, at which ther was a vast number of Ministers, persons of fashion, and, if my memory fails me not, some hundreds of coaches.

Hugh Stewart tells me, that in conversation with Professor Hamiltoun he heard him say, that a good many of the present Bishops in England wer more favourable to the Calvinist and Anti-Pelagian schem of late; and wer it not that a generall odium of misrepresentation was spread of it among the nobility and gentry, they would declare themselves that way. I fear this is some mistake in the speaker or hearer, for I can observe nothing like that in their writings. He adds, that of late Dr Clerk, wher he used freedom, was like to declare himself more sound than formerly. Things at present here and in England do not appear so promising like, but quite the reverse, though I oun the Lord may soon make a change to the better; but I fear we may have some shakes and desolating stroak before such a mercy come.

In the end of this moneth the election of Magistrates in Glasgou and other burghs come on. Ther continoues a struggle between the unhappy parteys we have been so long divided by.

October, 1728.—Our Synod met at Irwine in the beginning of this moneth. Mr M'Kneight, the Minister of the toun, was chosen Moderator. Mr R. Maxwell preached, and had some good things against Ministers involving themselves in state partys and politicks. He notticed, that, in some cases, every honest man ought to be a party man, and on a side; as, when truth and error were on the feild, Jacobitisme or the Revolution; but when the question was, whither such a great man or another should be most folloued, and have greatest sway in the country, it blacked a Minister's reputation, and was unworthy of their coat, to medle; and such who did so wer sinking, and would sink more and more, in their credit and reputation.

We had litle before us save Mr Orr's transportation from Muirkirk to Hoddam. It caryed almost unanimously, Not transport; and an appeal was made to the Assembly. Mr Orr sheued much aversion himself; his wife's relations seem to have brought about the process. The parishes are much about one, only ther is a Meeting-house in Hoddam.

Mr Finlater's unhappy affair was also before us. I have hinted at it before. One of the witnesses in the former process charged him with the former guilt on her deathbed. A visitation was desired, [and] complaints given in. These turned to a lybell. The first thing insisted on was the opening of the former proces, closed upon this neu scandall. This the Presbytery refused to do; and this was the precise state of the thing before the Synod. The Synod unanimously wer not for opening the former process, and so cast the appeal, on which the complainers appealed to the Assembly; but we recommended it to the Presbitry to go on as to the rest of the articles, and offered a Committy to joyn, if they desired, which they did; but they picked and waled* members. The rest of the articles are confessed; neglect of family visitation eighteen years, baptizing a child of a scandalous person privately, breach of Sabbath by his family, and a rash oath, bordering on perjury. The house of Hamiltoun, and many heretors, and all the profane in the place, appear for Mr F[inlater;] all the godly and serious have almost deserted him. I knou no place in Scotland in so lamentable circumstances as poor Hamilton, since Mr Wylie's death. Ther is a generall desertion of all from Mr F[inlater,] and uneasiness rising as to Mr H[amilton.] The affair of his bargain for teind, at twelve pennies per peck of meal, with a man in drink, though to-morrou the minute signed was given up, breeds much coldness.

The Synod also, finding a copy of Mr Simson's process directed to them from the Assembly, as well as to Presbitrys, appointed all Presbitrys within their bounds to appoint a dyet *in hunc affectum*, as soon as may be, and have their report and instructions timously in readines. I mind no more we had, save our common money affairs, which very needlesly spend so much of our time.

I hear litle considerable before other Synods in this country. We

* Selected.

had not one correspondent from neighbouring Synods. This part of our laudable constitution is very much turned to desuetude. In Dumfreice Synod I hear that Mr R.,* who made such a bustle about the Abjuration, and since joyned with the Separatists, came before the Synod, declared his sorrou for his separation, promised orderlynes in time to come. He was exorted to continou in his duty, and his case delayed till next Synod.

This moneth we have the accompts of the choice of Magistrates through the burghs. At Aberdeen, we hear that Provost Fordyce, Steuart, and that side who have carryed all before them since the Revolution, have left the balance in that toun, and their party turned out. Pr[ovost] Fordyce is continoued a counselor, but his party turned out, and he himself will be out next year. Midltoun's party and the Duke of Argyle carry all before them, and Principal Chambers is intirely in with them.

At Edinburgh ther has been a battail between P[rovost] Campbell and P[rovost] Drummond, who is forced to fall in with P[rovost] Campbell and D. Lindsay. It run but upon one vote, the Deacon of the Goldsmiths, which is like to be a contraversy before the Lords. All the contending partys are upon one side, as is said.

At Glasgou their election made less noise than I have knouen it nou for many years. It run, they say, generally on D[ean of] Gild Rodgers to be Provost; but it's said he would not yeild to it, being expensive, and he not for it. P[rovost] Stirling is chosen, and it's a question on what side he is. Both promise well of him, and yet none of them are certain of him. His B. [brother] Walter seems to have a considerable share, and seems pretty firme against Shaufeild and that side.

Last moneth Mr J. Millar was setled in Kilpatrick, and Mr James Millar in the Shotts. The rable there was taken in task by the Duke of Hamiltoun and Dalserf, the authors of it threatned, and the setlment

* Reid?

easy enough, for any thing I hear. These two wer pretty much spoken
of, when students and preachers, for setting up for a great latitude.
I wish they grou wiser when Ministers, and disappoint fears.

This moneth our difficulties, as to Renfreu, continou. The report is
made to our Presbytery that a vast plurality are for a free call, and against
the presentee. Three or four have named one, but all the rest hold in generalls. We had lauers again before us, and long pleadings. We had much
of the former pleadings resumed, and nou our difficultys run to balance
the heretors, and whither the toun counselors are to be considered as
heretors *per capita*. They are eighteen, and, joyned with five or six other
heretors, come pretty much up to the number of other heretors for a free
call ; and yet the heretors are supernumerary by one or two to the rest,
even taking in the councill ; and the heads of familys are some hundreds,
to ten or twelve. We wer keept so late with the pleadings that we delayed doing any thing till next Presbitery day.

Mean while, Mr Bruce's call is sent over to Ireland, and is in de-
pendence ther as to Killellan ; and Lochwinioch goes on very unanimously, and we [have] taken Mr William Broun, Mr Thomas' son, to
tryalls.

The Colledge meets, and at first are very thin, but afterwards they
meet better, and Principall Campbell takes up lessons of Divinity under
Mr Simson's sentence. At first feu came, but in the after moneths he
has forty or upwards attending lessons three dayes a week.

November, 1728.—This moneth begins with Glasgou Communion,
wher I helped in the wine, [Wynd ?] Offence, less than I expected, was
taken at my ser[mon] on Immanuell. It seems people are less moved
nou then formerly, and more used. Mr Robb has lately had severall
sermons at Glasgou, pretty much spoken of for the freedom of them.
Honest Bailay King dyed the Communion Saturnday. He was much
taken up in the duty of singing Psalmes, and sung in the family a litle
before his death. That same night my wife, and Pet* before her, wer

* Probably for *Pate*, Peter or Patrick.

throuen off the horse, by some shotts of some young sparks who left the sermons, and mercifully preserved both.

Some Ministers mett and aggread upon some things proper to be a subject of conversation and correspondence among Ministers, as to Pres-bitrys [and] as to Mr Simson's process. See my Letter to Mr L. this moneth.

Mr Brand of Borroustonnes tells me, that he had an account from Mrs Frazer, the Laird of Brae's wife, that Mr John Welsh dyed in her house at London, 1679. That next morning after his death, Lauderdale went in to the King, and told him his Majesty oued him five hundred pounds. He asked, For what? He told him one of the great disturbers of the peace in Scotland, upon whom five hundred pound was set, was nou dead! The King said, If he be dead, it saves so much to me. He was burried on a Sabbathe, and the Dissenters invited all their hearers to the buriall that day, from pulpit; and his burriall was the most numerouse that ever had been seen in the city.

He tells me ther is a pretty remarkable passage as to old Mr Simson, the father of him in Stirling, in his son's Commentary to the Penitentiall Psalms, about some fishers in Dumbar, and a remarkable judgment he predicted coming on them for breach of the Sabbath, which was very sensibly and suddainly accomplished. Consult the Book.

The Commission sat this moneth. I hear very litle of any importance before them. The affair of Mr Glass was out of their hands. They had advised a conference, which he slighted, and counteracted the suspension laid on him ; and I hear no more lay on them to do. I hear litle of any concert among the Ministers, either as to doctrine [or ?] instructions as to Mr Simson's process, though I imagine they had some conversation ; and the Warning, afterwards published, came thus to be published.

Presbitrys began this moneth to enter on Mr Simson's process. The Presbitry of Glasgou had some meetings as to the manner of their procedure, and so in others. But it was fitt that such as kneu that process from the beginning, and they who wer the Judicatory to whom he was most immediatly subjected, should enter upon this matter among the first. See Letters, this and next moneth.

As has been for many years nou, so a neu struggle, and as closly fought as many, comes this moneth as to the choice of a Rector. The boyes wer not a litle on their priviledges in point of a free choice. Ther was a designe formed, and severall gentlmen, particularly Blackhall and others, engaged they would be against the person named by the Principall, as contrary to their rights. Ther appeared a great scarcity of persons to be named. Aikenhead would by no means continou, neither was it agreable to regulations. The Master of Ross was pitched on by the Principal and his side. Mr Maxwell of Blawarthill was fixed on by the other side, but he would not be active, nor give the least encouragment; but he was gone into, and by far the majority of severall of the Nations was for him; but by cajolling the boyes, closeting of them, and many other litle methods of threatning and flattery, they were broke; and Mr Maxwell had between sixty or seventy, and the other upwards of one hundred; and by the charges before, and some litle promises to Mr Forbes, and making his son Colledge Advocate,* and some other wayes, the Principal caryes all in the Faculty as he pleaseth.

This moneth the Presbitry had Renfreu affair before them, and though the matter was brought to a pretty narrou point, yet we had long enough debates upon it. The precise question was, Whither allou the petition of the heretors for a free call, and that of the heads of families almost to a man, or to moderat a call to Mr M'Dermitt, the presentee? The three Brethren on the one side, Mr J.,† Mr C : . . . . t,‡ [and] Mr Turner, urged, *pro aris et focis,* we should only moderat a call to Mr M'Dermitt. The foolish pretence of two calls was insisted on, which was not the case here. It was urged, that we could not moderat a call indefinitly without naming a man; that this was contrary to the rights of the Presbitry, who should knou the man, and this was pushed hard, as what appeared most popular. It was answered, that there was no word of this till the call was drauen up; neither in a place wher ther wer different sentiments could it be : That the Presbitry's rights wer fully secured in their concurrence after the no-

* Counsel for the College.   † Johnston.   ‡ Carrick ?

mination. When, in reasoning, they wer forced from this, and its being
our received principle, [that] the free call of the people was to be alloued
notwithstanding of a presentation, was urged, which they would not oppose, they urged a reference to the Synod for advice, or to the Commission. The Commission was not a very favourable proposall, the Synod was more urged, but as to both the unreasonablenes of referring a
plain ouned principle of our Church for advice, was argued, and a reference was refused by a vote, and then we agreed to send two to Renfreu, to moderat a free call to Mr M'Dermitt, or any other whom the plurality of electors wer for; upon which the Provost of Renfreu, Lord and
Master of Ross, and others, appealed to the Synod. At night we gave
them instructions, and ordered them to go on, notwithstanding of the
appeal, the partys being in our bounds; from which Mr J. dissented.

December, 1728.—In the beginning of this moneth Mr J. Pinkertoun
was ordeaned in Lochwinnioch. Mr Hunter preached very well, on Heb.
xiii. 17, and Mr K. Millar off-hand preached to the people, "Hou beau-
tiful are the feet of those who bring good tidings," &c., exceeding well; Mr
Anderson, who should have preached, being deteaned. This hath been
a most unanimouse and harmoniouse setlment as we could wish for, and I
hope he will be an usefull minister.

I said somwhat on the state of the Meeting-house in Glasgou. By
the Magistrates' influence, Wingat, the Nonjurant, was sent off. Mr A.
Duncan is nou old and failed, yet he would willingly preach, but dare
not in the Meeting-house hired. When the Jacobites see they can do no
better, they resolve to take up with the English service at any rate, and
so nou the generality of such who would not joyn with Presbiterians,
R. Graham, and others, who incline to the English service, and do not pretend to Jacobitisme, go to the Chaplain of the souldiers, the English Regiment nou in Glasgou, and the Jacobites also are going thither, and such
who wer reconed so, Barroufeild and his family, Keir and his family,
Northside and his family, with others who winter in the toun. They
have got over their scruple at praying for King George; and, indeed, I
am of opinion this practise of theirs will gain them more countenance,

and tend exceedingly to the setting up of Meeting-houses, and the lau will protect them ; and under this scogg* Jacobitisme and dissafection will terribly be propagated.

This moneth the Presbitry of Glasgou come to an issue, and instruct their Commissioners that the Assembly depose Mr Simson.   This they did unanimously, save three : the Principal, who spoke in Mr Simson's defence but very faintly, whither in a faint or designe, or because of another reason, cannot be determined ; Mr Wisheart, who had a long discourse on charity, and other things of that nature ; and worthy Mr J. S., [James Stirling,] who, till nou, that his brother is dead, and is fallen under the managment of his son-in-lau, votted and acted in that affair in no publick Judicatory hitherto ; he, every body belives, with much sincerity, said several moving things : That he kneu Mr Simson from a child ; reconed him pious ; and if it wer not so, and if he did not think him sound, he would not appear in his favour ; but he thought he was hardly dealt with.   These three craved their votes against deposition might be marked.   Mr Wisheart, when the Presbitry was on the second lybell, had a pretty surprizing speech : That he thought the first lybell was not referred to Presbitrys ; that, as to the second, he was of opinion that Mr Simson had run to severall gross errours, and sheuen in his cariage a very great and surprizing measure of pride and innovation. It was said that about that time the proposall began to be made by some that Mr W[isheart] should succeed Mr Simson, in case of deposition ; but whither this be true or an assertion, I cannot learn.   Houever, Mr Simson's oun Presbitry being for deposition, who should knou him best, and had so stranously defended him before, and the storys of their being picked† at him, I knou are very ill grounded.   This, in my opinion, should have a great deal of weight, and I belive will throu‡ the Church. For accompts of their procedure, see Letters this m[onth.]

This moneth, or the last, we have the accounts of the Duke of Gordon's death in the North ; which, at first hearing, I reconed the

---

* Shelter, covert.   † Piqued, chagrined.   ‡ Overrule, turn the scale in.

greatest stroak the Popish interest in the North hath received since the Revolution ; and nou that we have certain accompts of his son's being educat Protestant, (see Letters in February,) we are encouraged under the prospect of having Reformation carryed on with more vigour in that country, and Popery more born doun.

All this harvest and winter we are in a perfect silence almost as to publick neuse. What may be the cause I knou not, but I never observed so much of uncertainty as to publick affairs. These about Court keep things in the outmost secresy ; and if that be a wise max[im,] as generally it's thought to be, it's, under Sir Robert Walpool's managment, as much keeped by as I have ever seen. We had accounts of changes in the Ministry, and the Duke of Argyle's being to be made L[ord] L[ieutenant] of Ireland, and other storys ; but they all come to nothing in eight or ten dayes.

We had the affair of Renfreu this moneth before the Presbitry. I did not go, knouing hou matters went. The two Ministers went through the heretors and elders, and called for their votes, and they all centered upon me, save those feu for Mr M'Dermit. The last had the draught of a call, but the Ministers upon the plurality filled up my name in their draught, and it was signed by twenty-five heretors and severall hundreds of heads of familys ; and the other side desired liberty to signe their call. The Ministers said they could not attest their call. Houever, they signed it in the same place, nineteen counselors, and four or five heretors, and two contraverted ones, among whom the Colledge of Glasgou as titular of the teans,* and ten or twelve heads of familys. The Presbitry had both calls presented. By a vote they approved the two Ministers' conduct, upon which was a second appeal. By another, they found no call to Mr M'Dermit ; upon which ther was another appeal. They delayed concurrence with it, or any steps, till next Presbitry.

* Teinds, tithes.

M.DCC.XXIX.

January, 1729.—This moneth I had a pleasant child born to me towards the beginning of it; and in the beginning of the next he was taken away, I hope to a better place and state. Houever, I have reason to observe the good and kind hand of God in preserving my dear wife in her labour, " who is better to me than ten children."

When my wife was in her labour, and she and I wer talking, she told me that, after the birth of Martha, she had a sweet time for some weeks, and a tract of more livlynes and communion with God that she used not to have. About this time the noise was beginning about Mr Simson, and his gross errours touching the person [of] Christ. One day, after this sweet time of more nearnes than ordinary for some moneths, she was in her closet at prayer and meditation, and was led out in the thoughts of the Godhead of the blessed Redeemer, and had a great multitude of Scriptures casting up on a long train with a peculiar, sweet, and convincing pouer, all confirming as to this great truth. In short, much of the substance of my sermon, some moneths after, in the Barrony [Church,] upon The Everlasting Father, was suggested, and came very fresh to mind. When hearing this, she sau a great light like a glance of lightning, (it was dark night,) and a gloriouse inexpressible brightness filling with aue and reverence. The thought which came in presently was—" This, perhapps, might be Satan transforming himself into an angell of light ;" and that filled with terrour and fright. This naturally landed in an earnest supplication that the enemie might [not] have his will. Upon which, that place of Scripture came in—" It is I, be not affrayed !" This came with much evidence, but still fear of a mistake, and its being the effect of meer rememberance remained ; upon which ther was an insisting in prayer to this purpose, as farr as is minded :—" Lord, I

desire nothing extraordinary; let me have Thy Word and Spirit; let
me knou this is from thyself, by an after set of seriousnes and nearnes to
thyself." After continouing some time at duty at that time, with some
sweetnes, litle more observable fell out; but, for some moneths following,
a very sweet, seriouse set of spirit continoued, with greater constancy
and feuer interruptions than ever she had formerly felt. And at the
Barronny Communion, when many particulars wer much forgotten,
though the sweet impression remained more generally, I went throu the
whole of the former things, and they wer reneued with yet greater sweetnes. She added, that she was affrayed I might be wrong, or found to
be so; ther was such a perfect agreement between what had formerly
run throu her thoughts and what I then [spoke,] with some additions,
that she had not cast up to her, was so great. This was certainly a singular vou[ch]safement, and a step of singular condescention thus to
confirm it in the publick preached Word.

I forgot, on the last moneth, or November, to notice worthy Mr William
Lau's death, Professor for thirty or thirty-six years of Pneumaticks and
Morall Philosophy at Edinburgh Colledge. He was the worthy son of
an excellent father, Mr John Lau, Minister at Campsie, and then of Edinburgh. He made a considerable estate, and was old before he marryed.
He was a person of great learning and solidity in his bussines, and much
gravity and piety. He was as [much] valued for his being master of
his bussines as any of the Masters, and was a great ornament to that
University. They say he had excellent prelections upon Naturall Religion,
and it will be pity if somwhat of his be not published. It's said that he
is to be succeeded by Mr Scott, of whom above; and that he is to be
succeeded by his son in the Greek Profession. If all be true, or the half,
that is said of Mr S[cott,] he does not seem qualifyed to be a Professor
of that part of learning.

This moneth Presbitryes fall in earnest about Mr Simson's process.
See Letters this moneth. We entered upon the consideration of it, and
though all wer ordered to read the process, yet we read a good deal.
The proposal was made by Mr J. M.* that, considering the difficulty in it,

* John Miller.

and fears of breaking among us, we should intirely leave the first process
to the Assembly, to do as they think meet.

This was greedily fallen in with by such who are reconed freindly to
Mr Simson ; and, indeed, it was a short work fitt for lazy persons.   The
great pretence was, that the remitting to Presbitrys was a hasty act, and
proposed by Mr Logan and Mr Haddo.   To which it was answered, that
it was gone into by the Assembly, without any struggle, and the Committy.
That nou it was the deed of the Church, and a most reasonable one.   It
was further objected, that the matter was not intire.   The Assembly had
gone throu the proces, and given sentence ; we could not renverse* what
they had done, and behoved to judge with their eyes, and not our oun.
To this it was answered, the Assembly had ripened it for us ; printed the
proces ; shortned the proces to us ; summed it up ; desires our opinion as
to what is to be further done ; that if we could find any flau in their procedure, we might humbly represent it, and give light on both hands.
Houever, all ended in a neu day in February, and letters to absent
bretheren to be present ; so we lost a day intirely on this matter.

The affair of Renfreu was delayed till March.   I was not present, but
left things to others, to do as they sau fitt ; only, in privat, I told my being
to oppose the transportation, when it came to my dore to speak.   I was
urged to be silent, and let the Presbitry go on and setle me.   That I
would not yeild to, and so they sau proper to delay concurrence with the
call, or a reference to the Synod, till March, which I went into ; and this
was agreed to in Presbitry.

This moneth we had The Allarume printed at Glasgou.   It galled the
freinds to Mr S[imson] and himself.   The printer was threatned, and
forced to abscond for some time, till he got a sist from Edinburgh on a suspension.   This step in Mr Graham, as Barron Bailay, was wondered at,
and by many reconed not agreeable to lau, and a considerable invasion
on the liberty of the subject.   Whatever be in that, it helped on the sale
and spread of the pamphlet.   The author, whom I take to. be a Minister
in Angus, hath defended the pamphlet, in an Appendix, six or eight weeks

---

* Fr. *renverser*, to overturn.

after, from the charge of disaffection and Jacobitisme, and stirring up dissention among Ministers and people and sessions.

This moneth Mr Patrick Bruce came over to Killellan, and was received by the Presbitry in the beginning of the next. I wish he may [be] faithfull and usefull, and not medle in party or innovations. He was once among the Non-subscribers in Ireland, but left them. We have very good testimonies of his sincerity in his change there from subscribing Ministers, and yet some things are talked that look as if he reteaned some warmnes to things which will not be so agreable here. Mr Anderson preached at his admission, wher I was not, from 1 Tim. iii. 1.

The Parliament sat doun this moneth. The King's Speech left us much wher we wer, as to peace or war. It looks as Sir R. Walpool wer firm in favour. He is certainly the former of the materialls of the Speech: and ther ar severall thrusts in it at Poultney, and the party who stand up against Sir Robert.

The affair of Mr Blackwood beginns to be talked of. Petitions, and very numerouse ones, from his Burghs of Glasgou, Dumbarton, Renfreu, Rutherglen, are formed in his favour. He moved soon for a day to be heard, and he was refused to be heard before the House, but referred to the Committy, which is said to be unfavourable to him; and a day for hearing it is named, in a long day, to which the Parliament cannot probably sit. Severall great men tell him they belive his cause good, but they cannot appear for disoblidging a great man. So that it's reconed he cannot be member this Parliament.

This moneth, the case of the election of the Magistrates of Dumbartan is before the Lords of Session, and both sides are declared unduly elected; and a person such as Doctor James Smollet, and his son, who have had the direction of that burgh since the Revolution, who are not trading merchants in the burgh, cannot be elected. This may come to be sauce for a gander.

Ther are warm debates about the election of the Magistrates of Edinburgh; Provest Campbell and his party *contra* Bailay Lindsay and his party. It comes before the Lords of Session as to the election of the

Deacon of Goldsmiths. My Lord Miltoun, Ordinary, delivers his judgment in favour of Bailay Lindsay his side, and the Lords confirm what he has done. The Magistrates appeal to the Parliament, and cary their point ther as to lodging the appeal to stop execution of sentence, and get it doun in a day or two before they should have been imprisoned for disobedience to the Lords of Session.

Shaufeild's oppression of the toun of Glasgou continoues this winter. The merchants are threatned with *Subpenas*, and this frights many of them; and those who are frighted form a supplication to Shaufeild to favour them. The Magistrates, and most by far in the toun, will not joyn in the adress; and at lenth they find out that the *Subpenas* cannot be executed for three years, which putts the people who truckled to Shaufeild to the blush.

Mr Alexander Duncan preaches to a feu of the upright, stiff Jacobites, who will not joyn in places wher the King is prayed for, in his oun house. The rest they go to the English Service, by the English Regiment Minister.

We hear of gross reports of the young Earle of Kilmarnock, who lives nou at Callender; of breaches 'twixt him and his Lady, and her being about to seek for a divorce. All these are flatly denyed by his freinds, and they say all is lyes, and they live in very good harmony.

This winter the merkates are very high. These severall moneths the meal is eleven pence and ten pence per peck, and not under. The straits of many familys and persons are exceeding great, and money is scarce to be had. Tradsmen make the most heavy complaints ever I heard, that they can get sell no manufactor, and nothing is to be had for yearn and spinning, and things look very judgment-like. If the Lord do not graciously interpose in sending a good season next, it's more than probable we shall have a very great scarcity.

The addresses of many Sessions to Presbitrys, to appear for the truth and against Mr Simson, are pretty generall up and doun; and they are a considerable check upon Ministers that incline to support him. See Letters this moneth. They are pretty common in the South and about Stirling, and they are even beginning this moneth to be talked of among us; but most Ministers are not very fond to encourage this step, it being a litle doubtful what may be the consequences of such a step ; and, in this case, the most part of Sessions can judge litle.

February, 1729.—This moneth we hear of most of the Presbitrys of the South and West. None yet are for Reposition save Irwine; and it may be Haddingtoun and Dunbarr, wher his relations are. Edinburgh Overture will readily be the louest feir* that will be struck ; and, generally speaking, hitherto Deposition seems to be the cheife and universall instruction.

This is a very ticklish time, and we that appear for the purity of doctrine had need to be wise as serpents and harmless as doves. We hear a stirr is like to be with relation to Mr G. C.† Session, some of them went to him, and wished he might give his testimony for the truth, and joyn with his brethren. He excused himself for want of health. He was told he might go doun, as he used, on a horse to week-dayes sermon, and at least give his testimony. He asked, " Unto what ? " they said, Against Mr Simson's errors. He seemed to doubt of the need of that, and expressed himself to the Elders that that was a question only about words. This stuck deep with them, and they and the rest of the Session sent two of their number to represent their stumbling upon that expression, and to signify to him their difficultys to joyn if he should imploy at his communion Mr H. F. and the Principal that appeared for Mr Simson's reposition. They went, but he declined conversation, and ordered things so as to have company with him while they were in the house, and so it yet stands. I very much fear that matters come to sad extremitys, if the Lord do not direct to wisdome and faithfulnes.

Matters lye over as to Renfreu as formerly, and Kilallan is setled, I pray it be comfortably. Mr Bruce seems resolved to medle in none of our present questions as to Mr Simson or Renfreu, and goes over the week after his admission to bring his family from Ireland hither. Houever, he seems to say in conversation, that the Ministers in Ireland are of opinion this Church hath gone far wrong as to Mr Simson.

---

* Degree of censure that will be proposed—from striking the Fiar, or average price of grain.

† George Campbell.

My Lord Ross tells me that it is generally belived that the Earl of Stairs, when at Paris, laid a designe, and hired a person, a Captain, to cut of the Pretender ; but the designe broke. When he came over, the designe was disliked, and he frouned upon for it ; but this story needs to be better vouched ere it be belived.

It's also said, by the same hand, that Sir Robert Walpole is more firmly setled in the favour of Court than is generally belived or knouen ; that he had one of the papers concerning the late King's secret Will ; that he prevailed with money with the Dutches of Munster to give another, and a third in the A[rchbishop] of Cant[erbury's] hands was gote up ; that he has prevailed to get funds for the Houshold [of] the Q[uee]n setled, larger than formerly ; and having the vote of the Commons in his hand, and the command of the money of the Nation, he will be either for peace or warr, as matters stand, and will be a necessary person in both cases. The Lord lives !

I hear ther are severall divisions in the Colledge of Glasgou upon more subjects than one. The nominating a Factor is what the Principal's party are particularly divided about. The P[rincipal] and Doctor Johnstoun and some others are for Wood, factor to the Duke of Hamiltoun's part of Dundonald, with a reservation of somwhat for Mr Carmichael's son, as under-factor, or somwhat that way. Mr Dunlop, Mr Dick, and R. Simson, are for Mr Thomas Harvey ; but he is a bankrupt, and he cannot find caution. Hou that will end, time will try. Another thing like to divide them is a designe in the Pr[incip]le to setle Doctor Campbell, in Paislay, Professor of Anatomy. He wants persons in the Faculty, to whom he can entirely trust, and when he spake to Doctor Birsbane and Doctor Johnstoun, they stormed furiously, and told him he must not take such steps as to encrease persons to vote for him. They are divided, they say, as to the successor of Mr Simson, whom they begin nou to dispair of carrying his point. The P[rincipal] and some feu they are for Mr Connell of Kilbride ; Mr Dunlope, R. Simson, and Dick, are for Mr W. Wisheart ; Mr Loudon, Carm[ichael,] and some others, for Mr Smith of Craumond. Houever, these are not yet come to any bearing, because the matter is not ripe.

This moneth a most melancholy accident falls in my family. At last term I feed a servant, Isobell Broun, who had been at Pearston, in Mr Mudy's family. She was recomended as piouse, and a good servant, by the Minister, Mr Sempill; and that she came only away on a debate with her mistress, and she was unwilling to part with her, was what we wer well informed of. She came in December, [and] caryed well enough. Soon after she signifyed her want of health to my wife, and that her [*catamenia ?*] since a heat and stress in kemping,* in September, wer not as usuall. She continoued this way, and went in to D. Thomson, her acquaintance, and advised with him her case, but took nothing. My wife's pains came on in the beginning of January, and the child's death followed on the beginning of this moneth, which hindered her from not-ticing her much; only we found her sleep litle, and frequently mourn-ing and groaning, which we reconed the fruit of her seriousnes, for which we had her recommended. She begun to speak of leaving our service. My wife told her she was not willing to be harsh to her, and did not complean since it was the hand of Providence. She spoke of going to Stranraer, wher her father is a guager and waiter, and using means for her health. At lenth she turned peremptory, and we found her exceeding concerned in the night time, and my wife began to suspect her, shee being turned bigg and round. We, in charity, supposed it a timpany;† but, on consideration, when we found she would go away, resolved to speak freely to her, to see if ther was any cause, or if she had been really guilty. She denyed, seemed very vexed we should sus-pect. Houever, I desired my wife to call a midwife, and told her I would do it, and that an innocent person would not be against a tryall; and, indeed, what swayed us was the fear of murder, in case of guilt. At lenth, on Saturnday before she went, my wife called J. F., who has skill, and told Isobell that they two would try her breasts, unles she confessed. She fell down on her knees, and confessed guilt with . . . . ; and declared it a rape, late when . . . . came from . . . . ; and that some attempts had been made before,

---

* Striving in reaping during the harvest.   † *Timpanites,* dropsy.

and once after: That she cryed, but it was late at night, &c. She seemed exceedingly concerned and seriouse. I once thought to have taken a judiciall confession, but did not think it proper to raise a scandall wher it was not; and so I spoke twice to her. She adhered to all. I laid the guilt to her dore, and advised her to take care of further sin. She acknowledged she felt life since January; regrated she had come to a honest family, but hoped she would not have been with child, the guilt being but once, and an absolute force. I wrote with her to Mr Sempill, assuring I would write by post to him. His Letter, this moneth, tells the event. The guilt was laid to another; he was told what she had confessed to my wife and me was a lye; and the reason was, that the true father said he would deny, and advised her to confess as she had, because she would be best belived. Many things must [be] left to the day of the manifestation of all things. She did not appear to me disingenouse, and wished I might keep her till she wrote to the person named; but I inclined to lay it rather before the Minister.

The end of this moneth Hamiltoun Presbitry met about Mr Simson, and agreed that it was highly unfitt that he should any longer have the education of youth in his hands. Ther is one thing told of a young member ther, Mr J. Millar, that I shall be sorry if true; that, in discoursing on naturall pouers, he said, he did not doubt but naturall pouers wer exceedingly mistaken and misapplyed; that he was [of] opinion it was naturally in the pouer of God to lye, though it was impossible he could lye. This choaked some, and he was interrupted.

We mett in the end of the moneth, according to appointment. After a teezing us with the former story of doing nothing, and referring all to the Assembly, I was called on to read what had been said to have been drauen up. I declined till it came to my turn, and afterward yeilded. In the afternoon we reasoned long and much. Mr Carrick had a longer paper than mine, and asserted that no error in judgment, when retracted, could be matter of censure, and, after renunciation, [it] could not be the ground of deposition; and that a heretick or erroneouse person was not to be rejected—that is, as he explained it, censured—till after two admonitions. He was told that error was a scandall, and to be censured even when confessed : That rejecting, ther, was undoubtedly the higher sentence. Mr R. M.* had litle of argument, but declamation, and severall places of Scripture, very unapplicable to the case in hand. Mr Jo. Millar argued more closly, but on things many times answered. The Elders said litle. It was moved to delay. This was again yeilded to, to make them the more inexcusable, if, after all, they would insist for waving. Reposition was not desired by any but Mr Carrick, so we delayed the consideration till the 18th of March, with a resolution to end it before we left the place.

March, 1729.—I hear lamentable accounts of the grouth of most corrupt and loose principles at Glasgou among the young people, merchants, and others ; and do not wonder at it. Ther is litle care taken in their education and founding in the principles of religion ; they never wait on catechising ; they have multitudes of corrupt books among their hands ; and clubs, wher every thing that is serious is ridiculed. And at Edinburgh, they say, ther are many turned Deists, and that it's exceeding common ther to mock at all religion and seriousnes.

The Commission mett the second Wensday. I hear they had litle before them. The affair of the Magistrates of Edinburgh, their appeal from the Presbitry to the Commission upon their setling Mr Kinloch in the Neu Kirk, as the Session inclined, and against the Magistrates, or a good many of them, their endeavours to have Mr Brown, who has been long noncollegiat, setled ther, or to the Synod of Lothian, which of them meet first. This seems an affair of great heat, and Mr Broun is talked of as sett up for by the keen Argathelians,† and opposed by the other. In the Commission it was managed with some warmth ; but at lenth, by a plurality, they caryed that the[y] wer not instructed to medle with that debate, and so they let it take its naturall course to the Synod.

Another affair came in unexpectedly before the Commission. Mr

---

* Robert Miller.   † The Argyll party.

Flint, and that in concert with some who are not reconed favourers of Mr Simson, moved a question to the Moderator for advice, Whither it was the Commission's opinion that Mr Simson was regularly sisted before the next General Assembly? He was in a doubt about it himself, and thought it would be a matter of ill consequence if Mr Simson should be absent, and the opinion of so·many Presbitrys concerning him come in, and their procedure stoped by his not being sisted. He ouned the reference to Presbitrys and to the next Generall Assembly, if they sau fitt to take it up, did·incline him to think Mr Simson was sisted; but this being a debatable case, he thought the Commission should consider if any thing wer incumbent on them. It was opposed by some feu, and said the Commission had never that affair remitted to them: That the Assembly had done what to them seemed proper. On the other hand, the generall clause and pouers of the Commission wer urged. In end, it was agreed to write to the Presbitry of Glasgou, that it was their opinion that Mr Simson should be present at the next Assembly, and require them to signify so much to Mr Simson.

They had an advice from the [heritors of?] Campsy sought by the Presbitry of Glasgou, hou to secure the stipend of Campsy upon setling Mr Govan's nepheu there, without a presentation upon the call; and they got, I think, an advice they should take the heretors bound to pay stipend. But it's hoped a presentation will be gote.

Mr Simson's freinds about Edinburgh are for his giving in a dimission to the next Assembly, but he delayes it till the Assembly meet, and he see hou matters go. Principal Wisheart is turned tender, was not at the Commission. It's doubted if he be able to preach to the Assembly. Mr W. Broun is talked of to succeed him. Professor Anderson, at Aberdeen, is said to be dangerously ill, and some speak of Mr John Walker, Canongate, to succeed him.

Our Presbitry met about Mr Simson on the 18th. We had Mr R. Maxwell caryed of from us. Houever, we caryed our point, after long reasoning and tugging. We had six Ministers against five, and eight or nine Ruling Elders for us, even when Mr J. Anderson was present, who had a short paper in favour of Mr Simson, but going quite on wrong facts. Mr Turner was absent, and Mr Bruce not come over: And instructed that the Assembly should declare it unsafe that Mr Simson teach, preach, &c.

In the beginning of this moneth we had the suddain and unexpected accompt of Agnes Luke's irregular marriage with Joseph Williamson. It was laid on me to acquaint parents, which I did; and immediatly I brought her home with me, wher she stayed till Williamson took her home with him to Edinburgh on the 20th of March. Expecting to be consulted in this most fashious case, I dashed doun my cursory thoughts upon it as folloues:

CASE.

A., of thirteen years and a feu moneths, is by fair speeches [induced] to have some affection for W., and under breach of trust when committed to W.'s parent for education. Under this affection, after many fears of A. her parents, she is made to belive that W. is so deeply engaged that he will dye unless they be married. Upon this, without proclamation of bands, they are irregularly marryed, and witnesses see them go to bed, and leave them there. When in bed, as A. sayes, they went no further, yea, can depone it if called regularly therto: That the marriage was not completed, and that she is as free of W. as the day she was born; and adds, that when W. rose without any attempts to complet the marriage, she thanked him, and said she resolved to have taken his promise, before marriage, that it should be thus. W. answered, She needed not be in pain that way, for if she should have proved with child, he would recon himself and her ruined, in that event, when parents wer not brought in. A. further tells me, that she had no thoughts at all of an oath; that she repeated some words read to her out of a book, and really did not [know] what she said. She added, she was still of opinion that it was in W.'s pouer, on her desire, to have loosed her and quitt her; and that, in the event of another's being proposed to her by her parents, a year and more after, when by this time she declared her affections wer loosed from W., and by what had hapned to her S. M. [Sister M. . . . . . ?] committed also to W.'s mother's care and education, she perceived that, without crushing and killing her parents, she could not but be miserable with W. She still judged [it] in W.'s pouer to loose her. Mean while, W. gives out the contrary, and sayes to me that all is done which was necessary for completing the marriage; and hath, by himself, or at least by a friend of his, spread the accounts that the marriage is completed, and they had many times cohabited. This is the case as it comes to me from both sides; and my opinion is asked, What parents should do in point of conscience?

In point of lau, upon which the resolution, *in foro conscientiæ*, in some measure dependeth, I am told that, by lau, a marriage-vou and promise [is binding] in a woman at twelve or a man at fourteen years: That the irregularity of the marriage; the want of parents' consent; the pretext, if a pretext, that fear of W.'s death brought her into it; that A.'s ignorance, nor any other circumstances, will do to render the marriage null; and, providing the witnesses sau them go to bed, and left them there, the lau (as I think it should) will find the marriage completed. In which case, I suppose summons of adherence will be got against A., and she will be obliged to adhere, or if she keep out of the way, W. will get a divorce, and she must live unmarried.

To me, I oun the lau of finding a vou and marriage promise in so very lou an age as twelve years, does not appear to be founded in Scripture or publick utility. I am sure in all other cases, almost, persons at twelve years of age need persons to act for them. I very much question if at that age they are *sui juris*, at their oun pouer and disposall; I am sure they could not in reason be admitted to give oath in a matter that is of any consequence, and required any reflection and thought; and such a lau, if any such be, appears a great tentation to irregular marriages.

Be that as it will, in point of conscience, after I have turned this matter all the wayes I can, it is very hard to me to see the binding force of an oath upon A. at thirteen years and a feu moneths, even allouing her to be one of more than ordinary smartnes and capacity. In this case, it does not appear, but the contrary, if A.'s word may be taken, that she had any knouledge, sense, or fear of an oath ; and she still thinks it is in W.'s pouer to free her. But waving this, when I consider the thing in generall, I cannot think that an oath lyes in words or pronouncing of them, but an oath must be in truth, knouledge, and rightiousnes. That, generally speaking, none of the qualitys of an oath can be found at thirteen years. That the tricking, in one of such an age, by professions of dying for affection, joyned with the presence of two witnesses privy to W.'s plot, to get money, (which I cannot help thinking was all in vieu, with affections subdolously and under trust raised,) together with the vile prostitution of the holy institution of marriage by a mercenary man under the name of a minister, and much more of the solem, sacred oath of marriage, and the tremendous name of God, which is worst of all, together with the prostitution of the great bond of human society by a man being, or pretending to be, in orders ;—that all this should make a reall binding oath upon A.'s part, is what does not appear to me. To say so, to me appears without all manner of ground, and the way to en-courage those unjust and unrighteouse attempts upon parents and poor innocent girles and boyes under age by the basest of methods.

What my advice shall be, in point of conscience, to parents or partys, I oun is one of the hardest cases I ever had upon my hand ; and I only dash doun my thoughts, as I comonly do, to get light in such cases, in sincerity, and without any byass I knou of, and to be matter of reasoning with others, and till I have more time to consult writters upon the case.

As to parents and partys, the choak to me lyes here : Upon the one hand, the lau, as I am informed, will find this a marriage, and completed ; and if the lau makes the marriage valid, I see not but it should also be found to be completed, because men can go no further than that which, it seems, witnesses will depone; but, then, A.'s positive, and seemingly ingenous declaration, when under no weight, and told the hazard of making further lyes on this head, that the marriage is not completed ; and W.'s as positive declarations, that all that is necessary for completing the marriage is done ; which, though a generall, yet I doubt not

but he will explain as particularly as is needfull. This being the reall
state of this matter, ther appears a very great difficulty here. Could I
be fully convinced that the marriage was not completed, and that A. and
W. are really free one of another, considering what danger the parents
are in of having their dayes shortned, by the cutting circumstances of
this unhappy matter, I would incline to think means might be laufully
used to bring partys to go no further during parents' lives; since, if
what I have remarked above hold, the oath is null upon A. her part, and
nothing folloued upon it. Indeed, upon W.'s side, the case alters, considering his different circumstances; and his oath, being twenty-three
years, was with knouledge and designe. Thus, about three weeks ago,
upon my first hearing this matter, I was peremptorly for keeping all
secret, as far as possible, for some time, save from the parents and a third
person concerned; but by this time matters have taken another turn,
and the thing is nou open, and in every body's mouth.

What is nou to be done, in conscience and prudence, and without
offending God, comes next under my thoughts; which I shall nou set
doun under the above restrictions.

As far as I can perceive, A. may be brought, (being not yet fifteen,)
notwithstanding her present cooling and aversion, to have her former
love and affection (raised in her artfully, and under breach of trust)
rekindled. W. is a person blameles, except in this matter, with whom
she may have a small competency, and not be miserable; unles it be
that the crush of her parents, or their death follouing upon it, or her
oun disappointment as to her portion, lay a fundation for after breaches
betwixt her and W. Indeed, these secret subdolous marriages are often
attended with miserable consequences even in this life.

W. insists, and probably will publickly intent a proces in lau. He
solemly declares and promises no alienation of affection in A. shall ever
alter him; that he recons himself happy in A., without a groat from her
parents.

I have a regard to them both; and though W. is no equall match
for A., yet since they are come this lenth, I see not much in their circumstances, (could I determine myself as to the completing of the

marriage,) but in that event they should live together, and make the best they can of their rash choice. But then, in the event of the marriage its not being completed, I confess my compassion to A., miserably imposed on, and unto the parents, inclines me to the other side.

As to the third person concerned, I take that to be nou intirely out of the question.

The great strait with me, in point of conscience and prudence, is as to the practise and carriage of A.'s religiouse, and to me, upon many accounts, very dear parents. I knou not, but my thoughts may be too much byassed in their favour in this weighty affair. They have one child happily setled; another of them, (and by an irregular marriage when under trust with W.'s mother too, though not in such cutting circumstances as this,) of whom they have lost [all] hope of comfort in this life; A. is their third and only child remaining, very promising, and, had the proposall of the third person nou out of dores taken, would have been the staff of their old age. That is nou broke; and the question comes, What is their duty in the above circumstances?

Their worldly circumstances, no doubt, allou them to enter into a lau process. They have got provocation so to do. What its event will be I do not knou. I am told lauers, and I see the generality of A. her relations and theirs, persons of greater piety, experience, forcast, and some of them of greater knouledge of the lau than I, are of opinion that, upon a process, the marriage will be found valid and complet. The event of that will, as I take it, be summons of adherence to A.; and, in that case, parents must either give up A. to W., or permitt a divorce to be issued out against her, which W. will, no doubt, carry, and get liberty to marry another, and A. must live unmarried. The parents only can determine themselves which of these hardships they will chuse. I see no sin on either side, save what may mix in, by not forgiving the injury, upon the one hand; or, upon the other, in their not pursuing all Christian, legall, and laufull measures, for their oun comfort, in their child, in their old age. I only observe, that the parents must be very much determined by A. [her] carriage and determination of herself, and her being easy and comfortable to them, and her affections being entirely

loosed from W., and her being free of him. W.'s circumstances are
certainly pityable ; but by this secret subdolous practise of his, full of
unrighteousnes and unjustice, in the sight of God and man, to A. in her
childhood, if her affections have not been greater to him than I can
belive, and especially to her parents, he brought them upon himself;
and is bound, by the lau of God, and as he would have his sin pardoned,
to make restitution, upon supposition that marriage is not completed.
And all that lyes on [the] parents, as to him, is to forgive what is
personall, and to pray for him that he may be forgiven by God on
repentance, which will keep him from further rash steps and sinfull
steps.

Upon the other hand, if the parents can bring up their minds, after a
legall tryall of the validity of the marriage—which, indeed, to me appears
to be a duty in persons of their opulent circumstances, both for their
own satisfaction in knouing the outmost which the law provides in such
cases, and to give a check, if possible, to such vile practises in W. or
others ; or without that, if the circumstances be doubiouse and hazar-
dous, upon the advice of lauers and freinds, they can bring themselves
to part with their child, and live easy, through Divine grace, under this
heavy dispensation, without going to lau, or, which probably may be
the case, without forcing W. to plead his claim. I can, at present, see
nothing sinfull in this.

Therfor, all I can say further is this : that the matter should be delayed, with mutuall consent of partys and parents, and any further procedure put off, if all concerned can be prevailed with, till A. be of age,
to think seriously, upon disposing herself, and upon what hath passed
in her nonage, as her case seemes to me to be. That, in the meantime,
there be a forgetting what is passed, with forgiving and praying one for
another. The delay I propose is till A. be of seventeen years of age,
which was the term parents at first set to themselves, in the event of the
third person, who was much preferable to W.; and, in the mean while,
the rights and claimes of all sides stands as they are, untill a publick tryall
of them, and ther be no disposall of either of the partys. And I do not
see where the hurt or prejudice of this lyes on either side.

The affair of Renfreu continoues this moneth as it was. The Presbitry formed answers to the three appeals, and referred the matter as it stood unto the Synod. I have not yet been befor them personally; but they took a further step, and concurred with my call, and gave their reasons for so doing. They ordered the call, with the reasons of it, to be put in my hand, and me to be cited, and that I cite the parish to the next Presbitry day. Houever, this was not done; the reasons wer not in a readines, nor read before the Presbitry, and so the call and these wer not put in my hand.

I am told by a gentlman that came from London, that the King hath been for some time in an ill state of health; that he is much sunk in his spirits, and is oblidged to be supported with drinking, and carefull dyet; that the load of bussines lyes much upon the Queen and Sir Robert. Some say he had an apoplectik fit, when the Prince was brought over last winter so very suddainly. Whither this be Jacobite neuse or not, I cannot say. The Lord prepare for his will.

Aprile, 1729.—The first day of this moneth our Synod met. Mr M'Kneight had a good sermon on, " He that is faithfull in litle." Mr W. Love was chosen Moderator. Ther was litle before the Synod save Renfreu and Mr Finlater's affair.

Severall motions wer made for a Fast, and, indeed, ther wer many obvious reasons for it. The generall sicknes this spring in very many places in these bounds; the scarcity and dearth, the merkets being exceeding high, eleven pence, twelve, and twelve pence half penny, per peck, and this, considering the present scarcity of money, makes it harder for poorer persons then when the meal was at eighteen and twenty pence per boll, [peck?] and ther was more money in the country; besides an extraordinary cold spring and strange saxoues.* A Fast seemed to be gone into in the Committy for Overtures by the most part, and was delayed till another meeting; but the affair of Renfreu turned so tedious, that ther wer no more meetings of the Overtures.

The affair of Renfreu came in on Wensday forenoon. Upon the Teusday's night, in our meeting in Presbitry at night, after our Synodi-

* Perhaps sicknesses?

call bussines was over, the Presbitry read the reasons of transportation given in by Renfreu for my removall from Eastwood. They wer but short, and then they called me, and offered to put them in my hand. Last day when the call was concurred with, they wanted the reasons; this day, when they have reasons, they wanted the call. It was delivered in, with other papers in process, to the Committy for Bills, and was not in a readynes. The Presbitry offered to put the reasons in my hand without the call, and ordered me to cite my parish against next day. I told them whatever they did or ordered me to do, I craved they might put in write, and give me an extract of it; and desired them to notice what they were doing, for I was nou on my guard, and would certainly improve every informality. They begged I might come over* the want of this peice of form, since I sau the call was not in their hands. I told them I was on my defence, and they might do what [they] sau proper, and I would act so as I thought most for my interest, and that of the parish; so they desisted. To-morrou I was called to meet with the Presbitry. They had, contrary to the perremptory demands of the appellants, got up the call from the Moderator of the bills, in order to present it in form to me with the reasons, but the meeting of Presbitry being in time of Synod, and not an ordinary meeting, regularly called in the intervalls of Synod, I declined meeting with them; so the call was not put in my hands.

On Wensday fornoon the affair of Renfreu was floored.† The first question that cast up was about the partys. Mr N. Campbell had subscribed a commission to Mr A. Dunlope to joyn in and prosecut Mr M'Dermitt's call, and he was desired to remove as a party; this he declined till he had the opinion of the Synod. The Presbitry of P[aisley] wer reconed partys in judging of the partys‡ in this cause, I think without all reason. Houever, he insisted to have the Presbitry removed as partys, and, without debating, they removed. The Principal urged that he was oblidged, as President of the Faculty, to signe a commission whither he was for it or not, and addressed the affections of the house, and begged their compassion. All did not do; the Synod came to a vote on it, and all, save five or six, voted the Principal a party. In the

---

* Overlook.   † Brought before the Court.   ‡ Who should be heard as Parties.

afternoon, and the after debates, I left the Synod and came home, because, though not a party, yet it was not so decent I should be present. And my dear Jamie fell worse, and so I went home. The two appeals wer after a strugle cast, and the third was referred for want of time to the Assembly, upon which those for Mr M'Derment appealed to the Assembly. I cannot but in all this observe the Divine Providence in conducting this matter, so as it never comes to my dore ;* and probably nou it will not come to my dore, but be turned into the Commission, and ther we will be either both laid aside, or it will be so determined as probably I shall not be troubled.

The other affair of Mr Finlaterr came in late on Thursday, when the Synod wer outwearyed with Renfreu. The Presbitry and Committy made their report; nothing was found proven but his neglect of visiting for many years, and for this he pretended want of health ; and his ultroneus oath, or asseveration ; for both which Mr Finlater received a Synodicall rebuke ; and so this process was again ended. Whither the compleaners will prosecute their appeal to the Assembly I knou not ; but that poor parish of Hamiltoun lyes in the most deplorable circumstances I knou any parish in the Synod.

By this time, it was so late that the Books and the Privy Censures wer passed† and referred to the next Synod.

Mr John Loudon, who was some time in the family of Rothess, tells me that the D[uke] of Rothess, though he put on a face of severity and persecution of the Presbiterians, partly to cover his keeping Bishop Sharp fast to him, and to keep the Clergy at his devotion, yet he was no enimie to them in his heart, and shoued them all the favour he could. Particularly one time the A[rchbishop] came to dine with him, as the Dutchess told my informer, and compleaned of David and James Walker, his oun tennants, two eminent Christians, one of them father to Mr David Walker, Minister at Temple, as keepers of conventicles, and supporters of that way. This complaint was made at dinner by the Bishop in very great wrath. The Duke seemed to be surprized with it, and said he should take an effectuall course with them, and see them both stringed.‡ The A[rchbishop] insisted that he might not forget them,

* Becomes my duty to take a part in it.   † Passed by and deferred.   ‡ Hanged.

for they wer incendiary throu all Fife ; and the Duke immediatly gave orders to his gentlman, standing at his back, to send immediatly to the toun of Leslay, wher they lived near by, and bring them doun to him after dinner ; and with many asseverations promised that they should give the Government no more trouble.   The orders wer obeyed, and they sent for.   This spoyled my Lady Dutches' dinner, the[y] being her Christian freinds, whom she exceedingly valued.   The twa honest men wer brought doun immediatly, and carryed into one of the roomes of Lesley.   The Duke after dinner sau the A[rchbishop] to his coach, and there again he minded the Duke of the two men.   The Duke told him they wer come, and he should not fail to handle them severly.   The Duke came up stairs, called for them, and spoke nothing of the matter to them, but asked the prices of the merkates, and what grain was best to him to sou in such and such places of his lands about Lesley, and dismissed them without a froun.   The Dutchess retired from dinner in deep concern for the men, and gave orders to a servant to bring them in to her when the Duke parted with them by a back gallery.   Accordingly, they came. The Dutches was all in tears, and almost trembling, asked what had past?   They told her, " Nothing but kindness."   Whither this was to be attributed to an answer to the Dutches' prayers on their behalf, or to the Duke's naturall temper, who was not inclined to violence, I am not to determine ; but the fact is certain.

Another instance of the Duke's lenity the same person informs me off was this : A certain persecutor, a broken* gentlman, who had got a commission to search for Conventicle preachers, and was very willing to the work, in the heat of persecution got notice of Mr R. Rule, afterwards Minister of Stirling, and another Minister whose name I'v [I have] forgot, who had been preaching near Lesley.   Mr Rule was a man of boldnes and courage ; the other Minister was of a more timorouse nature.   He passed under the name of the Minister's man, and generally caryed a brace of pockit pistolls with him.   The gentlman who had commission from the Bishop got nottice of them and of their characters, and that they wer in such a room in such a place, not far from Lesly.   He comes in to the place, and asked, If ther was a Minister and his man

* Broken down.

ther? It was a publick-house, wher they wer refreshing themselves. The people kneu nothing of them, and said ther was two men with them in such a room. The persecutor, who was no bold man either, ordered the people of the house to tell them that he wanted to speak with them. Mr Rule kneu his errand, and asked, if he was alone? They said he was, but he had a commission to seize suspect persons. Mr Rule bad her* tell him they had no bussines with him, and wer bussy. Upon which he came to the dore, and ordered them to come forth, for they wer his prisoners. Mr Rule told him that they would not obey him, they wer persons, free leidges, and he mistook his men. He threatned to break up the dore. The other Minister was at his witt's end. Mr Rule encouraged him, and went to the dore, and opned it, and asked whom he wanted? He said, " A Minister and his man, two rebells." He said, " I am the Minister's man; but if you come any further, (presenting his pistol to him,) he was a dead man." This dashed the gentlman, and he went no further, but called the Minister to him, and catched hold of him. The other being timorous, when Mr Rule went about to rescue him, begged he might not do any harm, he would go with the gentlman.

Thus he carryed away the other Minister prisoner to Lesley, and came to the Duke, who by this time had got the story from some other hands. When he came to [the] Duke, he told him he had seized a Conventicle Minister, and brought him to his Grace. He asked wher he was? " Doun stairs," said he. " Bring him up," said the other. When he came, and [the Duke] found by converse with him the story as above, he came out to the gentlman, and said, " You base couard! Go presently and bring me the Minister's man, whom ye have left behind. It's him I want." This made the other ashamed, and he went off; and soon after the Duke dismissed the timorouse Minister.

This moneth we have many variouse reports of the Commissioner to the ensueuing Assembly. The Earl of Loudon pushed very much for it, as is said, and had the two brothers† for him. The Earl of Buchan is also talked of; and Mr Simson gives it out that the Earle of Isla is coming doun to Scotland, houever, and he is to be Commissioner. Hou-

---

* The Landlady. † Argyll and Islay.

ever, at the close of the moneth we have certain accounts that Earl
Buchan is pitched on, which is not a litle mortifying to Mr Simson and
his freinds. The occasion of the Earl of Buchan's coming in, I am told,
was this : In the summer 1726, the Earl of Buchan got a promise from
King George to be Commissioner next to the Assembly. That excellent Prince had a great value for Buchan, as I am well informed ; and
when he was by, the courtiers scored out of the list of Scots Peers, about
the 1721 or 1723 ; and the list [being] brought to [the] King, he put
him [in] with his oun hand. In the year 1727 he had been Commissioner ; but Seafield got in by Sir Robert Walpool's means. He had,
by a warrand from the King, represented him the former winter, at admitting Duke Hamiltoun Knight of the Thistle, and gave in an accompt
to the Threasury pretty large. When he was put off, he proposed to
withdrau his account, if Sir Robert would get him named Commissioner
to the Assembly. This was done, 1728, on King G[eorge] the Second
his accession. Buchan pleaded his promise, but Loudon prevailed by
the interest of the two brothers. But this year, Buchan being very well
with severall of the English Nobility, by his relation and estate in England, insisted upon his promise ; and when Argyle and Yla continoued
to act for Loudon, he caused tell them he would not desist ; and if they
insisted to oppose him, they wer never to expect any more freindship.
So he carryed his point.

The midle of this moneth we had the accompts that D[uncan] Forbes
was to be President, and the presen[t Presi]dent to have his sellary
turned to a pension during life, and the Solicitor to be made Advocat ;
but they do not hold.

We have the accounts reneued about the King's ill state of health,
but I hope they are groundless, since nou we are assured that he is going
abroad to Hannover.

I am well informed that Mr David Williamson, when he was, a litle
after the Revolution, supplying at Aberdeen, was much hated by the
Jacobites and Episcopalls ther, [who] put all the obloquy and affronts
upon him they could ; particularly on Sabbath, when he was going to
preach, they hounded out a poor profane man to meet him on the pub-

lick street, and sing and dance on the Sabbath.   Whither he had [a] fidle playing also, I do not mind ; but the tune he sung in dancing before him was " Dainty Davie !"   Mr Williamson was greived at the profanation of the Sabbath, and said to some body with him, " Alace ! for that poor man ; he is nou rejecting the last offer he is ever to have of Christ !"   The wretch came not to Church, and before night dyed in a feu minutes.

Mistress Luke tells me she was present when Mr Gillies was examining in the Laigh Church, a litle before his death.   He called in his roll one Horn, a flesher, in his quarter.   He was not present.   He asked if he was present ? and was told he was not.   He said, with much gravity, "·Not present ?   He never was present ; he never shall be present with us till we be all sisted befor the Judgment-seat of Christ !"   The poor man was in perfect health, and, in a day or two, dyed suddainly, and was never again at Church.

The same worthy person, Mr Neil Gilles, was some times exceeding seriouse in his sermons.   On[e] time the same person heard him either preaching on these words, " Good-will to men," or he cited them, and enlarged on them in a holy rapture ; and was running out upon the infinite love and condescension in good-will to men, and repeated it once or twice :—" Good-will to men, and good-will to me ! O ! hou sweet is this !"   A woman long under distress, but seriouse, cryed out, " And to me also !"—and this was the beginning of her graciouse outgate.*

Ther is a very strange account which I have from severall hands, as what is really belived at Edinburgh, though the persons concerned decline to speak of it, and it's keeped very closs.   In January last, or two or three moneths ago, my Lord Royston, (M'Kenzie,) his daughter, lady to Coll. Cunninghame, this last winter, fell into a decay, and turned weaker and weaker.   For many weeks she was diverted by company, and playing at dyce, cardes, and the like ; and her hazard was keeped from her.   At lenth the physicians, reconing her within a feu dayes of death, took her father, my Lord, aside, and told him they thought his

* Deliverance from despondency.

daughter was lou, and it was proper she should be told she was dying. Her father took a proper time, and acquainted her with her hazard in the most cautious manner. She took the hint, and turned very seriouse, and could not bear any diversions. Her brother, my Lord's eldest son, a youth about seventeen, very rackish, and loose in principles, at best a Deist, came in to her room, and, finding her pensive and thoughtfull, fell a jesting with her, and, taking up a flute or some other musicall in- strument, fell a dancing and playing. She desired him to desist, for she had been to long diverted, and could not bear his dancing; and the less, that the beginning of her decay had been a wrest* in her arm, which she had gote by a suddain turn in dancing in one of their Assemblys at Edinburgh. The youth asked if she was turned whimsicall? She said not; but my Lord, his father, had been with her, and told her she was near death, and she was nou endeavouring to prepare for it. He in- sisted that she was roving, and should be diverted; and told her he did not belive ther was any thing after death to fear, and wished she might not belive any thing she sau not, and make herself easy. She answered, She did belive she had an immortall soul; that ther was a heaven and a hell. His words I do not repeat, being horrid, but ended with that :— " Girl, when thou dyes, if ther be any thing in those dreams, come back and tell me! I belive none of that preistcraft!" She, with difficulty, charged him off. In a day or two she dyed. Next morning, or soon after her death, her brother being in his room alone, it's confidently said she appeared to him. What passed is not told; but this is certain, the youth came running, like one distempered, to my Lord, his father, his room, in his shirt, as I am told, all in sweat, and told what passed. He was gote composed a litle, but keeped his room, and was not upon the street for five or six weeks. Of late, nou, he begins to come out. I enquired about the story at Edinburgh. I find ther is somwhat in it, but the particulars are keeped closs; and people stickt to enquire or to be particular about them.

Mistress Luke tells me that she is well informed that, some years ago,

---

* Twist, sprain.   † Hesitate.

John M'Gilchrist's wife, ... Smith, daughter to Bailay William Smith, had an uncle, perhaps in Kilmarnock, who was a seriouse, good man. His daughter dyed of a lingering sicknes, pretty much beyond expectation. Her father fell under great damps and darkness as to her welbeing after her death, and betook himself to prayer, whither by necessity or out of choice to quicken himself, I knou not; but he was wrestling in the room wher the corpse was lying, and, after prayer and much liberty in it, the corpse sat up in the bed, and said audibly to him, " Christ is all and in all to me;" and then leaned doun in the bed, and was cold and stiff as before. The good man was much astonished at this. These extraordinary things are a dangerouse dispensation to be under.

The same person tells me her mother, Agnes Guthry, was with her grandmother, on Mr Guthry's death, at Bogton, in the parish of Cathcart. That, at that time, her mother was exceeding seriouse, and used frequent[ly,] in the summer evenings, to go out in the walk of trees at Bogtoun, and continou late in prayer and covenanting. That, one night, she was there at twelve of the clock at night, and got much liberty in taking hold of God as her father's God, Mr William Guthry, and in covenanting. When she came in to the house, by the way, she was earnest with God that she might have a confirmation that what she had met with was not a delusion. When come in, she took her Bible to read, and that place casting up to her, " Go thy way, eat thy bread, thou art accepted !"—and, after it, Thomas' words, " My God and my Lord !"—and, last of all, as far as I mind, " My God, whose I am, and whom I serve, hath appeared to me !"—These gave her much consolation.

The same person tells me that, on the Friday afternoon before the Sacrament at Glasgou, she is wel informed that Mr William Wisheart, Mr George Wisheart, and Mr William Hamiltoun, who is in a decay, and probably dying, went out to Mr Wisheart's country house, at the head of the Green of Glasgou, and drank, as is supposed, most of the afternoon. At least, when they came in through the Green, towards the evening, they, especially the last, wer observed scarcely in case to

walk, and their eyes muddy, and staggering. I wish this may be false
and ill-grounded ; but such things, even when reported, wound religion
dreadfully.

May, 1729.—Ther was a meeting proposed upon the Munday, Aprile
28, about Mr Simson, when the Colledge wer upon Counts and some
other things ; and accordingly ther was [a] meeting of the Masters. Mr
Loudon, Mr Carmichael, [and] Mr W. Anderson, would not meet. Doctor B[risbane] was called and heard the paper read, and went off, and
would by no means stay. The matter, it seems, was before-hand dressed
up between the Principall, Mr Simson, and that side. Mr Simson dreu up
his declaration of his soundnes and orthodoxy, which is in print, and the
Principall had the draught of the Colledge paper ready likewise, which
is in print, and it was resolved to send both to the Assembly. Doctor
Brisban, being sent for most earnestly by the Principall, came, not
knouing the occasion, but when he heard the paper read, he took up his
hat and left them, telling he was no judge of such matters. He was
entreated to stay, but by no means would, though he was told it would
break the quorum. Mr Forbes reasoned against the Colledge making
any application to the Assembly, and declared himself dissatisfyed all
along with Mr Simson's doctrine, and that this paper was to him as un-
satisfactory as the others he had given to the Church. Mr Murthland
would not come. Ther was only Mr Wisheart, Mr Dunlop, and Mr
Dick, and Robert Simson ; the two last the Professor's near relations,
and yet the paper goes in name of the Colledge, when, indeed, there was
no quorum, especially for a matter of that weight. This paper was
caryed in to the Instructions, and ther throuen out, and brought in head
and shoulders to the Assembly by P[rincipal] Campbell, and very ill
treated there, (see Letters in May,) and therafter it was printed.

On this occasion, Mr John Hamilton tells me that Mr Simson undoubtedly at the beginning had altred his sentiments as to the doctrine
of Christ. That when urged, upon severall arguments, in conversation,
which related to the Son's independancy, &c., he said openly, " What !
will you make the Son rivall his Father ?" That letters passed betwixt

Professor Hamiltoun and him, wherin Mr Simson used such extraordinary freedoms that Pr[ofessor] Hamiltoun declined going on in the correspondence, and waved it. My informer is positive that P[rofessor] Hamiltoun was once of opinion, and ouned it to him, that Mr Simson had altered his scheme; and when he P[rofessor] Hamiltoun stopped writing, and declined to enter any further on these points, he advised Mr Simson to take heed of entering to Doctor Clark's scheme, in his last letter

May 1.—As to the procedure of the Assembly, which sat doun this 1st day of May, see Letters this moneth. I was not in till Mr Simson's bussines came in open Assembly. After that, ther was litle, save the classing of the Instructions, and the Overture upon the Instructions from Presbitrys. I did not hear the Reasonings. The Overture is in the papers this year. It was necessary, indeed, that the Assembly should come in* to some sort of declaration to that purpose, that they did not intirely go on Instructions from Presbitrys, but wer judges themselves, and sau with their oun eyes; and they say that no Suprem Civil Court, particularly the Parliament, will receive Instructions from countys and corporations; but that will not, in all respects, be a pattern for Suprem Ecclesiasticall Courts. It is hard, I oun, to describe the pouers of the Supreme Court, or to say they are bound up by Instructions from their inferiors; but, on the other hand, it's as plain that Presbyterys, taking them altogether, are the Church diffusive, the whole of the Ministry of Scotland, with the Elders; and I see not but the declared sense of the plurality of Presbitrys, by our Presbiterian Constitution, ought to be considered as the sense of this Church.

The precise question seems to be this, Whither the sentiments of the Ministry and rulers of this Church, mett separately and in Presbitrys, or the sense [of] the plurality of the delegates of Presbitrys met together in an Assembly, should issue† a matter of contraversy in [all] the Church? We oun both Presbitrys and a delegat Assembly to be Courts and meetings of Christ's institution; and both have the promise and [of his?] conduct vouchafed to them. In that respect, they seem to be on a

* Agree on.   † Determine; bring to an issue.

ballance.   On the other hand, prudentiall considerations will lead us, it may be, to preferr an Assembly to the plurality of Presbitrys; because there, the most aged, and knouing, and most experienced Members are there; and Members, not numbers, are to be weighed, and votes are to be pondered rather than numbered.   And, to be sure, when it's impossible that all the Rulers of a Church can meet together in one place and time, in the nature of things, there must be som. last ressort, and an issue and end to different sentiments; otherwise ther can be no order or society.   Upon the other hand, in Presbitrys, it's as plain that ther is much more time and freedome to consider a matter, at least of this nature as Mr Simson's is of, ther is room for amicable conference, considering the circumstances, and speaking of many things necessary to be considered, which are not so proper to be talked of in an Assembly; neither, indeed, is ther time and room.   Besides, every body that knoues matters, easily sees that in Assemblys, all matters of consequence must be done in a Committy, which, generally speaking, is as small in number as a Presbitry; and the Overture brought in by them comes pretty. hastily to be. approven or disapproven by the whole Assembly.   Upon the whole, though I am sorry I was not present to hear the reasonings. upon this head, which, no doubt, wer in the Committy of Instructions, I cannot altogether approve the generality of their conclusion, which the Assembly is indeed come into.   Their generall declaration, whatever regard is to be had to Instructions from Presbitrys, seems too much to lessen the regard an Assembly ought to have to the deliberate judgment of the body of Presbitrys, in a matter remitted to them by a Generall Assembly, after printing the whole process, and transmitting it to the consideration of Presbitrys.   The Presbitrys, no doubt, had all before them almost that the Assembly could have before them; and as, I hope, never a case of this nature will again exist, so I wish a more particular regard had been sheuen to such a solem and deliberat remitt as was made.   Houever, the declaration the Committy and Assembly have made is so far right, that the Assembly must certainly have a judicative power upon the Instructions that are sent up; and, after weighing the reasons sent up by Presbytrys, must, for themselves, and according to their light, form their sentence.   What offers to me, in this case, is this, under correction, that an Assembly, in such circumstances, cannot indeed be bound up from acting and passing a sentence as matters appear to them ; but in case, after mature deliberation, the[y] cannot be of the opinion with the plurality of Presbitrys, they ought not to come for the first to a finall decision contrary to the knouen sentiments of the diffusive Church, but may and ought to transmit the grounds upon which they cannot be of the mind with the Presbitrys, and [for order's sake] they may be alloued, in the mean time, to give their judgment till another Assembly, to bind till then : but, mean while, their intermediat act, with the reasons on which they go, should be again transmitted to Presbitrys, and their opinions be again required to the next Assembly. If, upon these reasons, the plurality of Presbitrys alter their sentiments, it's well ; if not, I cannot see but the follouing Assembly should give a finall sentence as they find cause, because at lenth ther must be a decision. Things have been, indeed, I hope wisely and moderately, and with the vast advantage of harmony, carryd ; but, on the whole, if Presbitrys take care to send up Members of the sentiments of the Presbitry, ther is no great hazard of dilators* and endles clashings in such matters as this, which I pray God deliver us from in time to come.

Other things that hapned in the Assembly, see Letters from this Assembly to my wife, to which I'll add nothing but a feu more generall remarks. At the beginning of the Assembly, it was given out that the Earl of Buchan, Commissioner, had Instructions from the King to see that nothing should be done against Mr Simson ; and that if any motions to depose him wer made, that he should dissolve the Assembly. As soon as I went in to Edinburgh, being allarumed with these accounts, I was glad of the first occasion I had to converse with the Commissioner, which I got the very day I first sau him. He told me that he was no way straitned by his Instructions ; that the King had never given him the least hint about Mr Simson ; that he would never have taken such Instructions as would in the least have straitned the Assembly ; that the Assembly was not in the least interrupted by the shaddou of an Instruction. Houever, he spoke favourably of Mr Simson, and thought we could require no more repentance and acknouledgment than he had

* Dilatory proceedings.

given ; and wished the Assembly might not run matters too farr against him.   I took the liberty to ask his Grace [if ?] his Lordship would trust [the] Education of his children to a person that had once corrupted them, and professed he would not do it again ? He said litle to the argument. I presumed to tell him that it was in the pouer of those for the truth to carry his deposition ; and unles somewhat effectuall to prevent his further teaching and corrupting of the youth wer gone into, they would carry a vote, "Depose him." He said he was no way straitned in his Instructions as to that, and if it could be carryed without a breach, he was easy. But if we broke upon it, this would be improven against him, the Commissioner, for he was not without his enemies. I said, for my oun share, I was for doing all with harmony, as far as possible, and wished for it, both for the Churches sake and his Grace's ; and if any thing could be harmoniously gone into that would effectually secure the youth from corruption in time to come, and unite the Church, I was for it ; and so we parted.   This made me very easy.

I find, from the beginning of this affair to this time, that either Mr Simson or his freinds have spread untruths to support their cause ; and, as is ordinary, when lyes wer discovered, their cause lost by it.

The first thing that cast up in Mr Simson's affair at this Assembly, was the class of the opinions of Presbitrys.   See this in the papers for this year.   Ther wer but two Presbitrys for reponing him ; a feu, very feu, for any thing favourable to him ; all the rest wer for laying him aside from teaching ; and the far greatest part wer for his deposition from teaching and preaching.   This was a considerable stroak (shoak ?) to his cause in the entry, which his freinds could not easily grapple with.

One of the most plausible defences that Mr S[imson] had, was that of his not being cited by the last Assembly.   It's true, in my opinion, the Reference cited him ; but I do not see any other thing for this save practise.   The acts of Assembly adduced do not appear very strong ; but it seems the Assembly [on] the first tabling of this affair came over* this, and sent a formall citation to him, and acquainted him they were to go on in his process.   When he came, he subjected† practically.   If he had not appeared, it is probable the Assembly would have gone on, and he

_____
 * Took notice of.   † Subjected himself; submitted.

might [have] taken it to be saffer to be present at the Assembly's meetings upon his affair ; and it was much more fair and frank, and like an innocent person, to compear and plead his cause.

In his discourses, Mr Simson and his lauers wer exceeding prolix. They wer heard upon what was called alleviations ; and, under that head, as they had done upon exculpation and probation, they dreu in the whole of the subject, and every thing that might breed favourable impressions of the cause. These took up three or four dayes. See my Letters.

When the Assembly came to advise what to do upon the whole, their speeches and reasonings wer decent, very calm, and with much feuer indecencys than I have too often seen in such a numerous meeting. It appeared to me, (and Ministers of very good experience and knouledge, not at all sided* in our debates, who wer present, made the same remark,) that the members who wer for further censure had very much the better in point of reasoning. Indeed, in my opinion, they had the better side, easier to argue upon ; but even in the managment and manner of reasoning I did think they acted a closser and clearer part then the other side.

I will not enter into a detail of the reasonings. Hints of them, as far as my frail memory served, are in my Letters. The act issuing† this affair is printed. If we may judge by Mr Simson's oun thoughts of it, it is certainly very grating to him, and he inclined rather to have been deposed than to have this incapacitating declarature pronounced upon him. What wer his reasons I say not ; but one is pretty plain, that this declaration, especially when unanimouse, can never with any decency be altered ; wheras a deposition, especially had dissents or reasons been given in against it, might have more easily be[en] reversed.

The second lybell was not at all considered by the Assembly. But the sentence of the Assembly run upon the first. This had severall advantages, and keeped this Church from neu breaches upon these subjects to which that lybell relates. Houever, it was moved in private, and appeared very reasonable, that this present sentence should not be opened, and the present suspension should not be taken off till the second lybell

---

　　: * Not taking a side.　　　　† Deciding.

should be judged, and the Church determine hou far he was guilty or not ; but that was not moved in publick.   It was also proposed in private, and I am sorry it did not go further, for in this Assembly I hope it might have carryed, that all Presbitrys and Synods should be by the Assembly prohibited to transport any to the profession of Divinity, till the advice of the G[eneral] Assembly wer taken, or of the Commission. This is a most reasonable motion, considering the influence a Professor of Divinity hath upon this Church, and what trouble this Church hath had from this Professor.

Upon the whole, this process as to Mr Simson is, certainly, happily off the feild in this Church ; and I think it's a token for good among the many evil tokens we have, that we have got throu such an intricat, quisquous,* and tender a proces ; so as I hope even the men of latitude† cannot, upon any tollerable grounds, blame us for a persecuting, violent temper ; since all done personall is but a continoued suspension, and the outmost lenth that is come is only a necessary provision for security of the doctrine and youth of the Church.   Our enimies expected a breach, and we our selves very much feared it, and an open breach by dissent or reasons publicly given in, on either hand, would have had ill consequences, and the harmony and unanimity of the sentence makes it the stronger, and every way the more desirable.

These three years, nou, as is to be seen in what is above, the Churches time hath been taken up with this affair of Mr Simson.   Nothing else almost hath been done of any weight.   We can get no advances made in forming regulations, acts, and constitutions, the proper work of an Assembly.   At this Assembly ther was no more save this affair, and a refused transportation of Mr Wilky from Uphall to Dundee, though the state of that Presbitry, having five vaccancys, made his transportation, considering his fitnes, very needfull ; but he was the Commissioner's Minister, and averse himself ; and it's but seldom, nou, a transportation is carryed (neither, considering the multitude of young men, is there any necessity, as indeed once was in this Church) wher the Minister is heartyly against it.

* Perplexing.   † Latitudinarian principles.

Principall Chambers' case was just the reverse. He was setled in Old Aberdeen, and seemed to have been too active, or at least too much passive in that matter. The Commissioner's daughter, L[ady] Kathrine Frazer, was particularly brought to oppose this setlment, and this helped on a considerable opposition to it. The Ministers of the Synod wer very keen against this setlment, and severall things in it did not look well. I did not attend the Reasonings, and so cannot state them, but his setlment was renversed.*

The affairs of Touie and Hutton, and some other transportations, with our case in Renfreu, wer remitted to the Commission; and, at the first Commission, Mr Orr was transported from Muirkirk to Hoddam, and the setlment by the Presbitry which had been by Principall Chalmers' influence and that of his party, reversed by the Synod, was affirmed by the Commission. Thus, at this Assembly and Commission, Principall Chalmers, and his side in the Synod of Aberdeen, are considerably shaken. Indeed, the Ministers in the North are exceedingly dissatisfyed, generally speaking, with his conduct. Hou well grounded their exceptions are against him, I do not judge. His changing sides, and his involving himself in politicks, are not to his advantage.

The Earl of Buchan, in conversation, told me that the bulk of the English Peers are, in their opinion, against the Bishops sitting and votting in Parliament, and very openly declare their sentiments. But at present the Bishops are so moderat, and medle so litle in what relates to State affairs, and generally are Whiggs in principle, that no nottice is taken of their sitting. But would the English Peers deal generously, this is the proper time for them, when the Bishops are upon the side of liberty, and yet by their office, or their grants of lands, have no claim to sit in Parliament, with the best grace, and the most disinterested way, to lay them aside from medling in Parliamentary affairs.

Ther is a considerable zeal and firmnes at present in our bretheren of Angus, Aberdeen, Murray, and Inverness, against innovations upon our

* Overturned. Fr. *renverser.*

constitution, against Patronages, for the purity of doctrine, and in prosecuting of immoralitys in Ministers, more, I think, by far than with us
in the West and in the East.   Professor Hamilton is extremly blamed
by the Ministers of the North with whom I have conversed, for patron-
izing Principall Chambers in all motions for patronages, and protecting
of viciouse and looser persons.   Processes that came up from the North,
(wher it may be some irregularitys and haste, on the side of opposition
to loosnes and vice, are,) never sooner come to Edinburgh, to Commissions and Assemblys, but he is blamed for siding with the lazer* side ; and
in Commissions, some younger Ministers, Mr John Walker, Mr George
Logan, Mr James Nasmith, Mr Hutchieson's grandchild and others, joyn,
and scandalous persons, deposed Ministers, and the like, are protected.
This is exceedingly greivouse to many Ministers, and in time, I am perswaded, will come to have ill consequences on our generall interests, and
at best will raise such jealousys as the generall concerns of the Church
will not run so as they have done under the managment of some of the
older Ministers.

The mixing in of lauers, Lords of Session, and others in Commissions
and Assemblies with so much keenness, in processes for doctrine, and calls
to parishes, and transportations, and party affairs, is a greivance we have
been long under, and it's still grouing upon us ; and the admitting of so
long litigiouse and forraign pleadings of Advocats, at the barr of our
Church Judicatories, is like to have such ill consequents, that it [is] a
wonder to me the leading Ministers in Commissions and Assemblys do
not observe them, and endeavour to provide some reasonable regulations
against them.

Mr Charles Masterton was with me in the beginning of this moneth.
He tells me ther is litle remarkable in Ireland.   Their Judicatorys are
nou again very peacable.   The Not-subscribers are much left by their
people, and make litle or no noise.   They have still a joynt meeting of
Subscribers and Non-subscribers about their money matters, and the dis-

---

* Laxer ; more indulgent.

tribution and securing of the King's Bounty. This spring, it seems, one Mr J. Hamiltoun, a merchant in England, who was their receiver of the twelve thousand* the Goverment alloues them yearly, has got an estate, and is chosen a Member of the Brittish Parliament. When thus a member of Parliament, it was not fitt his name should stand in the King's books as receiving L.1200 pension yearly. This, it seems, is the method. The Bounty is given to one whom the Synod intrusts, and comes not in the King's books under any other notion but a pension to a particular man. Mr Hamiltoun acquainted the Synod's Committy, or the joynt meeting for managing the Bounty, that his circumstances did not any longer allou him to serve them, desired another might be named, to whom he would give all the assistance he could, and moved that a minister on both sides, if they pleased, or one for both, might be sent to London, and his name insert in the books, and that one should yearly come to London and receive the money. This was gone into by the joynt meeting. Mr M'Bride was Moderator, and after some debates, whither one or two [should be sent,] for saving of charges, it was agreed one might do, and a neutrall person as much as might be, neither Subscriber nor Non-subscriber, should be fixed on. Accordingly, Mr Craighead was gone into, and sent over to London, to desire the augmentation of the fund, if it can be got, (and, indeed, they need this very much,) and to represent the greivances of the Presbiterians in Ireland. According[ly,] he went over in Aprile or March last.

He tells me, that Mr Halliday is very frank and open; and in conversation with himself ouned that the Calvinist scheme was not tenible: That at last he and many others are gone into the Baxterian scheme.

He adds, Mr Patrick Bruce, before his comming over last moneth to Killellan, preached with his B. [brother?] Mr M. Bruce, and baptized his child. This may be perhaps easily accounted for; but when he came to Belfast, he preached for Mr Halliday: He preached for Mr Kilpatrick, and conversed with them and that side: Never looked near Mr Masterton, though indisposed, and though he had been usefull to him in vindicating his character, and sending favourable representations, in

* So in MS. Probably it is a mistake for L.1200.

order to his setling with us. This method in his comming to Scotland
savours either of a very considerable remaining regard to the Non-subscribers, or at least not of very much prudence and reflexion, after the
declarations he sent to our Presbitry.

He tells me, Mr William Biggart is lately transported from Bangor in
Ireland to Inch in Galloway, the Earle of Stair's parish. He had one
of the best setlments in all the North of Ireland. His people and he
fell into some misunderstanding. He is turned infirm, and would have
had an assistant, and they wer not so forward that way as he expected
their former regard to him should have led them to be. The people of
the Inch do not seem to be altogether so earnest for his transportation.
A presentation was tabled before a call, and they wer fretted; houever,
he is nou transported, and by this time setled in Galloway. He is a
very considerable man, easy in his temper, and highly esteemed in Ireland; but my informer doubts if his setlment be comfortable.

Mistress Luke informes me that . . . . Colquhoun, a sister of Mr John
Colquhoun, Minister of Drone, a woman that was reconed religiouse and
seriouse, many years ago, in Glasgou, fell under great straits and poverty,
and the greatest penury for daily bread. She keept her circumstances
secret; and under the continouance of her strait, and under the violent
pouer of a violent tentation, was at lenth hurryed into self-murder, which
she executed. I knou not the circumstances, but I believe it was by
wounding herself mortally, so as she lived some hours. She sent for Mr
J. Gray a litle before her death. She was very penitent for the fact,
and narrated the whole circumstances, and asked his opinion if mercy
was possible for her? He was in a strait, in so extraordinary a case; and,
after safe generall declarations to her, asked her her oun thoughts, finding her a person of considerable knouledge. She expressed great diffi-
dence, without despair, and agravated her crime; and said, she sau no
place in the Scrip[ture] to build on but that, " I will have mercy on
whom I will have mercy." Mr Gray prayed with her. In a litle time
she dyed. She appeared to him to be a humble seriouse Christian, and
he had great hopes of her salvation.

Mr Colin M'Laurin, who was frequently with Sir Isaack Neuton, and very much valued by him and intimat with him, tells me that he has left pretty large papers upon the Scripture Prophesys. That he had severall peculiar thoughts upon them, and was not of the opinion that Daniel's Last Week was fully ended. Upon my shouing Mr M'Laurin some of Mr Whiston's reflexions lately upon Sir Isaack, and that he sett him on the head of the Arrians, my informer tells me that Sir Isaack and Mr Whiston these twenty years have been at great variance ; but, houever, he belived it might be fact that Sir Isaack was pretty much in Doctor Clerk's sentiments, and that he has heard him express himself pretty strongly upon the subordination of the Son to the Father, and say, that he did not see that the Fathers, for the first three or four centuries, had opinions the same with our modern doctrine of the Trinity ; but that Sir Isaack was extremly cautiouse in his discourse upon those matters, especially for some years before his death, when he compleaned of decayes and failours.* He thinks that Sir Isaack's papers on the Scripture Prophesys will be published, and that he heard Sir Isaack say, that he reconed the argument for the Messias, and the truth of Christianity, from the accomplishment of prophesys, was next to a demonstration. That ther is a great expectation in England of somwhat great and neu in these papers of Sir Isaack on the Prophesys.

I had not so much occasion of conversation in this moneth as I have had, our time being constantly taken up at the Assembly and meetings. I heard a very strange account of an apparition, of which I had some accounts in Letters from Mr Mck [Mack ?] about the 1724 or [172] 5, at Dumfrice, of the Laird of Coul, if I forget not his name, to a servant of a physitian at Dumfreice. Mr Ogilby, Minister at Haddington Presbitry, had the accounts of these, and being very frank in his temper, seemed incredulouse of it, and to say that he would have enquired severall things, if it had appeared to him. When he returned him [home ?] and was riding near his oun house, the apparition did appear to him; and told him the same story, and he conversed with it, and had severall meetings

* In his mind or memory.

with it. He discovered this to some feu of his bretheren before his death, which hap[pened] in some years after, but keeped it very closs. Houever, when he dyed this spring, and his Cabinet was opened, ther was found sealed by his seal, [and] with his oun hand was written on the back, " This bundell of papers is not to be opened till after my decease, and that in the presence of two neighbouring Ministers." Whither they wer named or not, I do not mind ; but they wer accordingly opened after Mr Ogilby, Minister at Innerweek, his death, by Mr R. Paton, Minister at Haddingtoun, and another. The papers, a sheet or two of paper, all written with his oun hand and signed, giving a full narrative of all that passed between him and the apparition, at severall intervieus. The papers are nou in Mr Paton's hands, and I am promised a sight of them.

This was talked of a litle at Edinburgh in time of the Assembly, and Mr Gilbert Anderson, Minister at Fordoun, told a story of an apparition to a Minister in that Presbitry, which stands in severall branches of it in their Registers (if I remember right.) The apparition discovered a secret adultery to a Minister, that had been overlooked by his predecessor, and, after some witnesses failed, discovered others, till at lenth the fact was proven by living witnesses, and the partys wer brought to acknouledgment, and to give publick satisfaction. Memorandum : To write to Mr G. Anderson to get a fuller account of it. See his Letter to me.

When I was enquiring at Edinburgh about Mr Robert Trail's papers, at London, his nepheu, Mr R. Trail, a Minister in the North, told me that he was at London about the time of his death ; that his books in Latine and Greek wer given to him by his wife, and but feu ; but she keeped all the English, and papers, save a feu scrapes of sermons she gave him. I enquired, what could become of the course of Letters betwixt his father, Mr Trail, Minister at Edinburgh, and Mr William Guthry, of which he speaks in his edition of Mr Guthry's Interests, London, 1705, or therabout : He said he could not tell ; and added, that his aunt Mss [Mistress] Trail had a neice marryed to one Mr Alston, and, as far as he can guess, they must be in Mistress's or Mr Alston's hands. It will be worth while to cause make enquiry about them, and, if possible, recover them ; for certainly a course of Letters on spirituall exercise between Mr Trail and Guthry, for some years, is a treasure.

Mr Randy tells me that when he was at London, as far as he could learn, matters wer intirely managed by the Queen and Sir Robert Walpool ; that the King was reconed a mere cyfer, and did no bussines ; that really, for all our present calm matters, by the most knouing persons we are reconed to be in the outmost confusion ; and, indeed, it is not probable but we must have some turn, if Providence prevent not. This state of things cannot long be hid, and we will certainly lose our influence in Europ.

I can mind litle more this moneth, save that, though our Moderator, Mr Alston, carryed pretty equall, and certainly acted outwardly a seeming fair part, yet I notticed him notting doun some memorandums, and handing them to Professor Hamilton, and Mr George Logan, and some others ; upon which we had some pretty suddain speeches and turns made, in favours of Mr Simson : But all would not do.

June, 1729.—This moneth some Ministers dye. Principall Wisheart has been long tender, and was not able to preach before the last Assembly. He was, first, Minister of Leith, and was ordeaned in time of the liberty.* He was then transported to Edinburgh, upon Mr Creighton's death. He was Moderator of the Assembly before, and of the Commission at the time of the Union, wher he had a difficult post, which perhaps was as well in his hand, than in one who would have managed that chair more cleverly. He has been Moderator three times since. He was disliked a litle for a sermon he had on Mr Meldrum's death, when he took some nottice, a covering his faults (Mr Meldrum's complyance with Prelacy) with a mantle of love. But I see not why he was so much blamed for that. He has printed many particular sermons, and his Theologia, which is reaconed a compend of Charnock on the Attributes. In his last years, he was very firm in the matter of the doctrine of the Trinity, and zealouse in his opposition to Mr Simson's innovations, notwithstanding the weight of his two sons. The greatest matter of objection ever I heard made to him was his too great exactnes

* Indulgence.

as to his brother's, the Admirall's, affairs, and too great narrounes.   His father's family is an instance of Divine retribution in this state.   His father was Minister in Linlithgou toun or Presbitry, and was persecuted for adherence to Presbyterian principles, and yet his children came all to have vastly more than he could have given them, had he continoued without trouble : His eldest son was in the army, and acquired a great estate of Cliftonhall.   Sir G. Wisheart, his other son, was Reer-Admirall in England, and left twenty thousand pound to the Principall, dying childless.   The Principall was a kind, honest, good man, and affectionat, seriouse preacher, and piouse.

Mr James Hart, first Minister at Ratho, then at Edinburgh, dyed in a day or two after him.   He was a worthy good man, and one whose sermons wer much haunted.*   He was naturally a litle warm and keen, but of considerable gravity and prudence with it.   He printed some feu sermons.

Mr David Fleckfeild dyed this moneth also.   He was thirty-eight years Minister of Balfrone, in Dumbarton Presbitry.   He was first marryed on my sister by my mother, Jonet ; and since twice marryed. He was a weak, to [though I] hope a good man, and has done good among that people.

I forgot to set doun an account Mr Ch[arles] Mastertoun told me of, a pretty odd passage which happned to a gentlewoman of his acquaintance, in Ireland.   She was aged, and used spectacles.   Her sight, on a suddain, so far failed, that her spectacles failed her.   She was very pious, and her comfort was much bound up in the Bible.   She had no knouledge of opticks ; but when her spectacles failed her, she concluded her reading was gone. On this she set apart some time for prayer, and came from it with much ease in her mind.   It came in her mind to look for a pair of old spectacles she had by her, and joyn them with these she last used.   She could give no reason for such a thought, but would try it, and the matter answered, and by the two pair she sau as well as ever.   A great many followed her way, and Mr Mastertoun had a pair of double spectacles with him, which magnifyed much, and wer very clear.

* Followed after.

Things are come to a terrible lenth among us. This moneth I am
well informed that lately, in Air toun, wher other sort of meetings wer
wont to be, ther is a meeting of men who deserve litle better name then
that of Atheists.   On the Sabbath, in time of Divine Worship, men of
some character, Mr Charles Cochran, James Dalrymple, Clerk, and
many others, to the number of seven or eight, who, instead of worshipping
with other Christians, meet in a tavern, and read Woolston's Discourses on
Miracles, and ridicule all religion.   That, ordinarly, in contempt, they
are seen to dismiss when the Congregation dismiss, and though Mr
M'Derment knoues of it, and Mr Hunter,* [no] nottice is taken of it; and
James Dalrymple, one of them, hath, since it was knouen, got a token to
communicat, though even otherwise he is a druken, loose man.

We are told of a designe of the leading men about Edinburgh (but I
cannot belive it) to lay aside Mr M'Dermitt and me as to Renfreu; and
to bring in Mr John Simson to his father's parish, when he is restored
to his Ministry, as they say is designed next Assembly.   But that is not
feasible, and will never go doun.

This moneth the Dean of Faculty comes to be chosen at G. Coll.
[Glasgow College.]   Ther is no struggle about it.   Their regulations, it
seems, allou him to continou two year, if the Faculty please; and so Mr
Wisheart is re-chosen.   He stayed his journey to London after his father's
death, till that was over.   Nou, he and his wife are gone up to order the
affairs of the Admirall's legacy, and are to go to the Bath.   Without ad-
vising with the Presbitry, he hath left a preacher to supply his Kirk, Mr
James Stirling, and they say he alloues him largely two gin[eas] a week
till he return.

Mr Mack tells me that Mr J. Hill, of whom in the former volume of
this, continoues very ill, though not to the extremity that sometimes he
hath been in; yet is at that lenth, that when he supplyed him last, he
would not bid him pray for him, only said he would not hinder him.
The same person tells me that he is informed that Mr Hill has told,
though persons cannot certainly judge but it may flow from his melancholy, that when young, he was only in one instance disobedient to his

* Ministers of Ayr.

mother, who had some imprecation upon him ; and at another time, when young, he was guilty of uncleannes, or somewhat tending that way.

My Lord Ross tells me this accompt of his carriage at the Assembly, 1704. By my Lord Wharton, his brother-in-lau, he was named at that criticall juncture. The Tolleration had been essayed the former year, and broke* by the Duke of Argyle's firmnes ; houever, the Jacobites and Episcopalls had taken great liberty, and made many encroachments in the North, and intruded on Churches. No other offered, who it was thought would be acceptable, and his B[rother]-in-lau, Wharton's interest at Court, wher he could cary what he would, encouraged him. When his being Commissioner was proposed, he told them he behoved to have somwhat openly favourable to the Church to bring doun with him, and what would satisfy the Ministers, and proposed a very strong act against intrusion into Churches. This was opposed by Sunderland, but Wharton carryed it throu. When he took his leave of the Queen, she told him her croun was nou in his hands, and upon his managment of matters it very much depended. If she lost Scotland, she could not be easy wher she was. That which put her in a fright was the last Parliament 1723, [1703 ?] wher Duke Hamiltoun carryed his point against the Court, within six votes ; and Wharton and the English Ministry wer of opinion that if the Assembly broke, and the Church wer disgusted, it would effectually strenthen the dissafected party, and next session they would be inferior by twenty. This made the English Ministry come in to whatever could be reasonably proposed in favour of the Church. When my informer came doun, he called to [the] Counsell, and laid the act against intruders before them. The Advocate, Sir James Steuart, when it was read, was pleased with it ; and said he had seen nothing that looked so much like earnestnes and effectuall dealing for a long time ; and when it was passed in Counsell, ordered it to be printed. This act pleased the Ministers much. The Assembly run very smooth. At the close of it, Mr Wilky proposed that my Lord would allou them to adjourn the Assembly, in Christ's name, first, in the termes which since that Assembly have still been made use of, as what would be of great

* Gave way ; was prevented.

use to allay heats and setle people's minds after Seafield's dissolving them, and their being ruffled. He said it was but a feather in their cap, but he belived scarce one thing would do the Queen more service. My Lord said he would consider it. He called the Counsell. There all the Presbiterian favourable Lords, Glasgou, Philiphaugh, in short, all of them, opposed it with violence. He debated the matter with them; told them there [was] nothing in his Instructions against it; that he sau it would be for the Queen's interest, and would much satisfy the Ministers, who had been maltreated. They continoued to refuse to concurr. A lenth he told them that he would venture on it himself; but being instructed to advise in matters with them, he would not do it alone, but then he would acquaint the Ministry and all the world that he was for it, and that they wer the hinderers. Upon this, though with no litle difficulty, they came in to it, and the matter was concerted, that the Moderator first dissolve the Assembly, and then the Commissioner; and this form has been keeped nou for twenty-five Assemblys.

Some time this moneth, I think, or in the end of the last, ther was a terrible fire in the Causyside of the toun of Paislay. The drought was great, and ther was no stopping it. Twenty-six familys wer burnt out, and they say about fifteen hundred pounds sterling damage done. These dispensations of calamitys should have good effects, and, consequently, ought to afford occasion of prayer about them.

This moneth the Colledge Factors are laid aside—Mr Murthland, Mr Carmichael, and Mr Loudon; and Mr William Wood, formerly at Paislay, is made sole Factor, and comes in to live at Glasgou with his family. If ther he be as active as at P[aisley,] he will corrupt multitudes with dissafection, and strenthen the Episcopall and Jacobit interest excedingly. It's a strange step to chuse him Factor to the Colledge, who, I doubt, will pretty openly disoun the King, whose house and rents he has among his hands. I cannot understand the P[rincipal]l's tentation. Indeed, Mr W[ood] is a man of smoothnes, sufficiency, and, for any thing I ever heard of, great fairnes and integrity. He has nou an estate, and hath four of the great estates in this country in his hands, and, consequently, a great access to bring many to his way of thinking. He has Selcridge's, [Selkirk's,] the Duke of Hamiltoun's, the Duke of Douglass, and Colledge of Glasgou.

In the close of this moneth the barbarouse murder of M. Purcell happens, and James Muir is blamed for it, and, in a day or two, laid up. He stifly denyes his share, and continoues in prison till his triall, of which afterwards. At the same time we hear of D. Robb's daughter's murder, but it holds not. A child in Catrart [Cathcart] is murdered, but it's uncertain hou.

Mistress Luke tells me that Mr N. Gille's last sermons were on Jer. iii. 19, Sabbath before Sacrament—" Hou shall I put thee," &c. Action sermon—" I'le give the a goodly heretage." Sabbath after, which was his last sermon ever he preached—" Thou shalt call me, my Father, and shall not turn away."

This moneth I was at Dougalstoun, throu whose ground the old Roman wall goes. I had the pleasure to see that old vestige of the Roman greatnes. The wall is levelled with the ground, or filled up with every year's grouth and dust many hundred years since. Houever, the tract of it is very plain; from Kilpatrick to Kirkentilloch it runs all along on an eminency. Dougalston getts all his stones for a large park dyke from it, and the people just digg under a foot of earth and find them in plenty for raising. At the place where they wer digging, the heuen stone with inscription, gifted by Dougalston, 1694, to the Colledge, was turned up. No other freestone has been gote. The workmen are bound doun to care, by the promise of a croun, for every figured and lettered stone they find. I sau the vestige of a ditch on the north side of the wall, then the wall itself, which, in as farr as can nou be guessed, has been about twelve foot thick. The hight cannot nou be knouen; and on the south side of the wall, from its root for about twelve or fourteen foot southward, there is a causie* of small stones about half a foot or therby diametter, [and] gravell among them. The wall itself has large stones at the sides of it, and the body of it is made up of smaller stones of smaller size, without any lime we can perceive, but just

* Causeway; the Roman Road.

earth or sand nou turned to earth among them. It has been faced with
these large stones on both sides of the wall, north and south. They are
all what we call whinstone, and I observe no freestone at [all] among
them. They seem to be another stone than those about, and brought
from some distance. This dyke is just nou a kind of loose quarry to
the gentlemen throu whose lands it runns. Dougalston tells me that
all the country houses therabouts are built of the stones of the Roman
wall.

July, 1729.—Litle offers this moneth. Our Communions this summer are sweet. The number of communicants is rather mo than usuall;
and, generally speaking, it's observed that ther are mo neu and young
communicants who never communicat before; particularly at Strath-
blane, where Mr Livingstoun is, they talk of more than two hundred
neu communicants from themselves and neighbouring congregations;
but, I fear, this is too great a number to hold. This, wer they all worthy—
and I hope many are so—would be one of the best tokens for good we
could have. At our Communion here, next moneth, (I mark it here
because of its sibnes* with this,) we had moe first communicants than
we have had for many years. I have observed thirty-six; and there
wer, I belive, some others not among us.†

The estate and family of Eglington is nou exceeding lou; not in
riches, for they wer never more opulent, but in freinds and representatives. My Lady, and her b[rother,] D. Kennedy, are like to have the
sole managment of all, and the education of the young Earl. William-
wood is continoued factor to the eastern part of the estate by the Lords;
and the former in the west.

On the other side, the estate of Dundonald is weakning; and, if care
be not taken, it's like as fast to come doun as it rose. The Earle is
bent on improvements, and they do not answer much in this country.
He has laid many of his best malins‡ wast. But his house managment will
run deeper still. This moneth he sells his paternall estate of Kilmaro-

---

* Relation; literally, nearness of kindred.   † Belonging to the parish.   ‡ Maillings; small farms.

nok to the Duke of Montrose, at a high rate, nine thousand pound ; but this did not hold.   The Duke, they say, is to sell his lands in Inshanan to help to pay it.   He is commended for buying a Highland estate, for, besides the improvements it's capable of, it makes him very considerable in the shire of Dumbartan and the borders of the Highlands ; and it was old Dougalston's advice that he should buy lands in the Highlands, and sell in the Loulands.   Houever, they say Gorthy is out* in this matter, and was so before at selling three votes for Parliament, which wer made independent of the Duke.

This moneth the Duke of Argyle comes doun to Scotland. He stayed litle in Edinburgh, but hasted to the Highlands, where, as many of his lands are to be of new entred, he is to drau a prodigiouse mass of money. It's given out that he is to drope D. Campbell of Shaufeild, and, they say, he would not see him at Greenock and at Inveraray, nor speak with him.   It's talked that Shaufeild, at London, vyes with the Duke, and recons he stands on his oun leggs ; and that the Duke cannot bear. His brother, Pr[ovost] Campbell, and G. Drummond, are to be dropt. Whither all this be grimace, to fank in† the Toun of Glasgou again to his interests, a litle time will try.   All airs,‡ I see, are laying in the watter this way.   P. Stirling, I find, speaks on this side, that it's fruitles to struggle, and best to keep in with all sides of great men, and be out with none.   At the Circuit, Lord Miltoun, a tool of Earl of Isla's, regrated the hardships on Glasgou, and said the toun had been maltreated, and the family of Argyle had been informed they bore a personall hatred at them, and would not bear any of the name of Campbell, and other such storys ; and, at Edinburgh, the Duke told the Provest he resolved to come by Glasgou and stay all night.

August, 1729.—This moneth Argyle is much at Inverary, with Mr Forbes, King's Advocat, and feu have acces save Sir James Campbell of Auchinbreak, and Sir John Shau.   He, about the end of the moneth,

---

* Dissatisfied.   † Entangle ; draw within the toils.   ‡ Oars.

came to Greenock, and stayed with Sir John some dayes. When he came to G[lasgow,] he stayed in the Principall's, whom some call his bastard brother; but I cannot belive it. The Magistrates provided an enterteanment for him, but he excused himself, saying he was indisposed, and Sir John Shau had drunk on him.* He generally refuses enterteanments. He has a considerable parsimony, and, they say, both dispises these things, and cares not for the gratifications which are proper at these times. The Magistrates compleaned to him of the ruin of trade, and impositions. He regrated it, and said he had been informed they hated his family, and would not hear of [his] name. This they denyed, and appealed to Blythswood, present, that they wer last election for him, in opposition to Shaufeild, and offered to chuse him. He asked Colin if it was so? He ouned it was. "Then," said he, "I have [been] abused." They offered him their greivances, in a discourse, and asked leave to give a note of them to his secretary. He said it would be a greater favour to put them in his oun hands, and promised to do all in his pouer for their good. Next morning he went early for Edinburgh.

I am told Argyle, at present, has not much to say at Court; that this may [be] one motive of gaining Glasgou; that he does medle very litle with Scots affairs; that his top ambition is the army, and he keeps himself by it; that all other things that relate to Scotland come throu Isla's hands, and he is sole manager under Sir Robert Walpool. The intimacy between the brothers is not great.

They tell an instance of my Lord Isla's interest above. Lately, in June or July, ther came up a proposall from the Commissioners at Edinburgh to Sir Robert Walpool for bettering the Revenue of Scotland. It was thought to be formed by Shaufeild, and sent doun to Mr Dr[ummond?] and by him modelled and given in as from himself. When agreed to and transmitted to Sir R[obert] W[alpole,] he put it in Shaufeild's hands, who said it was formed by one that kneu the Revenue better than he thought any in Scotland had knouen it; that it raised the Revenue thirty thousand pound or more per annum, and it was all right and highly reasonable. Then it was put in Isla's hands, who, after

* Probably, had led him to hurt himself by drinking.

perusing it, gave his opinion directly against it, as what, indeed, bettered the Revenue, but to the King's loss, for the subjects in Scotland wer already overburdened, and he would not answer for the consequences if that scheme wer insisted on; he thought it might land in a neu Rebellion, and so it was laid aside.

I hear, from a good hand, Sir Robert Pollock, that this while the Queen does all bussines with Sir Robert [Walpole;] that both the King and Queen are parsimoniouse and aboundantly saving. The matter of the one hundred and fifty thousand pound, last session, made a terrible noise. It seems this summ was alledged to have fallen short in the allotment for the King's eight hundred thousand pound last year, though ther is a quarter or more to run out in the funds, without which the quota could not be exactly determined; but a round calcul was made from the deficiencys in the time elapsed to what was to come, and that summ required to be made up. Ther wer free speeches made on this occasion, and Sir Robert was like to doubt of the event, and moved it should be waved at this time; but that would not be gone into, and high resentments threatned. At lenth it was promised that any surplus, if it should be, of the one hundred and fifty thousand pound beyond the quarter current, it should be accounted for nixt year. Thus the matter was forced doun with much difficulty and grudge.

The Bill for preventing Corruptions and Bribery in Members of Parliament their election, when proposed in the House, was scarce thought in earnest designed by the opposit side to Sir Robert, and jested at. They themselves had litle or no prospect of carrying it; yet the more it opened out the more it gained ground, and at lenth Sir Robert began to use his outmost efforts against it, but in vain. It's said to be exceeding weel worded, and to contean all human security, by oaths and such like, that it's possible to be given against Elections by Bribery. All depends on its execution.

The Prince is aboundantly smart and brisk. He is keeped much under tutors, yet my Lord Malpas and he are not in so good termes with him as wer to be wished. His restraints he somtimes breaks throu, and finds wayes to be from under his keeper's eye. The King's health, my informer tells me, is as good as ever, for any thing he could observe.

The Commission mett at the ordinary time. They had the affair [of] Mr Glass, and Neu Macher's planting with Mr Rea, and of Renfreu. I do not hear they had much more of a publick nature. As to Mr Glass, he was present; and his affair is sub-committed to some of the leading men about Edinburgh, and they seem to favour him. He is already deposed, as has been observed, for his contumacy, divisive courses, and spreading Independant schemes. He, though he alloues no judicatorys above a Congregationall meeting, and denyes Nationall Churches, hath appealed to the Assembly, and sayes, " I will take justice from it, as a meeting established by the King." The Assembly referrs him to the Commission. The strait as to him seems to ly here. He is not charged with error, save Independantisme, nor immorality; and to depose him for his opinion in Church Goverment, say some, will look exceeding ill in the eyes of other Churches; to depose him for the opinion of the great Ouen, the Mathers, &c. But [that] is not the question. His [he ?] is already deposed not meerly for his opinion, but his railing on our Covenants and Establishment, and divisive practises; and the question is, if the sentence should be taken off, and he encouraged. The Commission has discharged him to preach; formerly they would take small acknouledgments, and promises of amendment; but he will give none. He seems buyed up with the hope of being protected by leading men, and that keeps him from all temper. He goes on to preach publickly every where, and disseminat his principle. This is greivous to the Ministers of that country. Houever, the matter is still put of from time to time, and his affair is referred to the Commission in March.

The other affair is Mr Rhea, P. Chalmers' cusine, his setlment at Neu Machir. This was before the Assembly. Exceptions wer made against his acceptation of the presentation in its terms; and his character, it's said, was not very tender. The Presbytery of Aberdeen opposed him, and took his license from him. The Commission have restored

him, susteaned his call, and ordered him to be setled; and added a
Committy of the Synod supernumerary to the Presbytery, and ordeaned
the day of his ordination.   Thir superadded Committys to Presbytery,
especially from the Commission, are, in my opinion, dangerouse and
eversive of our constitution.   If a Presbytery malverse, let them be compleaned of to Synod, Assembly, and Commission.   Lett Superior Courts
appoint whom they will to execut their acts, but never appoint additions
to Presbyteries to over-vot them, and pretend to act in concert with the
Presbytery, when the Presbytery are against a thing.   This is scorning
and jesting.   •

   In the last room,• the affair of Renfreu came in before the Commission.
This affair was caryed by an appeal to the Synod, and by appeal and reference to the Assembly.   The reference of the whole was (if it be)
wrong in the Synod, since they could referr nothing but what was before them; and ther was no appeal made to them upon the Presbytery's
concurrence with my call.   This matter was referred to the Commission,
and should have come in when the affair of Neu Macher came in, as was
appointed by the Assembly, after Mr Glass's affair.   But the Managers
waited Lord Isla's coming up, and designed a thin Commission, when
the Elders should be brought in to overballance the vote; and so Neu
Macher was taken in first, though it's certain, morally speaking, had it
come in while the North Country Ministers and others wer in the Commission, it had carryed otherwise.   (This I take as a kind Providence
‘o me.)   When it came in, it was put off Thursday's night with reading
papers, and Friday fornoon with speeches, till the afternoon, that Lord
Isla came to toun, and came in with about twenty votes of elders at his
back, when they had waited an hour or two for want of a coram,† and
many Ministers wer gone away as not expecting another meeting.   When
it came in, the Commission slumped the matter, waved the appeals, and
susteaned Mr M'Dermitt's call.   Ther wer very warm speeches on it.

   Mr Will. Steuart of Perth compleaned of the managment, and of such,
be who they would, (he had Pr[ovost] Campbell in his eye,) that procured

---

* Lastly, in the last place.   † Quorum.

presentations, till a parish heard a Minister, and wer satisfyed with him, as acting against the principles of this Church; and compleaned of Patronages. My Lord Isla interrupted him, and said he had procured the presentation, and did think he did a service to the Church. The other said he had not his Lordship in his eye, but others; but since he had ouned his hand in it, he behoved still to be in the same mind, that it was ill service to the Church to get a man presented when people could not knou anything of his fitnes for them, and without concerting matters with persons concerned.

The Lord Isla answered pretty long and warm; that we sat here by an act of Parliament; the Revolution was by an act of Parliament; patronages was nou a lau; there was an act of Parliament for this presentation; it ought not to be quarrelled, otherwise the meeting quarrelled their oun pouer; and much to that purpose.

Lord Dunmore was about to back him, when Mr George Gillespy stoped him, and said he was up first, and he thought nou Ministers ought to speak, and that before Elders, in a matter that concerned the interests of Christ and the whole of Church pouer. He ouned the King and Parliament's goodnes that we had freedome to meet under the countenance of laufull authority, but could never think the Commission sat here by an act of Parliament. He reconed we sat in the name and by virtue of a Commission from Christ, the Head of his Church, and wished that Members might speak in another stile. He thought we might complean of an iniquous lau, and then entered in to the cause, and moved the vote might be "Sustean Mr M['Dermitt's] or W[odrow]'s call."

My Lord Grange declared he could not vote in that state, but was for waving both, and applying to the Goverment to concurr with the parish inclinations. The other state caryed, and Mr M'[Dermitt]'s call was susteaned by twelve Ministers; for susteaning my call eleven Ministers; but a majority of multitudes of Elders was on the other side. Among Ministers, P. Hamilton, Mr G. Logan, Mr Goudie, and some others, for Mr M'D[ermitt;] for the other, Mr W. Steuart, Perth, Mr J. Craige, Mr J. Davidson, Mr G. Gillespy, and others. Mr J. Smith, Principall Haddo, Mr A. Logan, and many others, who wer against Mr

M'D[ermitt's] call, wer not present. Some say P[rovost] Campbell
stayed in and voted. All the members of the Synod wer called save our
Presbitry of Paisley. It being a reference, Mr H. Hunter and the Principal had pretty warm words.

Towards the end of this moneth the Duke of Argyle, in his way to
Edinburgh from the Highlands, came to Glasgou about four of the clock,
and stayed all night in the Principall's. The toun had prepared a treat
for him, but he excused himself as near drunk, the two or three dayes by
his freind Sir John Shaue's kindnes, and really indisposed. This same
way he declined dining with the Principall. The Magistrates entered
upon a long conversation with him. They lamented that the toun for
some time had been under his Grace's frouns, which they wished to have
removed. The Duke said, he had no reason to take rubs and affronts
upon his family and name well. They protested they never wer guilty
of them. He said he had been told, and could not well doubt it, that
at the very last election they had said, " They would have none of the
name of Campbell to represent them." To that it was answered, it was
a hellish lye, and they wer glad they could disprove it by one near his
Grace. They ouned, indeed, they had opposed Mr Campbell of Shaufeild, and they thought they had good reasons, considering what treatment the community had from him ; but so far wer they from what had
been told his Grace, that before ever Mr Blaikwood was fixed on, they
offered their vote and interest to the Laird of Blythswood, standing by
his Grace ; for which they appealed to him. The Duke seemed struck
with this, and said, " Colin, was it so ?" He said it was. " Then,"
said the Duke, " never man was more abused than I have been ;" and
seemed to insinuat Shaufeild was his informer, though not directly ; and
said he nou found whom he had to deal with. When this was over, the
Magistrates began to open out the impositions, hardships, and greivances,
in point of trade, lying upon the toun, (which are indeed notour ;) and
after they had explained them pretty fully, the Provest begged the liberty
to lodge a memoriall of their impositions, he had in write, in his Grace's
secretary's hands, that when he had laizour he might call for it ; and

humbly desired his Grace might befreind the toun in getting them taken off. " No," said the Duke, " Provest, I'le take it as [a] favour if you'l lodge the memorial in my hand, and I'le take a care of it." It was given him, and [he] promised to do all in his pouer.

Thus, the peace, they say, is made up between the Duke and toun. Let me add here, because it relates to this, about three weeks after, toward the end of September, an express came from Isla to the Provest, telling him hou acceptable it would be, if he, and whom he sau proper to bring with him, would come to Edinburgh and talk over somthings about the state of the toun. The Provest went, and, as he sayes, Isla took out the memoriall and read it over to them, article by article, and desired them to add what they had to add. He disapproved every thing they had met with, and promised his assistance to a redress.

These are reconed great things gained by the toun and P[rovost] Stirling. The event will best sheu this. If the two brothers can releive them, good and well. By all this, it's said P[rovost] Stirling and his party are all gained to be for the family of Argyle, and the toun is nou theirs, very cheaply, if no more follou.

September, 1729.—In the beginning of this moneth, poor James Muir's tryall came. The particulars, see Indytment, in print, and Letters. The case came to be plain to the Jury and to the Judge. Ther was nothing of importance proven, so as to land on James Muir ; and three witnesses (of no good character, indeed, but these on the other side wer litle better, and whoor *contra* whoor) proved on oath, that they sau the murdered woman alive after the Saturnday's night lybelled. The Judge, Mr Graham, said somthings very home on the character of the witnesses, and went so far in his requests to one of them, that the Advocates for Mr Muir blamed him. When she had sworn, he called the Advocates near him, and told pretty audibly that he hoped they would not blame him, for the woman had declared the contrary to himself. James Muir was acquitted and dismissed from the Barr ; but still he has the misfortoun to be suspected ; and the witnesses who cleared him, by their *mala fama*, have but confounded people. Till Providence open a dore, and discover some other murderer, I fear the scandall lye upon him. I pity his poor mother and freinds, who are as much almost to be pitied as if he had been condemned. Many things must be left to the great day.

Earl of Isla continoues at Edinburgh regulating the debates in that toun referred to him. He, they say, is not to declare till the next election of Magistrates is secured to P[rovost] Lindsay and his side. They say the Earl would have P[rovost] Drummond turned out of his Commissioner's post, (which, indeed, is all he has to live on,) but the Duke sticks by him, and will not allou that. The Provest, they say, has engaged to medle no further on any side in the toun's affairs, and intirely lye by; and so he is spared for a time. P[rovost] Campble is no more to be alloued any share of things at Edinburgh, being Shaufeild's brother, whom the family of Argyle has either droped, or affects to drop at this juncture.

The Pr[incipal*] carryes all in the Faculty as he pleases, and nou beginns to make these who differ from him knou what they may expect. I belive I notticed Mr Wisheart's being continoued D[ean] of Faculty, and Mr Wood made sole factor. This step is much wondered at in a Minister, to choice a man a professed and knouen Jacobite, and one who hears no Presbiterian Minister, and doubts of the validity of our ministrations, to be factour to the Colledge of Glasgou. Indeed, he is a sufficient man for the bussines, but it's said that sufficiency is not restricted to him.

This moneth the Principal and Faculty have taken away Mr Murthlan's twenty pound of additionall sellary, and the Principal has quitt his twenty-two pound that he might have claimed; at least, P[rincipal] Stirling had it, and divided these among his freinds. Mr Dunlop ten pound, Mr Dick as much, Mr R. Simson as much, and the fourth to some other. They say, this year, the Principal has near one thousand merks of income, one way or another; two years' stipend of Renfreu, the Principal's sellary, forty pound for transportation, one hundred gineas from the Exchequer; and yet some think in this aboundance he is in penury.

* Campbell, of Glasgow College.

This moneth—see Letters—we have the accounts of worthy Coll[onel] Blaccader's death, the Deputy-Governour of Stirling Castle—a person of great value, integrity, and piety; a souldier of courage and ability, and a greater Christian; one that lived very near God, as his remaining Diary will sheu. He was exceeding usefull in that place, a firm freind to the Goverment and the Church, and a great terror to the Jacobites. He was son to Mr John Blaccader, whose life and memoires I have; a godly son of a pious father. Many instances I could give of suffering ministers' children, and Christians also, who have aboundantly inherited the reward of the parents' sufferings since the Revolution; but they are hapyest who inherit their virtue and grace. Admirall and Coll[onel] Wisheart, Mr Robert Blair's children, and Coll[onel] Blaccader, is another.

September 17.—Upon the 17th of September the toun of Glasgou susteaned a very heavy loss by the death of Robert Alexander, frequently Bailay in Glasgou. His health had not been so firm these two or three years. He was carryed off by bloody flux in eight dayes time. He had heard the Reformation sermon on Friday, and dyed Wensday after. He was, for many years, Governour of Hutcheson's Hospitall. He was a good, pious, bookish man, exceeding zealouse against all vice and immorality; a terror to evil doers, literally. When a Magistrat, he usually gave in five pound more to the session for fynes of vice than any others. In short, he was hearty and zealouse in a good thing, and, take him altogether, I question if he hath left his match for usefulnes against vice in the toun. Provest Peady's death and his are great, and the toun is like to sustean losses on losses of valuable men.

September 18.—Upon the 18th, Mr John Govan, Minister at Campsie since the Revolution, dyed. He was turned seventy, unmarried, and left a heap of money behind him, about which ther is like to be debate. He was buryd on Munday, September 22; and his nepheu, Mr Forrester, ordeaned Minister, September 23. He had been his helper, and, with difficulty, he got him ordeaned. He studyed physick, and practised by Receipts,* but took no money. He lived a retired, monkish life ; was usefull, I belive, among his people ; an excellent preacher, a person of some learning and knouledge, but lived exceeding narrouly ; and, save at his Sacrament, flesh was not in his house throu the year. No wonder he left five or six thousand pounds sterling.

This moneth, we hear of Mr Wisheart's being to be called to be Mr Cumming's successor in the Scots Congregation, London. He was up this summer, and preached once or twice there. His vast money and estate, from his uncle, the Admirall, lyes there ; and it's probable he will go.

Mr Muir, Minister at Orwell, tells me the present state of Kinross parish, which is to [be] before their Synod the end of this moneth, and because it's remarkable, and like to bring us on the look as to the unhappy debates on The Marrou, I'le set doun till I see what Providence brings it to. Mr John Craige, son to Mr Hugh Craige, Minister at Gallousheills, a good, honest man, was centered† on by the parish of Kinross. Mr Craige was a pious youth, under great deeps of exercise for some years. While a student at Edinburgh, when in the Lady Maitland's family, his serious exercise brought him to haunt with some of The Marrou Bretheren, and their follouers. When he came to the Presbytery of Dunfermline, he was sent to Kinross, and the people wer as one man for him, save one Bailay . . . . . who influenced another. The people prevailed with Sir William Bruce, of Kinross, to give him a presentation, or promise it, and allou them to call him. The more he preached there, the more they wer knitt to him. A call is drauen, and he is entered on tryalls in the Presbytery of Dumfermline. Sir William dyes. His brother, Sir John, succeeds ; who, by the influence of that Bailay, begins to oppose him, and to hint the refusing a presentation. The report was spread that Mr Craige favoured The Marrou, and unfitt to be setled in that Presbytery of Dumfermline, where so many of them

---

* Written prescriptions, *recipes.*   † Fixed on unanimously.

wer. This took some impression in the Synod of Fyfe, Principall Haddo and Mr A. Anderson soon took it by the end, and soon got a Committy added to the Presbytery, at Mr A. Logan's desire, none of the Presbytery opposing. Accordingly, the Committy joyn the Presbytery in the examination of Mr Craige; and being empoured by the Synod, they formed Queries, to the number of twenty, all of them upon the heads of The Marrou, turning over the act of Assembly 1720 or 21, against The Marrou into so many Queries. They had been prepared with care by Mr A. Anderson and others before the joynt meeting of the Presbytery and Committy, and wer read and approven in generall. He was called in, and they wer read to him. He desired time to bring in his Answers. The meeting would only give him till the afternoon sederunt.—He dreu up Answers, in that space, to all the Queries save the last, which was, whither he approved of the act of Assembly 1720 against [The Marrou,] and read them? Some litle difficultys wer raised upon some of them; but nothing of importance objected. In short, most ouned he was a lad of sufficiency, in so short a time to form such solid and well worded answers. As to the last, he desired to be excused, that it was not his bussines to approve or disapprove such an act. He ouned it the deed of the Church, and did not in the least contravert it. He was removed, and the Committy insisted upon an express answer in write to the last Query. He was called in, and desired to give answer. He again begged they might not insist upon it, not being the proper subject of a question; declaring his resolution not to medle with or oppung [impugn] the act, in publick or private, and do nothing against it; and he never inclined to medle with these things in publick. Mr A. A[nderson] insisted to have an answer, and was backed. It was put. His answer was to this purpose: That if the Assembly had taken due time, and fully considered all that was said by the Representers, and pro and [con] all concerned might have the more peace. He would not judge, but since he was put to it, and obliged to declare in a matter he inclined to have been silent, he declared, according to his present light, he was of the sentiments of the Representers, and was content to stand and fall with them. This was what they wanted. Sir John had come in before, and declared him-

self against his setled [settlement ;] compleaned that he was once crazed
in the head, and was a Marrou man.   Houever, after this declaration,
the meeting went on as above in their Querys ; and when they got this
answer, they referred the whole case to the next Synod.   What the
Synod did, see Letters October next.   In a word, they votted, " Stop
his tryall ;" and ane appeal was made by the parish, and a protest by
all The Marrou Bretheren in the Synod ; and a great many, not
favourers of The Marrou, joyned with them, and all comes in to the
Assembly.

The same person tells me that Mr Hog of Carnock has got Mr Hunter, Col[onel] Erskine's Chaiplain, to be his ordeaned collegue, being
now old and tender : That Mr A. Logan and Mr Hog are in pretty good
termes, and very kind and oblidging to one another.

This, as far as I yet see, is a most imprudent and unhappy step, and
is like to cast this poor, divided, rent Church into a neu labyrinth.   On
the one hand, the flames about The Marrou wer just dying out, and the
debates just ending.   This will revive the whole, and the Representing
Bretheren will get multitudes to joyn them that wer before opposit to
their peculiar wayes of speaking, which I am far from approving.   And
which, in some respect, is as ill, this especially, after what has been of
late as to Mr Simson's Queries, and the battail we had there, [will] expose the method of Queries, and stop any Overtures in dependance about
putting of Queries.   To urge and stop a man on his tryalls till he
give a direct consent to all complex acts of Assembly, and make that a
Query, after satisfaction as to his soundnes [in] the faith, is such a stretch,
in the method of Queries, as I do not see can be weel vindicat.   I doubt
not but this use of Queries [will] be very satisfying to Mr Simson and
his freinds, who with such keenness opposed this just method, when it's
regulat prudently.

The same person tells me that Mr Hog of Carnock has got Mr Hunter, Col[onel] Erskine's Chaiplain, to be his ordeaned collegue, being
now old and tender : That Mr A. Logan and Mr Hog are in pretty good
termes, and very kind and oblidging to one another.

Mr M'Alpin tells me that, in conversation with Mr Watts, at London,
last spring, he commended the Scots method of preaching, by doctrine
and use ; and said, God had very much blessed it.   He declared his dissatisfaction with the generall haranging way of sermons nou turning

fashionable, as what did not answer the ends of preaching to the most part of hearers.

He tells me he was in conversation with Doctor Calamy, at London. He has the distribution of the money and fund for support of many Ministers in the country. When my informer came in to the Doctor, ther was a old, decent, reverend country Minister with him, who me [whom he ?] treated with a great deal of freedom. He sat near the dore like a servant, and was spoke to with much distance. When he went away, the other scarce noticed. When he was out, the Doctor said to him, "That fellou would starve, if I did not keep him in bread !" After that treatment, which my informer could not but think supercilious, he could never since have the Doctor in that estimation he had.

October, 1729.—In the beginning of this moneth, or rather, this year, in the end of the last, the Magistrates wer chosen at Glasgou. Ther was no talk about them nor Clubs that we heard of. P[rovost] Stirling has the Counsell very much in his hand, they say, and Provost Stark's side is nothing at all nou ; but ther was a terrible debate about the conveener, I think. The Trades sent to the Magistrates as [a] lite* for conveener just the men the Provest had turned out of the Counsell. This he took ill, and returned the lite ; and would commence a proces against the Trades' right to give such a lite. They protested that if a proces wer begun, it should not [be] off the toun's stock, but out of the Magistrates' pockets. Protests and counter-protests wer taken, and the matter taken up. If I remember, a neu lite was sent up ; two others and the man they would have chosen, and the Magistrates chused the man the Trades wer for. Houever, the Provest has lost the Trades, and if he be not weel backed with his neu freinds, it's like he will lose more.

At Dumbartan, I hear the partys just continou as formerly ; and the two partys have made a double election, and none will yeild to the other.

The Synod met at the ordinary time. Mr Love preached the Synod sermon, on Ministers' duty to be faithfull, and their trust. He had some

---

* Leet.

pretty closs remarks on Patronages.   The Synod had no bussines almost before them, save that of Cambuslang, whose state is most lamentable. The Duke of Hamilton was writt to by the Synod, and Mr H. Finlater, we wer told, was nou to be setled at Lintoun, and then the people would have the choice granted them.   We had a Synodicall Thanksgiving for the good harvest; there was a struggle about it.   We had a current report that the Goverment had appointed a Thanksgiving for England, but it had never been in the Gazet.   It was urged ther would be difficulty in case we had two, and therfor it was best to delay and remmitt it to the Commission.   Against that, it was objected that the Commission ordinarly found difficultys about Nationall Thanksgivings and Fasts, and inclined to correspond with the Goverment as to them, and this would drive over the matter till December or January : That, nou, the sense of the mercy was fresh on our spirits, and every body looked for a Thanksgiving.   Accordingly it was yielded, and we appointed on October 23.   It was well we did so, for neither Goverment nor Commission have done any thing that way.

[*October* 6.]—Upon the 6th of October, Mr D. Brody, Minister of Dalserf, dyed pretty unexpectedly.   He was ane old man, and Minister between thirty and forty years.   I hope he was usefull among his people. He made litle appearance elsewhere.   He was a relation of the family of Brody in the North.   Ministers do not generally dye single.

[*October* 14.]—Upon the 14th, we had a very great loss by the death of Mr John Gray, Minister at Glasgou.   He dyed probably of an apoplexy.   He had been long and sore troubled with the gravell.   He was born in Glasgou, and an exception from the generall—" A prophet is not acceptable in his oun country."   He was setled at Glasgou in the year 1694, mostly by my father's influence.   There was a competition between him and Mr Blackwell, afterwards Minister at Paislay and Aberdeen, who was a preacher then very much folloued.   Mr Gray was about thirty-seven year a Minister, and, for what I knou, hath distribute the Sacrament of the Supper oftner to his oun flock than any Minister to one flock in Scotland.   He was a man of great learning, and weel seen in Polemick Divinity, and throughly sound in his opinions, which he had examined and fully considered. He would have made a good Professor of Divinity. He was an exact disciplinarian, and very usefull in the General Session and Presbitry. He was a man of weight and gravity in our Judicatorys, and a firm opposer of innovations in doctrine. He had a great weight* of the grouing corruptions of this time. He was a person of fixednes, courage, and boldnes, and not alterable and changeable. In Mr Simson's first proces, he stood by [him,] as he said to me, because, though he did not like many of his expressions and wayes of speaking, yet he did not suspect him so corrupt and variable as afterwards he found him ; and Mr Simson, in his first process, keeped himself, in most things, under the cover of approven and valuable authors, such as Dr Ouen and some others, and could not easily be reached without putting a tash† upon them. But, in his last proces, which began upon the Trinity, he appeared with firmnes against his novations ; and the storys of his personall pick‡ against Mr Simson, upon their disputing some points, and disagreeing, wer idle and groundles, trumped up by Mr S[imson] and his freinds. Indeed, he told me that he was dissatisfyed with Mr Simson's freedomes before he altered his way of teaching in publick ; that he used to cry out against and mock the systematicall Dutch Divines, and he doubted his soundnes from conversation with Mr Simson upon the imputation of Christ's rightiousness ; and that Mr Simson said positively to him, that the common Dutch systematicall sense of faith being imputed to Abram for rightiousnes, taken objectively for Christ's rightiousnes, was nonsense, or some such word. He added, that he found him so vain and variable, that he never kneu wher to find him ; but he never dreamed his unsoundnes upon the Trinity till the 1725, and that no difference between them ever led him to oppose Mr Simson. In short, the loss to that toun and Presbytery, and this Church, by his death, is exceeding great, especially at this juncture, when I doubt, as the Magistrates are situat, if his room shall be filled so as one could wish for. Mr Gray was a most ready

---

* Oppressive sense.   † Stain. Fr. *tache*.   ‡ Pique.

preacher ; and, as he greu in years, turned the more acceptable to the serious and godly people in that toun ; and, in his last years, was much more folloued than at the beginning.   He was a bold and free reprover of sin, and what he took to be wrong, in all ranks, and that even in his sermons.   He has left a plentifull subsistence for his family.

October 16.—My Lady Dundonald is brought to bed of a son, Lord Cocheran.   Mr Duncan baptized him the same day.   Our familys of rank, many of them, are like to continou in their disaffection to this Established Church.   The Lord give a better temper and spirit.

About this time, T[homas] Sheilds, in Sheilds, met with a very wonderfull preservation.   Riding throu the Sheil-muir, in a dark night, within a cry almost to his oun house, and a servant lad behind him on the horse, the horse steped into an old coal-pit.   The girth mercifully broke in going doun.   Thomas got hold, in going doun, of some old timber with which the coal-pitt was cased within, and stuck by his hold. The horse and boy went doun.   By some way or other, by the plunging of the horse in the coal-pit, the boy was throuen up, so as Thomas, sticking by the sides of the pitt, got hold on him, and pulled him out of the watter, and helped him up to the mouth of the pitt, and he got out. Thomas stuck there till the boy run home and brought out the family with lights ; and cords wer bound about a man, and he was let doun to the place where Thomas stuck ; and Thomas clasped about him, and got out.   The horse, of eight or nine gineas, was lost.

About the end of this moneth, we hear of severall persons, considerable merchants and traders, giving way and breaking.   Poor John Thomson, whom his father left worth about five thousand pounds, is quite given way.   He has had thirty thousand merks of plain losses at sea ; but he lived too high, and drunk too hard.   Baily Blair is spoke off ; but, they say, he has a ballance.   A. B., T. C., and severall others, are spoke off ; and really persons don't knou whom to trust.   Trade is so far decayed, and the burdens and losses so many, that multitudes begin to be doubted.

In the end of this moneth there are many suddain deaths, mostly of old persons. We hear of a sicknes at London, almost in every family, and near to a plague. In the last week of this moneth, ther are four or five suddain deaths. Old John Graham, son to Provest Graham, a pious man, while at sermon on Teusday, droped doun in his seat. He was carryed to the Session-house, in the Laigh Church, and there expired in a feu minutes. He was a single man, and spoke litle or none; a person of considerable learning in the tongues, and was master of the Syriack, Arabick, and other Eastern tongues; spent his time mostly in reading the Polyglott Bible, and prayer; attended on all the prelections in the Colledge, on Synods and Presbitrys, but conversed with nobody. He would have answered, " Yes," or " No ;"' but I could never engage him in a discourse, nor any other that I can hear of, these forty years. He was a perfect monk, and solitary, except when he came out to sermons, which he punctually keeped, and to meetings in the Colledge and Judicatorys. His paralel I never kneu nor heard of. He lived, one may be sure, unmarryed. A designe was laid to marry him [being rich] to a daughter of Mr P. Simson's; and he was brought to see her, but talked litle or none. She dreu back. He was educat in Holland, by Mr M'Waird, who marryed his mother, Provest Graham's widou, and came over with his mother at the Revolution, and since hath lived with a servant in this fashion. I reacon he was turned seventy. He was reconed very pious.

Next day, Stephen Crauford, coppersmith, and Bailay severall times, dyed suddainly. He has been still a counselour since he was chosen by the poll at the Revolution. He was most unhappy in his children. Another merchant droped doun in the street, and was carryed into a shop, and expired, and some others. Lord prepare us for death !

Mr Wisheart, Minister in Glasgou, who has been at London this last half year, in our riding together, entred upon his call to the Scots Congregation at London. He sayes he kneu nothing of it till that post which brought it to us in the English prints : That, at Mr Cuming's desire, he preached one day and an afternoon in that meeting-house ; but not one word was spoke to him, while at London, about the call :

That he is in a strait. His bussines leads him once a year to be in England : That he might manage it by a doer ;* but that wants not difficultys, since he is only in fee of the money and estate, and countable for every farthing, in case he have not succession, as he has none : That he entered into the Ministry against his relations (some of them) their mind, as the station he might glorify God most in, and be most usefull for his oun soul : That he has had the misfortune to be as a speckled bird, and to be thought of other principles then his mother Church, though he knoues it not, and he is sure he never concealed his thoughts ; but if he had any fault, it was too great openes. He is not so intire with his collegues as he wishes, but has no inclination to leave the Church of Scotland, she being the best he knoues, and would willingly stay, and take and mentean an assistant. I said what I thought proper to these declarations. He spoke much of his comfort and satisfaction in his people. He tells me that the sellary is by subscription, and not a legall setlment, as I took it to have been. He says it's some more than one hundred pound, not two.

He tells me that severall of the Dissenters are going over to the Church : That Mr Harrison, lately gone over, surprizes all ; he had no tentation, had a flourishing meeting, near two hundred pound of subscription, and has only gote a small curacy of fifty or sixty pound : He sayes, the Dissenting interest at London and in England is very lou ; many of their subscriptions are failing, by deaths and otherwise. Even Dr Calamy's subscription sellary is much decreased ; that he will not have much above one hundred and fifty pound ; and all the rest are decayed in proportion. The Doctor would have taken his son to be helper, but his subscriptions would not answer both, and therfor he is setled with another.

November [3,] 1729.—Upon the 3d of November, we heard of Mrs Glen's giving [way.] She has driven a very great trade, these many years, in silks and Hollands. A bill of three hundred pound, from London, came on her ; and she doubted of her circumstances, and let it

---

* Agent, solicitor.

be protested, that all her creditors might have as much as she had to give them, and not too much go to one. Many do themselves hurt by engrossing too great a trade, and not stating clear counts. She seems most concerned least religion suffer. He [she] is in debt, they say, to tradsmen in Glasgou, for working and manufacturing cloath, more then five hundred pound. We hear, after which I wish hold, that, on stating counts, she will have three or five hundred pound free.

[*November* 8.]—The suddain deaths continou, and it looks as if ther wer somwhat infectiouse in the air. We have nou had near six weeks rainy weather and hazie. On the 8th of November, three men, two boatmen, and a workman, in perfect health, standing on the key at the Brimmylau, droped doun speechles and motionles in an instant. Ther was a cart going up to the toun, and they wer lift up as dead, and laid on the cart. The motion of the cart was certainly of use to them; for by [the time] they got in to the toun they greu some better, but continoued sickly for some time. I don't hear any of them are yet dead, though all remain indisposed.

November 9.—A very sad accident happned at the Muir Heugh.* The day was Sabbath; and the English souldiers at Glasgou, as well as too many others, are ill keepers of that holy day. Three of them, who, they say, had a woman in common, came out of toun to walk on the Sabbath afternoon. They came out toward the Coal Heughs in the Muir of Glasgou. Ther was an old coal-pitt railed about, but the rail was old. One of the souldiers, in a bravado, would look into it, and trust to the rail. When he leaned to it, being rotten, it gave way, and he fell forward into the Heugh, and, some say, was first brained. Houever that be, he fell into the pit twenty or thirty fathom deep, and dyed. I wish idlers of the Sabbath would take warning!

Mr William Brown tells me the following accompt he had, when last [in] Perth, from Mr James Mercer, Minister at . . . .† as what was

* Coal-pit.   † Abardalgie.

generally belived as to Dr Rule, Principal at Edinburgh ; and the thing
was so notour, that it could not miss to be observed.   The Doctor hapned to be going to the North, to some Church meeting, and road with
a servant.   Came to knouen Carnie Mount, that lyes in the high and
nearest road, and belongs to the parish of Laurencekirk.   Before the
Doctor gote to the foot of the Mount, it was turning dark, and the
night drauing on him.   Ther is a change-house at the foot of the Carnie
Mount wher he expected lodging.   When he came there, the landlord
told him ther was not a bitt of room for him in the house ; that the
Shirrefe of the shire, and a good number of the gentlmen about, wer to
lodge with him, and he expected neither he nor any of the family could
have a bed that night.   The Doctor told him hou unwilling he was to
venture throu the Mount so late, and asked the landlord if he kneu of
no remedy for him ; that he would be glad of any place where he could
be free of the open air, and his horses have meet.   The landlord said he
could find room for his horses, and they should be weel enough.   For
himself, he kneu no place for him, unless he pleased to lye in yonder
large house about a quarter or half a mile distance, and he should take
care to send over bed-cloaths, and a fire, and candles ; only he told him
it had not been inhabited for thirty years, and it was said to be haunted
with an apparition.   The Doctor said, if no better might be, he would
rather chuse that than to stay in the open air.   His servant, houever,
would not go.

The landlord was as good as his word : sent over his servants with
bed-cloaths, fire, and candles ; and the Doctor went over.   The house
was a good house, and the rooms good.   After his room was ordered,
and every thing well, he was left alone in it.   He walked some time in
the room, and committed himself to God's protection, and went to bed.
Ther was two candles he left on the table, and these he put out.   Ther
was a large, bright fire remaining.   He had not been long in bed till the
room dore is opened, and an apparition, in shape of a country tradsman,
came in, and opened the courtains without speaking a word.   Mr Rule
was resolved to do nothing till it should speak or attack him, but lay
still with full composure, committing himself to the Divine protection
and conduct.   The apparition went to the table, lighted the two candles,

brought them to the bedside, and made some steps toward the dore, looking still to the bed, as if he would have had Mr Rule rising and fol- louing. Mr Rule still lay still till he should see his way further cleared. Then the apparition, who the whole time spoke none, took an effectuall way to raise the Doctor. He caryed back the candles to the table, and went to the fire, and, with the tongs, took doun the kindled coals, and laid them on the deal chamber floor. The Doctor, then, thought it time to rise, and put on his cloaths, in the time of which the spectre laid up the coals again in the chimney ; and, going to the table, lifted the can- dles and went to the dore, opened it, still looking to the Principal as he would have him follouing the candles ; which he nou, thinking there was somewhat extraordinary in the case, after looking to God for direc- tion, inclined to do. The apparition went doun some steps with the candles, and caryed them in to a long trance, at the end of which ther was a stair which carryed doun to a lou room. This the specter went doun, and stouped and set doun the lights on the louest step of the stair, and streight disappeared. Mr Rule, after a litle, waiting to see if any further should cast up, lifted the candles, went up, the way he came, to his room, and went to his bed again, wher he was no more disturbed.

Revolving in his thoughts what had passed, the Doctor began to think there was murder in the case. In the morning the landlord came over to see hou his guest was, and hou he had rested. The Principal told him he was very weel, and asked him if the Shirriff was still with him. The other answered he was. The Principal desired him to give his ser- vice to him, and to tell him who he was, a Minister and Principal at Edinburgh, and tell him he would willingly see him in the house wher he was ; but if that wer uneasy, he would come to him, because he had somewhat of weight to communicat. The Shirriff came over, and Mr Rule told him what had hapned, just as above, and that he was much of the mind ther was murder in the case. The Shirrif said it might be so, but it was certainly long since, for it was upwards of twenty, near thirty years since that hous was* uninhabited. The other begged the Shirriff

* Had been.

to cause lift the stone and open the earth where the candles wer left by the spectre ; and he yielded.   When the ground was opened, the plain remains of a human body wer found, and bones, to the conviction of all. Dr Rule next intreated the Shirrife that he would send orders to the country people, especially such above thirty or forty, to come to the place, and he would give them a sermon, and see [if] any hint could be had of the murder.   The Shirriff was not for this, and insisted that the murder was certainly so old that nobody nou could probably give any accompt of it.   The Doctor insisted ther was no hazard of their meeting for a sermon ; and we did not knou what Providence might discover. The Shirriff condescended, and that day warning was sent for some miles about.   The people conveened, the Doctor preached upon some subject suitable to the occasion, and told what had hapned, and earnestly dealt with the consciences of his hearers, if they kneu any thing of that murder to acknowledge it, nou that God, in his Providence, had brought it to light.   In the time of his sermon, an old man, near eighty years, was awakned, and fell a weeping, and, before all the company, acknouledged that, at the building of that house, he was the murderer.   He and one of his fellou masons fell into a debate and came to high words, on a summer morning, when the rest of the workmen wer not come up to their work ; and he killed the man with one stroak of a hammer, and buryed him under the first step of the stair ; and the matter was never knouen.   My informer knoues no more of what folloued, whither the murderer was punished ; and, as is probable, dyed penitent.

The same person told him that, in the spring or summer 1714, when he was in courtship of his wife, Mr Logan, of St Ninian's, daughter, he would needs come home to his parish early on Saturday morning, or late Fridayes night.   He had his servant riding before him.   It was dark when they came throu the Shirriffmuir, where, in November, the decisive battail was fought, and he sau two armyes of men upon the moor, with all military accoutrements, engage one with another ; and heard the gunns, and sau the swords, very much by the place where it hapned. His man sau the same, and stoped.   He bid him ride on.   He said he

durst not. He asked what he sau? He said, " Two armys fighting ;"
just as he sau. Mr Mercer rode by him, and bid him follou him. When
they came just upon them, all disappeared !

He adds to my informer, that, when he was a Preacher, he stayed in
Dundee, in a very good woman's house, Mrs Bell, a widou to the master
of a veshell, who dyed, a litle before, abroad, in America, I think. Mr
Bell was spoken of for taking up two young boyes that wer poor, and
carying them abroad with him under the notion of servants ; and, it was
said, he sold them for slaves. Houever, he dyed himself. His widou
was brought to set rooms in Dundee, and Mr Mercer took one of them.
He had not lyen in it many nights till he was no sooner in bed but
the room dore opened, and he heard it open. He took it, a night or
two, for the servant coming to take away his shoes ; but, on enquiry,
found it was not so. Next night the door opened, and he sau two boyes,
in seamen's habits, standing and looking into the room. Next night the
dore opened, and they came further in, and so every night for a fourteenth-night without intermission, only they made nearer and nearer ap-
proaches to his bed. They never spoke, and he resolved never to speak
to them. The last night they came just to the bedside, and then disappeared. He sayes he is very certain of the thing, and was under no
illusion. He was in a great difficulty what to do. If he should leave
the house, where otherwise he was very weel, the poor woman's way of
living would be broke, and he could not easily convince others. The
woman told him, when he had enquired about the dore's opening, that
the servants talked of aparitions, but hoped he would not scarr, and assured him nothing would harm [him.] He stayed out his time, and sau
no more.

[*November* 16.]—Upon the 16th, though it was the Saturnday befor
the Sacrament, the Colledge had an University meeting of their Nations
for the choice of a Rector. Many of the Masters and of the Students
absented. The Laird of Dunlop, of that Ilk, was chosen Rector without any opposition. That gentlman is unexceptionable, and is lately

marryed on a sister of my Lord Miltoun, Mr Fletcher of Saltoun's son, the great manager for my Lord Isla about Edinburgh.

November 17.—Mr Maxwell's lady is happily delivered of a son, this day, about ten of the clock. I baptized him, and his name [is] George. This is a great comfort to my old Lord Pollock, to have both his family strenthned by two sons, and to see a child called for his worthy and excellent father, Sir George Maxwell.

November 19.—Our Presbitry met. We wer expecting an application from Blythswood, to concurr with Mr M'Dermitt's call, but nobody came. Whither it was that the forces wer not yet mustered, (for we had none with us who favoured that side,) or that matters are not ripe, I knou not. Since the Commission in Agust, of which before, we have not had a sillable about that parish. At first we wer told that Blyths- wood was to go streight to the Presbytery of Air, and that the Commis- sion's susteaning the call was to be in the room of our concurrence ; but it seems that it was not thought sufficient, and Mr M'Dermit de- clares positivcly he will not come unless the Presbytery concurr. Blyths- wood said to some of us, that he was to be at our next Presbytery. What stops, we cannot tell. It's generally said that Blythswood is cooled ; and, indeed, he sayes openly, that Mr M'Dermit was never his choice, and, could he handsomely be off, he would heartily leave the matter, and that he is using endeavours to part handsomely with his freinds, and probably a third will be pitched upon. But I am rather thinking all this delay is but feigned, to cool the people in their opposi- tion ; and they are safe if they get in this matter, by appeal from us to the next Commission, in March. Time must unravell designes.

We had before us the affair of suppressing of vice and immorality, as remitted by the Synod to Presbyteries. We talked two or three hours. We wer all of one way of thinking, and this night's meeting put me in mind of our old Presbyteries before the 1715, when Mr N[eil] Campble came in, and we wer split into partys. We never kneu what different

sentiments almost wer. Ther wer seven of us, and we agreed that
Ministers should meet for prayer, with their Sessions, monethly; that
meetings for prayer in Congregations should be encouraged where they
wer, and set up under rules. They wer only stated in Eastwood,
Merns, and Neilstoun, and Inshanan. They are doun in Paislay, and
Lochwinnioch, and Kilmacolm, where they wer. These wer all of us
present. We agreed upon Congregationall fasts more ordinarly, but
remitted that to a concert with other Presbitrys and the Synod. We
agreed to set up our classicall meetings for prayer among ourselves, and
that essays should be made to set up a Society for Reformation of Manners in Paislay, Greenock, [and] Port-Glasgou; and invite the neighbouring gentlmen, that are blameles and weel affected, to joyn in the
Society; and that the Magistrates of Paislay should be spoke to.

When there, Glaud Simson told me a pretty odd story of his wife,
nou dead, Elizabeth Bogle. She bore him severall children, and never
kneu any thing like longing till the fourth or last. She was pretty near
her time, and happned to be in a house in Paislay before dinner, and
sau a sheep-head taken out of the pott. She took a great longing to
eat of it, but checked herself, and spoke not of it to any, but came and
dined. Soon after, she was brought to bed. The child was strong and
lively, but, soon after his birth, took a violent yauning and gaunting.
It was not much minded till it continoued near twenty-four hours, so
that the child they thought in hazard. They sent for the midwife,
Margaret Wallace. She asked the mother if she greened* for any thing
when with him? She said she had never before or since, and told as
above. The midwife ordered my informer presently to buy the best
sheep-head he could fall on, and boyle it weel, and take a bitt of the
flesh, when boyled, and rub the child's lips and mouth gently with it.
This immediatly was done, and the child never gaunted any more! The
fact is certain; the cause and connection I leave to others.

In November, about the 17th day, the Sacrament was at Glasgou.

* Longed vehemently.

In the Laigh Kirk there was a pretty odd case. When Mr Wishart came in to pulpit there wer but a very feu at it. He intimat his surprize, and earnest[ly] pressed that it might be filled. Some endeavours wer used by the Elders, but feu came. After prayer, before sermon, he gave another warning with the same succes. After sermon and prayer, he gave a long discourse on this, and earnestly pressed that communicants might come forward, but nobody stirred. After he came doun to the Table, it was not half full; and he expressed his concern, and signifyed hou indecent it would be if the work should be ended with the first Table! That he was ashamed to press them any further: That he would sing a litle before he began to serve; and if, in the time of singing, the Table did not fill, he was to serve it, and close the work. All this dealing did not prevail till, after singing more than three double verses, people began to come out of their seates, and some persons of distinction, Mr Wishart's great admirers, rose out of their seats and filled the Table. They had four more, and that was all. This is a neu thing in Glasgou. Whi[ther] this was occasioned by the ordinary feunes of communicants there since Mr Wishart's admission, or any fret at [the] call from London, or what was the reason, I cannot tell. But this I am informed it was.

The Wind* Meeting-house was, upon worthy Mr Grayes death, supplyed by the Session's choice, Mr Tate, and some others. I was writ to, but would not go, lest it should be misinterpreted, that I would be passive if I should be called, which the Session and people wer so foolish as to speak of. This way of a vacant Session's imploying, even under the conduct of a neighbour Minister, such as wer to help at the Sacrament, I do not knou if it should be encouraged. The Presbytery, undoubtedly, should name them.

This moneth, the Kirk building in Gorballs was finished, and they applyed to the Presbytery of Glasgou to have persons to supply it. The

---

* The Meeting-House in the Wynd, Glasgow. Mr John Gray, who had been translated from the Inner High Church, was succeeded by Mr James Dick, Minister of Carluke. This Church was abolished, and the congregation, in 1807, translated to St George's Church.

Magistrates of Glasgou took this hainously ill, at least appeared so to
do, and compleaned that Kirk was built without ouning of them, though
undoubted superiors of the Gorballs.   The people said, they had acquainted the Magistrates, [and] had the Provest of Glasgou's concurrence, when holding a Head Court in Gorballs.   It was said, they should
not have done it without an act of Toun Councill.   P[rovost] Stirling
was keen on the one hand, and Mr Ch. Coats* as keen on the other.
The Presbitry appointed a Committy to converse partys.   There, matters wer not like to be better ; hote words passed betwixt the P[rovost]
and Mr Coats.   At lenth it was compromised ; and the next Presbytery,
or that in January next, the Gorball people withdreu their petition, and
the Presbytery alloued Mr Coats to supply his people as he sau fitt.
This was the proper way, no doubt, for Mr Coats, or any Minister, may
preach [in] any part of his parish, and imploy whom he pleases, without
any act of Presbitry about it.   Thus, the neighbouring Ministers supplyed, after Mr Coats had preached first in it, and a collection was made
of twenty-four pound sterling that day.

[*November* 26.]—Upon the 26th of this moneth, at eight at night, the
worthy and learned Mr Gershom Carmichael dyed in his house in the
Colledge of Glasgou.   He was admitted Regent to our class, when
Magistrands 1695 or [169]6, so that he was about thirty-four or thirty-
five year a Regent in that University.   He was brought in by a publick
dispute,† throu the influence of the Lord Carmichael, afterward the first
Earl of Hyndford.   He was our teacher within a year after he had passed
his oun course at St Andreus, or therby.   He was son to Mr Alexander
Carmichael, who writes on Mortification.   When he came to us, he
had litle reading.   He was but very young, and was taken‡ from us by
his mother's death, and marrying his wife, a good woman, daughter to
Mr John Inglish.   His mother, I think, was relict of Mr Frazer of
Braes.   He was scarce six weeks in teaching our class.   He dictate us
severall sheets of peripatetick physics *de materia prima*, which I used
to jest him with afterward.   He was then pretty much Cartesian, and

* Minister of Gormo.   Gorbals is within the bounds of that parish.   † Disputation, or comparative
trial.   ‡ Withdrawn from his duty.

taught us Rohault.   Afterward he made himself master of the Mathematicks and the Neu Philosophy.   He was a hard student, a thinking, pooring man, and applyed himself mostly to Morall Philosophy.   He published an Abstract of Logick for his class, and Puffendorff *de Officio*, with notes, which took so well that it bore two editions.   But, above all, in his advanced years he was singularly religious, and I knou he was under great deepths of soul-exercise, and much the worse that he did not communicat his distress to any body almost.   I had a short hint of it from himself, about a year before his death.   He was a litle warm in his temper, but a most affectionat, freindly man.   His numerouse family was both a comfort to him, and he had great distress from one of them. In short, for these twelve or fifteen years last he was of very great reputation, and was exceedingly valued both at home and abroad, where he had considerable correspondence with learned men, such as Barbyrack, and other learned men abroad ; and he brought a great many scholars to Glasgou.   He might have lived much longer had not the trouble he dyed of spread much the two or three last years of his life. It began with a litle wratt* near his eye, which turned to a kind of cancerouse trouble.   Under this he remained a hard student and seriouse Christian more than twenty years ; but in the three last years of his life, it spread over his eye, and spread over his nose to the other, and, at lenth, killed him.   His death is a great loss to that society and this country.

Litle more offers this moneth.   The report continoues that P[rofessor] Hamiltoun is to be Pr[incipal ?] at Edinburgh, Mr Alston Professor, and Mr Gaudie to be called to Lady Yester's Kirk ; but nothing is certain, and things readily may take another turn.

I hear a lybell is formed against Mr Montgomery, come to Laswade, or some such parish in the Synod of Galloway, some years since, from Ireland, and that for intemperance and some other things ; and he is removed to Ireland, and will not stand a tryall.

They speak of Mr W. M'Culloch and Mr Walter Steuart to supply Wigtoun ; the Earl of Gallouway for the one, and the toun for the

---

* This seems to have been a cancerous wart.

other ; but there must be a vacancy there for a year, to get reparations from vacant stipend.

Mr Andrew Gray is called to preach at Tillicoutry, and the Laird and people seem for him. His father's congregation, Midle-quarter, Glasgou, are as one man for him ; but the Magistrates are for somebody on the other side, Mr J. Anderson or Mr J. Dick. The inclinations of people are not nou almost at all considered, but politicks and state partys, in setlments of Ministers.

Dougalston tells me that it is said that ther is some change at Court. Formerly the Queen did evry thing, and was generally applyed to ; but nou the King takes a great deal more on himself.

December, 1729.—In the last moneth, and the beginning of this, ther was the most generall cold and cough, with a feaver, seized almost every body that I ever kneu. Not one of fifty escaped. In Glasgou, they say ther was no hearing sermon, almost, for some time. It proved deadly to severalls, and yet very feu hereabout dyed of it. People wer seized with it in an instant, and somtimes they raved when on their feet ; and it was not many who wer confyned to ther beds by it. It began first in England, in the country, and it fell very heavily on London. See the prints. It came doun here in a fourteenth-night, and went over to Ireland. In short, it run throu France, Germany, and Italy, like a plague ; and, generally, the better sort wer seized with it. It's a mercy it went so soon off.

It's nou reconed that the peace with Spain is concluded, and that it has cost us a great deal of money ; and France and the Cardinall de Fleurie have made a fine merkat of it. It is said, (but, in thir things, one knoues not what or whom to belive,) that the merchants and trading part of England are exceedingly displeased with it ; and so they must, if it be true that folloues :—That they are [to] have no restoration for their losses, save what hath been seazed since . . . . . day by the Spaniards ; and very feu English ships, comparatively, since that time have been taken, and those that wer seized before amount to many hundred thousand pounds. Houever, the Parliament is to approve of it as honorable and safe : That both sides are to goe into it ; Sir R. W. particularly, because he made it ; and many of the others, in order to ruine him by this unpopular peace : That, in a litle time, a cry is to be raised against it, and the maker displaced, and the Parliament is to make up the merchants' losses ; and this is to be the first act of a neu Ministry, to render themselves popular : That the neu party severall times named, during this reigne, Scarburgh, Wilmingtoun, Carteret, and Chesterfeild, are to come in, and Sir Robert to go out.   It's said that Walpool has been, since June last, courting the Duke of Roxburgh and others called the Squad, and hath made many acknouledgments to them of his mistake in turning out them from Scots affairs, and joyning with the two brothers, A[rgyll] and Y[la :] That they stood it out two or three applications, and, in September or October, they joyned Sir Robert.

This is Glasgou accompts, wher nou the two brothers manage all. It's added, that these two great men wer awarr of this, and timously quitt Sir Robert, and are nou very well with Wilmingtoun and the rest. So that, in the event of Sir Robert's fall in England, they will still have the management of Scots affairs.   This is what is given out by Argile and Isla's freinds at Glasgou.   Time must discover what is in it.   It does not appear, three or four moneths after this, that Sir Robert is in any hazard ; and, in that event, I doubt not ther will be a change of hands again, for most part of courtiers are still ready to fall in with the Prime Minister.

I hear that, on Mr Carmichael's death, all the English Students have left the University ; and, indeed, it's very thin this winter, and his name and reputation brought many to it.   They say that, notwithstanding the late regulations, ther are some changes nou, and Books are alloued again to be lent out of the library.

[*December* 7.]—Upon the 7th of this moneth, my brother, John, has another son, in room of his former, that dyed.   He is a pleasant, sprightfull child, and bears my father's name.   I pray he may fill up his room in the world, and inherit his grace and covenant.

[*December* 16.]—On the 16th ther was an invitation sent by the Masters to Dubline to Mr Francis Hutcheson, son to Mr John Hutcheson, lately dead in Ireland; a worthy Minister and Anti-subscriber. It is said, that, by his name and reputation, [he] will, in some measure, fill up Mr Carmichael's room, and bring scholars, especially from Ireland, to Glasgou. But the immediat occasion of this is his relation to Mr A. D[unlop,] who nou has marryed his aunt's daughter. Mr Francis Hutcheson was educat here at Glasgou, and was Governour a litle* to the present Earl of Kilmarnock, and then went over to Ireland, and taught Philosophy privatly; and, at lenth, went to Dubline, and, for some time, hath had very many of the Dissenters' children sent to him to teach; and his scholars turned so numerouse, that he was oblidged to use a helper some years since. His book, Of the Beauty and Idea of Virtue, has bore severall editions at London, and hath raised his character, hou justly I cannot say. He has also answered The Fable of the Bees. Hou the principles he goes on agree with the truths generally received in this Church, and what influence his teaching them here may have, time will discover. It's doubted whither his encouragment at Glasgou will be equall to that at Dubline; but certainly it's more honourable to be a publick Professor than a privat teacher; and, I doubt not, he will accept the invitation. It's said, Mr Loudon, as eldest Regent, pretends to have his choice whither to teach Logick, which he nou teaches, or any other class that happens to vaike.

They say ther was a great strugle before this invitation. The Principall was not for Mr Hutcheson, both because he will strenthen Mr A. D[unlop]'s side in the Colledge, which is too hard for him already, and because he was for Mr D. Warner to succeed Mr Carmichael. It's said, both Mr A. D[unlop] and he wrott up to my Lord Isla, who is the *primum mobile;* and Mr A. D. prevailed, and the Principal was oblidged to drop his pretensions, when his patron failed him. The Principal has non in the Faculty throughly his, but Mr J. Simson; Mr Dunlop manages the rest of that side; and the five others wer for Mr Frederick Carmichael to succeed his father; and the P[rincipal] was so high that, till he was overborn by my L[ord] Isla's orders, he was inclinable to have

* Short time.

joyned the five who wer for Mr F. Carmichael; and if he had, he would
have cast it on that side.

[*December* 23.]—On the 23d, we had the lamentable accompts of
Lieutennant William Pollock, Sir Robert's youngest son, his death at
Dubline. The circumstances are so melancholy, that they ought not o
be remembred. It's a great breach to that family. He was the strongest and healthyest-like son left; and, taking all things together, I must
say the worthy mother of that family has met with as much for her
tryall from a mercifull God and Father as ever I kneu one of her religion and atteanments. I doubt not she has suitable and proportioned
supports, and truly she needs them.

About this time, (see Letters,) Mr John Flint, the eldest Minister
nou at Edinburgh, dyed. He was a worthy, affectionat, zealouse man,
of considerable learning. He was educat in Holland, in the late suffering times before the Revolution; and, I think, had a share in the Dutch
Edition of Pool's Criticks,* and was a tollerable linguist, and pretty much
about the famous Leusden's hand.† Whither he was sent over, and
menteaned some time while abroad, by the Society people, I cannot say,
but I have seen severall of his Letters to them, and he seems once to
have fallen in with the whims of altering the names of dayes and moneths.
But he soon got rid of these, and was Minister at Laswade; and from
thence, about twenty-six years or more since, taken in to Edinburgh.
His book, in Latine, against Mr Simson, as to the process betwixt him
and Mr Webster, sheues his reading and knouledge in the Arminian
controversy. He was a pious, warm-hearted, usefull Minister, very
aged, and troubled with a palsy in his head some years before his death,
and continoued at his work till his death. He was usefull among seriouse
persons ther, and near eighty when he died. The removall of so many
old seers and Ministers, at such a time, boads ill; but we should still be
thankful we enjoyed them so long.

Indeed, the Ministry of Edinburgh, the cheife watch-tower, hath,
within these feu moneths, had great breaches made on it; and, on the
matter, there are six vacancys in that toun. Mr Hart, Mr William

---

* *Synopsis Cricticorum.*   † In his society.

Wisheart, and Mr Flint, are dead within these six moneths, and ther are three others very near dead. Mr Greirson, who hath been almost laid aside by a failour and palsy for severall years; Mr Sandilands is superanuated, and not fully master of himself, and his voice so weakned that he is not heard at all; and worthy Mr Craig, they say, is very ill, and spitting blood, and threatned with death. Those falling in at such a time as this have a voice* to this Church.

[*December* 24.]—On the 24th, Mr M'Dermit's call, as susteaned by the Commission last, was presented to the Presbytery of Air. The Presbitry reasoned a good while on it, and found ther was no call before them, and gave it as their opinion, that since no Presbitry concurred with the call, it was not to be received, nor would it bear a process. The Commission had, indeed, susteaned it to be a call, and preferable to the other; and ordered it to be prosecute according to the custome of the Church; but the Presbytery of Air wer [of] opinion ther was no call before them, because of the want of concurrence of a Presbitry to it, and they did not see that the Commission had made up that defect. The Magistrates of Renfreu appealed to the Commission, but, as we shall see, did not prosecute their appeal, but it was cast in another channell.

[*December* 28.]—On the 28th of December, Munday morning, we had a most terrible and continoued thunder and lightning, some very great and fearfull cracks, and a continoued flash of lightning for some hours. I have not knouen so much of this at this season of the year. They say, winter thunder breeds summer's cumber and hunger.

* Of warning.

M.DCC.XXX.

January, 1730.—About the 8th or 9th of this moneth, R. Sanders, of Aldhouse, dyed and left the lands of Aldhouse, and money, to the Merchants' Hospital at Glasgou. It is reconed they have got, by him, about two thousand pound sterling. They are to have, also, about two thousand pound more by Mr Mitchell's death, Mr John Orr's relation his death, this moneth, at London; of which, just nou. Robert Sanders was exceedingly disoblidged by his relations, and so put all he had by them. He promised to me to leave a hundred pound Scots to our Session. He has been paralitick since his last fitt, about two years since.

We hear that P[rincipal] Campbell, finding matters like to go against him in Mr M'Dermit's setlment at Renfreu, wrote up to my Lord Isla that there wer so many difficultys like to arise, that he began to think of dropping it; on which my Lord made him a return, wherin, in a short and very peremptory oath, he swore he should be Minister there, who ever should oppose it. This letter, it seems, the Principal let his son-in-lau, Mr Sommervail, see, and [he] had not the closnes to conceal it, so that the whole toun of Renfreu has it among them.

Some time this moneth, the Principal, who teaches some, under Mr Simson's suspension, one day in the open Hall, among the students, regrated to them that he was so throng that he could not attend them so closly as he would, (they had no more but a meeting or two a week,) but he hoped that, shortly, the Professor, Mr Simson, should be restored to them by the ensuing Generall Assembly, and he would take a better care of them. This is thought a very odd step, unles he have very full assurance that his designe shall hold; and if ther be such a concert among his freinds, it does not appear so very prudent to blab it out so openly to a meeting of young students.

There seems to be a generall rumor, in most parts of the Church, much more than hereabout, at this time, of restoring Mr Simson by the insuing Assembly ; and the Ministers of Perth, Angus, and Fife, have formed a Representation to counter any such designe. It is very hard to say what can be in designe by such who talk so loud for a Reposition. It will inevitably run us in a breach. To prevent this, an assertory act is proposed of the doctrines opposed by him ; and, on the other hand, it will be urged that he be not restored till the second lybell be gone throu. I cannot conceive how he can be restored without a reason for his restoration and repentance ; and it does not appear what further lenth he can go, in professions and verball repentance, than he [has] gone already. I knou not in what shape his restoration will come in. If it be sought that the suspension from the ministry be taken off, it may be said that he was not blamed nor lybelled as to his preaching. And this will appear a litle modest ; but then, with what decency one who has been declared incapable to teach youth, should be alloued to preach the Gospell, I cannot see. If the shape be, that he be restored to be Professor, it will be a bold stroak, indeed, to counteract a judiciall declaration, in a way of compromise, and by way of ending his process so very soon ; and it will be an odd instance of the unsteadynes of this Church in a matter of doctrine of this importance.

[*January* 13.]—On the 13th of January, Mr John Logan, Minister at Neu Kilpatrick, dyed. He had been eight or ten years a Minister, and he was reconed a man of land and money ; but, by taking his father's land to his oun hand, and it being burdened with debt he kneu not of, and he paying the portions and giving away his stipend to his sisters, still depending on the paternall estate, he was sunk in debt. He marryed [Bailie] Murdoch's daughter, and got five hundred pound with her, much of which run to the paying his debts ; but neither he nor his wife's relations kneu the debts on the land till after his death. But melancholy and discouragment broke his naturall spirits. He was a well-natured easy man, and a good man. We that are Ministers should not involve ourselves in the things of time and of this world ; we have another work on our hand. And I see severall sad instances of Ministers that do so, who lose any small thing they have ; and really, by disappointment, (and we are not much acquaint with the methods of managing the concerns of life,) loss their health and life.

This moneth ther was a considerable struggle betwixt Mr Charles Erskine, my Lord Buchan's brother, and the Laird of Strichan, my Lord Isla's cusin, for the Commissariat of Edinburgh. Shaufeild, they say, used his interest for the first, his brother-in-lau, and the two brothers* for the other, and Strichan has carryed his point.

February, 1730.—Nou the talk is that the Toun of Edinburgh will not hear of P[rofessor] Hamiltoun to be a Minister at Edinburgh and Principall ; and without that, he does [not] care to quite his post as Professor, which has lately fifty pound annexed to it by act of Parliament, on the two pennys per pint to the Toun of Edinburgh. So he has two thousand nine hundred merk and a house. He would have taken a ministeriall charge with the Principall's post, because he is overburdened with the multitude of students ; but that, it seems, will not do. And the present Provest, Lindsay, inclines to have in Mr James Smith of Craumond to the Toun, as a popular act, and that will please both sides in the Toun ; so the project is, nou, which will hold. The Principall's place continoues vacand for another year. Mr G. Wisheart comes to the Trone Kirk, in his father's room ; Mr Gaudie to Lady Yester's, and Mr J. Smith to Haddoch's hole,† in Mr Flint's room.

This moneth Mr Dundas of Arniston goes up to Parliament. It is said he was not to be up this session, being on the discontented lay ; and our politicians at Glasgou are allarumed at his going up, as forbodding a change at Court : But I doubt ther is nothing that way ; but the bill

---

* The Duke of Argyll and Lord Isla.   † Haddo's Hold ; *i. e.* " The Little" or New North Kirk.

for the adjourning* the Session, at least, when he goes up ; I see he is chairman for it.

The talk is reneued of changes in the two Bords of Custome and Excise. That Mr G. Drummond is to go out ; but the Duke of Argyle stands yet for him, and the Master of Ross to come in, and Mr Thomas Cocheran to the Bord of Excise. The last gains it ; but I hear no change in the Customs at present.

This moneth ther is an accidentall fire at Leith, and a lodging burnt. A very strange passage is told relative to it. Mr George Shirrife, doer,† I think, for the Earle of Hoptoun, either had his house burnt by it,‡ or it was in imminent hazard, being next to the burning, and he had a strange premonition about it. The fire was about midnight, or early in the morning. Mr Shirriff was over in Fife : The day before ther came on a contrary wind, or storm, or some what that made it a litle inconvenient for the Boats to come from Kinghorn to Leith. He had no pressing bussines to bring him home, nor was he resolved to come over the watter till next day, when others wer coming also. But that night he took an unaccountable uneasines in his spirit, for which he could give no reason, but he thought there was somwhat or other, he kneu not what, that made it necessary to be at home that night, and went to the boatmen in the evening ; but they pretended difficultys, and said they could not that night come over the watter. His uneasines continoued to that pitch that he applyed to the Magistrates at Burntisland (I don't mind positively but it might be Kircaldie) for orders to the Boat to come over, and prevailed. When he came home to Leith three or four hours before the fire, he found his family well, and no apparent thing to support his anxiety. Houever, about midnight the fire broke out, and then he sau the need of the premonition he had. I have knouen severall instances of such kind premonitions in Providence, by impression on good men's spirits before hazards and dangers. He is a man of very considerable sense and learning, and of an excellent and fair character, not to be imposed on by fancy and vapours.

---

* Giving the Court of Session the power of adjourning. Next, adjacent to ; "hard by."   † Agent, man of business.

Last moneth and this we have the greatest number of unexpected legacys and huge heaps of money breaking out to persons generally very much needing them, that ever I heard [or] read of. I hear of severall in other parts of the nation, Scotsmen, that have been in Spain, and made some fifty thousand, some one hundred thousand pounds; and send over Commissions to buy lands for them in Stirlingshire, Perth, and Fife; two or three whose names I have forgot. But in Glasgou and the neighbourhood ther are five or six very strange and surprising ones.

Mr John Orr, late Bailay in Glasgou, his wife's uncle, Mr Mitchell at London, dyes, as we have heard, about the beginning of January. Mr Mitchell was born in Glasgou, and if I remember, had his prentice-fee payed by some of the Trades in Glasgou, at least was in very great straites. He left the place and went to England. There he marryed a rich Irish woman, and got forty thousand pounds with her. She had no children. He had another brother who folloued him, and he has a son who gets the one half of [his] means. Mr Orr's wife is a sister's daughter of his. Mr Mitchell was a paun-broker at London, and made a prodigiouse mass of money. By that, and his narrou way of living, which was almost incredible, he has left some say one hundred and fifty thousand pounds. About twenty years ago he made a will, and left his brother executor; and left two thousand pounds for a free school at Glasgou, and severall legacys to some naturall children of his. But he outlived his brother, and was so narrou as he would do very litle for his brother's son with him at London, during his life, and had not the pouer to make a neu testament. Thus he dyed intestate, the executor being dead, and no other nominat. Thus Mr Orr, in right of his wife, the neice, falls in co-heir with Mr Mitchell the nepheu, who, it seems, quites his claims of heirship, and divides with Mr Orr. Unless this incident had fallen in, Mr Orr would have been certainly quite excluded, or got very litle. Mr Orr has been my acquaintance since his youth. He was a student of divinity under my father about the 1700, and a lad of good parts, for whom my brother, Mr Alexander, had a great value, he being one of his parishoners. After my brother's death he quite* his studyes, and marryed his present wife, by whom he has a competency to live on, and took

* Quitted, left off.

himself to trading; and with Mr Harvey and some others, who had be[en] graduat and scholars, fitted out a ship whom they named Apollo, but they lost her, and wer reduced to great straits. His wife's uncle inclined about twenty years [ago] or therby to be chosen member of Parliament for Glasgou, and said he would leave twenty thousand pound sterling to the Toun. But that did not hold. Mr Orr then intirely broke, and had nothing left, paid all his debts honestly; and Mr A. Dunlop, Mr R. Simson, Mr Johnstoun, and some others, lent him fifty pounds sterling apeice, six or seven of them, and took his bill for it, and he set up a shop in Glasgou for cloaths, &c. and had many customers; and being a man of good sense and integrity, he got a livelyhood; and gradually cleared what he had borroued, and was chosen Bailay of Glasgou; he still continoued to read and was bookish. In his straits he went up to London, and communicat his straitned case to his uncle, Mr Mitchell, but he gave him litle or nothing, being such a narrou man, one that could part with nothing, and cooked his oun meat, and they say would never so much almost as keep a servant. Many wer the straites B[ailie] Orr and his family went throu these last ten or twelve years. His wife, a piouse good woman, had a trade of thread-making, and menteaned the family, and he keeped the shop, and they say she gave him eightpence a day for pocket-money, most of which he gave in charity. Nou, on a suddain, his circumstances are altered, and by his uncle's death he has got forty-two thousand pound, in good money. It's said that it's good to be sibb* to gear; but here I desire to observe the vanity and folly of the world, the uncertainty of riches, and the present strange turns of them, and even a present providentiall retribution of his honesty and fair dealing, and his and his wife's diligence, and I hope dependance on God, and their mite of charity.

Another great legacy is that of Mr John Grant, Minister at Afflect.† His wife is sister to Mr Colin Campbell, the great architect at London, who wrote Vitruvius Britannicus, and the two folios of Draughts of Fine

* Literally, of kin.   † Auchinleck.

Seats, and was to give an Edition of Vitruvius' Architecture. Mr Colin Campbell, I think, was Inspector of the King's Buildings, and made much money. And we are told that Mr Grant, who is at London this winter, gets twelve thousand pound for his share. Mr Grant, as is to be seen in this Collection, 1711 or [17]12, suffered a great deal from the Jacobites, was wounded in his head, and almost murdered. He has been Minister at Afflect since, and was still on the zealouse side, and a litle inclined to The Marrou. This great summ fallen to him is a retribution, and an hundred fold in this life, to a sufferer. There was an unhappy rumor raised of a woman he recommended, who fell with child afterwards ; but I hope it's altogether groundles, as to him. Whatever his circumstances wer formerly in straits, he is nou releived out of them.

Another odd thing of this kind is the above John Graham, who deceased in winter last. His papers, or rather those of Mr M'Ward, I have got. His lands and houses wer to go between Mr William Dennistoun and [his] cusine, and nobody interfeered with them, nor quarrelled the thousand pound left to Dougalstoun ; but Mr Dennistoun, to whom all was left, going throu old trunks covered with papers and pamphlets, finds to the value of fifteen hundred pound sterling in silver money, all antiquated, and never touched since the Union, and probably litle minded since the Revolution. It's a thousand pound good money, and there will be five hundred pound loss. This has been probably lying by him since his mother, Mrs M'Ward's, death. And Mr Dennistoun was so just, though he might have keeped all closs, all nou being committed to him by freinds, that he acquainted the Magistrates with it, and it was numerat. This has raised the hue and cry on all the relations of P. Graham, and many are nou putting in for the executry. This is another odd instance of John Graham's temper, as above narrated, to have so much money lying dead by him for near forty year !

Mr John Edmonstoun, Minister at Cardross, about the same time, has, or is to have, left him one thousand pounds sterling, or five hundred pound, as others say, by his uncle, William Edmonstoun, in Dumblane, who had an only daughter maryed to Mr Hugh Clerk, the Mountain* student; but both he and she are dead, without posterity; and John Edmiston is nearest.

Mr Bailay, of Monctoun, to his great surprize, has an estate in West Calder parish, possessed by one Buntine, about thirty thousand merks left to him, just as Major Buntine's heir, though ther was no relation between the defunct and the Major.

Ther is one that was born in the parish of Saltcoats or Stevenson, that has been long in the East Indies, and has more than one hundred thousand pounds, and wants to have an heir and relations, and [has] writt doun to Scotland; and one of them, a mason, M'Crea, Cree, or Crevoch, or some such name, is gone up. The event we knou not.

Ther is another—and all broke out these two last moneths—of the name of Semple, born in the parish of Cardross, worth forty or fifty thousand pound, to whom Mr James Semple, in Dreghorn, was said to be nearest relation; but another proves much nearer; and he has no relations at London, and has writ to Scotland for his nearest freind to come up.

Another servant lass is talked of at Hamiltoun, who marryed a Dragoun, who has left her; and, by the death of a freind, to whom she proves the nearest relation, she comes to possess fifty thousand pound sterling.

They speak of two old weemen, sisters, in the toun of Lanerk, very poor, who have fallen [heir to] five or six thousand pound; and one has quitted her part of it for about thirty pound a year presently secured to her; and it's all she needs to make her easy.

It's certain, a servant lass of D[ean of] Gild Rogers has fallen, by the death of some relation, a thousand pounds starling. This is as odd a chain of incidents, this way, in so short a time, as ever I heard of or read of, and is a very full proofe of the vanity and instability of human affairs.

March, 1730.—We have, this moneth and the last, the accompts of

* Student for the Ministry amongst the Cameronians, or Mountain Men.

a blind man in Kintyre, who hath visions of angells denouncing judgments on Scotland.   The account of which, see a paper by itself.

My wife tells me that she heard her mother frequently tell that Mr John Campbell of Craigie, Minister, whom I kneu when young, frequently told her that he had been abroad preaching, and generally at that time ther wer many hints of witches, and severall persons in proces for witchcraft ; (it was some years before the Restoration ;) and, in his preaching, he cautioned his hearers from hearkening to Satan, or credulity in beliving him, insisting that no regard was to be had to him or his creatures, he being a lyar from the beginning.   When riding home alone to his oun house, he heard one calling him by his name in the highway ; and Mr Campble looked about, and sau no body.   This was repeated a second or third time.   At the third time, he sau nothing, but heard a hidious laughter, and a voice saying, " The Minister himself must hearken to the Devil !"   He road on without any return.   In a litle he was called again by his name, which he did not nottice, but rode on : then the spirit cryed to him, that he had better hearken to him, for he had a matter that very nearly concerned him to impart.   Mr C[ampbell] still rode on, not seeming to mind what was said.   The voice continoued—" Well, belive me or not, it's true I tell you, and you ought to take heed to it !   When you go home, your wife is expecting you to supper ; and ther is a hen rosting at the fire for you, but do not tast it, for it's poisoned."   He rode home ; and when he entered his house, he sau a hen roasting.   He was then in some perplexity, and asked his wife where she had the hen ?   She told him the beast was brought in dead, though warm, and sold by a woman under a very ill fame for witchcraft. He went to prayer, and asked light from God.   He was in a great strait betwixt a just care of his oun health, and taking a warning from an evil spirit.   Houever, at supper, he cut up the hen, which looked well, and no way discolloured, which made him incline to eat her.   Just at this instant a litle dog came in to the room, and it struck him in the mind to try an experiment on the dog ; and he cast a peice of the hen to the dog, who had no sooner eat it, but he swelled and dyed !   This cleared his way, and he eat none of the hen.

There are some evil spirits, that, when permitted, seem to delight in freaks ; and yet, it seems, this devil has been forced to tell Mr Campbell his hazard, and used as an instrument for preserving this good man. The fact is sufficiently vouched, and may be depended on.

The Commission met the second Wensday of this moneth, as usuall. They had litle before them save the affair of Mr John Glass, which has been delayed and put off till this dyet of the Commission. We have seen above hou it stood. The Ministers of Angus wer well conveened, and had taken pains to gather the members of the Commission. The accompt I have of what is done, see Letters. I shall only add, that Professor Hamiltoun, with all his party, set up violently for Mr Glass ; and the vote run very narrou, and came within six or seven. It's thought that this determination of the Commission will weaken Mr Glasses party in Angus, and put an end to the divisions of the country.

The affair of Renfreu should have come in by way of apeal to this Commission ; but Principal Campbell waved that, and, in the close of the Commission, when it was reaconed ther was not a coram,* this affair was brought in in another shape ; and the Commission was desired to explain an act of the last Commission on this affair. They had susteaned Mr M'Dermitt's call, and ordered it to be proceeded in according to the rules of the Church. The Presbytery of Air stuck at proceeding, because it wanted the concurrence of a Presbitry. To supply that, the Commission declared that their susteaning the call to Mr M'Dermit was equall to a Presbitry's concurrence ; and they did concurr with the call, in the room of our Presbitry. A question was moved, (the number of members being very feu,) Whither the members of the Synod should vote ? They wer excluded from votting, though, in the former Commission, they wer alloued to vote ; and so the concurrence with the call was carryed. Ther was litle other thing but matters of form and common concern, that I heard of ; and, indeed, except party affairs, litle other thing is nou handled in the Commission.

* Quorum.

[*March* 14.]—On the 14th of this moneth, there was a barbarouse murder committed in the Brigend* upon one John Youl, by a villan who was in company with the robber, More. He was seized and tryed, and brought off in point of self-defence. This is five murders hereabout within this twelve moneth, and no punishment inflicted on the murderers. By some quirks in lau, they still get off, so that two very good lauers at Glasgou say that nou they belive that none shall be condemned for a murder, unles an instrument can be taken upon the murder in the hands of a publick nottar.

The . . . day of this moneth, my wife was safely brought to bed of a son, James, who, I pray, may repair the breach made on me by taking away my eldest and most hopefull son, of that name.

Aprile, 1730.—Our Synod met at Air, at the ordinary time ; see Letters this moneth. It is a perfect jest for us to meet at Air, for scarce any bussines can be done for want of members. There was but one member from Glasgou, Hamilton, and Lanerk, each ; two from Dumbartan, and three from Paislay. When the Presbytery of Air wer turned out, ther was not the face of a Synod, or of a Presbytery, not above fourteen. They had nothing before them but the minutes, and rose [on] Wensday, early.

[*April* 1.]—In the beginning of this moneth, Mr Wisheart offered a dimission to the Presbytery of Glasgou. I knou not but it might be proposed last moneth, and partys cited to this day ; but I shall give the whole together. I have remarked the state of his affair before. What hindered him to take the . . . .† of a process of transportation, I cannot tell. The callers of him at London, I heard, granted pouers to some in Glasgou to prosecute the call. But, at rights, and to shorten the work, it seems Mr W[isheart] chose to give in his dimission, though it may be doubted if this be a habile way for a Presbiterian Minister to treat his people and Judicatorys, when going to another Congregation,

* Bridge-end of Glasgow.   † Probably *course*.

especially in such strong terms as it's said he gave it in, " That he had received a harmonious call from London," without the least of his oun interposition ; and he was, after considering the affair, come to a resolution to accept of it, and had hereby declared his acceptance of it, and dimitted his relation to the Congregation in Glasgou.   Hou far this was the proper way for a Minister of this Church to do, without consulting with his people and Presbytery, I must leave to others.   The Presbytery, houever, supplied defects, and when the dimission was offered, (last Presbytery day probably,) they caused cite his people to appear, before they would give their opinion as to accepting of it.   This Presbytery day, Aprile, I think, the Magistrates appeared and his session, and declared their respect for him, and unwillingnes to part with him.   Mutuall complements passed, and he insisted that his affairs called him to be in England, and he could not manage what was in Providence entrusted to him by any other person.   He signifyed his great respect to his people, and his desire to continou in this Church ; but, all things considered, he was determined to follou the call of Providence.   He added, that he was to be in Yorkshire by the midle of May on bussines, which could admitt of no delay ; that he would give the Sacrament on the 19 of Aprile, and could preach no longer, and desired the Presbytery might declare the Church vacant the day after.   The Presbytery accepted the dimission, and appointed Mr J. Stirling to declare the Church vacant, Aprile 26.   Houever, I am told that in conversation with the Magistrates, it was found that they could not pay him the half year's stipend unless he preached after the term ; and so he altered his resolution, and, with the consent of the Ministers, the declaring the Kirk vacant was stoped. When the Presbytery in May came, there was like to have been a demelee* in the Presbytery, and an adherance to their former sentence, and to declare the Kirk vacant before the term ; but there was a compromising of the matter, and he sheued' some inclinations to leave that half year's stipend to pious uses in the place.   Upon which, the Presbytery went in to his preaching after the term, and yet I hear he has only left five hundred merks† to the poor.

* Contest, debate, difference. Fr. *demelé*.   † £27, 15s. 6⅔d !

[*Aprile* 20.]—Upon the 20th of this moneth the affair of Renfreu was tabled before the Presbytery of Air, by the Magistrates, nou that the Commission had put themselves in the room of our Presbytery, in point of concurrence.   The Presbytery, after reading the reasons and answers, unanimously refused Mr M'Dermitt's transportation.   It was said that a plurality of the Presbytery, some from one veiu, some from another, would have been for his transportation ; but the Magistrates being against it, and Mr M'Dermitt expressing his aversion, and the Presbitry finding that though they should transport, he and the Magistrates would appeal to the Assembly, they chused rather to be unanimouse, and refuse the transportation ; and so the Magistrates of Renfreu and Principall appealed to the Assembly.   I thought that they had designed, by the appeal, to have had the time of tabling it in the Synod, and that they designed to postpone it to the Commission, but the event sheued I was wrong.

Mrs Luke tells me that she has frequently heard my father express his regard to Mr William Guthry, and signify his satisfaction that his brother-in-lau was marryed to my informer, Mr William Guthry's grandchild.   Had he been alive, I belive he would have been yet more pleased at my marrying another grandchild of his.   Besides his great regard to Mr Guthry for his usefulnes, it seems Mr Guthry was the first that God used as the instrument of awakning him.   He was a young lad, at Egilsham, and went with others to Finwick, to hear Mr Guthry.   He was wearyed with the walk of some miles, and was warm and weary ; and in Mr G[uthry's] first prayer, he confessed, in name of the auditory, many sins, and among others, heavines and wearynes in prayer, and sleeping when at it.   My father heard this, and yet afterward he sleeped for some time in the first prayer ; and after prayer was over, Mr G[uthry] began his lecture or sermon with words to this purpose : That he belived some might be sensible that they had fallen into the same very sins that they had confessed in prayer to God, and wer guilty this very day of what they had been professing to confess.   His conscience smote him that he had sleeped, and this gave him matter of very serious reflexions.

This moneth, the Bill was brought in and passed in Parliament, empouring the Lords of Session to adjourn themselves, for what time they sau proper, any time from the 26th of December till the 29th of January. This is designed for a recess to the Lords, and yet so as not to fall in with the Youl vaccance, because Youll is excluded.* It is generally thought that this is preliminary to the Lords of Session their droping the summer session; and it's generally thought that the dropping of June and July, providing they sat in October to March or Aprile, would not be a disadvantage to the leidges; since very litle, as matters nou stand, is done in the summer session, and it brings more uneasines both to the Lords and leidges to be at Edinburgh in the summer time than can be ballanced by all the good that is then done.

We have, this moneth, accounts of one of the most attrocious villanys attempted that I ever almost heard of. The Laird of Aughtifardell, in the parish of Lesmahagou, has been for many years, since his killing Mr Houstoun, upon a terrible provocation, at the Cross of Edinburgh, about twenty years ago, been reconed a serious and most religious man. He is an Elder, and takes particular nottice of his servants. He had a woman servant whom he endeavoured to instruct, and frequently reproved for what he sau amiss. This servant took the gentlman's reproofes hainously ill. Ther was arsnick in the house for poisoning ratts. The servant asked, if that thing would kill men and weemen as well as ratts, at her fellou servants; and that is the only presumption against her. She was told it would. Next morning she was employed to make her master's breakfast, of bread and milk, and it's much suspected she mixed in the arsnick with the milk and bread. When Auchtifardell, his wife, and some of his daughters, eat the milk and bread, they reconed it had a peculiar tast, but suspected nothing. In a litle time they all sickned, and fell exceeding ill. Happily they got a physitian, who vomitted them, and it pleased the Lord to bless the mean. They all recovered, save one of the daughters, who, they say, is yet very ill. This is the most villanouse act ever I read or heard, almost.

* Its observance abolished.

May, 1730.—This moneth, we heard Mr Simson and his freinds wer exceeding pleased that the Earl of Loudon was Commissioner to the Assembly. From him, it seems, they expected all favour; but they wer out in their expectations. I belive I may have formerly notticed, that in January Pr[incipal] Campbell, when he taught the scholars, students of Divinity, that is, once or twice a week heard their discourses, and read a litle of a Systeme, he told them he was sorry he could not wait on them so closly as he inclined; but he hoped, against the next session, they would have their proper Master, Professor Simson, restored to them, and that the next Assembly would take off the sentence. This, two or three lads present tell with some positivenes, and the Principall, they say, refuses it. Be that as it will, the noise of this went throu the Church, and raised considerable fears of a designe to repone him. We heard that Mr Simson had proposed that the Colledge should address the Assembly to restore him, but the masters wer generally against this; and a litle before the Assembly, we heard that his freinds said, that they never had any designe to get him reponed to teaching; that they would not so much as ask that, but only to have the sentence of suspension from preaching and the ministeriall office taken away, that he might be placed in a Congregation. Meanwhile, Mr Simson is exceeding well in his health, never looked so well as he does, and seems to be perfectly easy under the censures upon him. He still enjoyes his sellary, and the youth in the West of Scotland are perfectly neglected.

[*May* 14.]—Thus matters stand before the Generall Assembly, which met May 14 this year. I hapned to be a member; and Mr Simson's case being the most important matter that we had in view, I laboured to state the matter to myself, and form the clearest vieu of it on both sides, and in my opinion it stood thus: The question might cast up in two shapes; 1*st,* Whither Mr Simson should be repouned to teaching divinity? or, 2*dly,* Whither, still barring him from teaching, he should have the sentence of suspension as to preaching and other parts of the ministeriall office taken off?

As to his being restored to teach the youth, I could find very feu arguments, I could think of, to be urged for this, except these that have been formerly urged against his being laid aside, which I have, in another paper last year, given my opinion of, the lamenes of the proof as to his teaching error, and his renouncing what was proven. It appeared, then, as to this, that the Generall Assembly could not in any decency go in to repone him to teach, for three reasons that appear very strong: 1*st*, That the last Generall Assembly, 1729, hath ended that process, which depended three years with a great eclat* in this Church, and given sentence, and a finall sentence, that it was not proper he should be, after this, intrusted with the care of teaching. Nou, when the Supreme Judicatory of any society ends a proces, ther can be no opening that sentence, otherwise ther could be no order, but plain confusion in the society. We find this strongly urged as to the pouers of the Commission in matters committed to them by an Assembly finally to determine, that whatever iniquity they committ in a sentence, unless they have done what is incompetent, and gone beyond their pouer, an after Assembly cannot, or at least ought not, to reverse what they have done, because they would thus open a dore for confusion, and nobody could be sure of a process being ended. If this be the case of a delegat sort of Supreme Court, the argument will be much stronger as to a proper Supreme Court. Let us suppose a Generall Assembly hath ended a process of transportation by a vote and sentence, or a process of scandall, upon a Minister. Shall the next, or any posterior Assembly, take it up and alter it ; especially if it be a declaratory sentence, on good grounds, that a Minister, by reason of some particular circumstances which still continou, shall never be Minister in such a place, or that such a scandall shall be so and [so] testifyed against ? To me it appears that that sentence cannot be opened by a succeeding Assembly.

2*dly*, Ther seems to me to be more in the sentence of the Assembly, 1729, than a mere declaration of his unfitnes to have the charge of the youth. It was a declarature from what was found in the process, and what affected the office of teaching ; it was a declarature that related to all times coming, without any reserve, and in most generall terms, and

* Noise.

fluuing necessarly from the gross things found proven and confessed; it was a declarature even with a vieu to what a Committy of the Assembly had found as to another lybell of teaching error and breach of an interdiction; which second process, indeed, was not finally judged, but by this declarature that process was to be droped and ended; but, lastly, it was a declarature, if I may call it so, by way of compromise among partys litigant, and a midse* struck by a harmoniouse consent of two different partys in judgment, and with a designe of kindnes and favour to the panall, giving him another year's (and nou it happens to be two years') sellary. In those circumstances, it appears very evident to me, that such a midse and compromise, which, I remember, last year was, by lauers from the throne, declared to be the strongest barr against Mr Simson's return to teach, cannot, without evident iniquity, be broke in upon and altered.

3dly, I think the Assembly can never go in to the reponing Mr Simson to teach the youth, because that will infallibly kindle a flame, and make such a breach in this Church as will be perfectly incurable, and of worse consequence than can be told.

For these reasons, I hope another Generall Assembly will never venture to repone Mr Simson to teach the youth.

The question is a litle more narrou and disputable, Whither this Assembly may not take off the sentence of suspension from him as to preaching, and other parts of the ministeriall function? It is plain that this suspension, in the act, is only continoued untill another Generall Assembly shall see cause to take it off. This, I knou, was quarrelled; but it was said, that whither it was in the act or not, such a supposition was in the nature of the thing, and another Assembly had it still in their pouer to take it off; and some went into this point of form, to give the greater force to the other part of the sentence, and [as an] absolute and unconditionall declaration that it was never to be found fit he should be restored to teaching the youth. This suspension from preaching and

* Medium, middle course.

other parts of the ministeriall office, did arise upon the proces on the doctrine of the Trinity, and was thought necessary till the proces was issued and ended ; and when the process came to be summed up, and it was not found proper to discuss the second lybell on doctrine, there was no reason appeared, but much on the contrary, to take off the suspension formerly laid on him.   Thus it was that that suspension came to be laid on, and continoues till this Assembly.

As to another Assembly's taking it off, no argument can be urged, as it would seem there may be as to reposition to teaching the youth from incompetency and want of pouer, but from inconveniency ther are many arguments may be severally urged.   But that I may give what offers to me on both sides of the question, as far as I am able to state them, I'le first consider what may be advanced for taking off the suspension from Mr Simson ; and then what appears of weight with me against the taking it off.

1st, It may be argued, in Mr Simson's favours, and for taking off the suspension, 1st, That Mr Simson was never lybelled nor blamed, in any of his processes, as to his preaching and the exercise of the ministeriall office ; and that the sentence of suspension as to this was not upon any thing pretended as to his doctrine in the pulpit ; but meerly because it was not thought proper a person under a lybell, in matters and point of doctrine so very high, should preach or exerce the ministeriall function, till it was issued.   And, indeed, I must do him that justice as to say, I have once and again heard him preach, and I could never blame his doctrine in the pulpit save once, and that was about the 1711, before Mr Webster's proces, and when ther wer no jealousy of his hetrodoxy. In the Wine,* on a fast day before a communion, preaching on Joh. iii. 16, he to me seemed to have some things which savoured of the error afterwards charged on him by Mr Webster, on the connection between morall seriousnes and God's giving of grace ; but it was so dark and indistinctly said, that I recon feu in the Church would observe it.   At other times since I have heard him preach at communions sound doc-

* The Wynd Kirk is here meant.

trine, and frequently refute the Socinians and others. It, *2dly*, may be said, that compassion to his numerous family, since the Church is secured against his teaching of the youth, should move Ministers to allou him to preach and have a country charge, or some other, wher he could not do much hurt, and have a competency to subsist him and his. This is plausible, and affects many. *3dly*, It may be urged, that the suspension was laid on during the proces upon the Trinity, and that and the second libell being nou ended, and no more to be taken up, it seems hard for ever to close his mouth, and forbid him to be usefull. *4thly*, That it wer injustice to him, without a lybell upon his preaching and his malversations as a Minister, to deprive him of that; and whenever he begins to vent errour, a check is at hand by the Presbytery, Synod, and Assembly; and ther can be no hazard in allouing him to preach and act as a Minister, till once he malverse. I shall not stay to answer those arguments. Materiall answers may fall in upon the next side of this state. Let me only, in a word, nottice, that though no lybell was given him as to preaching, nor instances advanced of his malverse,[*] yet his suspension was a consequent of his malverse in teaching, and nothing in that proces, when summed up, appeared for taking off the suspension, but much to the contrary. That his family circumstances are not straitning; that he is rather among the rich than the poor, and has enjoyed his sellary four year after gross errors in teaching cast up, which sheues much compassion to him and his family. That though the suspension was laid on him during the process about error in teaching, yet that being found, it does not follou that the suspension in preaching should be taken off, ther being a connection between errors; and if he entertean them, especially in foundation-truths, it will be hard to think but that he will mix them in his sermons, especially considering his rash, unstable, and innovating temper. That the proces is indeed ended as to the Trinity, and the other as to the second lybell is sisted; but the sentence of suspension is part of the sentence for his unsoundnes, and cannot easily be reversed without opening the whole, and really altering the sen-

---

[*] Malversation, or misconduct in that respect.

tence: For a suspension *sine die* was no small part of the sentence issuing both lybells, as well as the declaratory act, asserting him unfitt for teaching. But waving these, I come,

2*dly*, To give the reasons why Mr Simson ought not to be reponed, even to preaching and the exercise of the Ministry, very shortly: 1*st*, It's too plain that [if] a man found, after tryall, to have once taught errour in the schools, and for that cause declared unfitt to teach youth any more, should be alloued to preach in the pulpit and spread errour among the people, that if he act consistently and sincerly when he handle the points in preaching, especially those of the second lybell, he must (unles it appeared he had changed his sentiments, of which ther is no evidence) preach the same doctrine. 2*dly*, It does not appear possible that, with any kind of decency, a person against whom such things have been found by this Church, as tend to alter the object of Divine worship and the method of salvation, and affect all the Gospell truths that can be touched in sermons, should be permitted to preach, and have the charge of souls. One would think that it wer utterly unaccountable, that one who, in a very solemn manner, hath been declared unfit to teach youth, should be alloued to preach to young and old, and secretly to instill his loose notions to his hearers. What could bystanders conclude, if he who is reconed unfitt hereafter to teach, should be thought fitt to preach; though unfitt for the greater, alloued to be fitt for the smaller? 3*dly*, The Apostolicall canons will be found unalterable, especially when we are in no strait for aboundance to preach, that " a Bishop should be of good report, and apt to teach." Certainly, Mr Simson is found not to be of good report; yea, much as to foundation truths relating to Christ, the great subject of the Gospell, hath been found against him, and that plainly proven. And hou he who doubts as to the necessary existence, &c., of Jesus Christ, can be apt to teach and preach that Christ, is more than I can tell. 4*thly*, It does not appear to me that any grounds are offered, from any thing that casts up since the suspension was laid on, 1729, as to preaching, &c., for taking it off. It's, indeed, said that Mr Simson has renounced the errors charged on him, and professed sorrou for the offence taken; but as that was before the laying on the suspension, and so cannot affect it since, so it will be observed, that for all the plain proofe, he has never confessed that he was guilty of what was proven, far less professed any repentance for his teaching, as it hath been proven he taught. And it's said, as to the second proces, that the act 1729 puts an end to that second lybell; and any thing in the second libell, not being judged by the Assembly, can never affect Mr Simson. Upon this I only take nottice, that it's true the Assembly sists the second process, and declares the matter shall end here; but at the same time they lay or continou Mr Simson under the suspension; and that is the method they take to slump and end the second libell; and at least this will follou, that before the suspension be taken off, the second libell must be taken up and judged, since it's only on the supposition of a continouing suspension that the second lybell, for peace-sake and saving of time, and neu debates, was not entered into. Let me further add, that though, indeed, the Assembly did not judge the second lybell, yet ther is as much in that proces confessed by Mr Simson, as, in the opinion of many, very nearly affects our doctrine, besides what is proven by concurring testimonies and printed, and so open to all, as, till he purge himself by renounciation of these errors, as well as those of the first libell, and repentance, will be a sufficient ground for a suspension from preaching. And, indeed, if Mr Simson continou (as is more than probable he does) in these sentiments, he must preach another doctrine and Gospell than is preached in this Church.

But further, *5thly*, I wish it could be said in Mr Simson's behalf, that nothing has interveened since the Assembly 1729, which should justly hinder the taking off the suspension; and to us that live near him, and have occasion more narrouly to observe his demeanour, severall things have fallen out, that, when laid together, may amount to a legall hinderance of the removall of the suspension, at least till they be examined and judged. He hath since the last Assembly deserted his ordinary seat and Kirk wher he used to hear and has a seat and his family, and gone to another Church at a considerable distance from him. He and his family, though somtimes in the Church when others preach, yet seldom or never when Mr John Hamiltoun preaches; and they ordinarly, at least

Mr Simson himself, hears Mr Wisheart in the Laigh Church. *2dly,* I myself sau a testimoniall to one who had been his student, and was going abroad, signed S. T. P.* in July last. Whither that will be found a breach of the sentence he stands under, I must leave to others better seen in lau than I. Perhapps it will be reconed of the same kind with his sitting and votting in Faculty, and joyning in the deeds of the Colledge, which he has not ceased to do these four year he has been suspended. It's pretended, indeed, that the Assembly's sentence does not touch him as an University Master, and does not hinder him to vote in Faculty, signe testimonialls, &c. By the same way, for any thing I see, the Assembly's act should not hinder him from teaching Divinity, and keeping his lesson, which is as much an act as a Master, as his sitting in Faculty and signing testimonialls ; and some of the Masters, I hear, mentean he ought not to stop teaching for all his sentence. *3dly,* It is noture† that for all that is past he never has ouned any guilt. He sayes, openly, he has never altered his sentiments, and is just what he ever was, and guilty of no fault ; that the witnesses have intirely mistaken him. These, and such like expressions, *mutatis mutandis,* in the matter of immorality, where [or ?] scandall, would be reconed sufficient reasons not to take off any censure lying on a person. Lastly, in a word, he never converses with his bretheren, the Ministers in Glasgou, never expresses any concern for what hath hapned, or his sorrou that he is under censure and sentence ; and is openly sullain and sour to all that wer not of his sentiments in the process against him ; and his freinds, and such as are inward‡ with them, take all measures to blaicken them. These things, at least, are rather hinderances then helps to repealing the sentence [he] lyes under.

· *6thly,* If his sentence of suspension must be recognosced, in order to its being taken off, I think he should first be made to apply to his more immediat judges, the Presbitry of Glasgou, and lett them give their opinion on his suplication, and from them lett it come regularly to the Synod or Assembly, they being certainly the first and best judges of his per-

---

* *Sacrosancta Theologie Professor,* appended to his name.   † Notour, notorious.
‡ Intimately acquainted or conversant.

sonall character, and the fitness or unseasonablenes of such a desire, anent which a Generall Assembly can knou very litle; and if Mr Simson apply to the Assembly, unles his Presbytery joyn with him in his petition, I am of opinion the Assembly should remitt it to all Presbyteries, and the Presbytery of Glasgou in particular, to enquire into his character and circumstances, and report to another Assembly. This is the best way I could range my thoughts on this subject, as it comes under my vieu. But it's well it cast not up to this Generall Assembly, who, as far as I can guess, would have been more favourable to him than the former.

I shall nou set doun some generall hints as to the procedure of this Assembly, who did not medle with Mr Simson's affair. It was setled at London before the Commissioner came off, that if Mr Simson's affair was like to breed any disturbance, the Commissioner should discourage it, and do all he could, in proper methods, to prevent its coming in. My Lord Grange told me, that he, being at London, advised the Commissioner to setle this matter with the Ministry before he left London, which he did. So, as soon as I came to toun, Mr Alstoun told me there was not to be a mum* this Assembly about Mr Simson, unless it was cast up† by such as wer for his deposition last year.

The first thing that cast up was the Moderator.‡ The Commissioner was for Professor Hamiltoun, though it's but two years since he was in the chair, and had the sermon, last year, upon Mr Wisheart's death. I was for Mr Smith;§ and, I belive, he had been ready to have carryed it; but Mr Smith's freinds wer not for his competing with Mr Hamiltoun, since the Commissioner was for him, on a reason I may afterwards hint at, that a designe was formed they should be colleagues in another society. My Lord President, from what reason I shall not say, it seems, was not for Professor Hamiltoun, but proposed a young man, Mr Dickson,‖ to the Commissioner; but he stuck by his point, and nobody was

* Whisper.   † Introduced.   ‡ Choice of a Moderator.   § At Cramond.
‖ At Aberlady.

put on the lite* with P[rofessor] Hamiltoun who would have any votes; and he caryed it almost unanimously.

In naming the Committy for Commissions, and nominating of Preachers, I was sorry to see that all, except Mr A. Anderson,† wer of one side. It seems, a designe was formed to have Principal Chalmers' Commission, and some others, susteaned; and to have a set of Preachers before the Assembly that wer of the modish way. And so they did their bussines. Mr Wallace of Moffet, and Mr Telford of Hounam, [Hawick,] if I remember right, the two helpers to Mr W. Wisheart, at his first Communions, whose sermons made such noise in the West country, wer named, I doubt, on no good vieu, for the interests of truth and the method of preaching in this Church. Mr J. Dick,‡ as being Mr Simson's brother-in-lau, was mixed with them, and Mr R. Hamiltoun,§ who got himself excused, and Mr Patrick Cumming of Lochmaben was put in his room. I belive the namers repented their choice of Mr Telfair, as I'le afterwards have occasion to observe.

This was no very good omen in the entry of this Assembly. Mr Dick and Mr Cumming's sermons wer unexceptionable; but the other two young men wer too young and too confident to set up on such a speciall occasion as this. Ther sermons gave no good *vidimus* of a fleece of young men notted to have been students under the Moderator, and of the vitiated tast of the youth, and young Ministry. Mr Forbes of Deer attacked Mr Wallace's sermon in the Committy of Instructions, and moved that nottice might be taken of sermons upon morality, wher ther was nothing of Christ and the Gospell, and that the Assembly should provide against innovation in preaching. It was waved. Mr Wallace gave us flings at zeal, and attacked Queries, which the Assembly had ordered in some cases, and approven in others; and the prosecutions upon a *fama clamosa*, though prescribed in our Form of Proces, as rules established contrary to charity; and Mr Telfair gave a satyre of the former Presbiterian times, and our best times, as we shall hear.

The Instructions from Presbitrys came next in to the Committy appointed. I classed them, as I used. See the class, and my extracts

---

* Leet.   † At St Andrews.   ‡ At Carluke.   § At Hamilton.

from them, in a paper apart.   I shall only nottice, that ther is a pretty
generall inclination against Mr Simson being reponed, even to preaching,
in about eighteen or twenty Presbitrys, though ther was no pains nor
concert to make it universall.   On the other hand, by influence from
Professor H[amiltoun,] who was for Mr Glass, there is a great appearance from the Synod of Merse against the Commission's procedure
against Mr Glass.   Particularly, I am told, that The Marrou Bretheren,
Mr Wilson, Mr Bostoun, and Davidson, wer very keen against the
Synod of Angus' procedure, and, under pretext of liberty, and out of a
regard to the Independants, wer violent against Mr Glass his deposition ; and the flaming Instructions from the Presbytery of Jedburgh,
they say, wer drauen by Mr Ricarton, the author of The Sober Enquiry,
and the politicall disputant, who is thought to favour The Marrou ;
whereas The Marrou Bretheren in Fife are violent against Mr Glass,
and his opposition to our Covenants and Nationall Establishment they
give justly as the reason of it.   Whither this will creat any misunderstanding among the twelve Representers* or not, I cannot say ; time will
try.   Ther is likewise an Overture from the Synod of Fife about Queries,
which, I fear, be not got throu, and raise neu heats among us.   I was
called out of toun before the Committy of Instructions could meet, and
so knou not what is become of the Instructions.

I observe, these three or four years, the Instructions from Presbitrys
are read, indeed, and classed timously enough ; but though they are still
ready, on the first Munday, for bussines, yet, by art, and with designe,
they are shuffled off to the end of the Assembly ; and the occasion of
that is very plain.   During the last three Assemblys, Mr Simson's affair
took up the whole time, and nothing almost got in.   The Assembly before them, the litigious cause of Neu Aberdeen, shuffled them out ; and
nou, this [Assembly] the affair of P[rincipal] Chalmers took up all our
time.   Members of Presbyteries that have Instructions do not wait on
to the close of the Assembly, when dyets are appointed, and the leading
persons about the chair are willing to be rid of the trouble of them.   And,

* In favour of the " Marrou of Modern Divinity," condemned by the Assembly, 1720.

last year, they were found not to bind up the Assembly; and thus, from time to time, they are like to be altogether neglected.

The first cause that came in was that of Renfreu, for which see Letters this moneth. It was generally thought Mr M'Dermit's oun speech, sheuing his aversion, determined the Assembly to continou him. Houever, the people about the throne, and Mr Neil Campbell, got a very remarkable disappointment; and it was thought the Court, and my Lord Isla in particular, wer more set on this affair than any cause before us, and much more positive in that than as to P[rincipal] Chalmers.*

His affair was what fell in next; and it stands in Letters this moneth. It was exceeding warm. The Presbytery did their outmost, and the bulk of the weel-affected people there are against him, and his oun activity appeared very plain. We spend six long sederunts upon it. I fear the affirming the Committy of Synod's sentence, setling him ther, [will] have no good influence upon the state of things in the North. The Ministers do complean much of P[rincipal] Chalmers affecting a superiority, and pushing every thing in their judicatorys, and oppressing and overbearing his bretheren; and, I fear, the flames increase. The method of Synods overpouring Presbitrys by Committys is like to turn very troublsome. It's true, superior judicatorys must have a pouer to execut their sentences, in case inferior judicatorys refuse; and on this the hinge of this affair turned. But if matters go on at this rate, it wer to be wished that appeals from louer to higher courts should stope execution, till they be determined by superior judicatorys, especially in litigiouse matters. This, indeed, would bring a load of affairs upon the Generall Assembly, and to the Commission, but ther is no help for that; and they come by appeal, houever, with the disadvantage of execution of the sentence under an appeal.

The affair of Hutton† came next before us, and that stands at full lenth in my Letters this moneth. I shall only set doun what passed after the dissent was offered and refused by the vote of the Assembly, in privat among the Dissenters, as I have it from one of them. The dissent being refused, the Ministers and Elders, who dissented, resolved to drau up

---

* Principal of King's College, Aberdeen, presented to Old Machar.   † Viz. the settlement of Mr Robert Waugh.

the Reasons of Dissent, and subscribe them, and lodge them in the hands of Coll[onel] Erskine, to be keeped, in order to be published as circumstances call for. Mr A[ndrew] Darling and Mr Eb[enezer] Erskine formed two generall Reasons of Dissent. The one, that the Members of the Commission in the Assembly, who votted in the affair of Hutton, wer not excluded votting. It was, I mind, urged by Mr E. Erskin, that the Members of the Commission should not be called in the roll. It was said by the Moderator, they that proposed that would loss as many as they would gain, and there was no further insisting. But since, in looking the sederunts, it seems the Dissenters find that was a cheat put on them, and they would have gained more than the four votes, by which Not Reverse carryed. The other reason was, because this approbation is contrary to the principles of this Church, that a parish should not be setled upon a mere presentation, without the consent of the people. For these, and other reasons to be added, they dissent. The Dissenters are, Mr James Hog, Mr Ebenezer Erskin, Mr A. Darling, Mr Moncreife of Kilfergie, Mr Henry Erskin, Mr J. Forbes, and some others from the North ; Mr H. Hunter, Mr Allan Logan, Coll[onel] Erskin, Mr Ch. Erskin of Edenhead, and others. At another meeting, they brought in more Reasons of Dissent ; but not being agreed to, all wer put in Coll[onel] Erskin and Mr John M'Laran's hand, to be extended and sent to the different parts of the country, and Ministers and Members of Assembly to be dealt with to joyn in the Dissent ; and the Reasons of the Dissent, when the full draught was made up, to be published in print. Before the Assembly and Commission rose, ther wer twenty-one hands at the Dissent, with the two above specifyed Reasons.

This Assembly, four complaints wer tabled against the Commission, and the debate about reversing what they had done was pretty warm ; for which see Letters about Hutton. In that case, it came within four votes. In the affair of Touie,* the Commission wer found to have done wrong ; but the setlment was continoued, and the Minister continoues. Never wer ther such complaints on a Commission as this. The iniquity in Renfreu was not diped into ; and, indeed, it was palpable, though they wer found not to have gone beyond their pouers. I wish Commis-

* The settlement of Mr Andrew Moir.

sions afterward be more sparing in their sentences ; but, I doubt, it will not be so.

Somewhat has been said upon the Preachers set up to preach before this Assembly. I shall here nottice, that we had a very good sermon from Mr Dick, fornoon, May 17. In the after[noon] we had Mr Wallace's sermon upon " Charity thinketh no evil ;" the bulk of which was borroued from the Spectators, and ill put together. Last year we had a sermon upon Zeal, with a byass plain enough to one side of the question, and so as zeal was turned for Mr Simson's side. Nou, we have a sermon on Charity, with flings at zeal, very ill-worded. Next Sabbath, May 24, we had a sermon in the fornoon, upon Overcoming evil with good, upon forgivenes of injurys. It consisted of severall safe generalls, very weel and easily expressed, and, indeed, Mr Cumming has as happy and easy a way of delivery as I have heard. But in the afternoon we had one of the wildest out-of-the-way sermons that ever I heard. I pray God I never again [shall] be witnes to such a discourse and such an auditory, which looked rather like an audience at a farce than at the hearing the Word of God. Ther was almost throu the whole of it a smiling, laughter, and mocking at the Preacher. Mr Telfair, I am told, is Minister at Hauick or Hounam. His father was a Bailay in Edinburgh, and a Captain in the Traine-band. He is but a young man, and though I will not judge the spring of this discourse, it looked as if it proceeded from a designe to be taken nottice of for somewhat singular. He was not straitned in time ; for he had ten dayes warning before he preached, and therfor had time to choice his subject, and his method in handling it. His text was Eccles. vii. 10, " Say not thou, What is the cause that the former dayes wer better than these ? for thou dost not wisely enquire concerning this."

When I heard the text read, knouing somewhat of the character of the preacher, I expected a satyr upon the former times, and an encomium on the present, with biting flings* upon those who regrated the declining and grouing evils of this present age ; and I was not disappoint-

---

* Scoffs.

ed. The text I had some rau thoughts upon, in case (which I am thankfull did not happen to be the case) that I had been pitched upon to have preached at this Assembly, struck me strong in the mind, when Mr Telfair read his, as what appeared to me much more seasonable ; that was Rev. iii. 2, " Strenthen the things that remain, and are ready to die ; for thy work I have found not perfect before God." We had nothing like an explication of the text, and, had Solomon's words been fairly opened up, I doubt much if they would have been, without a violence, turned to the preacher's intended purpose. To me, I oun, they have a quite different meaning than he put upon them. He began with ane observation, that Ministers, in a particular manner, wer bound to encourage vertue and well-doing, and stirr up people to thankfulnes to God for his goodnes. Then it was observed that, in Solomon's time, it was a prevailing notion, against which he thought himself bound to appear, that the last age was still worse than the former that went before it ; that the world was still upon the decline, and things grouing worse and worse, in morall respects. This, he said was a very false and comfortles position. Here the speaker was certainly fighting with his oun shaddou, and impugning what I scarce belive any body ever asserted as universally true ; at least, it was far from being the sentiments of any to whom Solomon wrote, in his time. For, in Solomon's dayes, there was less ground for such a complaint, that the former dayes wer better then the present, that every body knoues things wer at the very hight of glory and prosperity under Solomon's reigne, and the decline hapned afterwards. So that I can never think that this can be Solomon's meaning. Be that as it will, we had a quarter of hour's discourse, to sheu the ill tendency of this position, which Mr Telfair thought Solomon struck at, that the former times wer better than the present. He observed that this position, that the present age was worse then the former, was not fact ; for many posterior ages wer much better than the former, and great improvements had been made. That undoubtedly the age, at the Reformation from Popery, was much better than the former. He notticed that this position was injurious to the Divine goodnes and Providence. And, lastly, that the laying doun this a principle, universally holding, was the way to discourage persons from all industry, vertue, and goodnes.

Here the preacher's work was easy in making to himself a man of strau, and pulling him doun. During this part of his discourse there was some tollerable gravity in the hearers, but in the succeeding part all bounds wer broke. He then came, next, to enquire what ground ther was for the complaint in the text, that the former times wer better then the present, in our present case at this day. And here he said, in the entry, that ther might be some feu cases wher things might be worse than in former times ; as the breaking out of vice, in some instances, ungratitude, and some other evils ; he hoped they wer feu, and was of opinion his text did not lead him to enquirys upon that side, but rather to sheu what improvments and bettering of matters wer in this present age, beyond the time before us in this Church and land. And these he gave us in the follouing particulars, which I shall give in the order he keeped, as far as my memory serves me. Many of his surprizing observations and assertions are escaped me, they wer so far disagreable to experience, and observation, and the common feeling of every one, that I have lost severall of them, and the loss is not great.

He began, first, with sheuing that the former times wer not better than ours, in point of religion and principle. And here he gave a short, poor, and ill-grounded satyre, upon the former times in this Church and land. He said, that in our fathers' dayes, it was a prevailing principle that nobody who differed from us in point of Church Goverment, Presbiterian Goverment ; that none who wer for Episcopacy, or any other form of Church Goverment, wer good men and good Christians. He ouned that the circumstances of things among us in former times, perhaps, made it more necessary than it's at present to enter into the contraversys about Discipline and Church Goverment, but that was a generall received principle, that nobody who differed from us in those matters could be good men and Christians. This is a figment of his oun, and a false asertion of our former Presbiterian time. But nou, sayes [he,] the generality are fallen into much more moderat and charitable principles ; and it's generally acknouledged, nou, that persons may differ from us in this respect and be good men and Christians. The next head, he said, former times wer not better than ours, was in point of liberty. Here he run out in commendation of the King, who was exceeding tender of the liberty of his subjects; and all his servants about him, though faithfull servants, yet they wer none of them slaves. This was an ill-said complement to the Court.

He came next to consider our bettering and improvment as to peace and warr, and that was as wild ane article as in his sermon. He observed that the prophesy relating to the Messia's times, that swords should be beat into plou-shares, was accomplished in our day : That we had forty years' peace : That there seemed to be a generall inclination throu Europ, at present, to peacefull measures : That the King and Ministry wer using their best endeavours towards this : That we wer much improven in this matter : In former times there was nothing but broyls and feuds between familys and persons, nou these wer at a happy end : That in former times ther wer partys and divisions among our Nobility and Gentry, nou ther wer no partys. Here was a generall smile and mock throu the Church, and every body sau hou far the speaker was stretching. He added a complement to our Nobility and Gentry. In former times, he said, there could be no meetings among gentlmen and neighbours for bussines or freindship in one another's houses, unles it ended in drunkennes ; and freindship in former times could not be compleat till the company wer deadly drunk ; nou, ther was no such thing to be seen ; when, I fear, drinking drunk is in many places as common as ever. This brings to my mind a passage he had upon the first head of bettering in point of principles and zeal. He said, in former times, Religion was so far driven, especially in Ministers, that it was a principle they should not be conversible, and they should only be taken up upon seriouse things in common conversation, but nou they wer more at liberty, and might talk about the affairs of human life, and be free and open in their conversation, as well as others ; or words to this meaning. He parted with this branch of peace or warr with a very impertinent, impudent, and false assertion, either proceeding from his ignorance of our history, or some what worse. He said, that the broils and stretches of our Ministers, and judicatorys and Ecclesiastick meetings in the minority of King James the Sixth, and during the beginning of his reigne, laid the foundation for the Civil Wars, broyls, and bloodshed, and confusions, in his son's reigne. A Clarendon, an Eachard, or one of the most violent Torys and Jacobites in England, could scarce have given this a falser and bitterer turn than he gave this !

He came next to assert we wer better than former times in point of trade and industry. That he pretended was so evident as not to need a proofe ; when every body sees an evident decline, even in this point. And next, he came to the bettering in point of riches ; here he was like to fall throu, and every body sau him straitned. He ouned ther wer complaints might be made, this way, as to particular persons and places ; but this was a native consequence of trade and industry, and our trade and improvements being grouen much since the Union, the other would follou. At least he might assert it, that the generous and publick spirit that run throu our Nobility and Gentry, in their encouraging industry, improvement of land, and our oun manufacture and produce, though the advantage was not yet sensibly felt, it could not fail to make the next generation rich.

He came next to assert that we wer better than former times in point of Lau and Justice ; and here he commended the honourable Judges and executors of the Lau. He ouned ther was some ground of complaint that lau-suites wer needlessly prolonged by people concerned ; but he kneu that the Judges wer very much in their opinion for the Scripturall rule laid doun, 1 Cor. vi. 2, 3, 4, and very much encouraged references and taking up of matters by freinds and neibours, and preventing lausuits. He came next to our improvments in knouledge, and arts and sciences ; and said we had come in to the method of true knouledge, and wer much leaving the scholastick formes of expression ; and this could not but have a good effect in time on practice. He ended this branch, I think, with morality and improvments in practice. He ouned we wer furthest behind in these, and some evils wer breaking out, and the dictates of reason, virtue, and the grace of God, wer not regarded as they ought. But the foundations laid in knouledge, he hoped, might afterwards come to improvment, even in this matter. Houever he, in the entry, had observed, and nou repeated it, that he was not to run the paralel in every thing. He ended this wild discourse with an inference or two, of the duty of praise and thankfulnes, and encouragment to go on in the wayes of virtue.

I have given a larger account of this discourse than it really deserves. It was an instance that this time is worse than the former good times of this Church; when I am sure such a sermon, if it deserves that name, would not have escaped without a censure. Upon the whole, one could not help wishing that his generall position, that we are on the bettering hand, had been true. But when it is evidently false to common observation, it is hard to conceive what could prevail with the man to insist at the rate he did. He seems to be a sour, confident man; and as his sermon was contrary to Solomon's words he read, in their proper meaning, so it was really a satyre upon our former Presbiterian times in this Church, ill-said, and worse supported; and the softest thing I can say of him is, the words of Solomon himself, " Thou hast not wisely considered this." Houever, this sermon may not want its oun use. I hope it will open the eyes of people to see what may be expected from the confident impudence of some of our young Preachers. They stretch matters so as to expose themselves; and I hear this discourse was displeasing to a great many of our young light Preachers themselves, and they condemn him. I wish it may open their eyes, and those of others, to see hou far we are declining !

[*May* 25.]—I came out of Edinburgh upon May 25, and I hear since that the Committy of Instructions met that day. Ther Mr Hog* and some others attacked Mr Telfair's sermon, but they wer not hearers, and wer not distinct in their charge. Severall desired the charge might be laid directly, but that was not done. Nobody approved of the sermon, save Mr George Ogilby, the Earl of Finlater's son, a foolish young elder, they say of very loose principles, [who] said he heard the sermon and approved it. The matter was droped, and it was said in privat that the best way to censure the sermon was to neglect it and contemn it.

Mr Moncreife of Kilfergie pressed much an assertory Act about Doc-

* Minister at Carnock.

trine, and had a long discourse in the Committy of Instructions to that purpose ; but he is young, and a litle unfit to manage such an affair. It ended, as I am told, in a recommendation to Ministers to preach against the errors and other evils of the times.

That afternoon, the Assembly met and referred most of their matters to the Commission. The affair of Kinross, of which above, was remitted to it. See the printed Case. Sir John Bruce, when meeting with some Ministers at Kinross to oppose Mr Craige, his horse fell with him, and broke his legg. I heard ther wer inclinations to be soft in that matter, by the Synod, and that Sir John Bruce was falling from his opposition ; but I doubt that will not hold. The matter is referred to the Commission in August.

[*May* 26.]—Next day, May 26, the Assembly rose with the common forms, and more references to the Commission. In this Assembly there was the greatest number of young faces I ever sau. Their very garb and habit was not what hath been in former meetings ; and nou I belive a plurality of votes in our Assemblys is but an ill signe of the sentiments of this Church ; and I would not wish any thing of considerable importance came to a vote ; for I am apprehensive a determination would as readily fall on the wrong as the right side of the question.

The matter of Mr Glass came not in to this Assembly. It was well it did not. He is sinking much in Angus since his deposition. The Laird of Teeling has left him, though his lady, it seems, sticks to him. Many of the people are leaving him ; and his setting up his Elders to be exhorters, and allouing them to preach, is what is much to the weakning of his party, and exposing his principles. No doubt, had he not been supported in his irregularitys by the seeming countenance that P[rofessor] Hamiltoun, and some others, gave at the Commission, he had probably sunk before nou, and I hope his party will dwindle to nothing.

The affair of The Marrou is at some stand. The appearance of these bretheren Representers in the Synod of Merse, in favour of Mr Glass, is disliked by Mr Hog and the Ministers' Representers in Fife, and I doubt [will] be the occasion of a coldnes among The Marrou bretheren. Ther seems to be an inclination in the Ministers favouring The Marrou in Fife, to conferr with the bretheren that differ from them, [and] to renounce the things charged on them as to assurance being of the essence of faith ; and of late Mr J. Hog, and Mr Logan,* and some others, are in tollerable terms ; and Mr Logan his joyning in the dissent as to Hutton is like to cement the differences in Fife. Certainly, if some neu thing fall not, in that affair of The Marrou, [the complaint of the] representing bretheren will come to nothing ; and the less it be notticed and medled with, it's like to dwindle the more away.

The bussines of Queries to Ministers was like to come in to this Assembly by the Instructions from the Synod of Perth, Fife, and Angus, but came not in, that I hear of. The affair of Kinross is like [to] bring that affair on the carpet, and undoubtedly Queries wer overstretched in Mr Craige's affair. The overture from Fife is well worded. See it in a paper apart. But this is not a season for any regulations to the better, and any thing that tends to the strict side of proceedure and discipline is scarce like to take, at such a juncture and time as we are at present in.

Most of the Assembly's time, these many years, hath been taken up in things quite alien from the proper work of Generall Assemblys, which is to consider what may be proper to be done for bettering of discipline, and what neu rules and regulations are to be made. But, nou, litigious and very idle debates as to calls and setlnents of parishes consume our whole time, with complaints against Patrons, without endeavouring to better matters as to Patronages. An act of Assembly as to the manner of calling Ministers, and determining when a call is to be found a proper call for setling a Minister, would save a vast dale of time and trouble to Synods, Assemblys, and Commissions. But though a draught of such an act, for some years, hath lyen before Assemblys and Commissions, the leading men about Edinburgh will never allou that act to come to any bearing.

These are the generall remarks that offer to me upon the matters before this Assembly, and things of a more generall nature. Ther wer

* At Culross.

feu complaints from the North of the insults of Papists and intruders. The change in the Family of Gordon* certainly makes the Ministers in that bounds much easier, though, I fear, Popery prevails still very much. And, for Episcopall intruders, many of them that qualify are coming in, and against them ther is no lau.

They tell a story, hou far it's fact I knou not, that the Bishop of London has offered twenty pound a year to such as set up Meeting-houses, and pray for the Goverment. But this neither appears to be Bishop Gibson's character, neither will his large sellary allou him to give twenty pound to every one who will pray for the King, and set up a Meeting-house. So, I doubt, this is an aspersion on that learned man.

They tell a story, quite reverse to this, of Bishop Talbot, Archbishop of York, and a freind of Bishop Gibson's, which makes me give less credit to the other : That Lord Kimmergame married a lady who was keen enough Episcopall. He had two daughters, it seems, educat that way, two or three years since. The two young ladyes wer at Berwick at the time when the Bishop of York, Talbot, was ther in his trienniall visitation, and many wer applying to him for confirmation, and Kimmer-gem's daughters applyed likewise. When B[ishop] Talbot heard of their coming, he signifyed his dislike at their coming. Houever, it seems they wer forward, and came, and waited on the Bishop, and wer earnest to be confirmed. He told them that they wer not of his charge, and they belonged to another Church, and wer born and educat in Scotland, and he was not over-fond of confirming such as wer not of his particular charge. The ladys insisted, and signifyed that they wer educat after the order of the Church of England; that they ouned the Goverment and Doctrine of the Church, and desired to be confirmed. The Bishop still declined ; and, when further urged, he said, " Ladyes, I don't blame you for asking confirmation ; it's a very ancient and decent rite ; but still you belong to Scotland, and if you want to be confirmed, there are nine hundred Bishops (he meaned the Ministers of Scotland) who can confirm you just as well as I. You must apply to any of them !"

* In their having become Protestants.

The setlment of the toun of Edinburgh, as to Ministers, is nou over. Mr Smith, Gaudy, and G. Wisheart, are to be setled without any opposition. The only remaining post is that of the Principall. Ther was a considerable opposition made to Mr Gaudie his call. The reason was, it seemed to have been the project laid doun to make him Professor of Divinity. This the Ministers in toun—Mr Matheson, Craige, Bannantine, and others, wer not fond of, Mr Gaudie having made no appearance but in favour of Mr Simson; and that seems to be all the merit he has. Mr Alstoun certainly had the offer of being Professor; but that did not altogether please him. He rather inclined to be Principall and a Minister. He was sensible of the importance of teaching Divinity; and that, being turned fifty, he was too old to change the course of his studys. Pr[ofessor] Hamiltoun, on the other hand, did not like to have a younger Minister than himself set up to be Principall, and therefore opposed Mr Alston's being Principall. He has taught Divinity now twenty or twenty-one years, and is weary of the toyl; and the Principall's post is an easy post for him, nou that he is aged and turned sixty. There it stuck. Mr Smith was agreed to by the Magistrates to be Minister. His party in the Presbitry inclined to have him Professor of Divinity. Pr[ofessor] Hamiltoun and Mr Smith have not been intirely one and of a peice these five or six years, and Mr Smith carrys his point in the Presbitry against all that P[rofessor] Hamiltoun can do. He crossed him in Mr Simson's affair; he crossed him in Mr Glass' affair; and carryed his point in both these, by stricking in with the stricter sort of Ministers, in both. P[rofessor] Hamiltoun nou sees that he cannot intirely mentain his significancy in the Church, if Mr Smith and he don't joyn more cordially then formerly; and so, it seems, inclines to fall in with Mr Smith's being Professor, and dropes Gaudie, and leaves Mr Alston, who is a man by himself, and will not come in to any particular set, and seems to incline to Mr Smith to be Professor, and himself Principall; and the rather that he has a son passing tryalls, ready to be setled in Cramond, when Mr Smith is taken in to Edinburgh. Provest Lindsay, it seems, inclines to be closer with the Ministers of Edinburgh than his predecessors in the Magistracy; and when he sau the opposition made to Mr Gaudie, he told the Ministers of Mr Smith's side, that he belived their opposition was not so much to him as Minister, as from their fears he was designed for Professor; and assured them that was not his designe, but only he should be non-collegiat at Lady Yester's; and alloued them to say, that, in his opinion, he was for Mr Smith being Professor. Upon this, they yielded to Mr Gaudie's call. Thus matters stand at present; and the designe is to settle Mr Smith Minister of Haddoch's-hole,* and the Professor Hamiltoun collegue with him in the half of that parish, and make Mr Smith Professor. If my Lord Isla come in to this, no doubt this schem will hold. What changes that will make, if he stand out, I cannot say; but thus things are at present. And on this score it was that Mr Smith declined being Moderator in this Assembly, in opposition to Mr Hamilton, as hath been hinted.

I am pretty well assured that P[rofessor] Hamiltoun is very willing to teach no more. Whither he be altered in his principles, I cannot say; but by severalls who knou him well, it's thought he is departed from the Calvinisticall doctrine, and the ordinary doctrine taught in this Church, though he hath the wisdom to keep himself in the clouds. Yet this winter, they say, he hath opened upon the head of the connection between morall seriousnes and grace, and other points. It's very plain Mr Hamiltoun is exceedingly bigg† with Doctor Calamy and the London Non-subscribers, and it's thought he is not far from them in point of opinion in other things. It's certain that the students and preachers that are most recommended by him, and most students that have been under his lessons for some years, are very much off the principles of this Church. His warm side to Mr Simson, his treatment of the Committy for purity of doctrine in the matter of Queries, and the second libell, in the Assembly 1729, did not look well; and it's pretty probable that it would be for Mr Hamiltoun's reputation to give over teaching before he farther open his change of opinion. In short, P[rofessor] Hamiltoun, who, since Mr Mitchel's death, sett up to manage all things in this Church, so as to keep fair with England, and the Court, and the Dissenters at London, seems to have fallen in with every thing that tends to

---

* The New North or " Little Kirk" of Edinburgh, of old called *Haddo's Hold*.   † Intimate.

depart from the usages and principles of this Church. The set of young Ministers and Preachers come from his hand for many years, if they have learned their way and principles from him, is not a good *vidimus* of their master. In short, he does not appear to be firm, but seeking the managment, and seeking his family's setlment.

Ther are some who want not their fears as to Mr Smith. Certainly he is a man, for easines of speaking, for distinctnes of thought, and appearances in judicatorys, far above the other. Some doubt if he is throughly firm in point of the connection and the Spirit's work in regeneration, of which hints have been given formerly ; and whither he has fallen in, in the case of Mr Simson and Mr Glass, to sheu his weight on whatever side he goes into, I am not to judge ; but, undoubtedly, he is a fitter person than Gaudie, and, I hope, is wiser and firmer than to depart in doctrine from this Church, if he be in the chair.

When I am upon doctrine, I have a very melancholy remark to make, that, since Mr Simson's proces began, the Lord, in his Providence, has removed a great many who wer firm in point of doctrine, and otherwise exceeding usefull in this Church, and opposers of him and his innovations. I have remarked their deaths above, and I shall lay them altogether here. Sir James Steuart, who was at first Committy ; Mr William Mitchell, Mr John Stirling, Mr Thomas Blackwell, Mr William Wisheart, Mr James Heart, Mr John Gray, Mr G. Carmichael, Mr John Flint, and Mr William Steuart of Kiltearn, and Mr M'Kenzie of Inverness. Perhapps I have overlooked some, but these make a dreadfull gap in this Church ; and I doubt,* if as many of their eminency and significancy wer removed, it would make a most terrible gap. When these and such as these are taken away, when error is grassent,† it's a very loud-speaking Providence, and looks as if the Lord wer taking away the standart-bearers and standers in the gap, and making way for evils to come in, with a terrible force and pouer, among us !

By the best accounts I can have, matters at Court are in the greatest

* Apprehend.   † Growing, increasing.

confusion.   Nobody can tell what to make of them, and it's hard to say if any of themselves can form a distinct judgment.   Wilmingtoun is certainly come in to Court, and Lord Carteret is come over from Ireland.   Tounsend is out, and yet Sir Robert stands as well as ever.   Wilmingtoun and Carteret are certainly antipodes to Sir Robert, and yet the changes that we have in the neuse-letters, and are fully confirmed, save Wilmingtoun, are all Sir Robert's creatures.   Time can only unridle matters.

The accounts follouing I can depend on.   My Lord Grange tells me that my Lord Tounsend is nou out of his post.   My informer was lately with him, and has the honnour of his freindship.   Tounsend told him that he was nou turning old, and in his master's favour ; his family was in good circumstances and provided for, and that he inclined to retire from the amusements and toyls of a Court, wher he had been so long, and enjoy himself in the country, or, when he pleased, in the city, with his freinds.   That this was the reason of his giving up.   But my informer found that he and his br[other]-in-lau, Sir R[obert] Walpool, had not been well* these two years, and ther wer misunderstandings betwixt them, though, as to outwards,† they stood fair enough.

My informer is exceedingly troubled at Tounsend's throuing up and retiring from Court.   He tells me he was the only one at Court that had any real concern about the interests of Religion, and might be depended on as to our Scots affairs, and was firmly for menteaning our present constitution and setlment.   That he has a great deal of the old English sturdines of spirit, and is scarce, in his temper, cut out for a Court, though, from a long being about Court, and in all the Courts of Europ, and being at the top of affairs, he is much smoothed from a naturall kind of ruggednes and stiffnes ; but somewhat of it sticks, and, he belives, is the spring of his throuing up :‡ That he has much of plainnes, and hates things that are not fair, and seems not pleased with the present managment.   He is not a professed free-thinker, though he has some turn that way ; but from politicall vieus, and from a hatred at Popery, he is for keeping things intirely on the Revolution foot.

He was one much depended on by the late King George the First.

* On good terms.   † Outward appearance.   ‡ His office.

I belive I have set doun above what passed as to Mr S[imso]n, and the
declaration he made in presence of . . . .   to my Lord
Grange, that he would not in the least protect that man. My Lord
Tounsend asked my informer very lately hou things wer going in Scotland as to doctrine, and if Dr Clerk's notions wer taking there? My informer said, he feared they wer too much. "Then," said the other,
" the Protestant Religion is gone in Britain;" adding, that [he] had still
hoped ther would have been a stand made to these notions in Scotland;
but since they wer corrupting* there, he thought the naturall consequence
would be the prevailing of Popery, and the overturning the Reformation;
for he was of opinion, that when the Scripturall doctrines, though he
would not say that they wer what he was stiff upon, wer quitted openly,
there was nothing could come in their room but Popery, and implicite
subjection, and perfect confusion.

He told my informer a very odd story of my Lord Sommers, who was
a pretty pressed [professed?] free-thinker, and inclined to Deisme, and
yet was much of the same way of thinking with Tounsend in this matter. The passage was this : About the 1710 or 1711, when Dr Clerk
began to discover himself Arrian, Tounsend made a visit to Sommers,
(I have forgot whither it was Lord Sommers or Cooper, but I think it
was Sommers,) and the conversation fell upon Dr Clerk and the Arrian
opinion that was breaking out. Sommers said, " Dr Clerk is gone mad;
and if these opinions prevail, Protestantism is at an end in England!"
Tounsend expressed his wonder that the other said so, seeing he reconed
his Lordship among the free-thinkers, and thought he would rather have
favoured the Doctor's way. Sommers ouned he was, in his opinion, a
Deist ; but added, that, " in the nature of things, Protestantisme, whatever way it was founded, was the only scheme of principles which could
keep things upon the Revolution foot, and make us hang together in
Brittain and abroad against Popish pouers." The ordinary way of the
Deists speaking of the Bible, then and nou, was to call it " The Book;"
and so Sommers added, he was for keeping by " The Book" in publick
doctrine, and he really wondered hou they could swallou all The Book,
and stick at a small verse at the end of it, which, he thought, came re-

* Becoming corrupt.

gularly enough in. He meaned 1 John v. 7. He ouned, in his oun
sentiments, the history of the creation, the deluge, and a good many
places of " The Book," wer as difficult to him as that little verse ; and
that the whole " Book" was to be taken complexly, and in a chain, and
was only tenible that way ; and he thought that such as ouned " The
Book," behoved to take it as it lay together in a body. But he was perremptory in it, that Dr Clerk's principles and those of the Arrians would
bring us to an unsettled state, and cast all things loose among us, and
effectually bring in Popery, which he hated. Tounsend added, he was
much of the same way of thinking, and still hoped that Scotland would
have been fixed, and a barrier against what tended directly to unhinge
everything : And if Dr Clerk's principles wer prevailing, he sau all
things loosing in Brittain, and the result behoved to be our throuing
ourselves wholly into infallibility : And an established guide for somewhat we behoved to have ; and if once the credit of " The Book" wer
destroyed, we could land nowhere but in the arms of Rome. This was,
he said, what made him so much in earnest to have our doctrine in
Scotland preserved.

My informer told me, further, that by his advice my Lord Loudon
setled matters as to this Assembly. He represented what it would be-
token if a breach fell out in the Church when his Lordship was Commissioner ; and that he would be importuned when he came doun to
repone Mr Simson, unles he was buckled.* My Lord, therefore, went
to Isla, and others in the Ministry, and represented the hazard of a
breach, if so soon Mr S[imso]n should be restored ; and got their opinion that his name should not be mentioned at this Assembly, unles his
opposers would hale† him in, and do somewhat further against him. In
that case, Loudon was alloued to declare for his reposition. By others,
I am told, P[rofessor] Hamiltoun wrote up to Isla to see if application
might be alloued from Mr S[imso]n at least to be reponed to the Ministry, and received a direct denyall.

The forsaid person assures me that, nou that Tounsend is out of
Court, he knoues none there who have any care about our constitution,

* Restrained, (by special instructions.)   † Drag.

and that all things tend to an unhinging and unsetlment : That it is equall to Isla and Sir Robert, whither we keep together or not : That our breaking in peices is what, when matters are ripe for it, they will make their oun purposes succeed by ; and he doubts not but, one time or other, they will make Mr S[imso]n an instrument to tear and rent us, when it makes for their designes : That my Lord Isla, houever he despises Mr S[imso]n, yet he does favour him ; and ther seems to be a designe, at some other Assembly, to throu up him, or some other bone of contention, to break and divide us : That when our Assemblys break upon this or other points, they will be prohibited by the King, and either Commissions, or some other select meetings, called by the King's writt, will have the managment of Church affairs : That their scheme is very easy in the plan laid down by King James the Sixth ; first delaying and deferring the Generall Assembly, or prohibiting them to meet, under pretext of preserving the peace, and then setling Church pouer in the hands of a feu, and naming three or four superintendants, such as Mr Neil Campbell for the West, Mr Chalmers for the North, Mr Hamiltoun for the East.   When I objected the Act of Setlment, my informer was of opinion, that the Court would make nothing of that at all, and could carry anything they pleased : That ther was nothing at all in the Act of Setlment excluding Superintendants : That the name of Bishops would not be pretended, and really was not liked : That Superintendants would have no claim to be in Parliament, as Bishops would, and so they would easily go doun : That, in England, nothing is made of our Act of Setlment, and all pouer is undoubtedly in the hands of the Suprem Court ;[*] and our oun representatives will not only concurr, but desire the change : That, at present, the designe seems to be to unhinge the Setlment, and cast all things loose, for politicall and party vieus.

The same person tells me that the Queen is exceeding loose in her principles, and quite another person than we take her to be : That she sets up as the head of learning and a refined tast, and such as are intirely loose as to all principles of religion : That, lately, when Generall Ross came to wait on her, she said, " G[eneral] Ross, you are a brave officer

* i. e. The Parliament.

and an honest man, but I cannot understand hou you are come into The Cant"—meaning of religion and seeming seriousness.

That the King knoues nothing but by the Queen : That nobody has access to him but such as Sir Robert alloues, and he takes care that nothing pass that may disconcert measures : That the method taken is this :—When Sir Robert would have anything done, he gives a hint, a transient one, to the Queen, and she gives a suggestion to the King, who thinks of it till the next day ; and then, when the Ministry come in to him, he tells them that such a thought has struck him, and asks hou such a plan would do ? The thing is humored, commended for an extraordinary thing ! It's wondered who has suggested it ; and when told that it's his oun thought, it's highly extolled, and the thing gone into ! That the King certainly recons himself the most absolute Soveraign Prince in the world, and recons everything his oun doing, and yet is perfectly under conduct :* That when the King goes abroad, it's perfectly surprizing to think hou litle he is noticed ; and, indeed, nobody almost regards him : That, in short, the King is very weak, and thinks he does everything, and does nothing ; and the Queen is extremely haughty and proud, and does all things ; and Sir Robert hath as absolut a pouer as ever a Minister had.

That the Pretender is nou generally hated throu England, and dispised : That he is perfectly abandoned to all wickednes, and the very blackest of vices : That now Mr Hay is taken in to his family ; and Mrs Hay, whom Princess Sobiesky was so much offended at, is no more talked of, and Mr Hay is said to be the Pretender's Catamite ; and these unnaturall, horride wickednesses are to[o] open, and both effeminat him and make him the common object of hatred and contempt.

That the Dissenting interest is exceeding lou at London : That Mr A. Taylor is a helper to an old Minister at Deptford ; that he has an estate in Kent, and another in Essex : That the Ministers who used to meet had very much given over their meetings—I mean those who stood for the old doctrine and principles of the Non-conformists : That the breaches among them are pretty much charged upon Mr Bradbury's heat and warmth : That Mr Bradburry's brother is marryed lately upon a

---

* Guidance; conducted or led by others.

very rich fortune : That things have a very melancholy and dismall aspect there and everywhere.

That the Bishops in England have very much lost their reputation : That the Nobility only consider them as a party that are just for going into the Court measures : That Bangor,* nou Sarum, is sunk into a hackney writter : That the Bishop of London and Talbot [Archbishop] of York are liked best ; but none of them being firm to any set of doctrinall principles, they are much dispised.

The same person tells me that Chub the tallow-chandler, or but a journeyman to a tallow-chandler, his book is highly admired : That the witts and Deists just admire it ; and my Lord Isla said to him, he wrote like one they called inspired, for the man had no education and letters, and writes strongly and connectedly : That he was taken in to be steuard to the Keeper of the Rolls, and continoued in that station with the ill-natured Sir J. Joseph Jekill, I think, while alive : That the story of his being put in the Custom-house, and getting two hundred a year setled on him, does not hold : That the Queen professes to admire his Tracts ; but, when dealt with to setle somewhat on him, declined that.

Dr Watterland is engaged at present in a contraversy about the Sacraments and Positive Institutions, with such as defend Clerk's Catechisme : That it's generally said that the Doctor is turned Calvinist, and must be so, if he will mentean his point against his adversarys.

It is ane ordinary thing nou to make applications to the Queen ; and when she is applyed to, her ordinary answer is, " Is Sir Robert for you ? If Sir Robert be for you, me be for you !" And that she is too much in conversation, when that falls in,† bantering and scolding the narrou principles of the Church of Scotland.

The same person tells me that he sau a letter just about the time, in February last or therby, from one present at the King of France his Bed of Justice, to an acquaintance at London. The Bed of Justice is when the Kings of France take upon them to enact laues and constitutions by their oun personall pouer and soveraigne authority. This spring, at the instigation of the Cardinall Fleury, and, as it is belived, to influence the

---

* Dr Benjamin Hoadley.   † When that subject occurs.

Election of a Pope, and bring the Cardinalls at Rome to go in to a Pope of the Spanish and French faction, the King declared his resolution to turn the Bull *Unigenitus* against the Jansenists into a lau and constitution of France, in a Bed of Justice. The Dukes, it seems, and Peers of France, are Counselours to the King, together with the Presidents of Parliaments, and the Presidents *à mortier; lauers* so called, from their capes they wear. Those are, in number, I think, near one hundred, and esteemed the ablest lauers in France.

When the King constitutes his Bed of Justice, the Nobility Counselours stand next him; the Presidents have seats or stalls according to their seniority. The King, having the Cardinall at his elbou, signifyed his desingne in this solemn manner, to adopt the Bull *Unigenitus* among the constitutions and laues of France. One of the Presidents, who was zealous against the Jesuites, and, in his opinion, a Jansenist, came out of his place, and fell doun befor the King upon his knees, while sitting in his Bed of Justice, and begged most earnestly he might consider what he was going to do: That he was bringing himself and his kingdom again under bondage to Rome: That he was infringing the libertys of the Gallican Church: That, in so doing, he would lose the hearts of the greatest part of his best subjects; and that he was affrayed he was, with his oun hands, pulling the croun off his oun head. He was removed, and, instead of further censure, he was only rebuked for speaking out of order, and till it came to his turn to speak. Then the arest* was read to the meeting. The Nobility, who have a right to advise the King in thir cases, wer easy, and would not oppose the King, though feu of them wer for the *Arrêt*. The first Presidents declared against the King's designe and the rest.† When it came to the President that formerly spoke before it came to his share, he again fell doun before the King, thanked him for overlooking his impudence, and begged his Majesty would consider what had been offered to him, and, in the name of many of his Majesty's subjects, humbly requested that his Majesty would be pleased to name that villan who had advised him to call this Bed of Justice, to do so ill a thing as was proposed to be done, that he might

---

* Arret.   † Arret.

be prosecut legally for giving his Majesty so bad counsell ! Every body
kneu that the Cardinall standing at the King's hand was the adviser.
The whole Presidents wer against it.   Houever, the King passed the
Bull into a lau, and sent it to the Parliament of Paris, to be registrate
there ; and they unanimously refused to registrat it, and protested against
it.   Thus ther seems a very great party in France against the Jesuits.

The same person tells me that he had heard that Mr James Smith*
had sent an offer of his service lately to my Lord Isla, and that he could
scarce belive it, till he enquired at Isla himself ; and he told him it was
very true, and he had accepted of it, and would serve himself of them
all, and they wer all of the same kidney !

That Mr John Hepburn, this last winter or spring, had come to Mr
All. Logan, and lamented to him the courses that seemed very fast to
be running into by Professor Hamiltoun, Mr Crawford, and others, at
Edinburgh, and said he had gone too far on with them ; and yet since
that time he was gone in gum† with all their measures, and was mostly
in all the clubs and concerts with Professor Hamiltoun.   That my Lord
Monie was pretty far gone into the notions of the Pietists, and that he
and Walter Pringle, my Lord . . . . . ., read the Books of the Count
Metenish,‡ particularly the Baron's Book *De Ratione Fidei* ; and that the
Lord Monie told him he did not understand the ordinary doctrine he
heard preached on Justification by the Rightiousnes of Christ : That he
was far from thinking of the doctrine of merit, but we wer justifyed by
a vitall union with Christ, and by becoming, in an unexplicable manner,
one with him ; which he explained some way by the rayes of the sun,
their enlightning and purifying the soul.   My informer told him, by anything he could understand of his notion, he confounded Justification and
Sanctification.   This error is what severall of the graver and more sober
sort of gentlemen and others are running to.   The Lord pity us, for
multitude of by-paths are running to, on right and left hand !

Mr James Wilson, lately come from Holland, tells me Dr Clerk's life

* Minister at Cramond.   † Displeasure, umbrage.   ‡ Metternich.

is writ, late[ly,] by Hoadly, Bishop of Bangor, and nou of Sarum ; and he has displeased many.   He comes to give account of his peculiaritys, and particularly upon the doctrine of the Trinity ; and when he enters on them, he sayes, we will not determine whither in them he is right or wrong.   This, people at London say, from the mouth of a Bishop, is a plain enough declaring himself of his opinion, and can be constructed no otherwise.

Mark and Wesselius talked with my informer about Mr J. Simson. They have no distinct accounts of him, and told him they wer not so much masters of the English as easily to read the proces, but they gave their opinion that Mr Simson seemed to be a stiff, peremptory man : That if he had, at first, given his bretheren the satisfaction that afterward he chuse when threatned with a sentence, all might have been ease, and much noise and debate prevented.

That they told him (see his Letter to me in March last) that Turre-tine, the son, had quite overturned everything in Geneva : That subscriptions to Confessions wer no more required in that city : That, while a student at Leyden, he was very forward, and opinionative, and headstrong.   His Letters upon Subscription to the King of Prussia are printed, and I am promised them in a litle.

It was in February or March that the affair of Coll[onel] Charters broke out, and it has made a great deal of noise.   The generality belive that he has met with no favour but the hight of lau.   A very ill woman, who had be[en] the Coll[onel]'s whoor many times, and, they say, stollen one hundred gineas out of his pocket, when he would force back the one hundred gineas, by the direction of Alderman Child, with whom the Collonel had a debate about five thousand pound, swore a rape upon him ; and the Jury, being impressed with the Collonel's ill character, brought him in guilty of death ; and the sentence was accordingly passed, though the Judges sheued their dislike.   His lands, coaches, lodgings, plate, &c., wer all seized, and he put in Neu-Gate, in the condemned hold.   I heard the solicitor, Mr Erskin, tell he went to see him.   He told the solicitor he was never so vexed as he had been that morning. The hangman had been with him asking money, and the Ordinary of

Neu-Gate came to him.   He got rid of the Parson, by saying he was a
Presbiterian, but the hangman was still dogging him.   He said he was
an old man, and was easy about his money and effects, but he was deeply troubled about the Earl of Wemyse, married on his daughter; his
children would be beggars.   He has this moneth got a pardon; and he
ouns that this scrape will stand him near forty thousand pound sterling.
No body pitys him.

Mr Steuart tells me that black John Walker, since he came into the
Society for Propagating Christian Knouledge, by his rashnes and for-
wardnes, has exposed himself.   He blames Mr Spence for changing letters, and Mr Cave for not accounting quarterly for what money he re-
ceives, alledging the interest will come to somewhat.   This foolish rashnes had fretted these two worthy persons and the members exceedingly;
but it was hoped it would be made up.   He is a forward, fiery man.

They tell me at Edinburgh, what I had not any accounts of at home,
that Mr John Simson is writting against Collings,* and writting a Systeme of Divinity, to sheu his orthodoxy, and convince the world of it.
He compleans we have no right Compend of Divinity, and promises one
exacter than any, nou that he is laid aside from other work.   They say,
Mr M'Laran, at Edinburgh, is writing another Systeme, and is to publish it.   It's probable they will not perfectly harmonize.

Alexander Voy tells me, that his father was born in Orkney, and he
heard him frequently tell this story, which was the occasion of his leaving
that country and coming to this.   He was educat at the Grammer School
of Kirkwall, and put an apprentice to a writter and publick nottar in
Kirkwall, of very considerable bussines.   His master was maryed upon
a very considerable gentlman in Orkney his eldest daughter, who wanted
the left arm from the elbou from the womb.   She was proud and severe
to him, and put him to work in the house, [which] he thought belou him
as his Master's apprentice.   When she insisted, he answered, It was not
work suited to him, she behoved to cause her servant weemen to do it!

---

* Collins, the Deistical writer.

She got up the kitchen tongs to strick him ; which perceiving, he got in upon her, held her hand, and bade her strick him with the other, if she pleased !—knouing she had no other. Upon this, he took the opportunity of a ship, and came away to Edinburgh.

The occasion of the mutilation of his mistress, as was knouen and fully belived in Orkney about sixty or seventy years ago, was this :—Her mother was a very short time maryed to her father, a Laird of three or four thousand merks a year, and lived in a Castle in Orkney. She was fond of children, and one day there came a poor woman with four pleasent children to the gate, begging. The young lady asked her whose children these wer ? She said hers, and their father was lost at sie, and she was oblidged to beg for her oun bread and theirs. The lady was much taken with the pleasent faces of the children ; and fell, in the hight of her temper, to scold the poor widou, and said, Wher had she got such well-favoured children, she that was a beggar ?—and added, she wondered that God did not put a difference between gentlmen's children and beggars' children ! The poor lady found her rash words had too visible effect. In some time she bore her eldest daughter, a very well-favoured child, but wanting the arm on the left side to the elbou, as we have seen. She next bore a son, and he was a very pleasent child, but wanted the penis, and in the place of it had a hollou passage for urine. She next bore another son who was perfect every way, but want[ed] the one eye, and in room of it ther was a smooth bone covered with skin. And she bore next a daughter, and I think she was maimed in a legg—and [then] left off bearing. Thus, Providence made a difference very remarkably between the beggar and the lady's children !

I find Mr G. Logan, Minister of Dumbar, is gone over to the Hague, to see his uncle, Mr Alexander Cummingham* of Block, who is fallen into a palsy, or some such distemper, and is a-dying. Mr Cummingham of Block is certainly of a considerable age nou. He was a comrade of my father's forty or fifty years ago. He had been governour,† and gone

---

* Cunningham.

† A pedagogue or private tutor to the Earl of Hyndford, the Duke of Argyll, and others.

abroad with young noblmen and gentlmen: He was in Scotland about the 1700 or 1703, when I keept the Library, and was a day in conversation with my father. He came into the Library, and understood the editions of books nicely. He was famouse for his skill at the chess, and one of the first-rate in Europ at that exercise rather than game. The Earle of Sunderland, one in France, and another in Italy, and he, set up for being most skilled in that study of the chess. He played a game with my father, and told him by way [of] a great complement, that he was in the thirty [third?] rate players, and he belived ther wer not many in Scotland above him: That he kneu my father's strenth exactly, and his oun; and that he was able to give him a queen and a paun, and no more.

When I was present he told my father, that he had read all he could find on the Christian Religion in generall, and that he was drawing up some papers upon it. He opned up his scheme; which I cannot fully, at thirty years' distance, recover. He designed to sheu that ther was not one of the laues of the Old Testament but what was absolutely necessary for the Jeues; and that, in the nature of things, they could have no other laues than God gave them; and even the laues about meats and the like wer bottomed upon necessary reasons. And as to Christ, he was to demonstrat, if my memory fail me not, that, on the supposition of God sending his Son as Messias, it was absolutely necessary that, when he came to the world in our nature, he should act directly the reverse to humane wisdom, and the maximes of the world. He promised to send a copy of his papers to my father when he had put them in order. He had a very great value and respect for my father. I remember my father made some objections against his scheme, which he said he would fully consider, and hoped to obviat. Some years after that, he set about the Edition of the Justinean Code, from a copy in the Duke of Florence' Library, and had some encouragment given him from our Scots Parliament to give a complet edition of that foundation of Civil Lau. Since that time he has been much in Holland. He had somewhat yearly from my Lord Summers, Lord Cooper, Lord Sunderland, the Earle of Oxford, and, more lately, from my Lord Isla, as I am told, yearly, for corresponding with them, and picking up the curious

editions of the Classicks, and other scarce books.   He has lived these
many years at the Hague, and has spent much time in giving an edition
of Horace, and making Remarks on Bentley's edition.   I hear no more
either of his designe on a Vindication of Christianity, nor of the edition
of the Code.   He was among the first-rate Criticks, and understood the
Classicks and editions of books, especially Lau, beyond many.   I belive
he may be nou about eighty years.*

Mrs Stirling tells me that the last time ever my father was out, that
she knoues of, was about June 1708, when he came in throu the Common Hall to her room in his goun, and asked if she kneu the place in
the Church-yeard where he was to lye when he dyed?   She said she did,
and went out with him throu the Principall's garden, and let him see it.
He lay doun on the grass on his back, and, fixing his eyes to heaven,
said, " O ! that thou wouldest hide me in the grave !"—and said he
longed much for it.   She said, he was happy that could long for it.
He answered, " I knou I am to have all my ill things here !" She said,
she was still affrayed to die.   He answered, " You are not yet near death ;
stay till it be near you, and then the fears of it will, it may be, [be] taken
away !"   After my dear brother, Mr Alexander's death, she was regrat-
ing his loss the next day.   He answered, " The loss is great indeed ;
but I knou who hath sent it—the good God, that cannot wrong me !
Sandy was a son that never displeased me ; he was my comrad, he was
my counselour, he was and would have been my helper ; but, since God
has taken him to Himself, I am silent !"

[*May* 17.]—On the 17th of this moneth, Mr William Wisheart
preached his last sermon in the Trone Church at Glasgou ; and, next
day, went towards London to setle there.   Ther is much speaking of
that sermon.   The text I have forgote ; but the discourse, they say, was
very artfull, and calculat to raise the passions ; and delivered with a
great deal of seeming concern, and in the manner of a tragedy.   He
gave them strong assurances of his sorrou to part with them, and fre-

* Mr Cunningham was born in 1654.   His father was Minister at Ettrick.   He was British Envoy
to Venice from 1715 to 1720, and author of a History of Great Britain, from 1688 to 1714, written in
Latin ; an English translation of which, by Dr William Thomson, was published in 1787.

quently wiped his face and eyes, as if he had been weeping. He commended the people very much, and declared that nothing less than the outmost necessity had prevailed with him to part with them ; that it was impossible, wherever he was, to forget them. There was a generall weeping throu the whole Church, and he himself appeared to be in tears. This was not formerly his way, and what he blamed in others, as a mechanicall way of stirring up the passions ; and, indeed, if anything of this sort be mechanicall, it's said ther was as much of mechanisme and labouring of the passions, [such] as is done in the Playhouse, as ever was essayed in our pulpites. People of rank, and who never weeped in a Church before, wer in tears ; and when asked, What made them weep ?—they could not tell, and ouned it was not the matter delivered, but the manner, and his and others' weeping about them, and his apparent affection. He gave them the character of the Minister whom he wished they would pitch on in his room, in a pretty extraordinary way ; and it was generally thought he pointed at Mr J. Anderson. But enough of this. His text was, " Only let your conversation be according," &c. He recommended charity, and love, and union, and very litle of faith, or its life. He preached over the sermon, with his brother, next Sabbath, at Edinburgh.

[*May* 20.]—Upon the 20th of May, ther was a man found murdered near Air. He was hid in the sand, and had been for some dayes lying there. He had eight or nine wounds in his body. It was thought he was a man come up with the cess from about the Largs, and was murdered for his money. Murders are turned exceeding common nou, and within this year we have had five or six. The woman, J. Muir was charged for, the man at Partick, Youl in the Gorballs, the Laird of Auchtifardel's family, and this. Blood toucheth blood, and we have reason to expect some very fearfull purging of the land from blood.

June, 1730.—Mr James Wilson tells me that it was generally belived the follouing odd freak of the King of Prussia was belived to be true :—About two years ago, or therby, that King was traveling, with two or three servants, about twenty miles from Berling, wher he met a coach with a young lady in it. He stoped the coach, and asked the lady wher she was going, with a great deal of civility; asking her a thousand pardons that he should use this peice of rudenes. She answered, she was going to Berline. He said he imagined so, and that was the occasion of his incivility; adding, he had a letter about a bussines of considerable consequence, that required speed and safety, to be given to the King's Secretary; and asked the favour that, as soon as she came, that it might be delivered. The lady, taking him to be some person of distinction, undertook to take a care of it. The King thanked her, and said he presumed further to begg that the lady might deliver it out of her oun hand to the Secretary. The lady was pleased to undertake to do so; and the King wrote a short line, and sealed it, and delivered it with many complements, and went off. The lady took her journey streight to Berline in coach. She was going to be marryed on a gentlman at Berline; and the gentlman mett her when the coach came, and offered to hand her out. She told [him] she behoved, having given her promise to a person of quality, to deliver a letter at the Secretary's office out of her hand, to drive forward to that, and then she would return. The bridegroom asked what he was; and, by the accounts, began to suspect ther was a trick in it; and being acquaint with the raverys* sometimes the King fell into, and jealousing a litle from the circumstances that there might be somewhat in it, desired the letter, and he would presently carry it or send it, with a sure hand, to the Secretary.

The lady yeilded, and was handed up to her room. The bridegroom took the letter, and went to the street and gote an old woman, and gave her money to carry the letter to the Secretary, and deliver it out of her oun hand, which she did. The Secretary received it and read it, and looked to her again and again. The letter was to this purpose : " Upon the recept of this, immediately marry the bearer to such an one, among the tall grenadeers, under the pain of my displeasure." He well kneu the King's hand, and that he must be obeyed. He asked the woman wher she got it. She told him from a gentlman she kneu not; and then offred to go her way. She was an old, ill-favoured, lame woman. The Secretary told she behoved to stay a litle, and he sent for the

* Extravagances.

Grenadeer, and read the King's letter to him, and told him it must be obeyed. The man was almost out of himself at the command, and the woman as backward as he ; but the thing behoved to be done, and they wer marryed, and, as the letter ordered, put to a room together. In two or three hours the King came streight to the Secretary, and asked if he got his Letter ; and when he heard he had, asked for the neu marryed couple. He was told they were in the room together. The King went in to them, and soon sau the change. He found them, the one at the one end of the room, and the other at the other, scolding and weeping. The King dissolved the marriage, and dismissed them ; and published a declaration, that if the person who received such a letter at such a place would discover themselves, they should be pardoned and rewarded : But the gentlman would not trust his Majesty, and none would discover who had thus tricked the King, knouing he is so absolute and capricious that nobody can depend upon him.

He tells me that the Prince of Nassau, or Orrange, is exceedingly beloved in all the Seven Provinces : That three of them have declared him Statholder ; that the other four stand out, not from any dislike, but because they would have him marryed to our Princess before they declare him. And our Court incline to have him ouned Statholder by all the Provinces before the marriage be declared. So that the youth is in a rack* betwixt the two, and thus that matter stands.

That the Criminall Jurisdiction in Holland is very odly mixed ; the Magistrats of their touns have the pouer of life and death, and in the country, except in some particular places, where Noblmen have it, the boors have this pouer in their hands. The boors, in such a precinct, meet together and chuse a number of themselves Judges, *in hunc effectum*, twelve or such a number, and they come into the Toun-house of the neighbouring city, and hear the lauers plead and pass their sentence, and the criminall is execute in the toun. He sau one of them, and the hangman is in the habit of a gentlman, with his laced hat, fine wigg and cloaths.

He tells me, that in Holland Cocceianism and Voetianism continou much as they have been formerly : That in touns and citys the people

* Strait.

and Ministers are generally Cocceians, and in the country places they are generally Voetians : That at Lyden and Utricht they find it their interest still to have some Voetian Professors, because forraigners chuse generally the Voetian Professors.

The publick in Holland and the Seven Provinces are certainly under prodigious burden and debt, but in case of any pressing necessity, they are in no difficulty, for they have multitudes of their magistrates and merchants who are immensly rich, and willing enough to advance money to the publick, when they see expenses or warr necessary.

That the nature of their Republick requires a constant standing army, and that ther are in all their touns great numbers of souldiers constantly ready, at a call, to keep the peace, and to execute the State's orders ; but ther is very litle need of them, save by way of precaution.

That the taxes in the Provinces, especially upon eatables and the common necessarys of life, are higher in Holland than any part of the world, and immense summs of money are raised for the support of the poor, and they are exceeding well taken a care of, and every body put to work that can work.

That in the Provinces Ministers are generally very rich ; and the occassion of it is not their stipends, which are moderat, though exactly payed, and encreased as their family encreases, but from this reason, that, generally speaking, Ministers make their marriages with very rich persons, and feu of the remarkable Ministers, and especially Professors of Divinity, marry under eight or ten thousand pound stirling.

He tells me that this last winter the noise of sodomy was breaking out, and it was talked of particularly among the young people and a club of students at Utrecht ; but ther was nothing come in publick about it when he came away, in March or Aprile last. Since that time, we [see] the tryalls there in the neuse papers, to that pitch that is shoaking to Christian ears.

Some of them, as well as of state criminalls, are privatly execute ; and if any executions are to be in privat, which, houever, seems not so consistant with the designe of punishment and executions-penall, (that is, the terrifying of others,) one would think that this unnaturall crime may be among that number.

He tells me, that there wer severall Deists come over from England, professed Deists. Some of them had been Felloues of some of the Colledges in England, and oblidged to fly for fear of being prosecute; and, this last moneth, we find that severall Masters are expelled Oxford for Deisme. They, generally, in Holland, study physick, particularly one . . . ., who was not knouen to be Deisticall till, last harvest, a merchant's sone in London, who had been his pupil, hapned to dye, and a course of correspondence between the Fellou and pupill was found amongst his papers; of which, when he heard, he thought fitt to withdrau to Holland this last winter.

In conversation with Dr Cumming, at Irwine, he tells me that Mr John Cumming, first Dissenting Minister at Cambridge, then at the Scots Congregation at London, and lately made Doctor of Divinity by the Colledge of Edinburgh, who dyed last year, was a relation of his. He had not heard of the story of his being converted by an old Dissenting Minister, which is narrated above in thir Analecta; but tells me that his father was an Episcopall Minister in the North, who was exceedingly violent for Episcopacy, in all its heights; and, for his warmnes and running things to all extremitys, was called frequently Jesuit Cumming. This Minister had a brother whose name was John, another Episcopall Minister, who quite* his parish because he would not take the Test. That, at the Revolution, this Mr John Cumming went to England; and when he sau the constitution of the Church of England, and their ceremonies, he turned Dissenter, and would not joyn with them; and he taught the youth philosophy. That he printed a sermon upon Queen Mary's death, which was very well liked. This Mr John Cuming, uncle to the last Dr Cuming, after the Revolution, mentained a correspondence with his brother, the Doctor's father, upon the Revolution and

---

* Left, quitted.

Episcopacy, which he had nou left.   His brother mentained Episcopacy in its height, and the unlaufulnes of the Revolution ; and there passed many sheets of paper on these subjects, wherein some who sau them say the subject on both sides was handled very closely.   After the Revolution, the last Dr Cuming being, for his violence, oblidged to leave Edin·burgh Colledge, went up to his uncle in England, and was educat by him.

The Isle of Arran hath about eighteen hundred examinable persons in it, and two Ministers, who preach in Irish and English.   The late Dutches of Hamiltoun established a helper, who preaches and catechises, 'and has five hundred merks a year ; and three schools, with a hundred pound a year.   Ther is a vast change upon that Island within these twenty years, or therby.   Mr Reid tells me there is twenty instead of one who understands the English tongue since he kneu it ; and, indeed, ther are not many nou but understand the English tongue.   Mr M'Lean, who was first Minister there after the Revolution, did not much propagat the English tongue.   He was reconed one of the greatest masters of the Irish tongue in Scotland in his day, and, I think, translated the Confession of Faith into Irish, and the Shorter Catechisme and Psalmes.

My Lady Eglingtoun, her brother, Mr David Kennedy, and three of my Lady's daughters, with their weemen, wer over in Arran at the goat-milk this moneth ; and a very odd passage fell out, which I have weel attested from two or three who had the accounts from my Lady and her brother, anent a disturbance they mett with.   They wer lodged in a house on the shore-side, the best house in that part of the Isle.   A kind of surgeon lived ther, some years since, and, it was alledged, a man who was sick and dyed in that house had not very fair play.   It's said that, severall times, noises wer beard about the house ; lights seen in it when nobody lived in it ; and the neighbours wer beat with unseen hands. Houever, these passages wer not much belived by persons who went over to the Isle, because the people, inhabitants of the Island, as all the Highlanders generally are, wer reaconed credulous and fretty.*   Ther

* Full of *freits*, superstitious.

had been severall lodgers in the house, who met with no disturbance; and care was taken to bear doun the storys, least lodgers should scarr at the house.

My Lady, and her brother, and the rest, wer one night disturbed with a noise in the night-time, a litle after they came to lodge there, which revived some former storys; but on enquiry it was found to be from two drunk persons who had some brandy in some of the cellars belou them. They wer seized by Mr Hamiltoun of Bardouy, the Duke of Hamiltoun's Bailay, and brought to the Countess of Eglingtoun. The Bailay offered to punish them at her pleasure, but she passed them, and the whole of the former storys wer knocked doun as groundles; and my Lady and her brother wer satisfyed all was but story and credulity. In some dayes ther wer frequent noises heard in the rooms, and when people wer sent nobody could be found. Some of the young Ladys' weemen wer frequently frighted; and some of them had stroaks, as they said, laid on them by invisible hands. My Lady and her brother, being fully satisfyed as to the first noise, would belive nothing after that, and endeavoured to jest them out of their freights, and caryed the matter the lenth that she frighted them herself by a suddain throuing a cod* among them when in company.

But the disturbances from another art† continoued, and at lenth they wer all convinced that ther was some what preternaturall about the house. One night, when in the room altogether, they hear a very extraordinary noise. Mr David, who is no way credulous, said to my informer, he could compare the noise to nothing but five or six squibbs bizzing and giving a crack altogether in the different corners of the room, and the young ladys and their weemen say they sau the head of a man sweeming over their heads in the room, which was pretty high, and his face looking doun on them. They wer all in the outmost consternation that persons could be in, and did not in the least doubt ther wer invisible pouers about them, and, as soon [as] a boat could be gote, left the house in a feu hours, and came over to Eglingtoun. This is a certain fact that may be depended on.

---

* Pillow or bolster.   † Direction.

Mr Reid tells me, that Mr John Wilson, Minister at Largs, was an excellent person.   He was once stoped, or, as we call it, really *sticked* a sermon in Ireland ; that is, his matter quite failed him, and he was oblidged to give over.   This made him, after that, constantly in fear. He was an excellent preacher, and, generally speaking, wrote every word ; and yet he was of opinion, that keeping the very words of what is written tended much to the breaking of a person's memory, when it was tyed doun to words and phrazes ; and yet, throu the forsaid fear, he never durst venture to the publick till he had mandated* word for word.   We fell a talking as to the method of writting and mandating sermons, and seemed to agree that ther are advantages in a closs writting of the matter of a sermon, and that the writing the enlargments† themselves is of very good use to make what is delivered exact and accurat ; but then it may be considered, whither, by mandating every-thing, the memory itself may not be overburdened, and really weakned, and that, perhaps, the best way may be for Ministers to study and write the heads of a sermon, and some pertinent Scriptures to each of them, and to mandat these ; but in mandating, to study and think upon the enlargments, without writting them.   This will both releive the memory from the bondage of the words and phrazes of the enlargment ; but, in thinking and meditating, the heart is impressed much more than in a transient glance in writting the enlargments, with the subject-matter it-self, and a savour of the truths spoken of will be reached.   These im-pressions, and this savour upon the mind in meditating on the enlarg-ments, will both strenthen the memory, and lead the speaker to suitable exercises proper to what is thought on upon his oun soul ; and what is spoken will readily, as coming from a heart impressed with these truths, have a great deal of more weight with judicious and serious hearers, than a feu quaint expressions writ doun in a hurry, and mandated as a school-boy's lesson.

My mother-in-lau was very suddainly taken ill, towards the end of this moneth, when Mr Warner was in Ireland ; so that I was necessitat

---

* Got by heart. Lat. *mandare*.   † Illustrations, amplifications.

to go West on July the 2d.   She was in a violent feaver, and yet it
pleased the Lord to carry her throu her trouble, to our great surprize.
She seemed to be under the expectations of death, and the more that
this was near the close of her seventy-fifth year, being born, I think,
July 7, 1655 ; and she observed that her mother, Agnes Campbell,
Mrs Guthry, her grandmother, the Lady Skeldon, and her mother,
dyed all of them precisely in their seventy-fifth year of age.   Yet the
Lord hath brought her into the seventy-sixth year of her age.

Mr Warner, who is lately come over from Dubline, tells me that he
waited on Mr Iredale there, who thinks the interest of the Dissenters in
Ireland exceeding lou.   Their divisions have exposed them, and they
complean of a coldnes even when they seem to be united, and a terrible
degree of decay in seriouse godlynes.   Mr John Abernethy was preaching there when he was at Dubline.   He heard him, and thought he did
not apply the Scriptures which came in his way to the Divinity of Christ,
but exceedingly waved that subject, when he had fair occasion for it.
A good many of the more serious sort are not for his coming there.
    They term the city of Dubline the fourth or fifth city in Europ for
bignes, and the number of inhabitants ; and in the year 1715, on the
Rebellion, when a list was taken up of the inhabitants, they wer reconed
thirteen or fifteen hundred thousand.*   Ther is exceeding great profu-
sion, and they live exceeding high.   They have aboundance of money
in great, but have no small money for carrying on of trade or bussines.
    He tells me, that we have relations there, by my mother-in-lau, his
mother ; two near cusins of the name of Campbell ; excellent weemen,
of great piety and sense : the one marryed to Mr Muir, who deals in
silver lace, whose sons I kneu when at this Colledge ; and the other
marryed to one Mr Caldwell ; both [of] them persons of great substance
and interest in Dubline.

The toun of Glasgow, this moneth, susteans a very great loss, as they
have had very many of late, by the breaking of a Dutch factor, a Scots-

----

* Probably a mistake in transcribing figures, for 130 or 150,000.

man. It's reconed upwards of two thousand pound sterling, but being divided among different persons, it's the less sensible.

This moneth the Heretors of the parish of Renfreu had a meeting, where, I am told, my Lord Dundonald, Blythswood, Walkingshau, and others, agreed on Mr Anderson, of Port-Glasgou, at Blythswood's desire; with his promise to them that, if he did not carry, he should come in to my Lord Dundonald's man, who is Mr J. Millar of Neilston. But I doubt if this come to anything.

As to Glasgou vacancys, it's said that Pr[incipal] Campbell is named to the Laigh Church; and the Provest would be for him, but the toun oppose it, because it would bring a burden on them still to make Principals Ministers in the toun, when a vacancy falls out.

Dougalstoun* is very ill this moneth, and some way in hazard. This is the second or third year his Rheumatisme hath attacked him, and I doubt he will not live very long. He will be a considerabe loss to this country, being not only morall, and a person of weight, but a great bearer doun of sin and vice, and a very usefull person in the toun and country.

Mr H. Steuart tells me a passage, that Mr James Ramsay, when Chaplain to their Regiment, told him and severall of the officers. When in Yorkshire, Mr Ramsay had the account from the first hands. The grave-diggers there, about twenty-five years ago, wer making a grave in a church-yard, and turned up a scull, which, when throun out, fell a shaking and tumbling up and doun. This very much allarumed the grave-diggers; and they went and vieued the scull, and perceived a large toad lodged in it, which was the cause of the motion of the scull, and certainly was lodged ther in Providence to make the follouing discovery :—When they had turned out the toad out of the scull, and wer veuing [it,] they found a large nail, of severall inches long, sticking in the scull. This very much allarumed them. They caryed the skull, and nail in it, to the Minister of the parish, (from whom, if I forget not, Mr Ramsay had the account.) He presently, by the parish books, found out the person last buryed in that grave; and, upon enquiry, got accounts that the man who was buryed there dyed very suddainly: That

* Graham of Dougalston.

his wife was marryed, soon after, to a servant of theirs, about fifteen years before : They lived still in the parish, and wer sent for, and confessed they had murdered that person by stricking a nail through his head. As far as I see, this relation may be depended on.

I heard a story, much of the same nature, that hapned in the parish of Luss, some years since, of a smith in that parish who was at variance with his wife, and dyed suddainly ; and when his grave was opened, a nail was found in his skull, about twenty years after. His wife was examined, who had maryed the servant, and the murder was confessed. Enquire at Mr Robison, Minister ther, and get the circumstances.

Mr M'Claurin, in Glasgou, tells me he heard of another discovery of murder in Argyleshire, when Mr John Campbell, of Mammore, lately dead, was Shirriff; upon which the man was taken and execute. Two persons wer traveling throu the shire, and one of them murdered the other. That same night, the wife or mother of him that was murdered dreamed that he* and another man, whom she kneu not, but gave all the marks, from his face, and hair, and cloaths, [who] murdered him. This dream made great impression on her, and she told it to her neighbours. In a little after, the accounts of the murder came. The dead body was found in the same place she dreamed of. The other man was gone away. Search was made for him, and he was found ; and Mr Campbell sentenced him to dye, and he was execute.

July, 1730.—This moneth we hear that Bailay Orr, of whom above, to whom so much money has fallen by his wife's uncle, out of his regard to the Colledge of Glasgou, hath gifted five hundred pounds sterling to the Library, the interest of which is yearly to be applyed to the buying of Books, whose authors have lived at least three hundred years ago. He has, they say, the Classicks and Fathers mostly in vieu, and thinks the Library is defective as to these. I wish many might follou his example in making donations to the Library ; with regulations of another kind, as necessary as this.

My son, Sandy, this moneth, at Blantyr-well, falls worse. He went out in a cart, and fainted ; and continoued so ill, that we found proper

* She saw him.

to bring him home. I do not see that the minerall watters have been of any use to him. He is in the Lord's hands, and it's probable his life will not be very long.

We hear some noise of a sermon preached by Mr Armstrong before the Synod of Dumfreice, at their last meeting, of a very odd nature. This young Minister, Mr Telfair, Wallace, and a brother of Mr Armstrong's, and, some say, Mr Cumming of Lochmaben, some years ago wer talked of as in a club, and having some meetings wherein pretty odd notions, pretty much favouring Arminianisme, wer vented ; and they strenthned one another's hands in them. It seems the effects of such more secret cabballs are nou coming out. We have heard of Mr Telfair's sermon at some lenth. I have not yet distinct accounts of Mr Armstrong's, but only that it was mostly taken out of The Rights of the Christian Church by Tyndall, and conteaned a satyre upon the Ministry of this Church for imposition ; when one would think we are so far from that, that we are running to the other extreme of latitude and libertinisme. Houever, I am told, after his coming out of the pulpit, being aprized of the Synod's generall displeasure with the matter of his sermon, he sau proper to withdrau, and ride off the place.

This moneth I have the very melancholy account of the open breach in my Lord Grange his family. Things have been very dark there for some time, since his Lady* took up a jealousy of him, charged him with guilt with another, and had spyes upon him in England, when last there about his son's process of murder. She intercepted his letters in the Post-Office, and would have palmed treason upon them, and took them to the Justice-Clerk, as is said, and alledged [that] some phrazes in some of her Lord's letters to Lord Dun related to the Pretender, without the least shaddou for the inference. Last moneth, it seems, his lady (being, for her drukennes, palpable and open, and her violent, unhappy temper, and mismanagement, inhibited by my Lord) left the family. This was pleasing to her Lord, and he did not use any endeavours to have her back, since sometimes she attempted to murder him, and was innumerable wayes uneasy. Upon this, my Lady gave in a Bill to the Lords

* The celebrated and unfortunate Lady Grange.

for a mentenance, and conteaning the grounds of her separation. But the matter was taken up, and my Lord entered into a concert with her freinds, alloued her one hundred pounds a year, and she declared she would separat from him, and be satisfyed with that; and so they live separatly. This man is ouned, by his greatest enimies, to have had the greatest provocations possible, and his family distresses have even drauen pity from them that (I hope) groundlesly have loaded him with the greatest calumnies and reproaches. I recon him among the greatest men in this time, and would fain hope the calumnies cast on him are very groundles; but they are exceedingly fostered and spread by such as dislike him for his zealouse appearances for this Church, and against Mr Simson.

This moneth, the touns of Glasgou and Edinburgh are at an issue* as to their vacancys. Mr Smith is transported to Edinburgh, and Mr Wisheart and Mr Goldie, and I suppose setled also, all being admitted by one sermon. Professor Hamiltoun's son goes to Cramond, and there is like to be a great heat about setling Mr Wisheart's place. Mr Jardin, in Glencairn, is what the Ministers and most part are for; but that is like to be defeated by a young man of the neu stamp, forced in from the Highlands by my Lord Isla and some others.

The toun of Glasgou have come to an issue as to ther vacancys, and have fixed on Mr J. Anderson from Port-Glasgou. For what I hear, P[rovost] Stirling, with Mr Wisheart, before he left the place, with the younger set of people in Glasgou, ordered matters so as ther was no difficulty in the particular Session, or in the Quarter, and all went pretty smooth. It was not so as to Mr Dick, who, at lenth, came to be fixed on for the Midle Quarter. The bulk of the Session, and the generality of the heads of familys, wer for Mr Andrew Gray, their former Minister's son; and the Ministers wer also for him; but P[rovost] Stirling and the Magistrates by no means would come in. Mr Dick was Mr H . . . nepheu, and Mr S . . . . had some vieu for his son, they say, to Carluke, whence Mr Dick was to come. So it was gone into. Indeed, the election in Glasgou is as much forced as in many places, and the sentiments of the people are very litle regarded. When a Minister is

* Come to a conclusion.

agreed on, and concerted, there is some shaddou of enquiry made whither the heads of familys are against him ; but he is not a whit their choice ; and, indeed, they have no choice, but to be for him, or to give objections against him.

The affair of Hutton has been notticed in May as it stood before the Assembly ; and, being there ended, I hear the conclusion and setlment of Waugh is equall to the strange and unprecedented steps taken by the Commission and others in that affair.   When the day of ordination was come, the dores of the Church wer barricadoed—the people as averse as ever ; and the Shirriffe of the shire, with upwards of a hundred armed men, wer present to force on the setlment, and protect Mr Waugh. Such procedure as this will be a blot in our history, when it comes to be writt ; and, I doubt, before that, the enimies of the Church will make a sport of us and our setlments of this sort.

Mr Thomas Finlater's setlment at Linton is like to be much of the same nature.   The people are opposit, the Presbytery for it, but not joynt.*   It was remitted to the Synod, and they ordered a Committy to joyn with the Presbytery.   When they mett in June, they wer on the matter rabled ;† and Mr Findlater (who was not there) was sought for, with threatnings to tear him.   Objections against him wer sought by the Committy and Presbytery.   The gentlmen, and heritors, and elders, said they would advance none but one, that at home, in Hamiltoun, where he was best knouen, he was not liked.   The Committy referred the matter to the Synod of Lothian.

This moneth we have our accounts first in the London prints, that the Colledge of Glasgou have made two Doctors of Divinity, *a la mode* Edinburgh ; Mr Grosvenor and Mr William Wisheart.   I have not talked with any about it.   Somewhat may be said as to Mr Wisheart, being their Dean of Faculty, and a member of their society, and going from them to setle at London ; but hou they came to pitch on Mr Grosvenor, I cannot conceive, unless it has been by Mr Wisheart's recommendation.   He is a very violent Non-subscriber ;‡ and, I fancy, Mr

---

* Unanimous.   † Mobbed.   ‡ Opposed to the subscription of Formularies, or Confessions of Faith.

Alexander Dunlop has not knouen that Mr G[rosvenor] was the writter of the Remarks upon his excellent brother, Mr William Dunlop, his preface to our Confession of Faith, Edition 1720, in defence of Subscription. Indeed, Mr Grosvenor there does, in his loose way, in that pamphlet, attack this Church; and, in his Occasional Paper (for he is reput the principall writter of the three volumes of Occasional Papers) upon the Trinity, he very furiously attacks that doctrine. This must strongly expose the Church of Scotland as departing from both doctrine and practise, when our University[s] are loading such men with their thin honnours and University degrees.

Last moneth, the Colledge of Glasgow, on Mr Wisheart's going to London, chuse worthy Mr James Stirling* for Dean of Faculty. The Principall designed Mr M. Connell;† but Mr Dunlop was not for him, and carryed his point by a vast majority. It was a meer off-put to the Principal's man. For Mr Stirling has not accepted, and will not accept of that post; and, indeed, neither his head nor heart lyes to mix in with their litle party-work.

This moneth, without my knouing any thing of the matter, a race was appointed and publickly intimat at Beith, to be run in the Shaues,‡ by R.... M...... and the gawger Anderson. I am so impressed with the profanity and loss of time and work by the convocation for races, which much more then ballances all the pretended charge, and disposall of ale and goods at them, that I thought it my duty to endeavour to prevent it; and, indeed, my Lord P[ollock] was active as I could desire, and stopped it effectually.

I mett with a pretty odd incident about the last [ninth?] day of this moneth. John Wallace, in the Shau, came to me in a great consternation for my advice. The day befor he came, July 8, he was early in the morning going to his taylor work in Deaconsend, and sau a herd, whom I had lately challenged for want of a testimoniall, as he thought in the act of bestiality. This struck him with the outmost horror, being a seriouse, knouing man. He being near him, went streight to him, and asked him what he was doing? The herd was seemingly in great con-

* Minister of the Barony.   † At Kilbride.   ‡ Probably Pollockshaws, in the barony of Eastwood.

fusion, but boldly denied any evil or evil intentions. He called out his master, when he was going to work, and told him what had hapned ; and they went both to the herd, and dealt with him, but in vain. He was dashed, but stifly denied guilt. Houever, his master called him that day, and payed him for what time he had been with him, and sent him off. John Wallace was in a deep concern, and desired my opinion whither he had done right, and what further was [to be] done? I approved his conduct, and told him I perceived no more to be done but a closs secrecy, and a charging his master to a secrecy, that the scandall might not break out. This very much strenthens me in my strictnes, for which I am by some blamed, in insisting for testimonialls. This is the second instance of this in herds without testimonialls in this parish ; one about a year after I came to the parish, who had been guilty, and fled from the Highlands to us without a testimoniall ; and this.

Agust, 1730.—Very little offers, this moneth, but what is in the prints and my Letters. The Commission met at the ordinary time, and their proceeding is in the Edinburgh Courant. The affair of Balfron setlment was before them, and they laid aside Mr D. Broun, and that though it was evident he had eighty heads of familys, and most of the elders, and near as many heretors as any of the other two ; and preferred the presentee's call, with thirteen heads of familys, and an equal number to Mr Buchanan of heretors, to Mr Buchanan, who had seven elders, (and the presentee none,) and thirty-five heads of familys, contrary to our received rules and principles. This is turning very common.

This moneth, we had our Sacrament at our ordinary time, the third Sabath. We had about one thousand and forty Communicants ; and I find that, generally, everywhere, this season, Ministers observe that ther have been moe Communicants than have been knouen. What to make of this, I cannot tell. It's good, in itself, that people are making a profession, and attending ordinances ; and if they all be seriouse, or many of them, it's a proofe that the Gospell is doing good. But this must be left to the day of manifestation of all things.

Mr Wilson tells me that, in Holland, the men and the weemen com-

municat separatly, at different tables, by themselves ; the men at one
table, and the weemen at another. He can give no reason of this usage,
and I belive it will be hard to give one.

The tryall of one Cunningham, a Kilwinning man, before Thomas
Orr, Barron-bailay, at Glasgou, for horse-stealing, made some noise at
this time. He was one of the men of the worst of character ; a resetter
of the Mores, and delated by Campbell, execute for murder. In short,
he seems to have been art and part in the most part of the robberys and
murders committed in the West of Scotland for severall years. B[ailie]
Orr was willing enough to do justice on him ; and when the jury brought
in an undistinct verdict, not answering the articles found relevant, he
desired them to return and bring in a fuller verdict. Some complean of
this as illegall ; others vindicat it. Houever, on their returning a fuller
verdict, he passed a sentence of death ; and the generall voice was that
Cunningham richly deserved it. Houever, the matter was tabled before
the Lords of the Justiciary. Before the day of the execution of sentence
came, Cunningham was taken in to Edinburgh, and the books of the
Bailay wer called for, and he ordered to attend at Edinburgh. There it
was pleaded, on the one hand, that the Lords had not pouer to open
sentences of the Royality Courts. One instance of their pouer was only
produced since the Revolution ; and the Lords found themselves Judges.
Ther was no fault found in B[ailie] Orr's procedure ; but the Lords
found they had reason to alter the sentence from that of death to per-
petuall banishment from the kingdom. This taking of causes by advocation from Regality Barron Courts by the Lords of Justiciary is much
questioned by lauers, and, they say, allarumes our Nobility a litle. The
Duke of Montrose, whose Court the Regality of Glasgou is, and the
Dukes of Argyle and Hamiltoun, it being a common cause, they say,
are agreed to oppose this step of the Lords ; and I am told that, upon
a complaint of this matter to the British Counsell, the Lords of Justiciary are called up to answer before them. What the event will be, I
cannot say ; but everybody regrates that, one way or other, the greatest
malefactors, murderers, and theives, and the like, escape nou.

September, 1730.—Sir James Campbell, brother to Provest Aird's wife, tells me this account, which he had from Shaufeild and his lady, and that ther is not the least doubt to be made of its truth :—About seven or eight years ago, Shaufeild and his lady wer going up to London, in the winter season ; and near to Burrou-bridge,* or some place on the road of a name like this, wher there is a bridge which, in great rains or floods, is, at one end of it, surrounded with watter, so that the passage is rendered dangerouse, if not impracticable, they met with this passage very remarkable. Upon a litle eminency very near it—it's in Yorkshire, I think—there lived a Popish lady, who, two or three nights before Shaufeild's coach came there, dreamed that she was looking out at her windou, which is almost within cry to the bridge, in the night time, and sau a coach, with a lady in it, almost lost, and that she sent doun her servants and saved them. This dream made such impression, that the lady got up and sent her servants immediatly to the place ; but ther was nobody there. Houever, the impression continued so strong, that, nixt night, the Popish lady caused her servants, some of them, to watch much of the night. Nothing hapned that night either ; but the third night, pretty late, the Lady Shaufeild came, and, of a suddain, the coach was overturned, and filled with watter. The coachman got upon one of the horses, to save his life. The good and religious Lady Shaufeild was for some time under watter ; and, upon the cry rising, the Popish lady's servants came to their assistance. With much difficulty, the coach and lady in it wer got out of the watter. Every body thought the Lady Shaufeild was dead ; her body was full of watter, and she was laid on a declivity on the ground till she voided some of the watter, and recovered her senses. She was caryed soon to the Popish lady, wher all care was taken of her ; and she recovered a litle, and stayed a day or two, and then went on her journey. Last year, when Shaufeild and Sir James [Campbell,] my informer, came that road, Shaufeild sent up his servant to see hou that lady and family wer, and still does soe every time he goes or comes that road.

Mrs Maxwell, at the same time, told us that shee had what folloues

* Boroughbridge.

from the first hands at Edinburgh :—About seven or eight years ago, Graycrookes,* the gentlman that left his estate by a mortification, for the support of indigent Ministers' widoues, and his lady, from whom I think my informer had the account at that time, had a servant man and woman.   The woman had some money scraped together ; and she was murdered in a cellar, as was violently suspected, and her chest opened and robbed ; and Graycrooks (if I remember) missed some of his oun money at the same time.   The matter was so secretly done, that ther appeared no presumptions at all against the man.   Houever, Graycrooks parted with him very soon.   A year or more afterwards, one night, the Lady Graycrooks dreamed that she sau the man murder the woman in the cellar, and carry off her money, and put [it] in two old barrells filled with trash.   When she awakned, she communicat her dream, which left a deep impression upon [her.]   Graycrooks was a lauer, and a wise man, and desired her to speak of it to no body.   He made enquiry about the fellou, who was nou set up for a smith, I think, some part in the suburbs of Edinburgh, and found that he had plenty of money.   In a feu dayes, he got a warrand from the Magistrates suddainly to search his house, which was done, and, in two old barrells, as his lady had dreamed, full of old iron nails and such trash, found some money, and his oun baggs, which he kneu on seeing them, and which had been amissing at that time.   The fellou was apprehended and tryed, and sentenced to dye ; and, if I remember, confessed the murder, and was execute.

I am told that the late Dutches or Countes of Rothes was one of the most extraordinary persons for religion, and good sense, and eminent acts of charity, that was in the last age.   That her life, could it be recovered, would make a beautifull figure in our Biography.   I have litle hope of recovering it.   In the late dear years, 1697 and [169]8, she was remarkable for her charity.   She distribut many bolls of meal among the poor every week, and it was calculat that she dealt out most of the

* This Charitable Institution, " Craigcrook Mortification," was left for " assisting old men and women who have been reduced in their circumstances, and for orphans ;" and is under the management of the Presbytery of Edinburgh, two Advocates, and two Writers to the Signet.   It was bequeathed by Mr John Strachan, W. S., who died about 1719.

yearly rents of the estate that way. She had a day in the week—Friday, I think—when sick and indisposed persons came to her ; and she spoke with them, and gave them medicines gratis ; and some cheats, pretending to be objects, she discovered, and severly punished them. She was most intimat with John Archer, Alexander's father, and many eminent Christians in that neighbourhood. She was eminent in prayer and wrestling, and had many singular answers of prayer. It's pity so litle about her can nou be recovered.

We hear, Mr James Craige is again fallen ill of his spitting of blood. He recovered a litle by going to the goat-milk in May, and has preached since ; but nou it's thought he shall scarce preach any more, for his concern and seriousnes in preaching brings nou his spitting of blood on him ; and though he may dwine* for some time, yet it's not thought he can recover.

The Master of Ross, this moneth, is translated from the Board of Excise to that of Customes, where he has one thousand pound a year, and an easier post.

Mr Walter Steuart, son to worthy old Bailay Steuart, in Nilton Merns, is nou on the way to be setled at Ashkirk, in Tiviotdale. Professor Hamiltoun's interest with my Lord Minto, and other Heretors concerned, takes him there. It's the Presbytery where three of The Marrou bretheren are—Mr Boston, Wilson, and Davidson. There Mr Tailford also is. A pretty strange mixture. It's the best benefice in Scotland, for what I knou, and reconed near three thousand merks a year. Mr Wylie was transported from that to Hamiltoun. Mr Charles Gordon, a man of great sufficiency and learning, was after him.

Mr William Maxwell returns this moneth, or the end of the last, from South Carolina, wher he went, being ordeaned by the Presbytery of Glasgou, on a call brought'over by Paul Hamiltoun, about 1724, as I belive has been notticed. His setlment there did not answer expectation. He had not what could even subsist him, though single, so that in seven years' time he has expended one hundred pound of his oun. The setlments there are very precarious. If a planter or two dye, or remove to

* Linger on, continue to decline.

another place, a Congregation dissolves—that is, the rest are not able to subsist a Minister, unless he has a vein for taking a plantation, and managing it by servants; and that way Mr Stobo, who went over to Caledonia, and when that project broke in the 1700, setled at Carolina, has made himself ritch, and is worth ten thousand pound of our money. They have in Carolina nine Ministers, which meet in a Presbitry. Mr Maxwell tells me he dispensed the Supper to about sixteen communicants: That some familys were twenty-two miles distant from the place of worship, and that his charge was not much above one hundred, or therby. The debates about Subscription are warm, and four of the one side, and four of the other, when he left them. One Mr Fisher is a most sufficient man there. The contraversy is in print. See pamphlets this year.

Mr Henry Fisher, one of the Ministers there—one who, by his papers, appears a very sufficient person—Mr Maxwell tells me, is upon a work that may be very usefull; and of a long time I have wished to see somewhat done that way. He is, in his opinion, for keeping only by David's Psalms in singing, or other Scripturall songs; and much against the practice of severall Ministers in England, and some in America too, who sing their oun hymns and composure.* Mr Fisher designes a dissertation against this; and, in the meanwhile, he is going throu the Psalmes of David, and considering every verse of them, with a vieu to what should be the soul-exercise in right singing of them; and sheues that they are all properly designed for praise; and hou we, in the Neu Testament, are to praise God in singing of them, and each passage. He has gone throu twenty or thirty of the Psalmes this way, by way [of a] directory in singing; being of opinion there is no branch of our worship wherin, throu ignorance and want of a proper directory, many are further behind than that of singing.

He tells me, that Mr Coleman and Dr Cotton Mather, when alive, in a particular manner approved of his designe: That those two endeavoured to prevent Mr Fisher and Mr Smith's debate on Subscription, &c., which is nou come to the press: That in pressing mutuall forbearance, Dr Mather, I think, in a letter, acquainted Mr Fisher with this

* Compositions.

step of the Ministers of Neu England. A person in Boston, of considerable repute, and one of their constant communicants, fell into very gross errors as to the Deity of Christ, either Arrian or Socinian. They used much pains with him, in conference, to reclaim him; but all in vain. At lenth they prevailed with him to keep his opinions to himself, and got him to engage not to converse save with the Ministers, when he pleased, on these heads; and advised him to withdrau from the Table of the Lord; and he yielded; and no further nottice was taken of him, and the thing was smothered, and had no ill effects among them.

I hear the Quakers at Edinburgh are considerably altered, and are upon a concert to fix upon one among themselves to preach to them, and no others are to offer to preach; and they are to give him a sellary; and they say he reads, studyes, and discourses very accurately to them; and the Magistrates are like to agree to grant them their protection, and give their Minister some sellary yearly. His name is Erskine, a breuar.

They talk of my Lord Isla's coming doun this moneth to setle things in Scotland, and the Professor's place, to be vacated by Mr Hamiltoun's being made Principall, is not to be filled till then. It's yet uncertain whither Mr Smith, Goldie, or some other, be professor. But nou that this moneth, or the end of the last, the Earle of Seafeild and Finlater is dead, it's doubted if Isla be to come doun till the election of a Peer in his room. It's thought Colonell Douglas, nou, by his brother's death, Earle of Mortoun, will be the man.

The Earle of Seafeild's character is the same at his death that it was throu his life. He was one of the cheif agents for the Union with England, and then Chancelour; and no side trusted him much further then his interest went. He has left a great estate behind him to his son Deskford, who is commended.

[*September* 16.]—Upon the 16th of this moneth, our Presbytery transported Mr J. Anderson from Port-Glasgou to the Toun of Glasgou, unanimously. Three or four wer silent. I was not there. I was not in health, nor very willing to be present or active in the transportation. I sau he was for it himself, and the generality of the Presbytery; and I did not think it decent we should transport him, but rather referr it to the Synod; and, in my opinion, I was positive the toun of Port-Glasgou, considering that numbers of people resort, of strangers and Glasgou people, to it, might have been laid in ballance with any of the Congregations of Glasgou. Mr Anderson declared he would take it as a favour that we should not transport him, and that he was willing to live all his dayes with his people, if he could but gain one soul to Christ. It's true his stipend is small, considering the dear way of living there; but that inconvenience will be to his successor likewise. I pray we may have a right one. I rather wished Mr Anderson had gone to Renfreu. I fear his temper is too easy for Glasgou, and that he may be imposed on there.

In the end of this moneth, we had an application from Renfreu, with a petition for a Minister to preach and moderat a call to one not named; but we kneu it was to Mr R. Paton, of Haddingtoun, in whom the different partys there centered. My Lord Dundonald was for Mr Millar of Neilstoun, the one-half of the Colledge for Mr Rouat,* and the Principal for Mr Bruce in Killellan: But Blythwood opposed Mr Millar, and fell in with Lord Miltoun, who had the presentation in his hand to fill up in concert with P[rofessor] Hamiltoun, who was, as is given out, for Mr Millar; but that came to nothing. Mr Paton is under uneasinesses with his collegue and the Magistrats of Haddingtoun, because of his mixing in their elections; and has but a very small stipend; and all the Heretors are come in to him. He came West in Agust, and preached twice at Glasgow, where the people [of] Renfrew heard him; many mo than ever heard Mr M'Dermitt, or Mr N. Campbell; and, I doubt not, he will setle there. The Presbytery sent Mr Millar to try the inclinations of the people, and session, and heretors.

In the end of the moneth, Mr Patrick Bruce called an occasionall meeting of the Presbitry, and acquainted them ther wer two gentlmen come over from Ireland with a call to him from his father's congregation,

* At Dunlop.

who dyed in the beginning of this year.   The Presbytery met and summoned the parish to the third Wensday of October, when, no doubt, he will be transported.   He was brought over to Killellan, with promises to provide better for him.   He was pushed for to be setled in Glasgou and in Renfreu, but without success.   He was made to hope, by Sir John Shaues means, and Collonel Cathcart, that he would be made one of the King's Chaplains or Almoner ; but no vacancy hapned, and that misgave ;* and so he returns to Ireland again.   He has spent some money in his transportation ; but his health is really ill since he came here.

October, 1730.—This moneth begins generally with the Magistrats' election at Glasgou.   Ther was much to do this year.   The party before headed by P[rovost] Stark† brought in the Stirlings, and they brought in the Buchanans ; but, in the course of managment, the Buchanans and Stirlings fell by the ears, and plotted one another's destruction.   Provest Stirling's managment does not please the toun, and he has not been popu[lar] : he has been reconed to bring in the toun to the family of Argyle, and brought in Ministers suspected to be on that side, and not very pleasing to the toun.   These two partys breaking, the old side wer stronger than any in the Councill ; and B[ailie] Murdoch was agreed on as Provest by both sides, as an easy man, who had no follouing‡ in the Councill.   When the election came on, the Stirlings joyned Pr[ovost] Stark's party against the Buchanans, and Walter Stirling was chosen eldest Bailay ; but then he has none save his brother in the Councill, and two or three more that he [can] recon on ; and John Culters, and one [James] Peacock, who is of Pr[ovost] Stark's side. The Buchanans seem intirely out, and have no man on their side ; all depends on the turns in Councill.

[*October* 6.]—Our Synod met October 6.   We had a very good and pointed sermon from Mr James Laury, Minister in Dalrymple, upon Urim and Thummim.   Mr John M'Lauran, Minister at Glasgou, was

---

* Failed.   † He was Provost in 1725 and 1726.   ‡ Supporters.

chosen Moderator.   At the last Synod at Air, there was not the representation of a Synod; not ten, if so many, beside the Presbyteries of
Air and Irwin; and, except upon speciall party affairs, we never have
an appearance of a Synod but at Glasgou.   The last Synod left the
absents to be censured by this Synod themselves, and not by a Committy; and about twenty-four crouns wer exacted.* This led the Synod
to consider what was proper to be done for remedying this evil, and a
Committy was appointed.   There the matter was reasoned at some
lenth.   The bretheren of Air and Irwine declared their unwillingnes to
separat from us on this side, and that they would not submitt without
an appeal to the Assembly.   They said, that, being such a large meeting as seven Presbitrys, our counsells, in ardous cases, wer better, and
had much more weight: That we had been together forty year and
more : That the touns of Air and Irwine had a claim upon us : That it
was lazines, which should not be yielded to, which hindered the bretheren in the five Presbitrys not to come to Air and Irwine, which
would still grou when yeilded to : That if our good laues as to absents
wer execut, as we wer beginning to do, they would secure attendance.
We urged, that our meeting with the Presbyteries of Air and Irwine
was really without rule : That there was no act of Assembly for it, but
only permissive in the 1638 : That, originally, we wer two Synods :
That the old Ministers at the Revolution wer for our separating : That
we wer too numerouse a meeting for bussines and any closs attendance :
That it was unreasonable to bring the bretheren of Air thirty-six miles
or more to our meeting at Glasgou; or force Dumbartan, Glasgou, and
Lanerk, to Air : That it was not to be thought of that Synods would be
keept at Air by the execution of our money-laues : That the very doing
of this, and examination of absents, took up the bulk of our time when
met at Synods; and it was a shame our time was so spent : That bussines was not at all done at Air and Irwine, and it was really lossing
that meeting of Synod; and, therfor, it was proposed that we should
still meet at Glasgou, because, without separating the Synods, which we
had not so much in our pouer as the fixing of the place, the face of a

----

* As a penalty for absence without a sufficient excuse.

Synod would be better keeped up; and the bretheren of Air that wer at distance from Glasgou, wer far feuer than these of Dumbartan, Glasgou, Hamiltoun, and Lanerk, from Air; and Glasgou much more centricall than Air or Irwine to the most part of members: That the touns in the West could not accommodat us: That they had no claim, and really litle profit, by our coming: That the bulk of Ministers in the West wer willing, once a year, or it may be twice, to come to Glasgou on bussines. Kilmarnock was proposed as more centricall than Air or Irwine; but then it was doubted if we could be accomodate there. In a word, it was urged by the bretheren of the West, that this proposall [of] meeting still at Glasgou was a forcing them to divide from us, which they wer unwilling to do.

To that it was said, that we did not urge a division; and, if they found meetings at Glasgou inconvenient, they might weel meet in a Synod by themselves, and have five Presbitrys—four of them of ten Ministers, and one of nine. After long debates, we came in, by a scrimp vote,* to propose to the Synod that there should be three meetings at Glasgou for one in the West; and that this was to be remitted to Presbitrys to bring in their report to next Synod. This the Synod went into.†

We had, next, Mr Dick's transportation from Carluke to Glasgou, referred by the Presbytery of Lanerk to the Synod. Mr Dick appeared alone—not one of his people with him. There was a letter from one of his heretors, telling that they valued their Minister, but wer hopeles to keep him; and so did not appear. Mr Dick, in two or three words, said he had a very loving people, and had lived seventeen years with them, he hoped not without fruit: that he was sensible of his unfittnes for Glasgou, but submitted to the Synod. Ther was no reasoning in the Synod about it, and he was transported, and the ordination appointed on the 28th of October.

We had the affair of Balfron before us, of which above. The Presbytery‡ read a representation of the affair to the Synod, for advice and their interposition. Therin they stated the case, and declared their unanimouse resolution not to setle the presentee, while matters stood thus,

---

* A narrow majority.   † Agreed to.   ‡ Of Dumbarton.

as what was contrary to their principles ; and, indeed, the representation was aboundantly pointed.   This came into the Overtures,* and it was yeilded that we should instruct our commissioners to the Commission to joyne the Presbytery of Dumbartan ; but I and some others urged a letter from the Synod to the Commission.   This was much opposed, as countenancing the Presbytery of Dumbartan in their standing out against the Commission's sentence, as making us partys, and what would make a noise, and what the Commission could not go into, it not being in their pouer to alter what they had formerly done in a prior meeting.   To that it was answered, that when a Presbytery took a resolution that they thought agreeable to our constitution, they should, if we wer of the same opinion, be supported in it : That all [that] was sought was a sist, and going no further till the Assembly ; which was very reasonable.   And so, the Synod went in to a letter to the Commission, wherin we represent the state as above, and declare that it's not from any want of respect to the Commission that the Presbytery do not fall in with their act in Agust ; and desire they may sist till the Generall Assembly take this matter in their hand.   What effect this will have, I knou not.   It will make a noise, and let the Commission see that Synods and Presbyteries will not still overlook their strange procedure in setling of parishes ; and if they proceed and clap a Commity to the Presbytery for setling Mr Sinclair, without an elder, and contrary to the whole inclinations of the people, it's probable our next Synod (at least I think it's our duty) will make a plainer representation of our principles.

We had a motion for a Thanksgiving for the last harvest ; but there did not appear such peculiar things, though our harvest be a great blessing, as to set apart a speciall day.   And so it was not urged much.   Ther is a hazard in going in to appointments of fasts and thanksgivings without very plain causes, and a hazard in neglecting them when ther are causes clear and evident.

The Heretors of Renfreu made an application to our Presbytery at the Synod for drauing up a call to Mr Paton on Munday next, and moderating next Wensday, that it might be ready against the Synod of

---

* Committee for Overtures.

Lothian, to meet November 2, which they reconed would be of some use to them, and would forward their affair. We compleaned that the heads of familys wer not duly advertised by Mr R. Millar. We wer all strangers to Mr Paton, but yeilded to send two to moderat the call, so as it might come in October 28. We thought it very suddain to do this Munday next.

The Synod of Stirling met the week after ours. I hear, from a Minister who was there some time, that they had very litle before them. There was one pretty odd case—one M'Cartney, or a name like this—a young lad that has been blind from his infancy, and has been a student at Edinburgh for some time, and every one ouns he has very uncommon abilitys, and hath made a great progress in all kind of learning. He has good testimonialls, and nothing I hear of is objected to his character, save some letters he wrote, or rather caused write, wherin he sheues some keeness to be licensed, and talks with some measure of freedom of the Ministers who wer not for his passing tryalls. Houever, these wer not insisted on. He was proposed to the Presbytery of Stirling; and they divided on this matter; and it came by a reference to the Synod. There the matter was argued. Litle could be said as to his letters. What was most urged was his face and countenance, which has somewhat (as generally all blind people have) uncomly about it. He has a protuberance on his one eye, and his face is spoted, and his other eye has a pearle upon it. It was urged that, under the lau of Moses, such wer excluded from sanctuary service; and his uncomlynes was pretty much insisted on. Mr Archibald Campbell, at Larbert, who has not yet been at Saint Andreus,* was the great reasoner for the blind lad; and argued, that nothing in his face was disagreable to his tast; that this was his misfortune; and he urged much that he and other students that had spent their means in four or six years attending Divinity lessons, and wer not disqualified according to the Rules of the Church, had a claim and a kind of tacit right to plead that he should have the benefit of a license to preach, if they had no other disqualification save their

* Where he was appointed Professor of History.

countenance. He had a fling at Mr Muir in Stirling, as was thought, when he added, that Ministers that in preaching and prayer disfigured their countenance, and, by their tone and singing, their voice, wer much more disagreable to him in the pulpit than this youth would be if he wer in a pulpit with all his disadvantages. Houever, it was the unanimouse opinion of the Committy that the Presbytery should delay entering him on tryalls.

He tells me Mr Campbell's Essay on the Apostles makes a great noise in that Synod. When Mr Campbell went to London this year, his freind, Dr Innies, seemed not to knou him; and till Mr Campbell had produced some letters of his, which [he] had with him, made him alter his method, the Doctor was like to have stood it out; but, hearing of these, he altered his measures, and, as I hear, gave Mr Campbell one hundred guineas to be soft and easy. It's said, when he got ac[cess] to the Chancelour, and ouned himself the author of the Enquiry, the Chancelor said he took Dr Innies to have been the author, and gote him a living of two hundred pound; and nou, since he was mistaken, he was ready to give it, or as good to him, if he would stay in England. Mr Campbell thanked him, and said, if he had any talents which might be usefull, he chose rather to use them in his oun country; and if his Lordship could help him to any thing consistent with that, he would be in his debt. So, the Chancelor got him to be Professor of History at Saint Andreus. My informer sayes he is reconed hardy, hasty, and forward, and imprudent in publishing his pamphlet at this juncture, because it will not recomend him at Saint Andreus.

The Synod of Stirling had another case before them of a student, Hepburn, in the Presbytery of Auchterarder. He was a Minister's son, and was in some post in Herriot's Hospitall, and fell out with some of his superiors there; and in a tavern, it seems, run out to passion, some say cursing, and drukenes. He retired, and was put on tryalls by the Presbytery of Auchterarder, where his father, they say, was a Minister. The Presbytery of Edinburgh wrote a letter to the Presbytery of Auchterarder, signifying to them that he was under scandall, and desiring them to sist; but, upon Hepburn's application to the Presbytery of Edinburgh, in six or eight weeks he brought a full testimoniall from them. This made a neu demurr; and when the Synod came, the book of the Presbytery of Edinburgh was revised. The Synod of Lothian, in their attestation, signifyed their disapprobation of the dissent that was entered into by a good many members against the testimoniall to Hepburn. Upon which the Presbytery of Auchterarder, still demurring, referred the matter to the Synod of Stirling; and they wer on it when he left Stirling, and had not ended the affair.

They had a reference from the Presbytery of Dunkeld, about one M'Laggan, I think, that is in hazard of joyning Mr Glass in his Independent notions. They recomended it to the Presbytery to deal with him by conference, and all proper methods, to prevent his defection.

[*October* 10.]—Upon October 10, the Colledge of Glasgou sat doun, as usuall. I have before notticed Mr Carmichael's death, and the Colledge calling Mr Francis Hutchison. They say, by an act of visitation upon a vacancy, the eldest master (when they wer fixed two years since to particular classes, and not to go throu with their scholars, Logicks, Ethicks, and Physicks, as formerly) was alloued upon a vacancy to chuse if he would take himself to that class or not. Mr J. Loudoun formerly had the Logick Class, and was not so much for Mr Hutcheson's coming. It was said he was easy,* since, being eldest master, he had his choice to teach Ethicks or the Morall [Philosophy] Class himself. Soon after the invitation of Mr Hutchison, he went to England, to the Bath, and passed the summer, and came home October 9. When Colledge mett, they say ther are about twenty English students come doun, expecting Mr Hutcheson was to teach Morality,† for which, by his enquiry into the Idea and Beauty of Virtue, and his book on the Passions, he is highly esteemed in England. Mr Hutcheson was not come over from Ireland. So great was the expectation of the students which Class Mr Loudon would choice. He and the Principall came doun together, and Mr Loudon went in to the Morality Class, wher his Logick scholars last year, such as wer come up, wer conveened. Upon this the English students wer disgusted, and did not enter. It seems to have been a concerted thing. In the afternoon a Faculty was called; and a paper was

---

* Indifferent.   † Moral Philosophy.

presented by the English students, signifying that they wer come doun in expectation that Mr H[utcheson] should teach Morality, and their parents and freinds sent them on this view hither, and if it was otherwise, they wer resolved all of them to go to Edinburgh. In short, Loudon was so dunned* by the rest of the Masters, that he yeilded to let Mr H[utcheson] have the Morality Class for this year. He† is used with teaching the Logicks. It's generally the stronger Class. He had asserted his right, as eldest master, to take his choice, and yet for the satisfying of his collegues and strangers, he quit his claim by an act of self-denyall.

Mr John Grant, Minister of Aflect, brother-in-lau to Mr Campbell, the famouse architect, has been, upon the account of his legacy from Mr Campbell, [away] from his parish (where he has left a preacher whom he satisfyes‡) about two years or less. They say he has offers of a meeting at London; but the reall cause of his stay, I am told, is a lau-suit he has with his sister-in-lau, Mr Campbell's lady, or some of his freinds.§ The case is this: Mr Campbell left by his will about twelve thousand pound to his sister, Mrs Grant, and her children. His testament was made and finished in deu time before his death; but within the term directed by the lau of England, he, ignorant of the lau, added on the margine of his testament a thousand pound more, or some such summ, to Mrs Grant or her children. This, it seems, is pretended to make the whole paper void and null by the English formes, and that all he has comes to his relict during her life, who offers Mrs Grant five thousand pound, or some such thing; but they can not agree, and are gone to lau. This is among the many instances we have of the vanity of riches, and high expectations from them, and the uncertainty of the most promising things this way.

[*October* 14.]—On the 14th of this moneth, the Dean of Gild of Glasgou was chosen. We heard severall named, particularly B[ailie] Orr, but it's said he declined it. But Mr William Cunningham, Craigend's son, is chosen, of whom we had no hints formerly; and they say he is

---

* Pressed.   † Mr Loudoun.   ‡ Pays for his services.   § Relations.

brought in against the mind of the Stirlings and Buchanans. Whither it's so or not, time will discover.

The same day, our Presbitry met and unanimously transported Mr Patrick Bruce from the parish of Killellan to his father's parish in Ireland, where he has no great encouragement either. That people wer earnest to have him. He was willing to go, and, indeed, his health hath been very ill since he came among us, and his encouragement at Killellan is very small. His freinds, Barrochan family and Ladiland, whose daughter he married, designed him for some better post, Glasgou, Renfreu, and even one of the King's Chaplains wer spoke of, but they could not be got done. He is a considerable loser by his transportation to Scotland and going back ; a thousand pound Sterling or more ; and his stipend at Drummore was better, I am told, than in the parish he is no[w] going to. It was given out that he was uneasy with his neighbours in Ireland ; and I hope he was sincere in his vieus in coming hither, being a grave, modest-like man ; but I never see changes by Ministers promoted by their freinds from secular and worldly vieus, and their changing and couping from place to place, as men do horses and merchandize, but it's witnessed against, some way or other, and people's expectations are often blasted.

About this time Mr Hutcheson came to Glasgou, and about eighteen or twenty of his former students at Dublin with him. He is well spoke of. He teaches Mr Carmichael's Compend and Puffendorf, and speaks with much veneration of him,* which at least is an evidence of his prudence. He is very closs in examining the lads on the Sabbath night as to the sermon, and seriouse in his sacred lesson on the Munday ; and he has many, not scholars, in the rest of the classes, who wait on his privat classes, severall tradsmen and youths in the toun.

There is a Highland gentlman, who is not throughly master of his reason, yet does hurt to nobody, who rides up and doun the country with a servant, Campble,† I think, of Glengyle, a stately proper person of a man, with this oddity about him, that from his birth one of his thighs is,

* Professor Carmichael, his predecessor.
† Gregor M'Gregor, (or James Graham,) of Glengyle. He was subject to occasional insanity. From the black spot on his knee, he was called Glune-dhu.

they say, coal black, and is generally termed the Gentlman with the Black Thigh. Some of the old prophesys, it's added, Rhymer* or others, speak of one in the Highlands to be born with a black thigh, in whose time great changes are to be.   The fact seems certain enough that his thigh is discoloured.

About this time I hear of a very melancholy accident, or Providence rather, in Glasgou.   One Robert Scot, a tradsman there, hath had his wife distempered for severall moneths, and the woman is under the reputation of piety formerly.   Lately she is turned furiouse.   Her husband used to have much influence upon her ; and in dealing with her one day she bitt him in the arm.   The man, in a feu dayes, turned distempered and mad, and dyed of the bite, and in a rage.   We are not suitably thankfull for our reason and senses ; and it's a very great omission we have not publick houses for distempered people.

October 28.—Mr Robert Paton's call was drauen to Renfreu.   The Heretors centered† in him, and the people wer willing to be setled.   A feu of them heard him, and some wer pleased, others not so much. Ther was no opposition made, no presentation spoke of, and, from different vieus, the Heretors concurred, and the setlment goes harmoniously on.   I wish them blessings one to another.

[*October* 29.]—Upon the 29th, Mr J. Anderson and Mr J. Dick wer received by Mr M'Laurin in Glasgou.   I have said already hou matters stood as to them.   It's plain the Ministers could make no other of it.   The people and sessions wer much overuled, as is nou too ordinary in setlments.   I doubt, in some feu years, they may be content they had been wher they wer formerly, among a loving and kindly people. The enterteanment was in Hutcheson's Hospitall, the company being great.

November [3,] 1730.—Upon the 30th of this moneth, Mr Francis Hutcheson was publickly admitted, and had his inaugurall discourse. It's in print, and I need say no more of it.   He had not time, I knou,

* Thomas of Ercildoun, so called.   † United.

to form it, and it's upon a very safe generall subject. I knou he communicat it to Mr M'Laurin and Mr Anderson, and some litle amendments wer made upon it, of no great importance. He delivered it very fast and lou, being a modest man, and it was not well understood. His character and carriage seems prudent and cautious, and that will be the best vidimus of him.

At this time I was surprized with the breaking out of the irregular marriage of K[atharine] W[odrow,] my cusine, about eight dayes before she brought forth her child to Somervail, a coppersmith. Nothing like this was expected from her; and if I could [have] promised any thing for any body for modesty and gravity, it would have been for her. Her concealing the marriage has dashed her reputation. Reasons are given for it; but her conduct has been suspicious; and it's well her worthy father is in heaven! The longer I live, the more unexpected things I meet with, and even among my oun relations.

The Commission met at the ordinary time. What is done by the Commission is nou generally pretty fully in the Edinburgh paper; and I mind little remarkable save the case of the parish of Balfron, wher things wer pushed most unaccountably. In Agust, Mr Sinclair's call was susteaned, though both Mr Buchanan's call and it were ordered to be moderat; and, by* all calculations, Sinclair's call had the minority, and not the shaddou of the parish with [it,] nor the other almost either; and yet they approve the worst call of the two, and that when the whole Presbitry and the whole Synod of the bounds wer unanimously against it, and declared so much to the Commission. Our Letter from the Synod was read, but laid aside. At this time the Commission adjoyn a large Committy to the Presbytery, and ordean them to proceed to tryalls; but before the Commission came to intimate this, they wer not a quorum, and so nothing was done in that affair.

They had Mr Archibald's case before them likewise. He is a follouer of Mr Glass in some things, but a better man, though not of such abilitys. Professor Hamiltoun was outvotted in Mr Glasses deposition. After his keenest reasoning, he could not get his freinds in England

* Contrary to, beyond.

gratifyed (as is said) in that matter ; though, I am ready to think, no Independant in England would stand up for Mr Glass his principles ; and it was not for Independency meerly he was deposed, but for divisive schismaticall principles. Nou, it seems, P[rofessor] H[amilton] would sheu his weight in Judicatorys by preventing Mr Archibald's deposition, though of the same professed principles with Mr Glass ; and, as Mr Archibald is only declared not Minister of Guthrie, and no Minister of this Church,* this plainly makes the Commission last year clash with the Commission this year, in different sentences upon the same matter, and very much exposes the Judicatorys of this Church in the eyes of on-lookers.

During the Commission's meeting, my son Sandy dyed, in the Thursday morning, as stands elsewhere. He was a smart and pleasant boy, with many excellent qualitys. He was long under trouble, and yet got much patience ; and had much peace and some comfort at his death, which should make me silent.

The Synod of Lothian had the affair of Mr Finlater's setlement at Linton. The heretors wer generally for the setlment, and the Patron, and, I hear, the plurality of elders ; but that is contradicted. However, the Synod ordered the Presbytery to go on, and added a Committy to them, at their desire, to setle him. When the edict was served, the people wer so averse, that they would not give the neighbouring Minister, who came to preach, liberty to preach nor serve the edict. They would not give him lodging in the parish the night before. They took† the copy of the edict, upon which soldiers wer sent out, and six or eight of them taken prisoners to Edinburgh, and some let out on bail. This makes great noise, and is turning a common thing. The setlment in January was peaceable ; the souldiers were quartered in the parish, but not in armes, at the ordination, as was given out. Our troubles are grouing as to setlments, and that cheifly by Ministers yeilding to Patrons and setlments direct cross to the inclinations of the people. I am affrayed, if things continou at the rate they are, Presbitry and Ministers loss the affections of the common people by thir setlments against the

---

* Without being deposed from the Ministry.   † Carried off.

plurality of heretors and people's inclinations, as ever the Episcopall Ministers were, under the late reigns; and when we loss the inclinations of the people, we are not much to lean to the affections of the noblmen and gentlmen, men whom we now strive to please in setlments.

This moneth, we hear, Duke of Hamiltoun, who had presented this Mr Finlater to Cambuslang, and keeped them vacant till he was setled these seven years, has nou condescended to Mr M'Culloch's setlment there, whom the people wer for. But nou Westburn* draues back.

December, 1730.—This moneth, John Luke, merchant in Glasgou, who has been tender and very brashy† these many moneths, turned very ill. He is astmatick, and under a complication of ill. I have been in his freindship these thirty years. He was my cautioner in the Library, and, ever since, a true freind; and, this moneth, gave me a fresh proofe of his freindship, under vieu of death. He was at the Sacrament in Glasgou this moneth, out of case to goe out any of the dyets,‡ yet had an earnest desire to communicat, and was caryed in a chair to Mr Hamiltoun's Church; and went in, and heard a Table served, and communicat, and came home the same way. This, I think, was the last publick worship ever he was present at; and he was exceeding easy after it, and met with his last feeding-meal§ there.

The designe of a Work-house for the poor was set on foot this moneth: See the papers printed on this subject. I took occasion to give a hint commending the designe, and encouraging to it in my sermon, Sabbath night, Laigh Kirk. It was not written, and only in a feu transient sentences. Houever, I had thanks for it by the Ministers and people concerned. See Mr M'Laurin's Letters this and following [month.] I was pressed afterwards to come in and preach on a week-day before the subscriptions; but that I declined, as very improper, and what was the work of the Mihisters of Glasgou.

Upon the Munday's night after the Sacrament, Mr M'Laurin, Hamiltoun, Rob, P. Maxwell, and I, met and talked of what was proper to do

---

* Hamilton of.   † Sickly, poorly; literally, subject to *water-brash.*   ‡ Week-day sermons.
§ Of spiritual nourishment.

as to Mr S[imso]n and the next Assembly. Mr Hamiltoun told us Mr Simson had visited him on Wensday before the fast, and had been four hours with him in his room. He told him before the Communion, he was willing to talk what had passed these three or four years over with him, thinking he had been exceedingly wronged by him and his bretheren. They entered to the detail, and Mr Simson had nothing but what had been again and again answered, both publickly and privatly. He said, that the most considerable Ministers in the Church, and some of the most pious, wer of opinion he had been hardly treated. When asked, Wherin? he had nothing to offer but what hath been said over and over, and as often answered. When urged that he was sensible ther was ground for all that had been done, in his very retractations, he said that he was still of the same sentiments ever he had been, and he was intirely mistaken when thought to be changed. On the whole, he and his freinds openly regrate their not applying to the last Assembly, who, they think, would have done Mr Simson justice, and restored him. We agreed to write to the different corners of the Church, and acquaint Ministers of the probable designes to restore Mr Simson next Assembly, and press them to be on their guard. It was laid on Mr Hamiltoun, Mr M'Laurin, and me, to write. See my Letters this and next moneth.

Mr Simson and his freinds give it out, that he had the offer of the Professorship of Ecclesiasticall History and Divinity at Saint Andreus, (which Mr Campbell, of Larbert, has since got,) and refused it. If so be as they represent, which I very much doubt, it looks as if Mr Simson wer very sure of keeping his post at Glasgou, and being restored to teaching; otherwise one can scarce think he would have neglected one of the best setlments in Scotland—one hundred pound, or one hundred and sixty pound, as some call it, and preferred an uncertainty to it. But I hesitate a litle if he had that Professorship in his offer.

Mr Francis Hutcheson is much commended since he came here. He carrys himself gravely, and will not meet in their clubs at night, nor drink: That he is not Arminian, but strictly opposite to these principles: That he sayes, on reflection he sayes, he is not throughly satisfyed in the principles, or rather some superstructures on which his book upon the Beauty of Virtue [is founded ;] and if he publish another edition, he designes to alter severall things : That he is most intimat with Mr William Anderson, Mr John M'Laurin, and uses most freedom with them : That he seems to be under some very serious impressions from his father's death, and that of one of his children : That he is very full and positive for the restoring the discipline of the College, keeping the students to rules, catalogues, exact hours, &c., wherein ther is certainly a very great decay ; so that, I hope, ther will be very good effects of his being at this juncture come to this country. In party matters, and some politicks, as to smaller matters, it's like he will be in the side with Mr Dunlop ; but, in the main matters, it looks as he would be very usefull.

Mr William Anderson tells me that, last summer, he hapned to be in conversation with a Deist, a person of considerable rank. They wer alone, and they very soon fell upon the debate betwixt us and Deists. After the person had used the best arguments he had, and Mr Anderson had given such answers as offered to [him,] the other fell upon the debates as to Church Government. The Deist said, " You will be, perhaps, surprized that I am intirely upon your side, and a Presbiterian in this matter ! But I see that Presbitry is the only constitution agreable to the libertys of mankind ; and I am really perswaded that Ministers in equality, and minding their proper bussines, are exceeding usefull in a society, and necessary to it."

In talking of Mr Wisheart's diploma for being Doctor in Divinity, I was told that the Colledge of Glasgou gave it to him meerly as a member of their society ; and when I enquired, How Mr Grosvenour came to be joyned with him in it ? I was told, Mr Wisheart recomended him, and it was from that intirely that they went in to him.

The above said person tells me that he is well informed that the two brothers, the Duke of A[rgyll] and Earl of Isla, take much pains to have some interest in all the variouse societys in Scotland, and to have some throughly engaged to their side every where. Every body sees it in the Members of Parliament, the Lords of Session, the setlments of Ministers, and particular Presbyteries in the General Assembly. Indeed, I thought the lauers had been pretty free from party influence, save by

other engagments ; but he assures me that, for these many years, a
young advocate never sooner appears in the House, and discovers his
parts and rising genius, but he has some favour sheuen him, or some
gratuity and pension given him by one of the brothers, or some promise
made to him   Thus universally carefull are they to spread and secure
their influence.

Mr Anderson tells me, that he was a scholar to, and most intimate
with, Professor Reeland,* about the 1720.   He gives him a high encomium for piety and regard to pious persons, for exceeding great diligence, and a peculiar regard to our Scots students, who did well.   My
informer observed a mistake in Mr Reeland's solution of the difficulty,
arising from the Scripture account of the brazen-sea ; its circumference
arising from the geometricall rules as to the proportion 'twixt a circumference and diameter ; and, one day, set doun another solution of it,
with a sort of demonstration of it from principles of Geometry ; and desired the Professor to read it over, and consider whither it was consistent with his, as it stands, I think, in the first or second edition of his
Antiquitates Hebraicæ.   Mr Reeland read it over, and presently sau it
was eversive of his oun solution, and told him he would think on it.
Next time they met he thanked him for communicating it to him, and
letting him see his mistake, that in the next edition he would correct it,
and insert his paper, and give him publick thanks.   Mr Reeland dyed a
litle after of the small pocks.   He had a child that fell ill of them, whom
he loved dearly ; and whenever he took them he had some kind of pre-
sensation that he was to take them, and was to dye of them.   He told
some of his freinds that such a thought had seized him ; that he could
not account for it, yea, he was easy under the thoughts of it, beliving
he was to make a happy change by death, if God was to order it out.
Only he took care to conceal it from his wife, who loved him dearly.
Accordingly, in eight or ten dayes he sickned, and in a litle time dyed
of that distemper.   My informer was with him under his illnes.   He
was most calm and submissive to the Divine will, but did not express
his fears of death, his wife being by him.

* Roland.

He told me, that Professor Mark was, though Anti-Cocceian, yet not a strict keeper of the Sabbath. That, on the Saturndays, he used to go out to his country house; and, on the Sabbath, did not spend his time after Divine worship but in his garden; and would be somtimes seen pruning his treas, and ordering his flouers.

That the Lutherans are eminently taken up in signing hymns of a sacred nature; and this has been used by them since the Reformation. They sing much in their publick worship; and, every morning before they fall to their trades and bussines, sing some hymns, each of them by themselves; and, through the day, frequently, when at their trades or day's labour, that alloues singing, they are very frequently repeting hymns melodiously when at their ordinary bussines, and when going from one place to another; and some (seem) to do this with much pleasure, and devotion, and seriousnes.

This moneth, towards the end of it, Mr Coats* and the people of the Gorballs entered to a concert for supplying the people there with catechising and sermon, as I hear, when they cannot get actuall Ministers, as they have got done pretty much for the year bygone. They agreed to give Mr W. Broun, and Mr James Sloss, six pound yearly, for examining the people, as an ease to Mr Coats; and that they should have, *per vices*, the care of supplying the Church with preaching, when not otherwise supplyed, and be satisfyed for this. The people are generally set on Mr Broun for their preacher, and Mr Sloss is likewise very acceptable.

They are going throu Glasgou and the neighbourhood for a supply for a fund to a Minister's stipend, and have considerable promises and gifts. Mr John Orr, who has done so many good things with his money, hath offered them one hundred merk; and, further, has offered to bind himself for them in five hundred merks a year for a Minister, and take his payment from them as they could give it him.

This moneth, and formerly, we have many storys about Mr W. Wisheart, his being in uneasy circumstances at London. Sometimes it's said that his wife does not keep her health at all at London, and is

* Minister of Govan.

advised to return to Scotland. At other times they say that he has
sent doun orders to enlarge his little house in the head of the Green,*
and that he is coming doun this spring to live in it. This seems to be
certain, that he and the Scots Congregation at London are not on very
good terms. I am told, by one who was his hearer, six or seven weeks
ago, that his auditory was exceeding thin; that ther wer not one hundred hearers; that his sermon was all upon calumny, and reproach, and
evil speaking. Some say, that his intimacy with Mr Chandler, and
other violent Non-subscribers, have much broken him and his people.
Others, that are his friends, deny all this, and say he is exceedingly
liked at London; that he hath an invitation to the Court end of the
town, where they offer to build him a neu Meeting-house. What to
belive, on these different reports, I cannot say; a little time may discover it. Houever, as I have observed, when secular vieus enter into
Ministers going from one place to another, I do not ordinarly see such
changes very satisfying to Minister or people. Whither this be the
case here, I do not knou.

Mr Loudon, who has been in England this summer, tells me that Mr
Thomas Burnet, nou the only surviving son of the knouen Bishop Burnet, who has his father's History, I am told, in his hands to publish,
i. e., the Second Volume, is in a strait for money, and, it's hoped, will
publish his father's book; and if he do, it's hoped it will be the more
uncastrat and unaltered, because, at present, he is malcontent and disgusted with the present Ministry. The case is this:—Mr Thomas
Burnet was taken nottice of, by the Courts of Hannover, in Bulingbrock's
administration, for his pamphlet, dedicat to Bullingbrock, intituled, " A
Certain Account of a Certain Person, &c., proving that the Pretender
is indeed James the Third." He was made, in King George I. reigne,
the King's Envoy to the Courts of Germany; and, in some time after,
he was the King's Resident in Genua, or some toun in Italy. Upon
King George II. his accession, and Sir Robert Walpool's administration,
he had no money due to him for his sellary remitted to him, and the
Government oued him L.6000 or L.8000. When he could have no

---

* Near where the Washing-house stands at present.

payment, without laying doun his character, he resolved to come home, and solicit his oun arrears. He came by Paris ; and there some villan, a Jacobite, attacked him, in order to murder him. Mr Burnet escaped, but sent over an express, with a complaint on the attack made on him. The murderer in designe came over to London sooner than his express, and applyed to Sir Robert last year, or the preceeding ; gave the story another turn, and pretended to reveal the Jacobites' secrets to Sir Robert, who is very much taken with such renegados. When Mr Burnet's express came over, Sir Robert parryd off the attack, and it came to nothing. Mr Burnet came over himself, but too late. Sir Robert was engaged ; and he had litle access, [and] no redress against the villan : and when he solicited for his arrears, he could get nothing from the Treasury, and came to be pretty much straitned. So that nou, they say, he is a discontented Whig, and has thoughts of publishing his father's History, by which he will probably get as much as may releive him of his straits ; and if it be published in his present humor, ther will be no amendments nor suppressions of truth.

The same person tells me, that Lord Carteret has been exceeding bussy against Sir Robert Walpool in England, and has formed a very considerable party both among the House of Commons and the Nobility, and has been gathering matter for an Impeachment. We have a generall talk, this moneth, of a double impeachment, on by Sir Robert, in the House of Peers, against Carteret ; and another, in the Commons, against Sir Robert. But when the parliament sits doun, no hint of this. The party against Sir Robert, in both Houses, seems not at all to be increased, but as litle as last year.

He tells [me,] the narrounes of the Queen is much talked of in England. Ther was a very rich stuffe that she sent for, the richest that has been in England ; and when she sau it, she liked it, but came not to the price by ten or twenty pounds, and it was returned. When it came back, Alderman Parsons sau it, and streight payed the price, and sent it home to his lady. In some hours she took a liking to the cloath, and sent for it again. The merchant told it was sold. The

Queen sent again, to knou to whom? It was told; and she sent to Mrs Parsons to have it; but that could not be done.   Another instance was a gold snuff-box the Prince, when he had got some money, bought in a toy shop, and gave seventy gineas for it.   In a day or two he gave it to one of his sisters.   The Queen sau it in her hand, and asked hou she came by it? That was told: the Prince called for, and asked where he got it? He told.   A servant was sent to the shop with a complaint that the box was too dear; and fifty gineas wer offered, otherwise the box was to be returned.   The people sent word it could not be afforded, and they had scarce a ginea of profite: that they sold it rather easier to the Prince than to another.   The box was returned, and the money taken back.   These things make some noise in Old England.

He tells that severall of the Dissenters in England are turning Arrian; and yet ther is a good body of them free.   Many more would, probably, discover themselves, did not their people's giving up with them, and calling others, prevent this. This makes them conceal themselves as long as they can: That the interest of the Non-subscribers is daily lossing ground, and severall of the Non-subscribers are going off to the Church.   Our publick prints bear this; one particularly, very rich, and having a good sellary, went over to a less in the Church.

M.DCC.XXXI.

January, 1731.—Ther is not much remarkable, this moneth, that I mind of, save what is in the prints, and Letters to me. The Parliament meets, and the King's speech leaves us in the same state of uncertainty that we have been in, as to publick affairs, these severall years. The partys in Parliament are much as formerly, and seem to gain very litle ground one upon another. We wer dunned with impeachments and warm speeches, but not much that way hath appeared. It's said, that money keeps all quiet; and an incident is fallen in, the end of this moneth, which makes matters much more easy to Sir Robert—the Duke of Parma's death; which will probably unite the Empire of Spain, and preserve our peace.

The beginning of this moneth, William Niven, younger, dyes suddainly; which, with the unsetlednes* of the remaining son, is a very heavy rod to that honest family.

Mr Andrew Gray's setlment at New Kilpatrick goes on. The Presbitry find his call good; and it's certain he has the plurality of legall callers, as they are termed, heretors and elders; and he has a good number of the heads of familys, near an equality with the other side. There is no opposition made but what floues from a particular disgust, not at him, but the Duke of Montrose,† and picks [piques] among the heretors themselves. The Presbytery resolve to go throu with the setlment; and though the opposers have appealed to the Commission or Synod, (which meets first,) yet they are going [on] with his tryalls, and will setle him before the Synod.

We have the accounts continouing of Mr Wisheart's uneasy circum-

---

* Unsteadiness.   † The Patron.

stances at London with his people; and his freinds at Glasgou do not deny but he has thoughts of coming doun; but they say he is to be made Principall of the Colledge of Edinburgh; but I do not think that probable, as matters stand, neither do I see wher his interest lyes to get that accomplished.

Principall Campbell, end of the last moneth, began to gather the students of Glasgou. He gave it out very publickly he was not to teach; but he altered on a suddain, from what springs I cannot say. But he proposed, in Faculty, Whither he should teach or not? The Masters said they wer not to advise him in that, neither had they formerly interposed. They desired to knou why he had nou communicated his designe with them. He insinuat, and afterwards more directly told, that he expected the College would consider his additionall trouble in teaching, especially that some other of the Masters had received gratuitys for their extraordinary teaching; as Mr Anderson for teaching Mr Carmichael's class after his death. That they peremptorly refused, and said, that if any body wer to consider his pains, and if he did not think he was oblidged as Primarius Professor of Divinity, it was Mr Simson's bussines, not theirs, who enjoyed the sellary. He has nobody nou in the Faculty who joyns him save Mr Simson. All the rest beard him in every thing. The meetings of Theologues* are but just a form. The Principall only hears discourses. He has not, this session, had above two or three prelections; he does not explain almost any thing, but only hears discourses; ther is none present but the bursars, and some feu Glasgou lads, and a feu about.†

I hear the toun of Stirling are upon getting a third Minister. Ther are severall considerable mortifications for a fund; and Collonel Blacader left some hundred pounds, and his Lady offers some more, if she be satisfyed in the choice. We hear, somtime after this, that the people generally are for Mr Ebenezer Erskine, one of the Representers or Marrou Bretheren; and she is for him to[o;] and it's probable that designe will go on. The Ministers‡ are against it, though they are thought very favourable to The Marrou, and decline to give their judgment till the Presbytery be advised with.

---

* Students of Theology.　　　　† From the neighbourhood.　　　　‡ Of Stirling.

[*January* 13.]—On the 13th of this moneth, John Peady, of Rough-hill, son to the last Provest Peady,* dyed, in four or five dayes illnes, of a pleuretick favour.† From his taking it, he laid his account with death. His lady, Blackhall's sister, about eight dayes before, was brought to bed of a son to him. I am well informed that he was under some surprize and damp‡ for three weeks before his death; the reason of which he signifyed to his lady, on her importunity; but really it should not have been spoke of; but being knouen nou, I set it doun. About three weeks before he sickned, he was going out to or coming in from Roughhill, in a dusky evening, and an oul crossed his way twice, and, some say, sat, or offered to sit, on his shoulder. This incident, he said, affected him much. It was his weaknes, and he was ashamed of it, but by no means could he get it laid aside; and the more, that the same thing hapned to his father, about three years ago, as the Provest told him, at the very same place, and in an evening, an oul came twice about him, crossed his way, and indeavoured to perch on him. He was in perfect health; and just about a moneth before his death, of which we have heard before, his father told him that he did superstitiously regard it, knouing ther was no connection betwixt [it] and any calamity on him or his, but he feared his oun death, or some of his, was near. Mr Peady, younger, meeting with the same incident, it affected him very much. He was a youth of great piety and good expectations. He has left a plentyfull fortune, more than twenty thousand pounds sterling, and an excellent lady. This is a very strange passage, but certain enough.

January 20.—Upon the 20th of this moneth, Mr Robert Paton was setled Minister at Renfreu. Ther was nothing but harmony in the setlment. I was keeped, by the children's ilnes, from being present at it. Mr R. Carrick received him; and he came immediatly, with his family. He is like to be tender.§ He had an ague, some years ago,

* Provost Peadie died in July 1728, while he was Chief Magistrate of Glasgow. He had been elected Provost October 3, 1727.

† Arising from inflammation of the pleura, then styled pleuritic fever.

‡ Depression of spirits.　　　　　　　　　§ Unhealthy.

and had the Jesuit's-bark given to him ; and it was well purged off, and his ague but half-cured, so that it frequently recurrs ; and he is troubled with a kind of vertigo and failour of memory, which, I am told, is the reason of his keeping his papers constantly in his Bible.

I have had considerable distres on my three youngest children this moneth ; and Lilly and Martha and litle Jamie are brought near to death with the chin-cough, a most violent renting distemper, in which parents tast of death, as it wer, for many weeks, not knouing but at every kink* the child may be carryed off to an unchangeable state ; and when the distemper comes to a very great hight, as indeed it has done with mine, it is a constant rack, as it wer, to a parent standing by. The two young-est have measles, small-pox, and teething all together. Lilly, that wants these, at least outwardly, appears in most hazard.

February [1,] 1731.—Upon the first of this moneth, Mr James Craig, Minister in the Old Kirk, Edinburgh, dyed, or at least we had the ac-counts of his death. He has been long ill of a decay and spitting of blood. He was, I think, an Episcopall Minister's son, and was Minister at Yester, and from thence transported to Edinburgh. He had once a very numerouse family, about fifteen or sixteen children, and nou they are reduced to two. He was a very grave, modest man ; a most fervent, accurat, and distinct preacher, highly valued by his people, at least the most judicious of them. I have heard him blamed for preaching morall dutys, without Christ ; but his hearers tell me that is very much wrong. He was the person at the Committy who straitned Mr Simson with a question which he refused to answer. He seemed to be a litle favour-able to Mr Simson, but was plain for his laying aside from teaching. He had a kind of burr in his speech, but when he warmed in the pulpit it was not much observed ; and his hearers reconed it rather a beuty. His sermons wer all very accurat and very patheticall. They talk of printing some of them after his death. He seemed to me, in conversation, to be a firm Calvinist, and much for the doctrine of the grace of God, in Christ. His poems are printed under the title of " The Spirituall

* The act of *hooping*, in this distressing complaint, is still, among the vulgar, termed *kinking*; and the disease is called the *kink-host*.

Life." Hou a foolish story came to be talked, that many of these poems wer composed by his son, who dyed about twenty or twenty-two years,* a youth of great expectation, I cannot conceive. His affection to him was singular, and his death seemed first to break his father's health ; and we parents, if not unnaturall, are ready to do every thing that may tend to the preservation of the memory of our children when taken from us, and to steal his son's poems, and put J. C. to them after his death, is a vile supposition. I sau some of them in MS. before his son was capable of making an English verse, and I kneu hou averse he was from publishing them. Indeed, I think they are the best Scots Poems ever we had published ; and in the poeticall flight, fancy, and strong images, are equall to most of the celebrated English performances ; and his preface to them is very good.

[*February* 3.]—Upon the third of this moneth my daughter, Lillias, dyed of the chincough ; and, I doubt, had the kind of small-pox the other two had afterwards begun in her, and probably dyed in the outstricking of them. She was a tender child, and when opened, had two or three polipuses in her heart, throu want of exercise, and her liver was very large. She could not have lived much longer. She was in a high feaver two dayes before she dyed. We thought her better some hours before her death. She was a smart, thinking child, litle more then six years, of a great spirit and considerable thought. Some time before she dyed, she declared her willingnes to dye, and that she chused rather to go to Christ ; and being as[ked,] If she would leave her mother and me ? she said, " It was better to be with Christ, and in heaven." She said, some dayes after that, she was feared she would rue, and was sorry for it ; but still thought it best to go to Christ. This is six children I have, I hope, in heaven, within these two years, or some less. May those that remain be fair in the way to it !

This has been a calm, still, and hazy winter ; feu winds, very litle rain as ever I sau, since September, and no frosts, save two nights, one of which was the sharpest I almost ever felt. I doubt the effects of it

* Of age.

on our bodies are not yet over.   I expect diseases in the spring.   Kink-hoasts* are turning common among children.   Ours had them first in this place, but many since; and persons of sixteen and eighteen years of age, and [they] tell me people of thirty and upwards, have it, which was scarce ever knouen in my time; the chincough being a distemper proper almost to children.

This moneth, the Gorbals people are supplicating for a contribution for paying the building of their Church, and many persons in Glasgou offer pretty frankly, and especially B[ailie] Orr, as has been notticed.   It's strange that the toun and Colledge, on a mistaken point of honnour, oppose a people that have exceeding† every one that I have heard of, almost, in this excellent work of Mercy to Souls.

[*February* 15.]—On the fifteenth of this moneth dyed Mr Michael M'Taggart, Minister at Glasfurd, at Kilbride, in his way home.   He had been in suit of a daughter of Mr Alexander Muir, and it had many ups and douns.   At lenth, the week before he dyed, the matter was ended, and a minute signed, and he was to have been proclaimed [the] Sabbath after he dyed.   When he was riding home he felt his legg swell and turn very painfull, and [he] alighted at Mr Connell's, in Kilbride, and dyned.   His pain increased, and he turned sickish, and Mr Connell sent for Mr Gordon from Glasgou.   Mr Gordon sau it was a gangren in his legg, and declared it uncurable, and that he would dye.   His legg had been spoyled some way when he was young, and cured, but it seems imperfectly, and the scarrs and a blacknes still remained.   He was not very apprehensive of death himself.   Houever, he soon fell a raving, and dyed a litle after.   When he was asked, to whom he would leave any thing he had? he added, " To whom but my wife, Christine Muir !" A writter was desired to form his testament, but before he could get it formed, Mr M'Taggart was not able to signe it, and soon dyed.   He was come to age,‡ a piouse man, of a very good gift of preaching.   He was the occasion, accidentally, of Mr Simson's first process; being born in the parish of Penningham, and, 1714, a student with Mr Simson, and

* Chin-cough, or hooping-cough.   See note, p. 200.   † Exceeded.
‡ Somewhat advanced in life.

Mr Rouan had his informations from him, and communicat them with Mr Webster and Mr Simson himself. He was, in the last process, pretty favourable to his old master, Mr Simson.

About the same time dyed Mr Hugh Thomson, Minister of Kilmares, but dimitted his ministeriall relation to that parish, as I belive hath been notticed about the 1712, having no freedom to take the Oath of Abjuration, and being affrayed of the fines being exacted. He studied physick, and came to have some reputation in it, and purchased land to the value of one thousand or twelve hundred merks a year. He took no money, while a Minister, for his advice; but his son sold druggs, and that way the family made money. He was with me a hearer and partaker at severall Communions, and at the last a helper; and it was the last time, I suppose, he communicat, unles at Kilmarnock, if he was there. His successor, Mr H. Cocheran, and he did not agree. He opposed his setlment as an heretor. He was the longest preacher ever I heard, and would have preached four [or] five hours, and was not generally under two hours; that almost every body expected. He lived for some time, till about a year ago, at Glasgou, and was pretty much imployed in physick, in which he had long practise, but could have no exactnes in the theory. He was a piouse good man, and a fervent affectionat preacher, and, when I heard him, he had a vast deal of heads, and a great deal of matter, and generally very good and practicall, but very long. He was exceeding ready, and would have preached long with very litle study.

This moneth the subscriptions for the work-house at Glasgou, for imploying the poor, begun. The richer persons signed twenty and twenty-five pounds; the ordinary merchants and shopkeepers ten and five pound. In short, in Scotland, I never heard of any thing so much charity and chearfulnes appeared in. In a week or two twelve hundred pounds sterling was signed for, besides two hundred pounds Mr Orr gives; and the Toun, Merchants'-house, and Trades, are [to] give largely to it. The toun, indeed, has susteaned great losses, impositions, and hardships, in their trade, and yet in this matter have done in some measure beyond pouer, and most liberally. I hope it will be an excellent

pattern to the shires about, and to all the kingdom. All will depend on
the choice of Managers, into whose hands this money, building the house,
and managing the poor in it, which they propose shall be severall hundreds of working poor, falls ; and it will be a thousand pitys if it shall nou
fall into wrong hands, or miscarry, after such noble and encouraging beginnings, and great progress made in it.

February 21.—The 21st of this moneth, being Sabbath, ther was one
of the most wicked and scandalouse rables and riots at the Neu Kirk of
Kilpatrick that I have heard of in the West of Scotland. Mr A. Gray
was appointed by the Presbytery, his tryals being nou well nigh over,
for that parish, as has been hinted, to supply them that day. The heretors, the Lairds of Mains, Succoth, Kilmerdinny, and James Graham
of Kilmanan, uncles to Dougalstoun, and ther sons, mett severall times
the week before to concert measures for the putting a rub on the young
man, and prevent the setlment before the Synod ; and at lenth fell on
this of a riot. They have nothing to say against the youth, Mr Gray,
and declare they like him as well as any other ; but are angry at the
Presbitry for hasting the ordination before the Synod, to whom they
had appealed. The Heretors are by the ears among themselves, and
privat picks [piques] and disgusts, upon the Duke of Montrose granting
a place to one of their sons and not to another ; and Mains, Succoth,
and some others, are upon Argyle's side, against Montrose. They hired
and hounded out thirty or forty servant lads in that parish, and some
neighbouring parishes, and some weemen, to joyn them. It's said Mains
got up early in the morning of the Sabbath, and road throu these of whom
he hounded out.

In the morning they came (feu or none of the parishoners, servants
excepted, and some weemen who wer parishoners, wer concerned) and
took the Church keeyes, filled the pulpit with stones, and hung up the
forms on the lofts, and barricadoed the dores. Carscadden,* Shirriff,
hearing of this, sent up the shirriff-officers about nine to disperse them,

---

* Colquhoun of Garscadden.

but they wer driven off. At the ordinary time, Carscadden and Mr Gray came up, and Hutcheson,[*] and the Church-yeard was guarded with thirty or forty young felloues ; no body suffered to enter. The people wer mostly conveened to hear sermon, and standing at some distance. Carscadden, hearing that Mains and other opposing heretors wer come up, and seing the opposition, went to them, and desired them to joyn him and keep the peace, and procure access to the Kirk, and prevent the profaning the Lord's day. They answered, they wer come to hear Mr Gray themselves, but would not medle with the people, to disperse them at the Church-yeard. Carscadden, with the shirriff-officers, and Hutchison and others, went to the Church-yeard. The officers again wer attacked by the rioters who guarded the Church-yeard. Hutcheson was beat doun with a club, and fainted, and was carryed off. Carscadden was struck, and forced off. Upon which he retired, without reading the King's proclamation ; which would have made the rioters guilty of death. Ther was no sermon. The two gentlmen wer bruised and wounded sore. Kilmerdinny and Kilmanan sons wer the only persons of note. Some weemen and men wer hurt in the confusion. Mr Gray stayed in the change-house, and went home with Carscadden, to whom and Hutcheson surgeons and physitians wer brought. Next week Councill letters came out, and severall of the rioters wer taken and imprisoned, and severalls fled. A man who was imprisoned, not as active in the mob, but found ther, the Miller of Garscub, who went to bring out his wife, Agnes Paul, a cheif riotter, from the confusion ; and she fled and he was taken, dyed in Glasgou three weeks after, being in an ill habit of body, and bailed.

This is one of the most outragiouse profanations of the Sabbath, and breaches of the peace, that has hapned hereabouts, and is designed to protract the setlment, and is the woefull effects of party rage and privat pick, [pique.]

In the end of this moneth, we had the accounts of a bill preparing by my Lord Isla for nailing doun Patronages on this Church ; see Letters this moneth It is to take away Presbyteries' *jus devolutum*, to lodge calling in Heretors, to exclude elders, and to take away Presbyteries'

---

[*] Hamilton of Hutchison.

pouer of second tryall, and ordering the present setlments on presentations. All the account of this is in a Letter from the Laird [of] Herron,
who is exceeding inward,* they say, more than any other Scots Member,
with Sir Robert Walpool. We shall hear afterwards all this is said to
be groundles.

March [10,] 1731.—The Commission met the tenth of this moneth.
I went in upon the allarume of the Bill about Patronages. At our
first meeting the setlment of Balfrone came in by the minutes. The
Commission in May ordered Mr Sinclair and Mr Buchanan to be on
the lites, and the Presbytery obeyed and turned out Mr D. Broun,
though the people wer evidently for him. The Commission, in Agust,
preferred Mr Sinclair to Mr Buchanan, against all rules, Mr Sinclair
having the plain minority. In November, the Presbytery sent a very
strong paper, and the Synod a Letter, urging a delay till the Assembly.
The Commission went over† both, and ordered a Committy to joyn the
Presbytery, and to take Mr Sinclair on tryalls ; they gave instructions
to the Committy, and finished all, to the intimation of the sentence.
When the partys wer called in, the quorum was challenged, and found
not sufficient ; and so all stood as it was till March. When we mett, the
minute was read, and the question was, Hou the Commission should nou
act ? It was moved, that they should go on to compleat the setlment.
Against this it was objected, that the setlment was not agreed upon at
the last Commission for want of a quorum. That was denyed, and it
was asserted, that all was good that was done before the quorum was
questioned, otherwise there would be no certainty in any sederunt of
the Commission ; and, therfor, all conteaned in the minute was the deed
of the former Commission, and could not be rescinded by this ; and so
nothing was to be done but the sentence of the Commission to be intimat
at this dyet. Then the minute behoved to be read again, and it was
found not clear enough ; and, therfor, the members present at the Commission in November claimed it as their right, exclusive of us who wer
not there, to rectify and enlarge that minute, it not being read till this
day. And so they did, and made it express that Mr Sinclair was to be

* On confidential terms.   † Disregarded.

setled before the Assembly, and some other clauses. This was a very strange procedure, and lyable to much mistake at least. In the afternoon we mett again, and resumed the affair. It was asked, What we wer nou to enter on, and what was intire and not already concluded? It was answered, the nomination of the members of the Committy, and their time and place of meeting. It was urged, that then ther was room to delay till the Assembly. That was denyed, and the minute, rectifyed in the fornoon, was cast up. It was said, that a delay to the Assembly was not a rescinding of what was done, but a delay. That would not be granted. Some members of the East country wer adjoyned to the Committy; the Moderator, Mr Smith, Crawford, Naismith, Walker, and others, wer adjoyned, with a designe to have a meeting after the Commission, and name texts to Mr Sinclair at Edinburgh. That did not please some of the proposers. Mr Smith said, it would be better that the Commission themselves execut their oun sentences, and name Mr Sinclair texts and subjects, *ex cathedra*; and nobody could except against that! It was [said,] That was taking the Presbytery's pouer out of their hand, and by that way of doing the Commission might engross all the pouer of planting of places in their hand, and pass tryalls, and ordean the Minister likewise, without the Presbytery. That matter was reasoned a litle, and put to the vote, and it caryed, " Delay till the meeting of the Presbytery," by nyne votes; which was a disappointment.

The affair of Patronages, and the bill about them, was what was very allaruming to us in the country. We had a meeting among some Ministers with Coll[onel] Erskine and Mr Charles Erskine, on Wensday, at dinner, wher we talked the affair over. Ther was no letter but the above from Herron, four or five weeks ago, and we hear of no steps that way taken since. It was the opinion of our two gentlmen, and some others, that the matter should be cast up* in the Commission, and an adress moved against Patronages, on this rumor; and, according to the Instructions by the Assembly to the Commission, the rumors we had wer thought ground enough for this application in generall, which might regularly have been made even without thir rumors. This was not to some of us so desirable. The Assembly was near, and application from

* Taken notice of.

them appeared much more weighty than from us. In case any such thing wer in vieu, at London, as the nailing doun Patronages, our Adress perhapps might irritat, and push some, who otherwise would be silent, to stirr. It was uncertain if we would carry our Adress in the Commission, and better not press it than loss it. On the other side, it might encourage ill-designing men at London, if, when they kneu hints wer given of the designe, the Commission met and did nothing; and confirm them in the thoughts that really we, the Ministers, wer not against Patronages. I moved a conference with bretheren on the other side, since we must have sides; and Mr James Henry and I wer appointed to speak with the Moderator, and Mr Alston, and some others. We did so, and they went into the thing.

Accordingly, that evening Mr Henry* made the motion, that the Commission might nominate some Members to conferr on a matter of some common concern. And, accordingly, the Moderator, Mr Smith, Mr Alston, Mr M. Crawford, Mr J. Walker, Mr Kinloch, the Laird of Pencaitland, Mr Henry Gustard, H. Maxwell, R[obert] W[odrow,] Colonel Erskine, Mr Charles Erskine, and some others, wer named. We met that night in a very freindly temper. The alarume was opened, and advice asked. It was moved by Mr Charles Erskine, that the Commission might address the King upon our greivances; that was thought not so advisable. It was asked, what was then to be done? Pr[ofessor] Hamiltoun said there was [no] letter but that of Herron's, and he was of opinion it was writ with a particular vieu to the West Kirk; but he did not think any thing would be done, at least he had no letters, nor kneu of any from Members of Parliament; and they used still to write when any thing was to be brought in that related to the Church. I asked, if there might not be a designe, in silence, to have no stirr till the Commission was up; and the bill might be passed in this week, and carryed throu before the Assembly, and so it might be passed before any applications could be made by the Church. To this it was answered, they would answer for no man; but only, if such a designe was in hand, it was strange that there should be no hints of it from any Members of Parliament to any body, save Herron's letter. Then it was proposed

* Minister of Kinghorn.

what was proper to be done to prevent the worst, and a surprize.   Mr Smith, Alston, and Professor Hamiltoun, said that they did not think an application proper from the Commission; but if we wer attacked, especially without acquainting us, we should make a publick application; and they declared them willing to joyn with us in it with the greatest vigour, because it was a plain invasion on our constitution, and such a bill would go near to ruine us.   The Commission meet quarterly for privat causes, and what is refered.   There have been instances of Commissions *pro re nata ;* but these readily must have six weeks advertisement, that members may at least have time to come up.   That would not hitt our case at present, and the only habil method was by short adjournments of the Commission, which we had been in use of since the Revolution. The Commission has adjourned somtimes a week, a fourteenth-night, three weeks, &c.; and if we heard account of the bills being brought in, then members would come up; if not, the members at Edinburgh, though not a quorum, could adjourn a fourteenth-night, and so on till the Assembly. This was gone into unanimously; and, accordingly, next fornoon, the Commission adjourned for three weeks.   Thus this matter passed harmoniously, and this was all could be done.

I remark only further, that it was observed, in our reasonings, that the people above seemed to be much encouraged to fasten Patronages upon us, by the procedure of the Commission in plain siding with patrons, against the plain rights of Presbitrys and people ; and gathered from this, that really the Church of Scotland, of whom they make their judgment from what is done in Commissions, would peaceably stoup* to Patronages.   Another thing I notticed was, that one made an observation that the reason why nothing was done upon our Assembly's proposalls to King and Court as to our greivances, was want of inclination, or perhaps want of application to our Members of Parliament : That the effectuall way to gett our greivances redressed was this, that the Assembly appoint Ministers to deal with all our Scots Members in the recess, and see if they can be gained to be freindly, without which all applications to King and Parliament are in vain; and then, if they can be gained, for the Commission to apply to the King, and send

* Submit.

up Members to agent the affair in time of Parliament, and hold hand to it.

I nottice that Commissions of our Assemblys are taking very wide steps, under the notion of executing their oun sentences, and this way evidently incroach upon Synods and Presbitrys, which will be of terrible consequence. An affair as that of Balfron, by a most irregular appeal, upon a most groundles pretence, is taken out of the Presbitry's and Synod's hand to the Assembly, not with any designe the Assembly should consider it, but [to] turn it over to the Commission. The Commission act as a feu about Edinburgh are disposed, to please Patrons [and] great men, and a feu make a false step, and then it's pretended it cannot be rescinded by a posterior act of the Commission, and so must be execute; and Committys of called-out* men are chosen by the Commission, and under the pretext of executing the Commission's sentence, refuse to allou the Presbitry to meet with them, unless they act as the Commission acted. This sapps our constitution, exposes us, hightens our division, and is the way to make the whole Church of Scotland stoop to a feu at Edinburgh, as if they wer Bishops.

This brings to my mind a story I hear of what lately passed betwixt Mr Cunningham of Boquhan and Mr Smith of Craumond, nou of Edinburgh, upon the very subject of Balfrone, though his brother-in-lau, Kilcrough,† is one of Mr Sinclair's side. Mr Cunningham, in conversation with Mr Smith, with much seriousnes asked Smith, what he and some others, men of reflection, sense, and knouledge of the world, proposed to themselves in violenting people and Presbitrys in the setlments? and told him he thought they acted very imprudently, and would soon loss the affection of the people and many gentlmen; asking what, under God, they had further to look to? It seems this raised Mr Smith's passion a litle, and he answered him, "Sir, we have done it, (Balfrone setlment by Mr Sinclair,) or we will have it done, and [it] must be done."—"Must be done!" sayes Boquhan; "that is an impertinent answer from any Presbiterian Minister, and unworthy of you;" and he run him doun fearfully, till he had nothing to say.

* Selected for the purpose.   † Napier of Culcreuch.

This is a grouing evil, which will undoubtedly in the first room divide us, and brings in a spirit of party amongst us ; it will sink our reputation in the eyes of persons of rank and influence; it brings in animositys and emulation among Ministers, and is a plain departure from our Presbiterian principles, and quitting the proper rights of Generall Assemblys, by sinking their pouer as to setlments in the hands of a feu Ministers ; and is what, in my opinion, Presbitrys and Synods should consider the tendency of, and endeavour to provide remedys against.

Ther was litle further before this Commission but some causes from Angus and the North, about matters of no great concern to [the] publick, and which must necessarly be ended.   There was a cause of divorce came before us, by appeal from our Synod at Air, in the case of James Caldwell.   His wife fell in adultery; he obteaned a divorce in Neu England, upon the notoriety of the fact of her being brought to bed of a child in his absence.   The woman, four or [five ?] years after the divorce, marryed, irregularly, another man than the person with whom she committed adultery.   The Presbytery interdicted them converse ; they appealed to the Synod : The Synod, when none but Air Presbitry and Irwine almost wer present, affirmed the Presbytery's sentence, and the Commission disannuled the Synod's sentence, without any opposition. They went on that principle of the Scots Lau and Canon Lau, that where there is a divorce for adultery, both partys may marry, even the *pars ledens*, save to the person with whom the adultery was committed.

My L[ord] G[range] was not in this Commission.   He has been ill in his health this winter, for severall weeks confined to his room.   I waited on him.   He is sore shaken, and appears heartles and sinking. The case of his family, and his lady's separation, I doubt sticks hard on him.   He is riding for his health.

I am told that, in the Presbytery of Edinburgh, Mr M[athew] Crawford said, in one of their debates, that Patronage was no greivance on this Church.   This, if true, was strange impudence, and not only contrary to the Churches declarations, but the declarations of all Churches which bear the name of Christians. The Bishops of England complean loudly of them, and so doe many of the Popish writters. Alace! what a lou pass are we come to, when Patronages are questioned to be a greivance! I hear, since the Commission, at the meeting of the Presbytery after the Commission, Mr Crawford read a paper in Presbitry, as his speech in defence of Presentations, which is a strange step.

Doctor James Crawford, Professor of the Hebreu tongue at Edinburgh—a man of piety, of excellent solid sense, but a recluse, modest man—dyed in the end of February, or the beginning of this moneth. Mr M[athew] Crawford, P[rofessor of] Hist[ory,] is using all his small interest to get into that post, and hold plurality of benefices. It's about sixty pound per annum, and in the hands of the Toun Councill of Edinburgh. Mr Mathew Crawford has, I am sure, (if not changed since he left us,) but a very ordinary knouledge of the Hebreu tongue; but I belive he could overcome that. He has one hundred pound, and really does nothing for it. He will give no privat Colledges* but for money, and nobody comes to him. His publick prelections are not frequented; he will not have six or seven hearers, they say: Not one of his Collegues favour his designe; and he will have very little interest in the Toun Councill, that post being designed for P[rofessor] Hamiltoun, when Principall.

Which brings me to set doun what I hear as to the filling of the Principall's post at Edinburgh. It has been vaccant since Mr Wisheart's death. In May last, I set doun what I heard about this. Since that, nothing is done that I hear of. Pr[ofessor] Hamiltoun is weary of teaching, and does not appear to care much for continouing. Mr Gaudie, it seems, he is inclined to, though he does not name him; and, poor man, he is in very hard circumstances with his family. His wife is distempered, and a great cross to him. She is gone to the country, but threatens every week to return. His son is his successor at Erlstoun, if I remember, where he was before. The Magistrats continou in their designe for Mr Smith, and must soon perfect it nou, being to go off

* Private examinations and instructions after lecture, &c.

next Michaelmass. Their project of Mr Smith and Mr Hamiltoun being joynt Ministers of one of the charges in Haddoch's Hole,* does not take. The people are not for it, and desire to have Mr Smith to have the charge of all. Mr Smith and Professor Hamiltoun are not very inward,† though they seem to act the same part in the Presbytery and publick ; yet Mr Smith knoues his superiority in the Presbytery ; in all cases where he and Pr[ofessor] Hamiltoun differ, the Pr[ofessor] cannot carry the vote without him : Besides, the Magistrats are not very fond to have the Principall in [a] ministeriall charge, but would rather have this custome interrupted. Nou, this occasion falls in well of the Hebreu Professorship being vaccant : The Principall is, indeed, as such, a sinecure almost, and has time enough to teach Hebreu. This will, with the Principal's post, make the Professor's sellary better than his sellary is at present. They say the Magistrates are all for this coalition, and that nou soon it will be done.

It's plain P[rofessor] Hamiltoun is one who has great interest among the young Ministers of the Church ; his interest among the elder is declining much. But Mr Smith, by falling in to some popular things, especially Mr Simson's discharge from teaching, and Mr Glass, is better liked, but he has the Presbytery of Edinburgh upon his side. I see Mr Alston beards Pr[ofessor] Hamiltoun and Mr Smith in the Commission. The complaints of the wildnesses of the students at Edinburgh continou : their haunting dancing-schools and publick dancing ; their night revells ; and the sermons of some of the younger preachers against the Spirit's work, under the notion of enthusiasme, and making their auditorys laugh by mocking seriouse religion in the pulpit, and smiling themselves. These give a very ill impression of their master, if he indulge such things in them.

In the beginning of this moneth, the Pension Bill, passed by the House of Commons, was throuen out by the Lords. Some used a very strange argument, that that Bill seemed to interfeir with the soveraignty of the

---

* Haddo's Hold, the Little or New North Church of Edinburgh.   † Intimate, on good terms.

Croun over the subject.   When it was throuen out by the Lords, the party for it in the House of Commons, who had lost it in that House, if the majority had not yeilded, knouing the Lords would throu it out, resolved to give them a bite; and proposed, the next day after the Lords had cast it out, that since the Lords had rejected it from being a lau, yet they had pouer over their oun Members, and moved that presently the House should enter to a resolution to make enquiry among their oun Members, who had Pensions and trusts contrary to the act they themselves had offered as a lau to the Lords.   But this was soon throuen out by a great majority of the House, though they wer, indeed, in so doing, properly contradicters of the Bill they had passed.   But this was Hackerstoun's Cou!*

I am well informed, that the English Strollers and Commedians are a prodigiouse summ of money to the toun of Edinburgh.   It's incredible what numbers of chairs, with men, are carryd to these places; and it's certain that, for some weeks, they made fifty pound sterling every night, and that for six nights a week; and they will, even of the Saturnday evenings, be coming home from them at one in the morning.   This is a most scandalouse way of disposing of our money, when we are in such a choak for money; and it's a dreadfull corruption of our youth, and ane ilett† to prodigality and vanity; and the money spent in cloaths, &c. for attending these is . . . .

The setlment of the West Kirk‡ makes a terrible noise all this winter; see Letters.   The state of it is there very fully.   I hear Mr Smith is not for Witherspoon, but he and P[rofessor] Hamilton joyn to have both— that is, [him and] Mr Jardin—laid aside.   Mr M'Viccar is blamed for writing up to London in termes to this purpose, that he did not wish for any presentation, but if ther was any, he hoped it would be for Mr Jardin.   This was sent doun to P[rovost] Lindsay; and upon this, as breach of the agreement, the presentation was sent to Witherspoon at the Magistrates' desire.

---

* Alluding to the proverb.

† *Eyelet*, a hole for admitting light, &c.

‡ St Cuthbert's Church, Edinburgh.

Sir John Bruce, Patron of Kinross, hath stoped payment of stipend to Mr Ebenezer Erskine and Mr Thomas Mair, upon the account of their Non-jurancy. Houever, the people pay their part, but he keeps sixty pound in his oun hands due to Mr Erskin. The reason is their oposing him in the setlment of Kinross. He intented a process before the session this winter, for a declarature of his not being oblidged to pay stipend to them, since unqualifyed; or attempted it, but was diswaded from it. Mr Ebenezer Erskin tells me he had advice of lauers he was in no hazard, on many grounds; but soon after this attack on them, Sir John's debtors [creditors] fell upon him for his debts, and he is like to run the country for his oun debts.

Ther has been a process between the Marquis of Tweddail and some Minister and parish, about a Reader and Precentor, which he claims pouer to put in as a Reader of the Bible; and the parish and session pretend pouer to chuse their oun Precentor, the office of Readers being abolished, which his Lordship's charters relate to. I have forgote the particulars; but the Marquise caryed his point before the Lords, and he was found to have the presentation of Reader.

I am perfectly informed that Mr Conduite, Sir Isaack Neuton's nepheu, or near relation, who has all his papers in his hand, is designed to publish his Life at a great lenth. Mr Conduite has lately write doun to Mr Colin M‘Laurin, at Edinburgh, desiring his allouance to publish, in his Life, a passage which Mr M‘Laurin is concerned in. It is this: When Mr M‘Laurine was upon the call from Aberdeen to Edinburgh, P[rovost] Campbell was then in the chaire, and had a mind to bring in Mr Campbell, but was disappointed. Many difficultys wer raised about paying a sellary to Mr Gregory, and Mr M‘Laurin also, by Provest Campbell, and some others in the Magistracy. Sir Isaack had recomended Mr M‘Laurin to Edinburgh, and had a peculiar liking to him. And hearing that the matter was like to meet with rubs, and the difficulty was hou to get a sellary to Mr M‘Laurin and Mr Gregory both, resolved to interpose, without any application at all from Mr M‘Laurin or his freinds, who never heard of it till Mr Conduit's letter informed them; and Sir Isaack informed himself whom in Edinburgh it was pro-

per to him to apply to ; and being told John Campbell was Provest, he
wrote to him, and reserved a copy of his letter among his papers, with
some hints on the back, giving the above occasion of it.   Theirin, after
complements, and expressing his concern for Mr M'Laurin's setlment,
he offers, for the encouraging of the setlment of Mr M'Laurin, he [Sir
Isaack] offered to setle twenty pound sterling a year on Mr M'Laurin
during life, and alloues the Provest to sheu this letter to all concerned.
This was a very high instance of Sir Isaack's regard for Mr Coline
M'Laurin ; and, no doubt, he will give his consent it be insert in Sir
Isaack's Life.   Indeed, it's a great deal of honour done to Mr M'Laurin.   Mr Conduit likewise desires Mr M'Laurin to drau up some account of Sir Isaack's mathematicall publications, and send [it to] him
to be insert in his Life, which I belive Mr M'Laurin will essay.

[*March* 16 and 17.]—On the sixteenth and seventeenth of this moneth
we mett, at Paisley, for our Priory Censures and ordinary bussines.   I
have not been with them since October, by reason of the indisposition
either on myself or family.   We had a good deal of ordinary bussines
before us, and in conversation with the Elders of Port-Glasgou, we find
that the people there are unanimously set upon Mr D. Broun, and have
petitioned the Magistrates to joyn with them in his setlment.   This is ill
taken by the Stirlings and Buchanans, though the toun sent him to them
to hear.   If they stand to what they have promised to be for him in
whom the people and Presbitry center, he will be the man.   Mr Turner
is continoually absent, and no course taken with him.   We agreed to
the Synod's meeting three times at Glasgou, and disliked the proposall
of the Assembly, about susteaning these who have votted in a cause to
vote again.   We chose, in common course, Mr Johnstoun, Mr John
Millar, Mr Pincartoun, members ; and Mr Maxwell, Elder.   We could
not make a better of it.   Two of them will be pretty favourable to Mr
Simson.   Mr Paton was indisposed, and not with us.

[*March* 18.]—Upon the eighteenth I went to Neu Kilpatrick, and was
present at Mr A. Gray's ordination.   I have notticed the unaccountable

rable, about a moneth ago, in that place. The setlment is discouraging, but Mr Gray would not throu it up, because he found the opposition was declared not against him, but against any his freinds would name. Since the rable the Heretors offered to joyn in the ordination if the criminall process wer dropped. Gorthie, the Duke of Montross' doer,* answered, that was not in his pouer to do. It was expected they would have been present, but came not. All was in peace, and a great multitude present from Glasgou. Mr Sidserff† preached from Heb. xiii. 17, very well. After the action was over, when discoursing to Mr Gray, he gave it him as his opinion, that nou, being Minister in the place, he should use any interest he could make for mercy to be sheuen to these guilty of the rable and confusion lately there ; for the most part of them, he said, he might make use of what the Scripture [says] of the follouers of Absolome, that what they did they wer put upon by others, and did it in the simplicity of their heart. When he spoke to the Congregation, after he had ended what he said to Mr Gray, he lamented the unaccountable disorder, breach of the peace, and horrid profanation of the Sabbath in that Congregation. He questioned if he had many of them personally guilty to speak to, but told them he reconed it a congregationall sin, and what they wer all to mourn for, that it was such a scandalouse breach of order that had not been knouen almost in the West of Scotland, and in his prayer he again regrated it, and asked God pardon for it.

At this time, we hear of John Walkinshau of Borroufeild˙ his death. He was a violent Jacobite, engaged in the Rebellion, and a person of considerable sense. It's said at the division of the West country, when full of hopes, 1715, he got my Lord Pollock's estate, and was angry because he had not the Aldhouse also !

[*March* 23.]—Upon the twenty-third of this moneth, John Luke of Claythorn, merchant in Glasgou, dyed. He was son to an eminent Christian, of whom I have said somewhat before in some of the former volumes of this Analecta, and on my father's life. My mother-in-lau,

---

* Agent, man of business.   † Minister at Dumbarton.

Mrs Luke's sister, is the only child of old Mr Luke nou alive of eight-
teen.   They all, who came to any age, had plain evidences of grace at
their death, and one of them, Ninian, who had litle evidences throu his
life, had his afliction sanctifyed to him, and seemed to get it in his last
period.   This is a rare instance of God's taking in a large and numerouse family.   I have knouen eight or ten of them remarkably pious;
and my mother-in-lau, the only remaining child, is an aged Christian,
and the eldest of any who came to age.   Mr Luke's character, who is
nou dead, is exceeding savoury in Glasgou, and knouen to all.   I scarce
ever kneu one more universally liked.   He was a lover of good men, a
person of a very peculiar talent of freedom in taxing vice.   He spared
nobody, and as he used to say, he was still on the side of the King and
Ministers.   He was remarkable for integrity and uprightnes.   He was
singularly zealous for the truth and our constitution, and against errour.
He was a true and fast freind, wher he had a value; he was generous,
and exceeding charitable to persons in want; he was a knouing, modest
Christian, and a closs walker with God.   I would say more of him,
wer I not under particular tyes to him.   As persons who live well ordinarly have much calmnes, and litle to do at death, so was he.

I talked frequently with him under his last ilnes.   He had a solid
satisfaction, a great deepth of thought in some things, and great modesty
made him speak softly.   He had not many fears, but much faith of adherance.   When I spoke some things about heaven, and seing as we
are seen, being lou in body, he said, one Sabbath night, " You must
forbear, for I am not able to bear the thoughts of what is coming.   I am
swalloued up, and my body fails me; I feel what I cannot tell, and put
in words."   And yet, though he had an opulent fortune, and pleasant
children, his crosses did arise from his children, and what he had to give
them.   His eldest daughter is, indeed, well setled; but the other two
wer perfectly crushing* to him, and, I may say, hastned his death.   He
carryed very Christianly under both their setlments; but, alas, they
stuck to him, and thoughtfulnes broke his health and constitution.   He
told me, and desired me to tell his youngest daughter, this moneth, that

* Oppressive.

she was his dear child ; and when [I] told him that I did not question of his forgiving what was past, he answered, " I knou she was torn fro me, and I do not blame her so much as others ! As to [that] affair, throu grace I never permitted my mind to allou any rancor ; and it never came to a hight against those who betrayed her."

I hear that the students at Glasgou, particularly Mr H. Millar and others, who are under the conduct of Pr[incipal] Campbell and Mr Simson, are handing about a petition to be subscribed to this purpose: " That whereas the Students of Divinity at Glasgou, and the whole society, are at a great loss for want of a Professor of Divinity exercising his office, these four or five years, that therefore the General Assembly would, in their wisdom, fall upon such measures as they may be taught Divinity ; and the rather, because many of the bursars there are oblidged to attend at Glasgou by their holding their bursary, and can go no where else." This proposall is, no doubt, suggested by wiser heads than the boyes, and is to be improven as matters cast up in the enseuing Assembly.

[*March* 24.]—Upon the 24th of this moneth, the Committy of the Commission met at Dumbartan with the Presbitery there. Ther wer only Mr N. Campbell, Mr R. Paton, Mr James Wilson, and Mr Sidserf, Minister of Dumbartan, who joyned from the Presbitry at this meeting. Ther wer eight or ten members of the Presbitry met with them upon the Commission's Letter. Upon their meeting, the first question was, Who wer members of that joynt meeting ? The Commission, by their act, called the Presbitry and Committy, or the Committy and such of the Presbitry as should joyn with them. The Presbitry wer met ; but the Committy, that is, the three named to joyn with them, for of near twenty named, and sixteen of them in this Synod, none would joyn save these three. Before they would allou the Presbitry to join them, [they] put the question, Whither they wer ready to execute the Commission's sentence of setling Mr Sinclair in Balfrone before the Assembly ? The Presbitry answered, They wer come there in obedience to the Commission's Letter, and ready to act according to their light : But the Committy insisted on the Commission's Letter, and would not allou them to act, unless they would declare for Mr Sinclair's setlment. On this they retired all, save Mr Sidserf and Mr M'Calpin of Arrachar, These, with the Committy, gave Mr Sinclair three discourses, to be delivered in the intervalls of the Synod at Glasgou. This is a very dangerouse innovation, come in but of late, to adjoyn Committys, a quorum, three or five, to Presbitrys, to execute the sentences of Superior Courts, especially the Commission, which is but a delegat Court, with exclusive pouers to cut off both Presbitry and Synods. This takes away all the proper pouers of Presbitrys and Synods, and lands all in the Commission solely, which is a direct infringment of our constitution, in my opinion.

At this time, ther was a Visitation by the Presbytery, in the parish of Govan, about the Neu Church built in the Gorballs, of which somewhat has been said above. The honest people of the Gorballs had got promise of considerable summs of money promised them ; and to compleat the matter, they asked a recommendation from the Presbitry, and by them from the Synod to the Assembly, for a voluntary contribution. The Presbitry divided in this matter. The country Ministers wer for granting their petition, but the toun Ministers dreu back, as thinking a collection could scarce be carried throu ; or, if got throu, would come to nothing, unless the Magistrates and College of Glasgou came into it. The Magistrates pretend they, being superiors, should have been consulted, and wer not, in building that Church : Wheras P[rovost] Stark* did allou that project, and promised to hold hand to it in one of their Head-Courts ; but nou it's pretended he had no warrand nor act of Council for what he did, and so it was void and null. At this rate, ther is no dealing with corporat societys. The Colledge pretend to be Patrons of that parish, and that the erection of a neu Parish there, and the building of a neu Church, ought not to go on, to the prejudice of their right ; and both opposed the collection, and protested against it.

This is a very hard case. The publick-spirited persons concerned have expended above twenty thousand merks, if not thirty, on the build-

* He was Provost in 1725 and 1726.

ing of that Church, upon the increase of the inhabitants of the Gorballs to above the number of two thousand, and, for many years, have and are like to ly out of their money and interest. The Visitation came to litle or nothing, and ended in a Conference, upon Aprile 6, between the Colledge, Magistrates, and Presbytery, and the feuers of Bridgend or Gorballs. Meantime, the persons in the Bridgend or Gorballs, to bring the matter to a narrou point, dreu up an obligation, subscribed with their hands, to be presented at the Conference, binding themselves, about twenty in number, providing a Collection wer given, to advance immediately thirty-three thousand merks for a fund for a stipend, and for ever to free the heretors, toun of Glasgou, and Colledge, for any thing laid out for the Church ; or, in time coming, for stipend and manse to an intrant, or reparations in time coming. Thus, these well-disposed persons, from beginning to end, burden themselves with more than five thousand pounds sterling for this piouse use of a neu Minister— an example that scarce has ever fallen out in Scotland ; and yet all is like to come to nothing, by the violence of the Stirlings and their party in the Council, in concert with the Colledge. The Colledge have no pretence but the reservation of their right of Patronage on the neu erec-tion, and the Magistrates' motive is to bring in the inhabitants of the Gorballs or Bridgend to bear scot and lott with them ; in which case, they offer to pay the expense of the building of the Church, to give a stipend and manse to the intrant. Thus, throu selfish vieues, this ex-cellent designe is like to be broken, the inhabitants of the Gorballs not being willing to be brought in subjection to the taxes of the toun of Glasgou. When the conference came, in Aprile, there was nothing but jangling, and they broke up without any issue, and so the matter lyes over.

About the end of this moneth, I hear, the lamentable state of Hamil-toun continoues. The dissatisfaction with Mr Finlater remains. They have but three Elders officiating, and Mr Findlater continoues in his offences and extravagances. About a moneth ago, some process of scandall was remitted by the Presbytery to the Session [of] Hamiltoun, that they might examine witnesses. Mr Finlater was on the side of the pannell ; and a letter, proving that he was not *alibi* at the time that was alledged, being produced, this put Mr Finlater in a passion, and he fell a railing, and, in his passion, swore, in presence of five or six persons— " As I shall answer to God ;" or, " By God, this shall not do the bussines ; he shall be acquitted !"—or words to that purpose. This is the second or third time he has broke out, as the people in Hamiltoun thing, [think,] in rash swearing on publick occasions, in the exercise of his ministeriall work, and yet he is still screened. *O tempora ! O mores !*

Aprile [6,] 1731.—Upon the sixt of this moneth, our Synod meet at Glasgou. Mr M'Laurin preached the sermon, on " Who is that faithfull and wise servant ?"—and had many sweet things. He was overtoyled with work, and not so well in health. He had litle or nothing upon doctrine and error, as was expected. Mr Dick was chosen Moderator. The votes wer equall betwixt him and Mr John Scot of Stenhouse, which has not fallen out in our Synod, save once or twice, since the Revolution. The former Moderator cast it in favour of his colleague, Mr Dick.

We had the matter of dividing our Synod into two before us, as has been notticed on the last Synod, where the arguments *pro* and *con.* wer hinted at. This subject cast up thus : Air and Irwine wer against this, and brought in strong papers against it. What they run upon most was, that ther had been an originall contract, at the provisionall joyning of thir two Synods, which could not be broken without the consent of both sides ; and that it was not in the pouer of the Synod to divide the Synod, or to bring them, without their oun consent, to meet three times at Glasgou, and once at Irwine and Air. The first of these was denyed ; and it was said ther was no concert, but with consent of the Assembly, a voluntary association on no termes, and that interrupted : That all the old Ministers at the Revolution wer for a separation of Synod, which could not have been had there been any contract : That it's true they might appeal to the Assembly ; but the Synod had pouer in themselves to separat, never having been united by any authority save their oun. But this was not the question at present, but only, whither we should meet three times at Glasgou for once in the West country ; and that was not beyond the Synod's pouer, and has been done in the Synod of Fife, and other Synods. The stating the place of meeting, houever, throu clamour and importunity, though the Presbitrys of Paislay, Dumbartan, Glasgou, Lanerk, Hamiltoun, approved the Overture, yet, by a vote, it was delayed till the Synod in Aprile 1732, and the next Synod in course was to meet at Irwine. Mr Campbell was very active for this delay ; much of his dependance and follouing in the Synod leaning to some young men lately ordeaned, and the Presbitrys of Air and Irwine. This is the third or fourth time I have seen this designe evaded.

Ther wer three appeals upon scandall, two which went, in my opinion, wrong, and upon the lax side. One Dumbarr, a custom-house officer, who had one accusation of sclander of adultry, which failed in probation ; but a neu scandall in the midst of it arose, and upon the Presbytery exculpating him of the first, with a reservation to go on with the second, he appealed ; and his appeal was susteaned, and the second scandall droped, for want of some formes. The other was from Stewartoun ; a scandall of fornication on an elder, remitted to his oath of purgation, which he offered in his oun termes, but not in these in the Form of Proces ; upon which the Presbytery wer going on to intimat the matter before the Congregation, and the appeal stoped that. The appeal was susteaned, and the matter dropped. The Minister made a favourable representation of the man, and an unfavourable of the woman ; and the matter turned to personall characters, and went off the *allegata* and *probata*, and the affair was droped. I am sorry to see so many Ministers advocats for scandalous persons, and that we are departing much from our forms of discipline. The last was an appeal of Gilbert Ware, adulterer, in Glasgou, once a shining professor, who craved absolution from adultery, which the Presbytery refused till he was reconciled to his wife, from whom he has lived separatly, by a kind of consent, these fourteen years. He summoned her to adhere, by a publick nottar. She refused. But when examined by the Synod as to his willingnes to receive his wife, he hagled* in his answers, and pretended she was not

* Hesitated, prevaricated.

willing. She and he both are averse to a reconciliation, and pretend hazard of life. The question was, whither, though morally seriouse for his crime of adultery, he could be absolved from it till he essayed reconciliation with his wife, whom [he] injured. The Synod thought he could not be absolved till he sheued himself in earnest to live with his wife; and remitted the affair back again to the Presbytery of Glasgou, that they might essay a reconciliation. He appears a knouing, cunning man.

The Synod sent instructions to the Assembly for urging our releife from the burden of Patronages, and falling on some uniform rule for planting of Congregations in the mean time.

During the intervalls of Synod, the Committy of the Commission above named, (and no moe would joyn them from the Synod,) with Mr Sidserf and M'Calpin, took Mr Sinclair's tryalls in three dayes, and appointed an edict to be served; but would not acquaint the opposing partys in the parish with the day of it: Yea, any hints given to them wer not as to the day which was agreed, but another, as one of the Elders told me. I shall here give the whole of that affair as transacted this moneth before the Assembly, such a setlment never being knouen in the West of Scotland before.

The day the edict was served was keeped closs from the people, that no objections might be made. Mr M'Calpin, Minister at Arracher, came to the parish, under cloud of night, the Saturnday before, and did not advertise the parish he was come. Ther wer no bells rung till the people wer gone to other Churches, and so the Minister had none present but the thirteen, or a feu more, who wer for Mr Sinclair. On the 23d, when the ordination was, ther opened a very unusuall scene. When the Committy, Pr[incipal] Campbell, Mr Paton, Mr James Wilson, (Mr Sidserf soured on the ordination, though he joyned in the tryalls;) but Mr M'Calpin continoued with the Committy, and not another from the Presbytery of Dumbartan; and Mr David M'Colm, Minister at Duddistoun, was accidentally there, and joyned; when these met at the Kirk of Balfron, on the 23d or 25th, at ten of the clock, the heretors and elders came into them, when the return was called for, and gave in their objections by way of complaint or lybell against Mr Sinclair. The heretors and two elders, for Mr Buchanan, with some lauers, and advice from Mr Grant, at Edinburgh, their advocat, gave in their complaint, in three branches, against Mr Sinclair; of which, see Letters this moneth : That Mr Sinclair had dealt actively with the elders for his oun setlment, and used pretty severe threatnings against them, if they stood out. The next was, that he hired a horse on the Sabbath day, or desired that one might be provided for him, on the failor of one the night before : There was litle in this. The last was, that in the park of Bandaloch, Mr Sinclair was seen kissing a woman of an ill fame, and, after that, went in with her to a thicket of treas ; and what passed ther was not seen. They offered witnesses for every point, and had them present. The Committy made some objections, as if the witnesses wer ultroneous, because they came to bear testimony not called ; but that was soon removed, they being only in a readines, if called. The lybellers desired the Committy should give their judgment on the relevancy of the articles given in, to prevent unnecessary swearing : There was a long debate arose on that. At lenth, upon Mr Paton's desire or proposall, they concluded to delay the judging relevancy till they called and deposed the witnesses, as in Civil Courts is somtimes done. When this was intimat, the heretors, for Mr Buchanan, reconing themselves lesed,* appealed from them to the Assembly, and left them. After this the Committy went on and called some of the witnesses, and interrogat them as they sau good, in the absence of partys, and found the complaint groundles, and designed to postpone the setlment till after the Assembly. After this, which took up till two or three in the afternoon, the elders came in, and gave in a paper conteaning reasons why Mr Sinclair should not be setled ; a modest, discret paper ; but it was not nou to be heard, and they resolved to go on ; whereon J. Edmond, in name of the session, protested against the setlment, and appealed to the General Assembly. This took up till after six at night. The people continoued in the Church and church-yeard, and not many from Balfrone except for

* Injured, hurt.

curiosity, but from neighbouring parishes, from nine of the clock to six at night. Ther was likewise an Independant company, not with their arms with them, but they wer at hand, they say, to keep the peace; but ther was no disorder that way. After six, the sermon began, by Mr James Wilson; and they went on, almost after sunset, to ordean him. Multitudes of the people left them when they began sermon. Houever, they ended their work after it was dark, to the great discontent of that country. Very feu of the parish stayed. This is the shortest vieu I could give, from my information, of this very melancholy and extraordinary affair.

We hear of great heats and contentions in the toun of Stirling about a third Minister. The Magistrates and toun are for a third Minister, and Coll[onel] Blacader's lady hath given somewhat to be a fund for it. The Ministers are not for this, or slou; and Mr Muir gave the Magistrates hard words, and called them " Michaelmass Lairds."* The veu is to call Mr Ebenezer Erskin from Portmoak thither; and the Ministers and Presbytery are against him, as being one of the Representers.

In the election for the Presbytery of Edinburgh, this year, Mr J. Smith was left out. He was against being chosen himself; and his party in the Presbytery spoke to Professor Hamiltoun, who voted for him; but his follouers, Mr M. Crawford, Mr Jo. Walker, &c., they scattered the votes, and Mr Smith lost it by three. But when my Lord Loudon came doun,† he would have Mr Smith; and, it seems, was not for Mr William Millar's being Moderator, which very probably would have been the case had not Mr Smith been gote in; and so Mr Thornburn, one of the members for Edinburgh, made his excuse that he was going to the goat-milk, and the Presbytery chose Mr Smith; and, even in this case, Pr[ofessor] Hamiltoun's party wer not cordiall, and it was a kind of force on them, so high do their humors there run.

It's talked, nou, with much assurance, that Mr William Wisheart is

---

* In allusion to the brief tenure of their dignities, from Michaelmas to Michaelmas.

† To be Commissioner.

to be made Principall at Edinburgh.   His freinds give it out that ther is nobody at London so inward* with the Earl of Isla as he : that he is very uneasy with his people at London.   It's certainly so ; and his meeting very thin.   Some say they take ill that somtimes he goes to the playhouse ; but I doubt if he will indulge himself in what is so openly unfitt for his ministeriall character.   I rather belive the reason of their coldnes is the company he keeps, and the Ministers he is intimat with ; and his people give it out, that the only Ministers he haunts with are Mr Chandler and Mr Foster, and a feu more Arrianized, young, hot-headed Ministers.   Whatever be the ground, it's plain the breach 'twixt him and them is great ; and, they say, my Lord Isla is to provide him of the Principall's place at Edinburgh ; but I yet doubt of this.

They tell a very odd story of a dogg belonging to the famouse Mr Tolland, whom he either gave to Sir John Shau, or he continoued with him when Sir John left London.   The dog Sir John took in to the coach, and keeped him closs with him all the way ; and as soon as Sir John came to Greenock, and the dogg was loosed, he got off, and, in three dayes time, as Sir John found, by a letter from Tolland, he run from Greenock to London !   This is an odd passage, and I may enquire further about it at Greenock.

When Dr Calamy heard of Mr Hutcheson's being called to Glasgou, he smiled, and said, I think to Thomas Randy, that he was not for Scotland, as he thought from his book ; and that he would be reconed there as unorthodox as Mr Simson.   The Doctor has a strange way of fishing out privat storyes and things that pass in Scotland.   He told my informer all the storys about the students at Edinburgh—their meetings, going to the dancing-school, some of them being apprehended, drunk in the streets, in the night-time, by the guard, and Pr[ofessor] Hamiltoun's interposing for their releif—in a clearer way than my informer, who was in Edinburgh at the time, kneu them.

This moneth, my Lord Grange went to England.   He was called up

___
* Intimate, confidential.

by letters bearing that his sister-in-lau, the Lady Marr, was recovered her reason, and nou to be dealt with. He hopes to bring her doun to Scotland, for the advantage of the family. His health is much broken this winter and spring. He is to be again absent from our General Assembly, and so is Collonel Erskine.

Dr Bentley, in England, some years ago, in conversation with Dr Watterland and others, said, he hoped, ere long, to give the Neu Testament as exact and genuine as it was sixteen hundred years ago. Dr Watterland pulled off his hat, and, lifting up his eyes to heaven, prayed that God might preserve to us the text of that holy book !

Ther has been, of late years, a paper warr betwixt Dr Bentley and Professor Burman, at Leyden, who teaches the Bell-Lettre. Dr Bentley is wearyed of the squable, and sayes he is fairly beat at Billingsgate and scolding by Mr Burman ; that, in that sort of writting, he is not at all able to hold it out against his adversary. He adds, that nou the tast of this age is corrupted, and we have no such learned men in Europe as Heinsius, and Scalliger, and Lipsius, to appeall to, otherwise he would make a publick appeal, and leave the matter in their hands : But he resolves to publish an edition of Ovid, with notes, (it's on criticismes on such authors they are tearing one another,) and that as a lasting specimen of his criticall learning ; and leave it to the coming age, which he hopes will be better judges than the present, to end the contraversy between him and Burman.

Ther is a neu edition of the N. T. [New Testament,] to which an appendix is printed, at Amsterdam, last year, beginning to be published. The author of it is a learned German. He pretends to restore the text, but the rules he layes doun very probably will deprave and pervert the text, and ther seems to be a present run and endeavour, by the licentious use of criticisme, to wrest from us the originall text of the Holy Scripture. Every thing that is valuable to us [as] Christians seems at present to be struck at ; Christ, his Spirit, his Grace, and his Word.

This moneth, the affair of the setling of Port-Glasgou, vacant by Mr John Anderson's transportation to Glasgou, comes to a bearing ; and I shall set doun a detail of it, as far as it yet hath cast up. When Mr

Anderson's call was drauen, the people of Port-Glasgou wer unwilling to part with him. He was not unwilling to go, but would not break with them. All the interest [that] could be was made to break them, but in vain. When they came up to our Presbytery in September last, as I am told by the person immediatly concerned, they* desired a sight of the answers drauen up by Port-Glasgou to their reasons of transportation. They wer communicat to Provest Stirling and Alexander Finlason, Toun-Clerk, commissioners from the toun, Provest Montgommery of Hartfeild, commissioner from the session who called Mr Anderson, and Mr Hamiltoun and Scot. When they sau them, and hou peremptory they wer, that if the Presbytery did transport their Minister they would appeal, and carry the matter to all the higher Judicatorys, P[rovost] Montgomery told P[rovost] Stirling that, unles that paper was smoothed, they would miss their designe, our Presbytery would never transport, and it was to be doubted if other Judicatorys would; and, therfore, they travailed with the elders and fewars of Port-Glasgou to smooth the paper, considering the Minister's inclinations to go to Glasgou, and the Provest and Clerk gave them the strongest assurances in name of the toun of Glasgou, that if they would be easy in the matter, they should have their free choice of another Minister, and the toun would come in to whomsoever they should be for.

Upon this, throu much importunity, they amended their paper, turned out the strong expressions in it, and gave in this altered paper to the Presbytery; upon which Mr Anderson was transported. The same assurances wer given to the Presbytery that the people should have their choice, and nobody should be fixed on for that parish but by the consent of the people, and in concert with the Presbytery. Thus matters stood; and, with the consent of the toun of Glasgou, they got a hearing of Mr D. Broun and Mr Moody. After they had heard both, they unanimously fixed on Mr D. Broun, and, upon the faith of that promise, made to them in so solemne a manner, they deputed two of their number to wait on the Magistrates of Glasgou with a subscribed petition, that they might concurr with them to get Mr Broun to be their Minister. Pr[ovost] Stirling, and his brother the Bailay, struck out, and represented this as a

* The Presbytery.

hainous insult upon the toun, who wer Patrons, and had the sole pouer,
as they speak, of calling and presenting, for them to subscribe their
choice of a person to be their Minister till they had consulted them;
wheras ther could be no want of decency and respect to the toun, in
going upon their oun grant and promise, and only in a petition to themselves. It's said, that P[rovost] Stirling and his brother* had their eye
to one Mr James Stirling, who would never have gone doun there. But
that seems out of dores; and the opposition seems meerly for opposition's sake, and to sheu their strenth in the toun. The bulk of the
toun of Glasgou who have bussines in Port-Glasgou appear to be for
Mr Broun.

Things went on till our meeting at the Synod, wher the Presbytery
wer inclining to speak to the Magistrates; but wer assured, by Mr Finlason and P[rovost] Montgommery, that [if] a little forbearance wer
used, Mr Broun would be amicably gone into, it being thought the plurality of the Councill wer for him. The Provest Murdoch and Mr Finlason both assured me of this, and yet that very week, as is suspected,
Principall Campbell and Pr[ovost] Stirling, when they dispaired of gaining the Councill to be against Mr Broun, without a trick, wrote in a
letter to Lord Miltoun,† and desired him to recommend Mr Moodie to
the toun by a letter. Upon the Munday after the Synod, a letter came
from him, signifying that he had received theirs, desiring his advice as
to their setlment; and he and their freinds above wer for Mr Moody,
and he was sorry he could not be for Mr Broun, whose character, he
heard, was very good; and, for eight dayes time, Pr[ovost] Stirling, his
brother, and Mr Finlason, dealt among the Counsellours, and insinuat
that they behoved not to disoblidge their freinds, considering they had
the *subpenas*, and the neu grant of the two pennies of the pint to carry
throu in the year 1733; and, by all means, they must be for Mr Moody,
Argyle's and Milton's man. So a Council was called, and there ther
wer very free speeches. D[ean of] Gild Rogers declared the promise
made before Provest Montgommery, who desired him to acquaint the

---

* Probably George Stirling, who was elected one of the bailies, September 30, 1729; though, on the
following year, the first bailie, along with Provost Murdoch, was Walter Stirling.

† Justice-Clerk and Minister for Scotland under the Earl of Islay.

Councill that he was never engaged in a smooty* and unfair thing, as this would be. Houever, they carryed it in Councill, by sixteen votes, against eight for Mr Broun, that a presentation should be given in to our Presbytery to Mr Moody. Accordingly, Instruments wer taken in the Moderator's hands, and the presentation and letter of acceptance lodged with him. These he tabled before the Presbytery, at a visitation, the last Wensday of Aprile. The Presbytery remitted it, to be received with the ordinary *nota* of its being a greivance to us, and reserved a pouer to judge next day, or any time therafter, whither the presentation was not undue, after the six moneths, and *a non habente potestatem*. With this the toun gave in a representation, bearing that, by the act of erection 1716, by the Lords of the Session, they wer the sole callers and presenters of a Minister to Port-Glasgou. Thus the matter stands this moneth.

As things are stated with us, I do not see hou irregular marriages can be well prevented, as long as ther are irregular Ministers to celebrat them for money. It's not to be expected that any fines will prevent mercenary men, hired by money, from venturing upon any thing; but I am told ther is no such thing in Holland as runaway or irregular marriages, for in all marriages the partys compear before the Magistrates of the place where they are. There, the objections against the marriage is heard, if parents be against it; and a writt is granted from the Burgomaster, for instance, or proper Magistrate, to the Minister, and he marryes none but such as have this writt. With some alterations, this, or somwhat like it, might be of use among us; but, indeed, the Justices of the Peace, who can pass an irregular marriage when made, might, perhaps, be prevailed with to connive at one to be made.

Mr Francis Hutcheson tells me that his grandfather was a Minister in Ireland before the Restoration, and very intimat with the Lord Forbes, afterwards the Earle of Grenard, in Ireland. He was a great courtier in King Charles the Second his reigne, and had the managment of all Croun revennue in Ireland, and was not unfreindly to the Scots Presbiterian Ministers, and had a particular kindnes for Mr Hutcheson.

* Smutty, dirty.

His grandson tells me, his father had this story from his grandfather's mouth, and he has heard his father tell it often. One day, old Mr Hutcheson was with the Earle of Granard, and the Earle gave him account what pains he had been at in setling the Civil List; and that nou all the Croun rents and revennues wer disposed off and collocated* to proper services, save six hundered pound. On this, a thought came in Mr Hutcheson's mind, which he ventured to propose to the Earle; and this was the occasion and foundation of The Royall Bounty to the Presbiterian Ministers in that kingdom. Mr Hutcheson ventured to tell the Earle that all the King's freinds wer provided for, and taken a care of; only the Dissenting Ministers, who had been firm Royalists in Oliver's time, wer still under incapacitys, though they would never joyn with the Usurper, pray for him, or countenance him: That they had been considerable sufferers for their loyalty, and had no small share in forwarding the King's Restoration; and the allocating of that small matter of six hundred a year, to be divided in small portions among them, for the support of their familys, would be an act of generosity, and worthy of the King. The Earl kneu what Mr Hutcheson said was fact, and promised to use his interest at Court to get the thing done; and he accomplished it. A warrand was procured for it, and the Dissenters in Ulster had this all King Charles' time. It was taken from them on King James' accession; and, at the Revolution, King William, knouing their firmness to the Brittish interest, and that of the Reformation, and their being firm supports of the Government, advanced it to twelve hundred pound a year, which was exceeding usefull to them, and continoued all Queen Ann's time. Upon King George his accession, he, knouing their appearances for the Protestant Succession when in hazard, in the end of the Queen's reigne, was soon prevailed upon to add eight hundred pounds yearly to the Royal Gift to the Presbiterian Ministers there, four hundred to the Ministers of the North, and four hundred to the Dissenters in the South. He adds, that that was punctually payed till the two last years of his reigne; and, at his death, these wer resting,† and they continou unpayed; and nothing has been payed of the addi-

* Allocated.   † Owing, in arrear.

tionall Bounty during this reigne, though the former twelve hundred pounds is payed.

The same person tells me, that his father, Mr John Hutcheson, was the occasion of ane incident which was very gratefull to King George, the then Elector of Hannover, and the occasion of his addition.* About the 1712 or [17]13, when the Torrys wer at the tope of their pouer, and doing all they could to overturn the Succession in the Protestant line, Mr Hutcheson made a proposall to some feu of his bretheren, the Presbiterian Ministers in Ulster, and very feu wer let in to the designe and secret; but means wer found that every Minister made a secretary in his Congregation, [to enrol] what persons might be depended upon as ready to rise in favour of the Protestant Succession, when called and authorized to appear. And, accordingly, ther was a List formed of about fifty thousand fencible men, who, if an attack wer made on the Succession, and if they wer provided with armes and ammunition, wer ready to venture their lives in defence of the Family of Hannover, and with the list of persons able to bear ends,—[arms ?]—Gentlmen and others wer pitched on in the severall parishes and countys fitt to command them, and whom the people would trust, and with whom they would venture their all, if called. When this calculation was made, they had a difficulty to get the Court of Hannover made acquaint with it, it being most inconvenient that any of the Ministers should go [to] Hannover; and so they deputed one Du Board, a French Minister, and bore his charges, and sent him over to Hannover, where he had quick access to the Elector, King George the First, and let him see the List and their officers. The Elector was very fond to hear ther wer fifty thousand stanch freinds to him. He promised, as soon as possible, to endeavour to provide them armes, and received the proposall with many thanks.

May, 1731.—This moneth, our General Assembly sat doun at Edinburgh, and continoued sitting as usuall; and I shall here set doun what hints offer unto me of things most observable.

The first thing that cast up was Mr John Dundas of Philpston his illnes. He hath been Clerk to this Church twenty-eight years, and

* To the *Regium Donum*.

lately was seized with a jaundice, and has been in an ill state of health for some time. When the Assembly met, the Moderator produced a letter from him, intimating his not being able to attend, and his desire that the Assembly might allou Mr Paton, Clerk to the Synod of Lothian, to officiat for him, till he sau what the Lord would do with him, seing he kneu that the Assembly needed two Clerks. At the same time, I had a verball message from him to give Mr Paton any help I could, especially in the affair of the classing the Instructions, which I did, and likewise in the Committy of Overtures. There was interest made, in the mean while, for a successor to him. His post as Procurator and Principall Clerk is worth near four thousand merks per annum; and those who set up wer, Mr John Millar of Neilston's son-in-lau; Mr William Grant, son to the excellent Lord Cullen; Mr Archibald Murray, Cringlety's brother, an Advocat; and Mr Michael Menzies, Cullerea's brother. The second was not so acceptable. The third is a person much commended for his piety, and, by some papers of his drauing, appears a person pretty good at forming papers; but he has no great interest. Philpstoun continoued sickly and dwining for some dayes, and then we had the account of his death by an express. That very morning the Assembly entered upon a choice of another Clerk; and Mr Grant was named, and the other two. It was feared, considerable interest would be made for the three different persons, and the Lord Miltoun and others, perhapps, interest themselves in the choice; and so, without any further,* a vote was entered upon. Mr A[rchibald] Murray, when he was named and put in the lite by a member, (when Mr Menzies also was put in the lite,) stood up and thanked the Assembly for the honnour done him, but declined to stand—he kneu he had not a backing; and Mr Menzies did the like. So the lite was left at large, and every member voted as he pleased. Three or four voted for Mr Murray, six or eight for Mr Menzies, and all the rest for Mr Grant,† who was called on, and gave his oath *de fideli*, and took his place, and desired two favours of the Assembly,—that he might be alloued to plead

---

* Delay.

† Mr Grant became successively Solicitor-General, Lord Advocate, a Judge, (Lord Prestongrange,) and Lord Justice-Clerk.

the causes he was engaged in at [the] barr for this Assembly, because partys had no time to imploy another lauer, nor inform him of their case; and because, in severall affairs he was to be at the barr, he begged that Mr Paton might be alloued to assist him.   Both wer alloued.

I shall not give Mr Dundas of Philpston's character.   I have enjoyed his freindship and much intimacy with him nou these twenty-six years. He was a pious man, and still* on the side of truth.   He was not so good a reader of papers, but a very good former of them.   He was a most diligent and indefatigable person in the affairs of the Church.   He and Niccol Spence have, indeed, had in their hand the current affairs of this Church these twenty-eight years, and have most faithfully and regularly managed them.   These two, with Sir H. Cuningham, Sir Francis Grant, afterward Lord Cullen, James Steuart, Clerk of Edinburgh, Commissar Broady, Dr Dundas, Sir Francis Pringle, Mr George Meldrum, and some others, wer members of a Praying Society, and set up [a] society for prayer, and a kind of correspondence for religiouse purposes, about the 1698, as I sau by the records of their meeting. This privat meeting laid the first foundation of that noble designe of reformation of manners in King William's time, and Queen Ann's time, that did so much good.   They held a correspondence at London with the Societys there.   About ten years after, they gave the first beginnings to the Society for Propagation of Christian Knouledge and Reformation of the Highlands and Islands, which has come to so great a lenth. Hou great a matter doth some times a litle good fire kindle ! They concerted subscriptions, they formed the charter to be expede by [the] Queen, and brought the matters to an excellent bearing ; and all as a litle weekly society for prayer and conference upon Christian purposes ! There wer but eight or ten members, lauers ; generally speaking, men of knouledge, solid piety, and estates : and, nou and then, some of the Ministers of Edinburgh met with them, and all they did was in concert with them, joyned with prayer, and flouing from great measures of a publick spirit—love to God, to souls, and abhorrence of sin ; and the Lord wonderfully countenanced their honest essayes, and hath nou

* Always, uniformly.

blessed and crouned them with great and publick success. Their memory deserves to be transmitted to posterity ; and if I can have the perusall of the MS. Register of their weekly meetings and procedure, if I live to bring doun our Biography this lenth, their procedure, and the graduall steps they wer led to as to the Societys for Reformation, and that for Propagating Christian Knouledge, this will make a gloriouse part of our Biography in that period.

But, to return to Mr Dundas of Philpston, he and Mr Spence, yet alive, had much of the burdensom work in all these great matters ; and, by their diligent application and continouall attendance upon these purposes, with the advice and influence of the rest, many of whom are nou got to heaven, helped on these great designes in Scotland. Besides these, Philpston was continoually taken up in doing things of publick use as to ecclesiasticall affairs. He formed the Abridgment of the Acts of Assembly ; a work of great labour, and very usefull. He published Directions for setling schools and manses. He, as Procurator for the Church, had the great weight of Ministers' processes for their stipends before the Lords of Plantation of Churches and Valuation of Teinds. He wrote a little tract about the Laues as to the Poor, and restraining of Beggars. He formed severall valuable memorialls about the pouer and incroachments of Patrons, in the case of East Calder ; memorialls about sists and citations of Presbyteries and Synods, before the Lords of Session, in Ecclesiasticall matters. He has brought the Registers of the Assembly, since the Revolution, to an excellent bearing. I cannot but here remember hou active and encouraging he was to me in my work of The History of our Sufferings. In short, ther was nothing of a publick nature in the Church but he was foot and hand to it, as we use to say, and heartily engaged in it. As the Church has a very great loss in his death, so it's a great mercy he has been spared so long, a faithfull, zealouse, and laboriouse servant in all our publick affairs ; and it's a favour Mr Spence outlives him, and will be in case to let in his successor to the state of publick bussines, and the thread of managing our affairs. I take it to be a kind part of Providence to this Church, that a good number of piouse and religious gentlmen and others about

Edinburgh, the seat of our publick Church Judicatorys, engaged in Societys for prayer, and some of whom wer sufferers, who kneu the lau, and had interest with people of influence, wer raised up after the Revolution, and continoued so long in this Church. Alace! many of them are taken away, as well as the old Ministers with whom they acted in concert. The Lord grant, that when such are removed, who keeped all things regular and in a consistency, under God, He may raise up a neu sett of piouse, prudent, diligent, laboriouse, and publick-spirited persons, at the helm and direction of our Church affairs; and that the publick interests may not suffer by the change of hands! The residue of the Spirit is with Him.

To return to the Assembly. It was opned with Mr Hamiltoun's sermon on 1 Tim. i. 15, where he had severall open declarations as to Christ's Divinity, and some hints against a spirit of persecution which wer variously applyed. Ministers are to be pityed who preach on such occasions.

Ther was nothing singular in the King's Letter. The Moderatorship fell upon Mr Smith; *vide* Letters, and to what is above. Mr William Millar was the person who would probably have been Moderator, had not Mr Smith be[en] a member; and, as it was, he had a considerable number :* but I observe Mr Millar is considerably failed since his last sicknes, and Mr Smith has not that vivacity and readines that once he had. He is a litle deafe; and his warmth and heat somtimes, on provocation, even discovering itself in passion, appears; which is no small token of his failour in naturall parts. His being chosen Moderator will, it may be, pave the way to setle him in the Divinity chair. It is certain he was not the person Professor Hamiltoun was at first for.

In the entry, let me observe that Mr Simson's affair came not in to this Assembly. I have notticed hou this matter stood above; and by the votes for Mr William Millar, and, afterwards, by the many warm and keen Instructions which came up from the North, in point of Doctrine and Patronages, it was soon seen that the meeting would not probably favour Mr Simson; and so no application was made. The

* Of votes.

Commissioner declared he was against its coming in, and so did the Moderator; so we have no heats upon this matter. Houever, the Church suffers, and the youth are neglected, and he enjoyes his sellary without any body's looking on the youth.

I have notticed that the Instructions that came up from Presbitrys to this Assembly wer many [and] vigorouse. An abreviat of them was taken, I suppose, by Mr J. Williamson, when they wer reading, and printed in half a sheet. I had them committed to me, and I am sure nobody ever sau them. They wer mostly from the Synod of Fife, of Stirling, Angus, and Aberdeen, and Murray, and related to doctrine, ane assertory act as to Patronages, notoriall calls,* and the Commission's members, and meeting-place, the method of preaching, and setlment of Parishes. See the copys of them this year.

Before I enter upon the bussines of the Assembly, let me begin with the Committy for revising Commissions, and nominating preachers. These wer Pr[ofessor] Hamiltoun, Pr[incipal] Chalmers, P[rincipal] Campbell, and Mr Crawford, and some feu such. Ther wer severall Presbitrys absent in Glenelg, and Argyle, and other places. The Presbitry of Orkney, I think, send up the Lord Aberdour, the Earle of Morton's son, and no Ministers. Ther was a double election for Haddingtoun or Dalkeith by a double set of Magistrates to the same person, both attested by the Presbytery, and Mr Gordon of Ardoch had a Commission not attested, and he was once throuen out as a member by the Committy, which I never kneu done since the Revolution, but all chosen wer susteaned *pro hac vice*, and Letter writt to the wrong choicers. But they designed to throu him out; yet another regular Commission from another Presbytery came up to him, and so they altered their report.

In their nomination of preachers they continou to nominat, as has been ordinary these severall years, mostly young men, who bear the name of " Bright Youths," and " Oratoriall Preachers." This is a considerable change within these feu years. For twenty years or more, since I keeped Assemblys, none but the elder, graver Ministers wer set

---

* Calls subscribed by notaries, or mandatories.

up to preach before the Assembly and Commission.   What the motives are for this change I cannot divine.   I am sure it's not a prudentiall step, and lookes as if the leading men, who have the direction of this matter, wer wearyed of the elder Ministers, and their way of preaching, or are inclined to please the vitiated tast of those about the throne, and inclined to set the neu way of preaching and harranguing against zeal, and other things, as [the] pattern to be folloued by other Ministers, or that they are affrayed, lest, if others wer named, they would perhaps touch on some truths that are not moddish and complaisant enough for this time.   Whatever their motive is, I thought they had got their bellyfull of such Preachers before the last Assembly by setting up of Mr Tailfour; of whom upon the former Assembly; and yet, this same year, they generally fix on such to preach.

Upon the first Sabbath we had Mr George Wisheart, who both in his prayers and sermon has more of a gospell strain then most of the younger celebrated preachers.   He hath a decent, grave delivery, a neat and flouent stile, and very good matter.   His text was, "Judge not"—a subject exceeding seasonable to the most part, but perhaps not so necessary at this time of a Generall Assembly, whose proper work, certainly, it's to judge, and set matters right.   In the afternoon we had a good, grave man, Mr James Chalmers, Professor of Divinity in the Neu Toun of Aberdeen.   He must be excepted out of what I am blaming.   We had a seriouse and solid discourse on, " If ye be Christ's, ye are Abram's seed, and heirs according to the promise."   He preached the Gospell, pressed preaching of Christ, and an interest in him; and I am sure, houever he pleased the great men, he had suitable. matter for the enterteanment of those who wer in earnest about their souls.   Next Sabbath there preached before the Commissioner Mr William Robison, Minister at Borthwick.*   I did not hear him, neither this time nor last time he preached, about three or four years since; but I heard nothing much blamed in his discourse on " The unity of Spirit in the bond of peace." He had some things, but pretty cautious, upon doctrine, and pointing a litle favourably to Mr Simson's prosecution; that retractations should not be uncharitably judged of, and the like; and pressed peace very much.

* Father of the celebrated Principal Robertson.

In the afternoon I heard, in the Commissioner's Church, Mr William Armstrong. He is the son of a worthy old Minister, but of another character. One Mr Burn, Minister of Fetteresso, was named; but he pleaded want of health, and this young [man] was named in his room. He is said to be a cusin of his, of the name of Armstrong, [who,] with Wallace of Moffat, Mr Telfair, and some other young men in that country of the Merse and the Dail, (Teviotdale,) [are] members of a Club, who do not favour Confessions, and seem to verge towards a latitude not consistent with the interests of this Church. He preached after the last Assembly, or before it, as Moderator of the Synod of Dumfreice, and had his sermon levelled against Church pouer and authority, much out of The Rights of the Christian Church.* Mr John Scot preached the next Synod sermon, in October last, and countered him without naming him, save under the generall, as the opposer of Church pouer, with the author of The Rights of the Christian Church. Mr Armstrong's sermon was so obnoxious, (as I am told, and if I be misinformed, thir things, as to particular persons, must stand in thir privat Collections, as if they wer not set doun,) that hearing that the Synod wer to take nottice of it, he took his horse streight after sermon and left them. Nou, what wisdom it's for P[rofessor] Hamiltoun [and] those he directs, to set up such persons on such publick occasions, I cannot understand. He preached to us upon doing good. He read his papers, in his Bible, in the grossest, most indistinct, and undecent manner ever I was witnes to. The writet was so large that I sau the letters at a good distance when he turned the leafe; but at every six or seven lines he mistook the line, and read a wrong one, and called himself back in a very undecent manner. The matter was very common and generall. He had some scrapes and sentences from Tillotson's Sermons, very ill put together. He had some flings at melancholy gloomy devotion, in the words of Mr Archibald Campbell's pamphlet on Enthusiasme. He said, pressing doing good, " That our good works would go in before to the aufull barr of Divine justice, and plead our cause there, throu the merits and rightiousnes of Christ," with severall other expressions lyabel to exception: But his heavy manner of reading, without the least decency, was obvious to all.

* Published, in 1709, against the independence of the Church.   † Handwriting.

This day, in the fornoon, I went to the Trone Church, and heard Mr Archibald Campbell, Minister at Larbert, and Professor of Ecclesiastical History at Saint Andreus. I have formerly hinted (and, for more accounts, *vide* Letters since October last) at his pamphlet about the Apostles not being enthusiasts, and the noise it has made in this Church. Five or six answers are come out to it by Mr Hunter, and Hog, his father-in-lau, Mr Steuart, and [Mr] Wilson, Ministers in Perth, and some others. It was talked, that Mr Campbell, chosen by the Presbytery of Stirling member of this Assembly, was to ask liberty of the Assembly to vindicate himself in the Assembly by a speech against the aspersions cast upon him by these pamphlets ; but, it seems, that project was not acceptable to his advisers, and it was droped ; and no wonder, unles he had been attacked by the Assembly for the propositions advanced in that pamphlet. He had liberty, unsought, to vindicat himself in the press ; and so nothing of this came in publick. I was fond to hear a person who made so much noise of late, and the rather that we heard he was to make a sort of recantation and retractation. His text was, Rom. viii. 9, " He that hath not the Spirit of Christ is none of his." He had a grave, distinct, solid, pointed, clear delivery. The substance of his discourse [was] this : After he had notticed that the Apostle had laid doun the doctrine of man's generall apostacy and depravation in the first three chapters, and drauen, as a consequence from it, that no man could be justifyed by the works of the lau, by which we wer to understand all things done by us after the commission of sin, he sheued the necessity of a propitiation and satisfaction ; as the pardon of sin necessarly went upon that, so justification, in the fourth and fifth chapters, could only be by faith in the rightiousnes of Christ. The Apostle, in the eighth chapter, came to the priviledges of the justified, among which this was a cheife one in the text, that they had the Spirit of Christ. And so he considered the priviledges of the disciples of Christ, or justifyed persons that have the Spirit—access to God, pardon of sin, the redemption of the body, and eternall life. Then he opned up the character of justifyed persons, their having the Spirit of Christ. By " the Spirit of Christ," he said, we behoved to understand the third person of the Trinity ; and, consequently, Christ was God : and the having Him did not, could not, relate to having Him in his essence, since that was impossible to men to have, but in his influences, and works, and operations.   He did not touch his indwelling.   But I blame nobody for not having all that is to be said on a subject in three quarters of an hour.   Then he considered the influences and operations of the Spirit of Christ as either universall, and common to all rationall creatures, yea, to all creatures : " The Spirit moved on the face of the watters," and " in Him we live and move," &c. ; or his miraculous operations for the confirmation and spreading of Christianity.   These wer not meaned,* but the ordinary influences and operations common to all belivers and disciples of Christ : These wer necessary, he said, because of our naturall darknes and confusion on our minds—" the natural man knoweth not," &c., " for they are spiritually discerned," and our passions and irregular affections.   He did not touch on the corruption of the will, but, it may be, he thinks that is a consequent of the depravation of the mind.   For this he cited, " the carnall mind is enmity against God ;" which, perhaps, hitts not the passions so much. This work of the Spirit he described by a neu creation ; a forming the mind to all rightiousnes, goodnes, and truth ; and enlarged a litle on it ; at the close of which he said, that all this work might fail, and be ready to dye, by our quenching the Spirit and vexing Him.   The phraze of " failing" may be taken charitably.   It was the only exceptionable phraze I observed.   Then he dreu some inferences : The first was the necessity that all wer under to have this Spirit of Christ, which he expressed in pretty strong expressions ; that as creatures had their being, and wer constitute creatures by the Divine energy and pouer, so Christians wer Christians, and had their very being from the influences and operations of the Spirit of Christ ; and that we should walk in the Spirit, and depend on him, and take heed what manner of spirit we are of, and pray to God for the Spirit.

Let me only add, that when he came to Saint Andreus, he presented his patent to the Principal in November last ; and the Principal called an University meeting, where they agreed to receive him upon a certi-

* Intended, in the text.

ficat of his having taken the oaths, and subscribed the Confession of Faith. In order to this last, the Presbytery was called *pro re nata*. The meeting was thin. The Principal and he applyed to the Presbytery for liberty to signe the Confession of Faith. Mr Anderson* was the only person that made any difficulty. He said, that he did not think that the Presbytery could allou him to signe as one of their members, till he was loosed from his congregation of Larbert, otherwise he might keep both benefices. He adduced many instances, [as] of Mr Neil Campbell, who was transported from Renfreu before he was received into the Presbytery of Glasgou, and inaugurat; and so every one who wer setled in Colledges. He and another wer sent out to converse with him on that matter. Mr Campbell told them he did not think it proper to give them, as a Presbytery, any satisfaction as to that; he had opened his designe that way to Pr[incipal] Haddo, but would give the Presbytery no answer to that; his patent gave him a right to demand liberty to signe; if they refused, he knew what to do. This was pretty magisteriall with the Presbytery. Houever, Pr. Haddo told the Commissioners from the Presbytery, that he, Mr C[ampbell,] had told him he designed to give in a dimission of his ministeriall charge at Larbert at Whitsunday, and remove with his family from Larbert to Saint Andreus after that—his circumstances not allouing him to remove sooner. The two Commissioners represented all to the Presbytery. Mr Anderson declared himself not satisfyed with the treatment, [statement?] but the rest alloued him to subscribe. After he had signed, he had his inaugurall discourse, and was admitted by the University. He preached none at Saint Andreues; and, in a feu dayes, left them, and has not been there since November. This is all that passed as to his reception.

I return nou to the Assembly. The Instructions† brought in the generall bussines of the Assembly. The particular transportations need not be notticed. Ther was nothing very remarkable in them, save debates about regard to the heads of familys, in opposition to the Heretors, and Elders, and Patron; and, generally, the Patron's side caryed it.

* Minister of St Andrews.   † From Presbyteries to their representatives.

By the Instructions, an adress against Patronages, an adress against Error, and the act about Setling of Parishes, wer the most considerable things the reasoning run upon ; and I shall give what I remember most materiall on these heads, and the rather that nou nothing of a publick concern, properly speaking, has been before our Assembly these four years. Mr Simson's affair took up three Assemblys, and the contentions about Principal Chambers' setlment, which wer so tediouse, took up the last Assembly, so that nothing of a publick rule or generall concern could get in.

To begin with Patronages, and our other greivances, ther wer Instructions from many Presbitrys to adress and take all proper wayes to have the Church freed from them. This has been a long continouing Instruction for twenty years, and nothing done upon it, save in the 1715 and 1718, when the clause about acceptations was added. The Commission hath been every year impouered to make adresses in order to removing the Churches Greivances ; and after all the reasonings this year, this landed likewise in that, and in the act about Setlments, of which afterwards. We wer, as we have heard, upon March, threatned with neu pressures, and the tying the yoak harder about our necks, last session of Parliament ; and that was made a handle of to keep us quiet, lest a neu lau should be made ; wheras, it may be, had a wise appearance been made by this Assembly, in a modest manner, to sheu the Goverment hou much we groan under the burden of Patronages, this would effectually have prevented further impositions, unles the leading men at Court incline to have the peace of the Church broken, which is scarce supposable. What many Ministers fear is, that such countenance is given by Commissions and General Assemblys to setlments by Patrons, and such favour is sheuen in the more publick actings of the Church by the influence of some of the leading Ministers at Edinburgh, and the Ruling Elders there, to every case wherein a Patron is concerned, be the people and Presbytery never so averse, and the man never so unworthy or unacceptable, that the Court, which take their rules from what passes at Edinburgh, may readily judge that Patronage is turning easy to us, and no longer a burden. In conversation and reasoning on this head, I find it observed, what, perhaps, I notticed before, in March, that if we be in earnest to have Patronages removed, we are in the wrong channell.   We make a bustle at our Assembly about adressing the King, who, indeed, has it not in his pouer to help us, ex[cept] when the Parliament is sitting ; our adress is out of head till next Assembly, and so nothing is done.   If our Scots Members of Parliament be not brought over to favour us in this matter, all adresses to King or Parliament are idle things.   Our road, then, would be for the Assembly to appoint persons in every Presbytery to deal with our Scots Members of Parliament in the time of reces, when they are here in Scotland, and to bring them to be sensible of the hurt that lau brings to the Church, and hou it sours people's tempers, and is the occasion of breaches of the publick peace, and really alienats the common people not only from the Establishment in the Church, but the Civil Goverment, which bears so hard upon them in their religiouse concerns, and the choice of their Ministers, nothing than this being dearer to them.   And then, when matters are prepared this way, the Commission, in November before the Parliament meet, ought to adress the King, and some of our Members apply to the Parliament, in a regular way, for redress ; and, if need be, Ministers should be sent to London, who are in earnest to have this greivance helped.   This is the only feasible way, to my apprehension ; and, indeed, could we prevail but with the two brothers, A[rgyll] and I[sla,] there is litle question to be made but all the rest would come in to it.   Hou to prevail with them is the difficulty ; but this [is] plain, wer they in earnest, ther would be litle or no stop from the English Members of Parliament.

This brings to my mind a passage Mr Robert Stewart tells me he had from Mr Carstairs, who was sent up with others—1714 or [17]15—about the Greivances.   When he came doun from Court, he told my informer, that they had a fair lay* to be eased of Patronages ; but the Duke of Argyle stood violently against them in this, and could by no means be got to yeild ; and I think I have formerly notticed, in thir Collections, that Pr[ofessor] Hamiltoun told me, that when he, with others, wer up, in the 1717 or [17]18, that the English Ministry wer most ready to ease

* Prospect.

us of this burden ; and desired them to speak to A[rgyll] and Isla, and if they gained them, they might depend on their concurrence. When he waited on the Duke, he frankly told them that, for his oun share, he needed not stick,* for he was sure of having his inclinations folloued in all his parishes, whether he wer Patron or not ; but, he was of opinion, Patronage was a civil right, and a point of property, which he would never give up ; and if it wer endeavoured to be wrested out of his hands, he would oppose it with all his pouer. The same was Isla's answer ; so that, indeed, the continouance of this burden upon us may justly lye at their dore ; and we knou it was their worthy predecessor in the 1649 that struggled hard against the rescinding of them, and from the 1638 till then prevailed to have them continoued.

There was not much reasoning in the Committy and Sub-committy of Instructions, about an adress to ease us of Patronages. The affair of the act about setlments was thought more of weight to take up our time with, as what was in our pouer, and what might calm the generall cry at present from so many Presbitryes. Ther wer some reasonings, indeed, upon acceptations of presentations by intrants, for some time pretty closs† in the Committy of Instructions and Overtures. Severall Instructions came up from Presbitrys, that the Assembly should pass an act discharging Ministers or Preachers to accept of presentations, as being a plain greivance to this Church. Mr Gordon, Minister at Alford, opened the debate, and said that he still took the clause of adding acceptations, 1719, to be designed as a favour to this Church ; and that our freinds that added it wer of opinion, that Patronages being declared contrary to the priviledges and principles of this Church, no Minister nor Preacher of this Church, acting agreably to our principles, would ever accept ; and so Patrons' pouer would fall, and, therefor, we should take the benefite of that favourable act, and discharge all to accept. Prof[essor] Hamiltoun answered, that he would not disput at present whither Patronages wer contrary to the principles of this Church ; he would allou them to be a greivance, but thought it hard to set our principles in opposition to the practise of the Ministers of this Church in

* Resist obstinately.   † Closely debated.

her purest times, from the 1637 to 1649: That it was evident that the Ministers, Mr Henderson, Gillespy, Dickson, &c., wer not in principle against acceptation of presentations: That by the acts of Assembly, 1643 and [16]42, upon concert with the King to name a lite of six, and these reduced to three, the Assembly appointed all Ministers and Preachers that wer in the list to accept of the King's presentation. To this it was answered, that the list was made by the consent of the people, and prior to the acceptance, and that the choice was made before the acceptance was enacted; and so it did not at all come up to our present case. It was further urged, that the Assembly, 1565, declared they wer not to act against the Queen's civil right of presentation, and only claimed the judging of the intrant's abilitys and qualifications. To this the Book of Discipline declaring the Churches Patrimony to be disposed of by the Church, and the plain declarations in the second Book of the people's right to choice their own pastor. Indeed, in the first period of our Church, the people's consent was all along stuck by by the Church.

Professor H[amilton] added, that as to the clause, 1719, about acceptations, it was designed in our favour, but not in the sense was urged; that by non-acceptance Patrons' power should fall. This he was very sure was not, he said, the designe of the act, but to prevent sham presentations. This, as I have more than once observed, is a fact, that persons who wer at London at that time differ about. Colonel Erskine, L[ord] Grange, and others, assert that act run upon the knouen principle that no Presbiterian would accept presentations. P[rofessor] Hamiltoun still asserts the contrary. The President and Solicitor said that an act of Assembly discharging acceptations would be very like the old way, ane act of the Commission against an act of Parliament, which they would be very sorry to think of: That it would be a material rescinding of an act of Parliament, and in our present circumstances would undoubtedly bring an explication of that Brittish act, and neu enforcements upon us.

To this Mr Gordon answered, that he could by no means see the justnes of that reasoning. He still considered the clause about acceptation as a favourable clause for this Church, and designed for our benefite, and it was not a flying in the face of lau for the Church to take the benefite of a lau in her favour: That he considered this case much as the case of Tolleration. The lau about tolleration of meetings for the English Service, and the lau about Patronages, wer brought on us at the very same time, and with the same vieu, to break* us in this Church for our attachment to the Protestant Succession in the present Royall Family. He put the case, that the act of Tolleration and the act of Patronages still continoued, but with this difference, that that of Patronages had the favourable clause, a saving clause added, putting Patrons, as it wer, in a tollerated state. He thought that it would not at all be a flying in the face of the lau about Tolleration, if the Assembly should make a declaration and act, that whosoever, Minister or Preacher, should forsake her communion, and wait on the tollerated meetings where the English Ceremonies are used, and joyne in them, should not be alloued to be planted in a parish. Just so, the act and declaration craved, that accepters of presentations should not be alloued to be ordeaned, could never, in his opinion, be reaconed an act of Assembly against an act of Parliament; if so be we wer agreed, as he hoped we wer, that Patronages wer a greivance, and contrary to the principles of this Church, which he thought the Commission and Assembly aproving their adress against them, 1711 and [17]12, had directly declared. I did not perceive this reasoning answered, save what is above, and that the members of the Brittish Parliament would not be of the same opinion with us that Patronage is unlaufull.

The Laird of Aflect interposed in this debate, upon another foot and manner. He observed, that he had not observed it questioned before, that Patronages wer unlaufull and a greivance, and that he took it alwise for our principle in this Church, and hoped it would still be so: That he still considered patronages as a branch of Popery and Episcopacy: That as they came doun from Popery, so they wer still accounted unlaufull in Scotland, save in the periods when Prelacy was crammed doun upon us; as soon as we reformed from Prælacy and Popery, the First Book of Discipline declares against them; after Tulchan Bishops† wer cast out, the Second Book declares yet more against them; and they

* Crush.

† This singular phrase, by no means uncommon after the period of the Reformation, alludes to the practice of placing a *tulchan*, or stuffed calf, beside a cow deprived of her young, to prevail on her to give her milk.

came in again with Prælacy, and wer declared against when Presbitery was set up, and brought in again at the Restoration, and cast out at the Revolution : That he still thought that a very essentiall difference betwixt Presbiterian parity* and Prælacy lay in the matter of setling parishes. Under Prælacy the Bishop setled whom he pleased, without consulting the people ; but under Presbytery the people's consent was alwise sought ; and if we loss this, we loss our Presbiterian constitution and parity.

The Lord Drummore answered him again, and said, he for [his] share reconed Patronages a greivance, and that not only upon the people but the Heretors ; but could not think they wer contrary to our principles, because they wer used, and acceptation of them common, till the 1649, the plan of which act he heard was objected to by some of the best of the Ministers. But he should have minded it was not Presentation being removed which these Ministers excepted against, Mr Calderwood and others, but the manner of Election by Sessions. He observed even in the 1649 the plan was not by poll, but the Heads of Familys wer alloued to make exceptions and objections : That, for his part, he would never consent to elections only by Sessions : That at the Revolution the Heretors and Elders named, not Heads of Familys ; and that was the plan he thought most reasonable, and wished we could obtain it.

Thir reasonings ended in the act about Setling Parishes *tanquam jure devoluto*, when the right falls ; see the copy of the act. Ther was an Instruction from the Synod of Glasgou, that the Assembly should lay doun a rule for uniformity in planting of vacancys, since in different places different methods wer taken. This matter was sub-committed, with all the Instructions relative to Patronages, Acceptance of them, &c. This Sub-committy entered upon the consideration what rule to lay doun in an Ecclesiasticall way, since we had no stated Church rules this way. Ther was some time spent upon the plan laid doun in the Act of Parliament 1690 ; and, at lenth, by a vote, this was agreed upon. It was said that was, till the 1712, that Patronages wer imposed, the ge-

* Equality of rank among her Ministers.

nerall practise of this Church.   It was observed, that that plan was the
sentiments of the old Ministers at the Revolution ; that we may be sure
they got at that Parliament every thing which they asked ; and that
what was in that act might be considered as the Ministers' desire, and
what they agreed unto.

Some said that it was formed by a meeting of Ministers then at Edinburgh waiting upon the Parliament ; but above, in this Collection, I
have set doun the accompt of it from Sir James Steuart, who formed it ;
and I am at this time further assured, that the first part of the Act 1690
was formed by Sir, then Mr, James Steuart, and was presented to the
Parliament by his brother, Sir Thomas Steuart of Cultnes ; and the
after part of the act, allouing the parishes to buy, and ordering the
Patrons to accept of six hundred merks, was added by my [friend ?] the
Lord Whitlaw, Mr William Hamiltoun, brother to the Laird of Houshill.
The Act 1690 was read ; and instead of " Heretors being Protestants,"
it was moved it should be in our act, " Heritors of our communion ;"
or, " a speciall regard being had to Heretors who joyne in ordinances."
By others it was moved that it should run, " Heritors signing the Call ;"
by which signing they oblidge themselves to subject to ordinances.
Against these additions, it was reasoned that this was too much limit-
ing : That, at the Revolution, the North was as much disaffected in its
heretors as nou, and yet no more was found needfull than " Heritors
being Protestants :" That this was the most probable way to gain Heritors to come to be of our communion : That the clause, " subscribing
the Call," would not be of great security, for subscription to subjection
might be made, as the world goes, without follouing attendance on ordinances.

Then the clause about naming and proposing was reasoned upon.   It
was said that it was to [be] understood of electing and choicing, as is
plain from the follouing clause, " as Royall Burghs wer," is used. Here,
indeed, the strait of severalls lay, whither Heritors, as such, and non-
residing Heretors, had a right to elect and choice.   It was thought that
this was the determining a very nice point, which had not yet been determined by this or any Reformed Church ; and, therfor, in the first

draught, we keeped " named and proposed," though in the Committy of Overtures, " elect and choice" was put in the room of it, for the above reason.

Then the clause of recomending this method to Presbitrys before the *jus devolutum* fell in their hands, and discharging them to delay unnecessarly, was reasoned upon. After this, it was sub-committed to Pr[incipal] Haddo and me to extend the Act, and put it in form of a Church Act. When we did this, and it was in some time brought in to the Committy of Overtures, ther wer severall debates and amendments. We had put in a clause of Patronages being a Greivance; that was turned out by the Ruling Elders, President, and others, as what, though true, yet it was not proper to put to an Ecclesiasticall Act; then a clause about the Presbitry's meeting, and calling the Heretors and Elders, (whose designation we had made " representatives of the people,") and the clause naming and proposing to the people was altered, by Pr[ofessor] Hamiltoun, to " electing and chusiug." Upon this there wer long debates. It was urged, that the Christian people wer the proper choicers and callers: That this was the practise before the 1649; and at the 1649, the Session wer appointed Electors, and the people to give in objections: That in the 1687, where Aflect cited a paper of the Resolutions of some generall meeting of Ministers, from my History, that Heretors, Elders, and Heads of Familys, should call; that this had been the constant practise till 1712, when the lau 1690 was in force.

It was urged by the Moderator, that Poll elections wer warranded by no practise in the Christian Church, and not to be gone into: That Heretors wer not to be put on a levell with their tennants. Pr[ofessor] Hamiltoun, when this was like to come to some heat, interposed, and endeavoured to sheu, though the plan of the Act 1690 was the fixed interest in a congregation, and that was the midse,* that the people, by this Act, had their approbation and disapprobation alloued, with the reasons, of which the Presbytery wer judges, that this was the proper midse we wer to keep. The bretheren in the North wer generally

* Medium, means.

against this plan, by reason of the disaffection of their Heretors, and
urged that, for the sake of the peace of the Goverment, somewhat
should be added to exclude Jacobite and disaffected Heretors.   It was
answered to that, that taking the oaths was the proper test of affection
and disaffection ; and as the Parliament 1690 did not think fitt to put
even that in, so it was not proper for the Church to do it.

Under all these variouse sentiments, it was agreed that the Act should
be transmitted to Presbitrys, and under their consideration till next
Assembly, and in the mean time have the force of an Act.   Mr Willison
of Dundee added a clause, which, he thought, might ease the minds of
many as to acceptations, that the Assembly should recomend it to Ministers, Preachers, &c., not to encourage any other method of setlment
but in the form of this Act ; which was gone into without opposition.
Pr[ofessor] Hamiltoun was for making this a standing Act at present,
as having long been under Presbyteries' consideration ; but he yeilded.

This is all the lenth this method of setling Congregations could be
brought.   It's probable that, by the opposition the North country Ministers made to it, that it may not be passed to a standing Act next
Assembly.   To me, indeed, it's hard to determine whither one method
will fully answer, in point of expediency, to the South, where the Heretors are not openly disaffected, and the North ; but it seems necessary
that some rule should be fixed.   It is scarce to be expected we shall be
relieved from presentations, and it's pretty hard to fix what should come
in their room.   One would think that the King might order the presentations in the Croun's pouer to be setled in this manner, and that would
be a copy for all well disposed Patrons.   I find it a debate among lauers,
whither the King be Patron in most places where he claimes it.   In
Erections made and doled by the Royall munificence, it seems yeilded
that he is ; and it's added, that where ther is no Patron, the King, as
last heir, is so ; but that is flatly denyed by lauers ; and they observe,
further, that the most of the King's Patronages are by his succession to
the Abbayes and Monastryes under Popery ; and the Patronages of
many laymen and Lords of Erection come this way ; but [they] say

litle as to the Patronages of these who have the lands and teinds of Religiouse Houses, since their tenour* of the Patronages may be much questioned. Many of the King's Patronages are where others have the lands and teinds. In England, indeed, the case is otherwise, when all Religiouse Houses wer put in the King's hands, and all Church pouer vested in him as Suprem Head of the Church, and flouing from him by lau. But this is not our lau, and the Croun's right may be questioned in most of his presentations. This is what lauers should clear to us.

Mean while, it's observed that King George the First gave it as a rule to the Court of Police, which have the Croun's Presentations in their hand, to present, with concurrence of all concerned, which was done in most cases ; and the Church had litle trouble with many of them. But when the two brothers, especially Isla, came into the managment, that instruction was left out to the Court of Police, and the King's servants. It was moved, by some, to the Commissioner at this Assembly, that it would be of great use, if so be he could procure such a clause to be reneued. He smiled, and said, My Lord Isla might be spoke to ; but he doubted it would not do, for that would loss the interest the managers inclined to have in the disposall of the King's Patronages, which he was affrayed they would not easily part with ; and, indeed, there our choak† lyes. Certain persons incline to have the planting of Churches, and the bringing in Ministers depending on them to the Church, that all may be as they would have it. And this, as, I believe, I have formerly observed, has been the politick of a great and noble family, to have the Ministers of this Church at their devotion, both from the 1638–1649, and since the 1715, that our party work came. *Hinc illæ lachrymæ,* and *origo malorum !* Could we get any ease this way, by an adress to the King, when we can scarce expect the Patronage Act will be repealed, I knou not ; but it might have a good deal of influence on subject Patrons, providing Ministers would abide by the plan 1690. But, alace ! our times are far from being on the bettering hand.

* Tenure.   † Difficulty.

Let me only further remark, that this Act as to Setling Parishes, *tanquam jure devoluto*, has been very long before Presbyteries, Commissions, and Generall Assemblys. It began about the 1711, and was resumed again about the 1721 or two, [1722,] and an Act printed and transmitted to Presbitrys. It was before Commissions and Committys of Assemblys severall times; and, I think, I have notticed some reasonings about it in the preceeding Volumes of thir Analecta. I shall only remark, that the leading men about Edinburgh did not seem to be for any such act its passing. Ther wer many difficultys, indeed; and my Lord Grange seemed to push matters very far against all heretors, as heretors, being electors of a Minister; and to lodge all in the hands of the Christian people and communicants. This was one of the things he was blamed for, as tending to rent and divide this Church. In severall meetings—1723 and [172]4—where I was, the Sub-committy of the Commission to which this Act was referred to ripen, by the Assembly, seemed to come pretty near one another; but I observed Pr[ofessor] Hamiltoun and some others desert such meetings, as if they wer not pleased with the plan of this act; and so, indeed, it came to no bearing, though I think it was still continoued, before the Commission, by the General Assembly, from that time to this. I am told, Mr Chalmers, last summer, got this Act, as amended by many Committys of the Commission, with him to Aberdeen; and it was not come up to this Assembly when we called for it.

The first open difficulty upon this affair of setling parishes was in the case of Lochmaben, 1723; see Letters and papers that year. That affair was made easy by the King's servants, and a neu presentation was procured for Mr Cuming, and Mr Carlisle was setled elsewhere. In the 1725, the affair of Mr William Chambers' setlment of Minister of Neu Aberdeen, in opposition to Mr . . . . . who is there at present. There the Commission, and I among [the rest,] out of regard to the Whig Magistrates, and interest there, joyned in it; and he was setled by a Committy of Commission, contrary the plurality of the Presbitry, and the elders and heads of familys wer dubiouse. Indeed, we restricted the Committy to our oun members; but, since that time, I have not voted in any affair wher Committys wer clapped upon Presbitrys, nor probably will, for what I knou, till I see matters in another channell; though that setlment, as far as I see, hath indeed proved, in the event, happy enough.

By this time, some about Edinburgh came to take the affair of calling really to heart; but the directors of affairs, as I have said, lay off, and, it seems, inclined to have this pouer of calling left loose, that it might really be in the Commission's hand to setle according as partys would have it; and so no rule was agreed to. The Commission after that, till this year, had really all the Churches setlments in their hands, the Assembly being so taken up with Mr Simson's affair, that there was no room for setlments save that of Aberdeen. And in the affair of Aberdeen, of Old Machir, of Touie, of Renfreu, of Hutton, [and] of Crimond, they took odd steps, sometimes on the one side, sometimes on the other side, of the question, as partys led them; they having no fixed rule to act by. But especially last year, in the affair of Balfrone. Multitudes of these setlments wer without any consent of the people, or such as are to be reconed proper calls. Sometimes the Commission wer disapproven, but their wrongouse setlments wer never reversed; so that nou, really the spirits of people are perfectly soured by these arbitrary steps, meerly to serve courtiers and partys. This present Act is the only generall [Act] that ever the Assembly has yet agreed unto; but then it needs great amendments, some of which wer reasoned and pretty much agreed upon in Committys of the Commission, which had the Act for setling *tanquam jure devoluto* under consideration, as has been said. Ther it was agreed on, that speciall regard should be had to heretors that attended on ordinances, otherwise certainly it will be a great hardship on well-affected heretors. Heretors also would be defined, and somewhat of their paying cess, or some other rule, should be fixed; and, further, it was there agreed that heretors and elders should act in two separat bodyes; and that heads of familys, in case of a difference between those, should be taken in to make the ballance. Many other regulations would be needfull to make; but I doubt this is scarce a time for it; and I see some leading persons are not fond of rules.

Pouer is sweet, and such who get it in their hands are not willing to part with it.

The other affair of consequence before the Assembly was an act and warning against Error and Infidelity, so much grouing. Instructions for this, as has been notticed, came in from Fyfe, Stirling, Angus, Murray, and some particular Presbitrys. Because this matter had been urged by many Presbitrys ever since Mr Simson's affair, and, indeed, the grouing infidelity and loosnes of principles in Tindall and others, very much taking among the gentry and others, seems to raise the concern about this, the Synod of Perth and Angus had adresses synodicall, and commissioners named by the Synod subscribing them, directly to the Assembly, by the Committy of Bills. This matter came in to the Instructions, and was sub-committed twice ; but the Committy did not meet, the directors not being inclined to medle in it ; and, on some pretext or other, they keeped not the meetings ; and when it came in in open Assembly, by the Bills, it was in the last sederunt, and went to the Commission, where it's probable it will never come to any thing.

The matter was pretty much ripned, and termes agreed upon by the Synod and Presbitrys, who sent them up, with much exactnes. See the copys of them, papers this year. In them, which seems to be the choak of the thing, there is a particular deduction of Mr Simson's errors, in the termes of the Assembly's declarations. This was one sederunt debated, in the generall, in the Committy of Instructions, before it was sub-committed. The substance of the reasoning was this : When the Instructions wer read, it was said, by such as favoured them, that the matter was much formed in the Instructions from Saint Andreus, and Synod of Angus and Murray, and might be sub-committed.

Pr[ofessor] Hamiltoun was of opinion, the termes, at least severall of them, in these draughts, pointing to some phrazes against the errors charged on Mr Simson, if adopted by the Assembly, would be an enlarging our Standarts, and making additions to our Confession of Faith, which, he thought, was a work very tenderly to be gone about, and with much deliberation. This is the great bugbear that is used in this matter ; and some of the Ruling Elders, who, I doubt, understand litle of our doctrine, made large declamations on the excellency and fullnes of our Confession, and hou litle need there was to give any warning in terms different from that. Mr J. Sanderson, in Elgine, answered : That enlarging Confessions has been what was ordinarly done in all ages ; and it behoved to be done, as hereticks and evil-minded men scogged* themselves under scripturall and standart phrazes, and yet vented neu and unsafe terms of expressing themselves : That this was what all words [which] men could contrive wer lyable to ; and when perverted, they needed explications.

Mr Alexander Anderson, in St Andreus, observed : That had been done already in Mr Simson's process, and it behoved to be done when circumstances made it necessary : That he had observed very feu or none proposed in any of the draughts of a warning before the Committy, but what wer either directly or by very near illation† in our Standarts, and in Acts of Assembly ; and he hoped, that if once we came to particulars, that would soon be made appear, if once we wer come to particulars.

It was urged that many of the errors pointed at in these draughts wer not among us, but in English Writtings, which would be best answered by overlooking them. It was answered, These books wer among us, and much read, and infectious : That, besides this, ther wer many assertions by writters among ourselves which wer out of the common road, and lyable to exception ; here ther wer pointings toward Mr Campbell's pamphlet.

My Lord Drummore hoped those errors, write and vented in England, wer not taking here : He belived they wer dispised, and reconed contradiction and nonsense : That a Church was not bound to give a publick warning when an author and pamphlet-writter to[ok] it in head to vent some old error, otherwise we would have work enough to doe : That, if errors wer vented among ourselves by Members or Ministers, the proper way was to raise a process, and lybell the writters, and censure them as

---

* Hedged, sheltered.   † Inference.

the proof came out: That he thought that a far more habile way than to give any publick warning, which he did not take to be a remedy proportioned to the disease at all. Answers wer given to these, That error and infidelity was evidently grouing, and innovations in point of doctrine among us: That the two wayes wer not inconsistent, and the publick warning reached other ends than a process, and a lybell was a pretty difficult thing in points of doctrine. So the matter was referred to the Sub-committy, who had the act about setlments in their hand; but, as I said, what for one cause, what for others, and the throng with the affair of Setlments, nothing was done but a reference to the Commission by the Assembly.

Ther was a direct address from the Synod of Aberdeen about Notoriall Calls, that is, acceptance of and approving by the Synod of Aberdeen, and the Commission of the Assembly, of subscriptions of people under the hands and attestation of publick notars,* and not supervised by Ministers, yea, in opposition to the call supervised by the Presbytery. It only happened in the affair of Crimond, and Mr Forbes of Deer made a great bustle about it. It was said that the Presbytery refused to take in those subscribers, and they had no other way to verify their subscribing but by calling nottars to attest. The members of the Synod of Aberdeen wer very loud against [each] other on that address; Pr[incipal] Chalmers and his party on the one side, and Mr John Forbes and Mr James Gordon on the other, and wer litle better than giving other the lye in the face of the Committy of Instructions. This matter went no further.

Ther was mostly from the Synod of Aberdeen strong instructions against Superior Judicatorys, Synods, Assemblyes, and especially Commissions appointing Joynt-Committys, Correspondents, and other such meetings, to overrule Presbitrys. This related to the affair of Old Machir and Neu Machir, and was sadly abused in Balfron. This is, indeed, a taking the whole pouer on the matter from Presbitrys by a superior party in the Synod or Commission, and is like to have very ill

* Notaries public.

consequences. It was said, that where Presbitrys are rebellious to Superior Judicatorys, they must be quelled, and in other cases they wer not appointed. But this is certainly a dangerouse thing, and has been much abused of late by the Commission.

[*May* 15.]—There was a very shamefull squable betwixt the Moderator and Mr Gordon of Ardoch in the Committy of Overtures, May 15. Ardoch alledged the Moderator had given a wrong state of a thing. Some others had compleaned, particularly Afflect, of peculiar treatment from Mr Smith, which was reconed ane attacking the chair and the Judicatory, but that was soon over. But Ardoch and he came to an undecent hight. Ardoch is a man of great passion, and still interposing ;* but when he contradicted the Moderator, and said he had mistated it, the Moderator being pushed to it by P[rofessor] Hamiltoun and Mr Crawford, would leave the chair and come to the barr. No body in the Committy was for it save these two. He would be to the barr, and Mr Gordon† was unwilling ; the members of the Committy opposed. They wer so loud, I heard them at the distance of the street and Kirk ! When I came in they wer not done. I heard the Moderator call Mr Gordon " a madman !" The Solicitor interposed, and Mr Gordon made some kind of acknouledgment, and Mr Smith closed with prayer, where he lamented weaknes and passion very much.

Mr James Bannatyne tells me, that, as has been notticed, P[rofessor] Hamiltoun very plainly opposed Mr Smith's coming in to Edinburgh, till he was forced to it, to get in Mr Gaudie : That since, he has, till of late, opposed Mr Smith's being Professor, and seems to be for Mr Gaudie, though he does not speak out : That this Assembly he thought to have prevented his being a member, but nou his being Moderator, though against the grain, was designed to sheu the interest Mr Smith had : That Professor Hamiltoun layes all the blame of any hights he goes to on Mr Cranford :‡ That he sayes he cannot hold up with him.

Mr Alston and I had a long conversation ; and he told me all that

---

* Constantly interfering.   † Mr Gordon of Ardoch, the party alluded to.
‡ Professor of Ecclesiastical History, Edinburgh.

passed as to his being Principall and Professor. After he was last Moderator, 1729, when it was thought by the courtiers that he had managed that difficult post at that time without a breach, and before Mr Wisheart's death, Mr Innies made a proposall to him of coming in to Edinburgh, and succeeding Mr Wisheart, in my Lord M[ilto]n or I[sl]a's name. He declined talking of it till the vacancy should come. When that came, my L[ord] M[ilto]n sent messages to him ; he still waved it for some time. At length they met, and he proposed his coming in and being Principall and Minister. He answered, that would meet with difficultys, and he could give no answer till he kneu hou the Colledge stood, and Pr[ofessor] Hamiltoun. If partys consented, he would take it to consideration, but would never come in to a flame, and till all wer satisfyed, nor be a bone of contention. Thus matters stood till my L[ord] I[sl]a came doun. When he waited on him the same proposall was made, and the same answer given. He was severall times with my L[ord,] and no more passed on it. After he was gone off he wrote a letter to another, desiring him to intimate to him, if he would take the Professor's place it was in his offer, and half of the ministeriall charge, with the Professor as Principall. He offered, for which he was sorry afterward, to take the Professor's post without any ministeriall charge, or the Principall's post with half the charge. Thus the thorn was put in the Professor's foot.

This was taken to consideration, and not gone into, but still keeped in suspense till the vacancy by Mr Scot's son's death. By this time he reued* the offer he had made to take the care of youth, as being unable for it, and it's putting him to a quite neu course of studys, and [he] acquainted L[ord] M[ilto]n, talking on the subject to him, that he would quite all pretensions and promises for any supposed service he had or could do, and live private where he was, and extricat them out of all the promises and difficultys from different claimes, if they would put his son, if he wer found qualifyed, on tryall, in the Greek Regent's place. This was frankly promised by my L[or]d. But nothing was

* Repented.

done ; he was excluded and dropt, and from that time to this he has not been spoke to. He is of opinion [that] nou the matter is made up betwixt Pr[ofessor] Hamiltoun and Mr Smith, and that he is to be Principall, and the other Professor, and is very thankfull the snare is broken that was laid by his hast and simplicity. He never sought any thing ; he was still courted, and stood off, except in the offer of being Professor, which greived him afterward. He recons the story of Mr Wisheart is nowise grounded, and is of opinion Mr Hamiltoun will never goe into it ; that it will be long before Mr Wisheart's influence in the Church can be so great as to be laid in ballance with Professor Hamiltoun by the courtiers ; and that, therfor, Mr Wisheart will be dropt. Thus matters go at present, in disposall of places to such as they think will have most interest and influence for a Court party. May the Lord, who lives, overule all ! else we shall soon run in confusion.

I mind no more I heard at Edinburgh, save that Mr Adam Colt, the old Minister, called up by King James, 1606, used to pray that he might dye at his work of preaching ; and it was notticed that he was honoured with a long course of preaching, and, according to his wish, he dyed very soon after his last sermon.

The affair of Balfrone made a great noise this Assembly. See what is above. The Commission was disapproven in severall of their steps, but they wer not condescended upon. What was most spoken against was their going in to the call that had a minority, over the belly* of Presbytery and Synod, and their shamfull hasting of the affair, to prevent its coming before the Assembly.

The affair of the complaint of the Synod of Angus and Mearns, of the Commission's reponing Mr Archibald to his ministry, though not at Guthry, contrary to precedents and acts discharging Commissions to renverse† Synods' sentences, and just the reverse of what they had done in Mr Glass' case, came in [and] was referred to a Committy. Ther wer many conferences between the members of the Synod and Commis-

* A singular phrase, then usual, meaning in defiance of, in spite of, or "in the teeth," as we now say.
† Overturn, set aside. Fr. *renverser*.

sion. The Synod compleaned of the irregularity Mr Archibald would
and did commit, being a Minister of this Church, and so having pouer
to baptize and marry. The Commission was instructed to support the
Synod in prosecuting him for future irregularitys. The Assembly did
not approve the Commission, but left things to stand as they are ; so
that one knoues not what to make of the case of Mr Archibald, he
[being] deposed by his Synod, and reponed by the Commission to the
Ministry at large, though they had deposed Mr Glass for the same irregularitys. The Assembly does not approve what the Commission does,
and yet leave matters to stand as they are. Such intricacys and mazes
does the different tydes of men's humors bring us to ! Mr Glass' deposition was carryed by Mr Smith's interest in the Commission, contrary
to Pr[ofessor] Hamiltoun. In Mr Archibald's case, Mr Smith and he
agreed, and Mr Hamiltoun (as is said) would please the English Dissenters again by reponing Mr Archibald to his ministry, though the case
was the same, and the Synod as much vexed with his irregularitys as
with Mr Glass. Thus publick interest sometimes yeilds to privat vieus.

Ther is much talk of a man (see the publick prints this moneth) who
hath left ten thousand pound to a Hospitall at Aberdeen. He was exceeding narrou, they say, and hard to his relations.

[*May* 10.]—On the tenth of this moneth, my Lord Justice-Clerk and
Lord Poltoun keeped a Justiciary Court at Glasgou, wher the Riot at
Kilpatrick came before them, which was hinted at above. The gentlmen cited—Mains, Kilmanan, &c.—came before the Lords in privat, acknouledged their offence, and asked favour, and promised to encourage
their Minister, Mr Gray, and wer passed. There wer five or six weemen who did not appear, and wer fugitat ; and four men appeared,
[and] pleaded guilty at the barr ; but the matter was concerted. They
wer condemned to some weeks imprisonment ; but, upon the Minister's
application, the Magistrates of Glasgou wer alloued to liberat them,
which was done in a feu hours ; and all this is hushed over ! I wish it
have good consequences to the interest of Religion, and that all be
encouraging to the Minister afterwards, and attend on ordinances.

[*May* 26.]—Upon the twenty-sixth of this moneth our Presbytery met. We had a discourse from Mr Ferguson, who was presented to Killellan by Barrochan. When the affair of that setlment [was] before us, the Patron desired Mr Ferguson might preach; and we sent him two dayes. At the same time, we had a petition from the Heretors—Dundonald, Fulwood, and the Elders, desiring one to be sent [to] try the people's inclinations. This was counter to the Patron, and we granted it. This day the Provest of Glasgou and Mr Finlason came in, and insisted for Mr Moodie.* They desired their Representation to be read, which they had given [in] last Presbytery day: This was done. They allege that they pay the half of the stipend, and bind for the whole; and, by the decreet of erection, they are the sole presenters and callers. I remarked this was a strong and unusuall clause, and wished to see the Decreet: That was not produced. The people of Port-Glasgou insisted for Mr David Broun, and desired one might be sent to try the inclinations of the people. The Magistrates alleged they wer sole callers. They promised, at least hoped, they would have a popular call for Mr Moody. We sent two to try the inclinations of the people, and report; and, in the meantime, reserved our judgment whither the right of presentation was elapsed or not.

June [16,] 1731.—I shall begin this moneth where I left. On the sixteenth the Presbytery met. The persons, Mr Mitchell and R. Maxwell, brought us in a Report of the state of Port-Glasgou. The Heretors and feuers wer called; the Toun of Glasgou did not appear, nor any for them. All the feuers, all the Elders, and heads of familys, to the number of two hundred and seventy, or thereby, declared for Mr David Broun. Ther wer many of them weemen, which was neu, about forty or fifty; but then it was said they had commissions from their husbands at sea to appear for their interest; and the rest wer heretrixes. For Mr Moodie, the Custom-house officers and their dependants, with a boatman or two they imploy, wer for Mr Moodie, to the number of thirty-seven; but we scarce reconed them parishoners. The Magistrates

---

* To be Minister of Port-Glasgow.

of Glasgou and the feuers, for Mr Brown, compeared. These desired a
call to be moderat for Mr Broun. The Magistrates declared they continoued for Mr Moody, and would go into no other, and craved a delay.
We sent out a Committy to converse them, and to ask what they meaned by a delay? They declared it was to have time to bring the people
to Mr Moody. We asked, if they would not come in, if they would
yeild? They wer very positive they would not, and yet insisted for a
delay. The feuars yeilded to a delay till next Presbytery day; and so
the Presbytery yeilded to it, with this declaration, that though they referred the consideration of the presentation in their hand, and find almost all the people for Mr Broun, yet they delayed, at the Magistrates'
desire, till next Presbytery, when they resolved to go on to a call.

As to Killellan, the Ministers, Mr Carrick and Mr P. Maxwell, brought
in a petition, signed by the Patron Barochan, Dundonald, Fulwood,
most of the Elders and heads of familys, for Mr W. Pollock to be their
Minister. There wer ten or twelve for Mr G. Adam, but they wer in-
considerable; and so we appointed a call to be moderat betwixt and the
next Presbytery day. Mr Ferguson sent a letter, declaring, that since
the persons concerned in the parish wer not for him, he renounced his
conditionall acceptance of the presentation. Barrochan was brought in
by Glencairn to be for him. The Heretors, headed by Dundonald,
bandied against Mr Ferguson, and Craigmuir prevailed with Dundonald
to be for Mr Pollock; and so the setlment will go on, the Patron being
easy, and neu come in. I have not so much hopes in our other
vacancy.

This moneth, I hear from Mr Jervey, Minister of Camphire,* and
Mr Thomas Hamiltoun, student, who is come this season from Holland,
that old Professor Mark is dead, at Leyden. He was near eighty, and
has been near sixty years a Professor of Divinity. He has writt a great
deal, as the Dutch Professors generally do. He was Calvinist and
Voetian, and very laboriouse while he was able; but, for some years
since, very much failed by age.

* Campvere, in Holland, where there was a Scottish settlement, with a " Conservator of Scottish
Privileges."

I hear also another famouse Professor Rush, in Physick, is dead. He was old, and turned, as it wer, a child again. He was very curiouse, and much valued, in his time, for his anatomicall preparations.

Monsieur Saurine, Minister at the Hague, I hear, is likewise dead. Some things about him have been already notticed in thir Collections. Last year, the Synod where he was, the Waloon Synod, who have all the French Ministers under their jurisdiction, had a process against Saurine for what he had published about lying, and God's allouing it [in] some cases, last year. See the French Journalls. The States interposed, when he was like to be censured; and the matter was shuffled over without a direct retractation. He declared to the Synod that he had published a Catechisme some years ago, which was generally approven; and he stood by what doctrine he had delivered there, and desired that if he had writt any thing, in any of his writtings, inconsistent with that, that what was in his Catechisme might be considered as his fixed sentiments; and so the matter was hushed. He was a person that was a kind of politician, and much valued by the States at the Hague, and consulted much by them. He had many friends, and two hundred pound Sterling, in pension, yearly, from England, from the Queen, when Princess, and since, and [from] some others.

I am told that Le Clerk is yet alive, but very much failed, and turned almost a child; and so that great man, in France, Abbe Vertot, so knouen by his Historys, is likewise superannuated, and quite failed. It's hard for men to stand out under closs writting and much study, which is a wearynes and wasting to the flesh; and really some of them die before their life be spun out. So did Mr Alexander Cunninghame, and others I could name.

Mr Thomas Hamiltoun tells me ther was not much remarkable in Holland last season. Ther was a Minister in North Holland prosecute before their Synod for Socinianisme, or doctrines tending that way. He has forgot his name; but when the proof was like to come out against him, he retired and went over to England, the sanctuary nou of Latitudinarians.

The same person tells me, that when he was at Amsterdam, he was very near seeing the person who has published the Apparatus to the New Testament, of which before. That Apparatus makes a great noise abroad, and is generally displeasing to all sober persons. The author of the neu edition of the Neu Testament [that is] promised there is one Mr Wetstein, brother to the famous Wetstein who published the beautifull Neu Testament, 1711. This man was Professor of Divinity, or Minister, at Bale, in Germany ; and for somewhat, (error I suppose,) was laid aside ; and nou, for a long time, has been giving himself to this edition of the Neu Testament. His brother, or, I suppose, rather his nepheu, the present Wetstein, printer at Amsterdame, undertakes to print it, and, I belive, has begun the impression. At the information of the Ministers, the Magistrates took some umbrage at such an Edition of the Testament, and, some say, the printing of it was discharged ; but nou that is evaded, and the ordinary text of the Neu Testament is to be printed in one column, and the neu text designed to be given is to [be] printed on the other colum or page ; and so this work is like to go on. Dr Bentley, in England, as some say, had his first hints from this learned critick and man, Wetstein ; and, for some time, they went on together in concert ; but the Doctor and he fell out, and now Wetstein is to stand alone.

. Mr Randy tells me this account of Mr Alexander Hamiltoun, Minister of Edinburgh, (of whom, in some of the volumes of thir Analecta,) as what he had from good hands, and may be depended on. I knou he was son to the Laird of Houshill, near this place. His brother was Mr W. Hamiltoun, Lord Whitlau, a considerable lauer. His father had seven sons ; and he used to say they wer all among the best of their profession—lauers, physicians, ministers, &c. ; and he had somewhat of all their skill ; and, I think, for physick, he said, " Beans, differently used, wer what he would prescribe for most distempers in man and beast." This was his merry, jocose way of speaking. But, to come to what Mr Randy tells me. Mr Alexander Hamiltoun, when he had passed the schools, resolved to study physick, and did so some years ; and was going abroad to France to be graduat, and compleat his studys, and his chest was put aboard, but himself never went. It pleased the Lord to visit him with a heavy sicknes, and therby brought him very near the gates of death. Houever, he was recovered; and when he recovered, he turned exceed[ingly] concerned about his salvation, and, for near a year's time, he scarce ever came out of his room, save to hear sermon, and he did nothing almost but studyed the Scripture; and, indeed, he was eminently seen in it, and master of it. At this time he laid aside the thoughts of physick, and took himself to Divinity; and Divinity is indeed founded in an exact knouledge of the Scripture.

At the Revolution, he was of very great use, and a person very highly valued among the Nobility in the time of the Convention of Estates. When Duke Hamiltoun was President, he was the person that broke a designe the Duke had formed, and which was like to take very much; and that was, a comprehension of all Ministers who would take the oaths to the Goverment, and setling the Church Goverment in their hands. This the Duke and others wer fond of, as what would please England, and be a peaceable way, as was thought, to setle the Church. Many had dealt with the Duke to bring him off this foot, but in vain. At lenth Mr Alexander Hamiltoun, who was a very strong and closs reasoner, went to the Duke one morning, and argued the matter with him on every side, and sheued him so many hazards in this comprehension, and dangers to himself, that the Duke (who was a man of strong sense) ouned he was convinced, and dropt his designe. Mr Hamiltoun, in his old age, used to say, For as old as he was, he would be content to travell to London to understand some dark passages in the xiv. and xv. of John's Gospell. His book on the viii. of the Romans was but short notes dictated from his mouth, on the Saturndays, to one that wrote them for him, not being able to write himself; but his sermons wer full of enlargments. What he said on the difficultys in the Epistle to the Romans, and his four volumes of sermons on the Epistle to the Hebreus, and his stoping in a sermon before the Convention of Estates, and breaking of his purpose, and encouraging the Members, who wer his hearers, to go on, notwithstanding of a difficulty, unforseen, very soon to cast up to them, and then going on in his subject; and, next meet-

ing, King James's Letter was presented to them, or else the defeat at
Dunkeld, or some remarkable rub fell before them, as my informer, my
L[ord] Pollock, who was present, informs me : These, I belive, and
some other remarkables about him, I have formerly set doun.

Mr Stewart tells me, that he was lately informed by Mr Hoarsly,
minister and teacher of Mathematicks in Northumberland, that, of late,
since the publishing of Mr Tyndal's Book, a great many of the English
Bishops and Clergy are returning to the doctrine of their Articles, which
we call Calvinisme ; and, he sayes, that severall of them oun, in conversation, that, upon the subject of the doctrine preached by Tillotson,
Sherlock, and others, as to the sufficiency of man's naturall pouers, it
will be very hard to defend Christianity against the Deists.

He tells me, that he was never in conversation with the late Mr
James Craige, Minister at Edinburgh, (and he was ordinarily several
dayes a week,) but he was bettered and edifyed. That he had a happy
way of mixing in somewhat seriouse in conversation. That he was still
uneasy almost in Church Judicatorys, from the heat and contention in
them, and frequently he left them. He used to say to my informer,
that of all the branches of his time, he had least peace, upon reflexion,
on the time he necessarly spent in Church Judicatorys. My informer
asked him his opinion of Mr Campbell's pamphlet, On the Apostles'
Enthusiasme ; and he said, it was an abominable paper. He used, not
without reason, to express himself in so high termes.

The same person tells me, that Mr Daniel Douglass, Minister at Hiltoun, was a man of great piety and considerable learning : he was of
perfect ability till, by the death of his son, about twenty or twenty-two,
a youth of great hopes and expectations, and the melancholy which fell
in on him upon this loss, he cracked,* and, some way, lost his reason.
That the story is very true about the denuntiation upon the Laird of
Hiltoun, as I have (I think) published it ; and ther is a man yet alive
who was witnes to it, and in the Church at the time : That when re-

* Became crazy or insane.

moved from his church, and restless in his head, he went abroad to Holland, and wandered about the country, and wandered up to Prussia, near Conningsburg. He had not the language ; and after he had wandered all day, at night he came to woods, and was like to meet with no house ; at lenth he discovered a light, and directed his way to it. It was late ; and he found it a gentlman's house. The gates were shut, and he knocked. The porter came, and, not understanding him, and fearing he might be a robber, he put him up in the gatehouse till he acquainted the gentlman. When brought before him, having neither the Prussian nor French, he spoke Latine exceeding weel ; and so he told the gentlman what he was—a banished Minister. The gentlman enterteaned him kindly. He told him it was a very singular Providence Mr Douglas was directed to his house, for otherwise he had been in great hazard, ther not being another Protestant family for severall miles round. He soon discovered Mr D[ouglas]'s disorder, took a care of him, and sent him with a servant to Conningsburg. He sau Mr D[ouglas] could neither use nor keep money, and therefor wrote with him to ane acquantance at Conningsburge to take care of him, and, at his charges, supply him in necessaryes, and to put him in the first ship that went thence to Scotland, and pay his freight, which was done, and he was brought home. Thus Providence remarkably watches over his oun people and servants, and makes provision for them in all straites !

He tells me, that he is informed, that in Holland, in some places, white wine is used at the Table of the Lord : That it was thought necessary, at the Reformation there, to drive persons from the folly of transubstantiation, and is yet continoued : That, in the Northern remot parts of Norroway and Denmark, where they can not have wine, the Sacrament is dispensed in malt-liquor : And he has been told that, at Aberdeen, yet, they use their wine at the Table mixed with watter. Enquire about this.

I find it observed, that, very soon, Scotland must be drained of money, in specie ; and really it's a wonder any almost is left with us. Indeed, except it be coals, and that is a trifle, linning cloath and black cattell, which may bring in a litle, we have scarce any other branch of trade that brings in money to us in specie. Add to this, that there is twenty-four thousand pound yearly in the Civil List and Croun Rents [which] is carryed away, after all pensions, posts, garrisons, and officers are payed, [and] what a prodigiouse quantity of money is every year expended by every family of any rank, for body cloaths of English or Forrainge produce! and to this may be added, that the greatest estates in Scotland, in land-rent, are all taken out to England in specie; Buccleugh, Roxburgh, Argyle, Montrose, Queensberry, &c. &c., besides Members of Parliament, who spend at least more then they get.

July, 1731.—As to the affair of our vacancys this moneth, we had a pretty unanimouse call brought in to Mr Pollock from Kilellan. Some feu heads of familys wer for Mr Adam; but the Patron, heretors, and elders, and most of the people, wer subscribers;* so that setlment goes on. As to Port-Glasgou, it continoues as it was; the people universally for Mr Broun, the Magistrates against him; see Letters this moneth. We have granted a delay till next Presbytery day; and a very ill use was made of it, as we shall see. The Magistrates want their director and manager, Mr Finlason, at present in Edinburgh, and want to have him in this country; and so we meet nothing but off-putts. Meanwhile, Mr Moodie is really† on the matter off the feild, and in the road of setling at Saline, where his relations, they say, are.

Mr Stewart observes to me, that Mr William Colville, whose moderation, piety, and learning, are noture,‡ and Mr Andrew Ramsay, Ministers at Edinburgh in the year 1648, after the Duke's Engagment, wer very roughly treated. The Commission, I think, had made an act cross to or against a Declaration of Parliament, and the Assembly follouing approved this, and would have all Ministers to signe a Declaration in the termes of that act. Mr Colvil and Ramsay declined to signe it, and wer deposed by the Assembly for this. Mr Colvil was called before the Assembly, and called on to give his reasons why he would not signe the Declaration. He modestly declined this, saying the Assembly was better judges of this matter then he, yet he had not freedom to comply; and being still pressed to give his reasons publickly, he refused, saying,

---

* Of the call.   † In point of fact.   ‡ Well-known, notorious.

this was most unfitt to state himself a party to the Assembly, and that the giving his reasons in publick could do no good, and would probably do hurt, to propale* reasons before people who were ill judges of those debatable points.   When he continoued, he and Mr Ramsay wer deposed for not signing, and not giving reasons for it.   My Lord Eglingtoun, Graysteill, left the house in a pett.   That same day, John Gilon, a piouse but illiterat man, who had no language but his mother-tongue, was ordered to be ordeaned a Minister.   My Lord, when he came out, said the Assembly wer going quite wrong.   They had put out two great lights in this Church, and had set John Gilon at Linlithgou, a ruff and dark lantern in comparison with them.

After this Mr Colvil went abroad to Holland, and was at the Hague during the Treaty of Breda, and there knouen to the King, and very usefull to the Ministers in their dealing with the King.   When he came home, and when the sentence was taken off, I cannot say; but, after the Restoration, the King wrote doun a letter to the magistrates of Edinburgh, ordering them to choice him to be their Principall, and dispensing with his signing the Declaration, or taking any Oaths, save that of Alledgeance.   Mr Colvil at that time had the offer of any Bishoprick save that of Saint Andreues, if he would comply; but that he refused; and Mr Leighton, who was violent for the Declaration Mr Colvil scrupled at, was made Bishop of Dumblain.

Mr Randy tells me he had this account from persons alive in Mr Guthry's time.   Mr William Guthry, when writting his treatise of a Saving Interest, endeavoured to inform himself of all the Christians in all the parts of [the] Church who had been under great deepths of exercise, or wer under them, and inclined to converse with them.   Ther was one Bahan, who lived in the Abbay of Haddingtoun, about a mile from the toun, who had been under great deepths and distress, and was got out of them.   Mr Guthry, as my informer was told, came once errand† to see him at Haddingtoun.   He went to the house, and stayed all night and next day, much taken with the conversation of this poor man and his wife.   Next morning, after breakfast, Mr Guthry said he

* Give publicity to.   † Of sole purpose.

would divert himself a litle, and proposed to go to the fishing. The goodwife said she wondered hou such a man as he could spend his time so. He answered he had pleasure in it. " Well," said she, " Solomon sayes, He that loveth pleasure shall be in poverty!" Houever, he and the goodman went to the fishing, and, when they came in, Mr Guthry was very facetiouse in conversation, as he used to be; and then they went to worship. When Mr Guthry left them, he said to the goodwife, " I hope you do not mistake my freedom in conversation?" " No, no! Sir," said she; " but I observe that, after all the freedom in talk and conversation, when you come to prayer you seem to lament it to God." Great was the freedom Ministers and Christians used one with another in former times.

We are like to fall under very great difficultys from the Setlment of Congregations over the belly and cross to the inclinations of the people. It's nou many years since Kilmares was setled by Mr Cocheran, contrary to the liking of the bulk of that people; and a great body of them still stand out. Some of their elders wer at me some years ago, with heavy complaints that they could not oun him as their minister; and, upon that score of not hearing him, they wer excluded the benefite of the Sacrament. Two of their sons wer with me this moneth, and are under the same difficultys, and from his ungaining carriage they grou in their aversion to him. They will neither hear him, nor ask tokens from him to communicat at other places, because they pretend that this would be a practicall ouning him as their minister, which they say they can never do, since he came not in by the right dore, and for the stipend's sake came into place, contrary to Gospell rules. It is almost fruitless to reason with them that the Church hath determined the matter, and that he is certainly laufull Minister in the place, and may be ouned when they have borne their testimony against what they recon sinfull in the manner of his admission. The urging of the Churche's authority with them is but to encrease the scruples, and to enlarge* to the Church in generall; and they·are in hazard to separat from ordinances altogether. I am really in a strait hou to reason with them.

          * Extend their dissatisfaction.

The very same day one of the Elders of Neu Kilpatrick came to me on the same difficultys, as to Mr A. Gray, setled as above there. If he may be belived, matters are not much mended there. The dissenting elders do not joyn, and his* sullen temper hinders him, it may be, from the gaining methods [which] should be taken with them. I urged conversation between them, and that naturall tempers must be borne with, especially modesty; and I thought I gained my point. The man† difficulty was, though he should joyn, yet none of his people in his proportion‡ would; and so he could no longer be usefull as an elder among them. I said that was uncertain, and his example would probably have influence; and, if he had clearnes, certainly it was his duty. He lamented their letting doun their meetings for prayer since the rabble, which he condemned very much.

The confusions are yet more open and scandalouse, in case of Lintoun and Balfrone; where, indeed, the setlments wer much more irregular, and, if I may say so, unchristian, as has been notticed above. This moneth or the follouing, as I am told, Mr M'George at Penicook invited his neighbour, Mr Finlater at Lintoun, to assist him at the Sacrament. He was to have preached on Saturnday, but, in the morning, Mr M'George his elders came to him, and told him they would not serve at the Tables if Mr Finlater preached! On which another supplyed his room on Saturnday. Houever, he was present, and Sir John Clerk took him home with him on Saturnday, brought him back on Sabbath, and set him above him in his oun seat. But when he came doun to the Table, it could not be got filled, though he was only to be a communicant. Some say he sat doun, and the bulk of the people arose and left the Table on his sitting doun! Others say that he was only at the head of the Table; and, upon that, though another Minister [was] with him and serve[d] it, there would none come to it till he removed from it! Whatever way it was, there was a terrible confusion, and he was oblidged voluntarly to withdraw.

And Mr Sinclair in Balfrone was invited to the Sacrament by Mr

---

* Mr Gray's.   † Main.   ‡ In his district or division of the parish.

Edmistoun in Cardross, and preached on the Fast-day.   When he came up the most part of the people went away, and left the place.   He was to have assisted the whole time ; but next day the Elders came in a body to Mr Edmistoun, and told him, that if Mr Sinclair was imployed on that occasion they would by no means serve at the Tables.   Upon which he thought it advisable voluntarly to withdrau and go home.   These things are very sad and lamentable, especially at Communions ; and, indeed, I see no other way remaining, almost, to discourage these cross-setlments that may come to prevail nou, as matters stand at present, but [the] people discountenancing such irregular impositions upon them ; though ther is great danger here, and we shall run to much confusion.   But I cannot but wonder that Ministers, who cannot but see the consequences of such unaccountable setlments, should not be deterred from them.   Indeed, if the common people be lost, as they are like to be, to our generall interests, I doubt our Nobility and Gentry are not much to lean to.

August, 1731.—This moneth, we hear of the affair of the toun of Monross ; see Letters.   The toun, that is, the Magistrates, wer for one Mr Hopper, Allanbank's Chaplain ; the rest of the toun wer for another. Magistrates wer willing to let it come to a call, without using their interest as Patrons ; and when it came to the Moderation, the Presbytery went on to count the votes ; and, by their votes, laid aside three heretors, because they attended not on ordinances, and others, for other causes, perhaps not tenible.   Upon this, within due time, the[y,*] on a suddain, threu in their presentation.   This did not mend the matter. The Presbytery went on to lessen the votters for Hopper, till they brought them to a minority, and concurred with the other, on which the Magistrates got a sist from Lord Drummore, Ordinary.   The Presbytery went on, and gave their answers ; (see them in print ;) and, on the 28th of July, they wer brought in before the Fifteen.†   Great pains was used, by Mr Grant and Mr Smith, to ward off this blow at the Church of giving sists ; and much going about among the Lords.   The

---

* The Magistrates.   † Before the Court of Session, Inner-House.

President was very stiff and keen, that the Lords had a negative, and pouer to stop any but the presentee to be setled, though he ouned they had no pouer but as to the civil right. The opinion of others was, that the Lords had no pouer to stop the Presbitry in their Ecclesiastical procedure, and that they might go on; but the Lords had pouer to stop the stipend, and refuse it after the Presbytery setled the man, if contrary to the Patron's civil right. All that could be done, at the close of the Session—and, Mr Grant sayes to me, they reconed it a considerable point gained—was, that a delay was granted till November 1, that the matter be heard by the Bench; for though sists have been granted by the Ordinary, yet the matter has never been done by the Bench, nor the merits of the cause of sists heard by them *in foro*. The Lords delayed it till November, but continoued the sist till then, and discharged even the Synod to settle another than the presentee, till they judged of the civil right. See the Interlocutor in print. This, I am of opinion, is a sore thrust, and a real sist to both Presbitry and Synod. Houever, it was all that could be got, as things nou stand. Thir clashings and ridding marches,* between the Civil and Church pouers, in setlments of parishes, is a most unhappy affair, which I wish had never cast up; but, every year, in our present gravaminous circumstances, new encroachments cast up. I cannot yet perceive that the Civil Courts can do any more, especially when the Church is still compleaning of this burdensome lau, put on us by our enimies, and the enimies of the Government, but stop the stipend in case the Patron's right be found good, under pretext of a call and setlment on it, for which we have lau. It's unaccountable to hale in what is ouned to be an Ecclesiasticall matter before Civil Judges, so as to stop their procedure proper to themselves; and suppose a Presbitry should be pretended to injure a civil right, which they do not by a setlment, for the Patron has still pouer to claim the stipend till his civil right be determined, to bring in an usage of stopping Judicatorys of Christ in what is their proper work, this, to me, appears an evil of worse consequence than a stipend or particular Mini-

---

* In allusion to the old custom of riding the marches or boundaries of parishes, baronies, &c.

ster's setlement can balance ; but certainly the civil title is still entire, and can be vindicat fully without stopping Ministers in their proper and spirituall pouer.   Be this as it will, the precedent is now begun ; wher it will land, I do not knou ! We hear, since, that the Presbitry are going on, and come the lenth of the serving the edict ; upon which the Magistrates of Monross came in to Edinburgh, to take advice what to do ; and it's said that lauers advise to take the assistance of three Justices of the Peace, and get a warrand to their officers to guard the pulpit, and not suffer the Minister to enter it, untill he promise not to do any thing to the prejudice of the presentee.   This, in former times, would have been thought strange advice and procedure ; but it was done in the case of Old Machir, and, it seems, it's what some leading Ministers are not averse from.   I hear, since, that the young man who has the call will not enter to such a flame, and that this will probably put an end to this unhappy affair.

[*August* 18.]—We in this Presbitry are like to meet with the same difficulty, though we have the advantage that no irregularity nor undue steps are chargable on us, as most part charge on the Presbitry of Brechin, in Monross affairs. Our Presbitry met on the 18th of this moneth, when we entered on the affair of Port-Glasgow.   The Provost of Glasgow and Clerk Finlason compeared, and the Moderator asked them their sentiments nou as to the setlment of the vacancy, after the Presbitry had delayed so long as they had done, and were ready to plant the place.   The Provost said, they were willing that the Presbitry should moderat a call to Mr Moody ; and the Clerk said, their final answer was, that they adhered to their call, and their representation, and presentation to Mr Moodie.   Next, the elders and feuars were enquired, and they unanimously desired us to moderat a call to Mr Broun.   When parties were removed, we went on in the usual step, to moderat a call, on September 6, to Mr Moody or Mr Broun, for which [soever] the plurality should be.   In this we all agreed, save Mr Paton, who only said he was affrayed of inconveniencys. When this minute was read unto them, Mr Finlason gave in a sist from the Lord Cooper, Lord Balmerinno's son, dated Agust 14. It was read ; and when he had read it, it was desired back again, as what was not to be in our hands, but their paper. We asked, if we were not to have a copy of it ? Mr Finlason answered, a copy might be had at the proper office, the Clerk of the Bills. So it was returned to them, and the partys removed.

The Presbitry took it to their consideration. We all spoke very fully on the head. Mr Paton said, he forsau inconveniencys, but never had the least apprehension that the Magistrates would take this extraordinary step, which he was extremely sorry for. All the rest spoke fully against it. It was observed, that ther wer severall palpable untruths in the bill of advocation, (see the copy of it, and papers relative to it,) as that some elders wer for Mr Moody, and that we wer going to ordean Mr Broun : That this was asserted to the Lord Ordinary before we had taken any steps at all, and when maters were under conference and compromise : That our moderating a call to the presentee, if it should come out* to him, was far from this. It was notticed that this was a new step on this side of Tay, and would have very mischievouse consequences ; and very ungratefull to the Presbitry, when under communing, after so many delayes, and condescentions, and professions of an amicable issue on their part : That it was sinfull and unlaufull to sist and interrupt a judicature when acting according to rules : That it was sinfull especially in Elders, and when given us by an Elder in our oun bounds. Wherupon we all agreed to alter our Presbitry day till September 1, that we might, before the moderation of the call, give in answers to the sist, and get advice in this extraordinary case. Houever, we adhered to our moderation of a call, notwithstanding of the civil sist.

When partys wer called in, we intimat this to them, upon which they appealed to the Synod, and craved extracts. After this, we ordered answers to be drauen to the bill of advocation, and given in to the Lord Ordinary, and lauers to appear; and a Testimony to be drauen up, to be insert in our Registers, against this invasion upon us ; both which, see *alibi*. This was done accordingly ; and the answers presented by the Agent for the Church, in name of the Procurator, Mr Grant. The

* Turn out favourable to him.

Lord Cooper stuck a litle on them, and desired two other Lords to advise with; but they wer not to be had in toun; and so, by himself, he continoued the sist till the 10th of September, from its expiration upon Agust 27.

I have put all this affair together this moneth.

The Commission of the Assembly sat at the ordinary time. See Letters this moneth. The affairs of West Kirk, Kinross, and Ketle, wer before them, and they caryed all upon one side by a great majority; especially [in] the affair of Kinross and West Kirk, ther wer very warm speeches, and some indecencys among Ministers. Mr M'Vicar was plainly surprized, and had not got up his side, expecting the matter would be delayed, as had been agreed; but, it seems, P[rofessor] Hamilton pushed the matter, and would have the matter delayed no longer, and shewed in this his strenth and ability to carry the matter as we [he ?] would.

Since the Commission, in the end of the moneth, when Lord Isla is come doun, I hear that he has desired three Ministers on each side of the West Kirk affair to reason the matter before him, that he may have a full view of it; for he must determine in it, it seems. This is a lou pass we are brought to! I mind no more, but an intimation made that the time of taking the oaths is prolonged for Ministers till January next. This, I fear, will breed new difficultys in the present broken state of the Church.

This moneth, the Communions are very much over. I have litle to remark as to them. For many years it has been to observe that Ministers have not wanted very sensible assistance at these times, but it has not been felt that a proportioned fruit in many hearers has followed. I hope many are bettered. I do not, at least in the places wher I have been assisting this season, observe so many Tables this season as last year. In this place we are near an hundred communicants short; but that may flow from variouse circumstances.

Mr Foster, Minister at Calder, a grandchild of Mr Foster's, who fell in to his uncle, Mr John Govan's, his predecessor's, his means, thirty or forty thousand merks, about a year and a half Minister, dyed of a feaver after 28 dayes sicknes. About the same time, we hear of Mr Patrick Lin, Minister at Dumfreice, his death ; see Letters this moneth. He was constantly at odds with the Magistrates, and was a man of strong passions.

Mr M'Culloch, Minister at Cambuslang, communicat to me his case, which needs very much sympathy. I think ther seems a mixture of bodily and heavy spirituall distress in it. He ask[ed] me whither I thought it warrantable and laufull, and if [it] was not the better side for a Minister who knew he was not called of God, and who was nothing but a hollou hypocrite, to demitt his Ministry, and give way to another, who might be usefull? He opened his mind, as I thought, very fully to me. Since his ordination, he has been preaching on Conversion, and the nature of it, which, he tells me, he had not throughly considered and gone to the bottome of before ; and nou he thinks he is perfectly a stranger to this great work : That he had some beginnings of seriousnes when about seven years of age, and continoued to have a liking to good people and the formes of duty till about thirteen years : Then the Word, under Mr Ker's ministry, very much awakned him ; and about that time, by the Minister's advice, he communicat : After that he went on in a form of duty and godlynes, but nou is made to raze* all ; and asked if I knew any in such a case ? I told him I did, and a Minister of much longer standing than he ; and asked him if he had any shakings during the time of his call and second trials ? He told me had, though not to the hight he nou is under : That when he was entered on them, he was made very much to question matters, and came to a peremptory resolution to leave the country, and go wher he was not knouen ; and, one night, he came to fix himself, and resolved to leave a Letter giving some hint of his distress to a confident comrade to whom he was to leave his books ; and was going to write his letter, but resolved to take some time to pray and consult Scripture before he did it that night. After prayer, at the opening of the Bible, the first chapter of Jonah was the place that cast up to him, which stunned him very much, and made him lay aside that designe intirely : That, before his ordination a feu dayes,

* To regard all as effaced, to obliterate.

his doubts recurred ; and he set apart some time for prayer and meditation ; and being under very sore trouble and distress, that place, " If
Thy presence go not up with me, take me not up hence," was made
very sweet, and what he thought he got leave to plead and wrestle
upon ; and, after that, the 2d of Malachy, about the Covenant of Levi,
offered to him in reading with much pouer ; both which gave him much
releife.   I presumed to say he had more of a call to the Ministry than
severalls had atteaned to ; and I took him to be of a thinking, melancholy disposition, and ready to dip too farr into things.   I asked him if
he could deny but the glory of Christ and the good of souls wer not in
his eye in entring on the Ministry ? He could not deny it, but said,
" Much went to sincerity."*   I said, I thought this was the greatest instance of sincerity ! I notticed, that it was Satan's way to raise distress
and sore battails when Ministers first enter on their work, and it was a
token he was called to it.   He is exceedingly haunted with Atheistical
thought and blasphemouse injections,† in meditation, prayer, and when
essaying to act faith.   They are exceeding hideouse and strange ; and
though, at first, and some time, they wer extraordinary burdensome and
hatefull, he thinks they are not so much nou so as they wer once.   I
observed to him, that thoughtfull, studious persons wer mostly, I supposed, haunted with these ; and I likewise belived that they had many
disadvantages beyond persons who wer not of their reach ;‡ especially
studiouse persons, and melancholy in their temper, ought to guard
against them at the beginning.

  He is also much damped in conversation with his people, and their
telling him experiences he has been a stranger to ; amidst all, he wants
not like seals of his ministry.   One, [particularly,] tells him he had
peremptory assurance, three or four year, that he was to be Minister
there ; and, one would think, run it too far, when he said that his assurance was as great as for his oun salvation.   I hope the Lord has good
to do by Mr M'Culloch, and is training him to be usefull ; but he is, at
present, in great hazard, and has bodily melancholy mixed in.   He is
jealouse and suspicious of his freinds ; compleans of pride and workings
of self-carnality, and thinks his case singular.   He has a violent pain in

---

* It required much to be sincere.   † Suggestions.   ‡ Extent of attainments.

his hind-head, with the rack of thought and contrary tydes. I advised him to riding-exercise [and] conversation ; but that, it seems, he much declines, and gives himself too much to thought and solitude. His life has been, all along, grave, serious, and contemplative. We who are Ministers have need of such an instance to quicken and awaken us !

September, 1731.—The first day of this moneth we met in Presbitry pretty numerously. The people of Port-Glasgou insisted for the moderation of the call. We had the reasons of the Magistrates' Appeal, in a letter to our Moderator, in due time.* Non of the Magistrates wer present this day, nor any from them. Their second sist was not presented ; perhaps they are ashamed of it, or advised to drop it, for their interest. Certainly, it would have done their cause much hurt at the Synod, and the dropping it will be pleaded as meritoriouse. However, we went on in our way. We had the report of the answers to bill of advocation, and the draught of the Testimony, which was approven unanimously ; only Mr P[aton ?] said he could not judge of so long a paper on first hearing. Then, according to advice from Mr Grant, we went on to declare the *jus* [*presentandi*] fallen in our hand. I did not oppose this, but was not much for it. I have an aversion at Presbitrys or Ecclesiasticall Courts medling that way in civil rights ; besides, I think this gives a handle to the Magistrates to procure another sist from the Lords with a better face than they had.

The point we go on is [a] pretty narrou point, Whither a parish is vaccant at a transportation, or at the Minister's setlment in the parish he is transported unto ; and whither the presenting of the Presentation to the Moderator preserves the right till the Presbitry meet? We had a debate, whither, in our declaration of the *jus* falling to our hand, we should delare that we had no evidence Mr Moody was qualiffyed.† Mr Paton and the Moderator wer much against this. I was unwilling to speak on it. I only said, I did not knou that any Church Judicatory had taken hold on the matter of Nonjurancy as an argument against an intrant, and I was not for our doing it first ; and I questioned if [we] should declare that it did not appear to us that Mr Moody was qualifyed,

* *i. e.* Within ten days from taking the appeal.   † By taking the oaths to government.

was a sufficient ground to us to go on for the *jus* being in our hand, since, in charity, we wer bound to suppose he was, and we had no proof he was not; neither was ther any lau oblidging him to have extracts of his being qualifyed still* with him. The Presbitry generally seemed to be for taking this advantage, when we wer pushed to it, by the Toun's treatment, but it ended in a generall.† We named the six moneths being elapsed, and reserved a pouer to urge other things that might be legall objections, such as this (though we name them not) of not being qualifyed, of his letter of acceptance, and the Magistrates' compromise. After this, we ordered the moderation to go on September 6, and a Committy to answer Glasgoues reasons of appeall September 8. This far we have gone.

[*September* 15 ?]—About the fifteenth of this moneth we met at Paislay in a Committy, for the answering Glasgoues reasons, anent which we had no difference. We dreu answers pretty smooth, but hard enough upon the Toun. We had the call very unanimouse to Mr David Broun, and a protest by Mr Walker in the toun's name. We heard likewise of the second sist, which was not intimat to us, because, as is alledged, ther was no need, since we had compeared by our advocat; and so what is above, as if a second sist had not been, is to be considered as wanting a foundation. This second sist is signed by three Lords; see the copy of it, with the other papers relative to this process, in the Manuscripts this year. It was a surprize that my Lord Neuhall's hand was at this sist; but he has either done it on wrong information, or upon a surprize. Sists, indeed, are things that go a course, and the Lords are not very nice about them.

[*September* 20.]—Mean while, about the twentieth of this moneth, we wer informed that this affair was taking another [turn] at Edinburgh, (see Letters this moneth,) and that my Lord Miltoun was willing to come in to Mr Broun's setlment at Port-Glasgou, and resolved [not ?] to setle Mr Moody at Port-Glasgou, and that the Magistrates wer to drope the appeal and joyne. If this was so, as I doubt not it was, since Mr Grant,

---

* Always.   † A general claim of the *jus devolutum*.

who made the concert with my Lord Miltoun, and let him see hou wrong it was to break with Judicatorys on such a plain point as this, and what a noise it would make, assures me, it seems Mr Finlason broke all when he went in to Edinburgh about the end of this moneth.

Our Presbitry met again toward the end of this moneth, and approved the call unanimously, and resolved to enter Mr Brown on his tryalls, and ordered him an exercise at the Synod. Here Mr P[aton] left us, though he approved the call, as reconing it unfit to go on under an appeal. The reason of this is, we had a third sist intimat to us, in name of the Magistrates, till November 5, and this put us to hasten tryalls, and resolve to fix him before this matter came before the Lords themselves, which we wer not willing they should have the trouble of.

I forgot to nottice, that by the concurrence of the Presbitry, though not Presbiterially met, I drew a memoriall, (see the copy of it among the papers this moneth in the MS.,) acquainting them* with the state of this affair, and begging them to come up to the Synod, since the case of a sist was neu, and of common concern. Those I dispatched about the 9th, with an abstract of the Testimony we had given, and about the 22d I sent a second memoriall to each Presbitry on the third sist we got, and repeated our desires that members might punctually attend at Irwine. This is all I mind, except what may be gathered from the papers themselves, which lye all together in the MS. this year.

[*September* 8.]—At our Presbitry, September 8th, we had another very fashiouse† affair before us, not in judgment, but in conversation. A terrible flame in the parish of Lochwinnioch, about leading stones to build the neu manse, to be built upon the excambion‡ with Colonel M'Dougall, of which nottice, I suppose, was taken above. The parish banded against this, and got out a suspension. Letters wer execute in Mr Pinkartoun the Minister's name, as they behoved in form to be, and some of the Elders had letters execut against them. This made a terrible noise. The Elders took it ill, refused to stand at the plate, for a Sabbath or two

---

* The other Presbyteries within the Synod.   † Troublesome. *Facheuse*, Fr.
‡ Ground exchanged.

the kirk was deserted by too many, heavy complaints wer made of the excambion, and it was pretended the Lords would disannull the bargain. However, this storm abated, and the Collonel took the service of three dayes* from the most part, and excluded some of the ringleaders, and all things came back to their former channell, which is a mercy to the Minister and people. Mr Finlason, in May last, led in the presbitry to the branch of their act at Lochwinioch about the leading stones, which was quarrelled by the Lords.

[*September* 10 ?]—About the tenth or eleventh of this moneth Mr George Park, Minister at Killearn, dyed. He had been Minister ther thirty-seven or thirty-eight years, and has been failing and tender for severall years. He succeeded, I think, Mr Thomas Foster, who preached somtime there, at and after the Liberty, and Mr Park marryed his daughter. He was a very ready and popular preacher, and pretty much followed for severall years. His Communions wer much frequented, especially during Mr Forrester's life, who was his helper. He lived sparingly, though he had a good income, and has left a round summ of money behind him; but his sons are not like to be promising, and will probably soon get through it.

We heard about this time of Mr Andrew Darling, Minister near Perth, his death. He was a very awakning preacher, and a zealouse, forward, honest man. He has left a very large family behind him; at least, once he had sixteen or eighteen children living at once.

Mr Robert Stewart tells me, that I may depend upon what folloues, for he minds it distinctly, and had it from severalls present. In the year 1685 or 1686, Mr Samuel Arnot dyed at Edinburgh, after all the persecutions and sufferings he had gone throu since Pentland, in much peace and joy. Ther was generally much company came and sau him on his deathbed; among others, Mr James Rouat, Minister at Kilmarnock before the Restauration, came in to see him, and, among other things, he

* The feudal service of leading stones for kirk and manse, &c., for three days.

asked Mr Arnot if he had any hopes the Church of Scotland would get out from under this dark cloud she was under for twenty-five year, or therby? The other answered he had, and he was assured she would. "Yea," added he, "I knou more, and that is, that you shall live to see and partake of the Church's delivery!" And so it came about. Mr Rouat lived till the 1690, or a year, it may be, later or two, and sau the great work of God at the Revolution. I think Mr Rouat was succeeded by Mr Osburn, afterward Minister and Professor at Aberdeen. Amongst other present, when this was spoken, that good woman, Mrs Durham, relict of Mr Zachary Boyd, and Mr James Durham, was there, and she got up, and said to Mr Rouat, "Mr James, I am younger then [you,] I hope I shall see the day of delivery as well as you;" and she danced and skipped for joy; and so it came about. I was at her buriall, at Glasgou, about the year 1692 or 1693.

The same person tells me he has what folloues from Mr Gilbert Kennedy, son to him I am to name, a man of learning and excellent sense: That his father, John Kennedy of Thorntoun, (or his daughter was Lady Thorntoun, and another daughter Lady Langshau,) surgeon and apothecary at Edinburgh, an eminent Christian, lived to a vast age, I think I have been informed, upwards of an hundred years. He was surgeon to Mr Robert Blair, and heard him predict the Revolution many years before, as I think stands in the First Volume of this Collection. His son, Gilbert, tells my author, that when he was a boy at the Colledge, he lay in the same bed with his father, who was then about ninety-five years, or upward: That, as to every thing save Religion, he was turned perfectly as a child: He never sought meat unless it was offered him, nor drink: He kneu not his oun children in the house with him, and would have asked who they wer: He minded nothing at all. For some time he remembered ancient things pretty weel, but nothing present, not the dayes of the week, or the like; but by this time he quite forgot every thing, though he had noe sicknes nor pain, but just a decay of nature, and eat and sleeped well enough; yet, when he was put to ask a blessing or pray in his family, he was most serious and distinct. He never missed one word; yea, he [had a] pleasant variety in expression, in his petitions and arguments in prayer.   One would think this is not only a good argument for a real distinction between soul and body, but a proof next to a demonstration of the reality of Religion, and the abiding nature of a work of grace, and the supernaturall habites and gifts of it in the soul, when the ordinary naturall pouers of the soul, memory, knowledge, and even the naturall apetit after meat and drink decay, and come to their first impotency and weaknes, during the state of nonage, infancy, and childhood.   Here is Religion and graciouse actings towards God, fresh, active, and vigorous, when all other things are failed ! When his son came to bed to him, he would have ask[ed] who is that ? and when he told him, he would [have] embraced him, and said, " O Gibbie ! it's a good thing to be good and religiouse !" and then given him severall very religiouse advices.   Then he would have sung a Psalm, or some lines of a Psalm ; he had them all by heart : Then he cast the bedcloaths over his head, and fell a praying, till sleep interrupted him. This was generally his way every night, as the gentleman, his son, remembers well to this day.

The same person tells me two remarkable instances of two Parishes, served almost by three Ministers since the Reformation. The Parish of Dirletoun was served by father, son, and grandson, one hundred and nineteen years, without intermission.   Mr M'Gie was their name, and the last dyed or went out for [the] Test in the year 1685.   The other Parish is that of Dalziell, in the Presbitry of Hamiltoun, hath been served by three Ministers during the space of one hundred and twenty-five years or more.   Old Mr Main, who was a very long time Minister there ; Mr John Lauther, who was near forty years Minister there, I kneu him at the Revolution ; and now Mr Alexander Adamson, who succeeded Mr Lauther, and was ordeaned about the 1691, or therby, has been another forty years in that Parish, and may live some time yet, if God have service for him.   These are rare instances.   I belive the medium of Ministers' living, by a common calcule, will scarce be above twelve or fifteen years.   So it has been in this Presbitry since I came to it, and I am ready to think that Ministers live shorter, generally speaking, than men of any other office, of which severall reasons [might] be given.

October, 1731.—This moneth begins ordinarly with the election of the Magistrates of Glasgou; Provost Murdoch continoues, and Bailay James Hamiltoun, eldest Bailay, an English merchant, who is half of the year in England, and the rest litle of it in toun, Mr Aiton, P. Stirling's son-in-law, and B. Peacock, a shoemaker. This turn is quite ouing to Pr. Stark and his party. They have nou another hitt for it, if they manage it, which they have not hitherto done, when more than once they had the ball at their foot. This election was so managed, that the other side kneu not of it till the night before the choice, and could not gather any great opposition to it. It is said P. Stirling and his freinds went into it when they sau they could do no better, because this weakens the Buchanans, and their side wer afterwards turned out of the Councill; and nou P. Stark, as I am told, has the next choice in his pouer, being seven or eight to five. It is said the management of the toun, very generally displeasing in our affair of Port-Glasgou, wanted not its oun influence at this time. Mr Finlason has lost much of his interest by his carriage in our sist, and, if he be not misrepresented, deserves to do so.

In the toun of Edinburgh, Provost Osborn is chosen, and he is the former Provost, Lindsay, his intimat. I know not what to belive as to that choice. Some represent it as concerted with my Lord Isla, who was at Edinburgh at the time. Others say it was not so, and that he was for another sort of persons more obsequious to himself. Time will best determine. Provost Osburn, it is said, is for Mr Smith being Professor, as much as P[rovost] Lindsay was, and will endeavour to have that carryed through.

The Synod met at Irwine the same day with the election at Glasgou. We had the Synod opened with a very good sermon on " Who is sufficient for these things ?" from Mr Dick. He had some things that looked as if he wer not perfectly pleased with our procedure in Port-Glasgou, but they wer safe generalls, so cautiously worded as no just exception could be taken. The Presbitry of Irwine generally chuse the Moderator in their oun toun, and designed it for Mr J. Montgomery, but he came not up, being willing, I think, to decline at this time; and so Mr

James Semple, at Dreghorn, was chosen by a scrimp* majority, Mr Scot of Stonehouse being within a few votes of him.   We had severall lesser things before us.   Some of the pretty quick decisions in matters of scandall, relating to Irwine, want not their bad effects there since the last Synod ; and that Presbitry, it seems, inclined to have some stop put to them.   But it's easier giving things a wrong turn than right, and it's hard to get a wrong cast mended.   Litle petty lauers wer waiting on to see hou matters went, and they take the worst of causes by the hand, and harden scandalouse persons by their quirks of lau, and consume our time abominably.   Our case in Neilston, with Isobell Erstoun, took up some litle time, and Mr B. of Muncton screued things to a poor pitch, by his fetches in lau for her; houever, we wer unanimously aproven.   He had nothing to plead on, save an omission in our Clerk of our sentence being intimate to her, with which he made a fearfull sputter ; but that was soon got over.   He made a prolix speech, and so lessned the evil of any crime by words omitted, as was exceeding offensive, and very hardning to a number of spectators, none of the best of people ! It's wrong that lauers are allowed such a liberty to extenuat [and] palliat sin before our Judicatorys, especially R[uling] Elders.

Ther was a process came in from the Presbitry of Air, about a man in Maybole guilty of incest concealed, marrying a woman who was his grand-neice, or some such relation, in the parish of Barr or Muirkirk.   Some lauers had drauen up some virulent, ludicrouse papers, exceeding offensive.   Mr Alexander Stevenston was blamed for them, lampouning the Scriptures and the Divine lau.   The Synod aproved the procedure of the Presbitry of Air, and declared the paper scurrilouse, blasphemouse, and ludicrouse ; and ordered a retractation, under pain of excommunication   This is a neu instance of the unbounded liberty that lauers take, when employed about scandalls, where, indeed, they have nothing to do. Habit and reput will execut a man in other crimes ; and yet, by no means will habit and reput, if we belive lauers, be proof of too near degrees of consanguinity : The matter, I thought, turned much on this.

* Narrow, slender. ,

But the cheif thing that took up the Synod's time was our affair of Port-Glasgou. I have not much to add to what is commonly knouen, and a hint of which is in the Letters this moneth. This affair came two ways before the Synod. The appealers brought it in the Committy of Bills the ordinary way. I proposed, in our Presbytery, and it was gone into, that we should separat the common* case of the sist, from that of our procedure in appointing the moderation of a call, on which the Toun appealed; that being a matter of no very great concern, though perfectly agreable to our rules; but the matter of the sist is a matter of generall concern, and, indeed, of the [last] moment besides. This mode† might be of some use to our cause, as well as it was naturall and just; and the members of the Committy of Overtures would hereby have some occasion to knou the cause, at least in its more important part, before it came in by the other papers. I was ordeaned to form a Reference to the Committy of Overtures, which I did, and gave it in, representing our treatment by three sists, and desiring the Synod's advice and direction in the generall case. When I gave it in, ther wer very full and free speeches by the eldest and gravest men. Our Presbitry was commended. It was moved that the Synod should go straight‡ in to our Testimony, or some equivalent. Mr Montgomery of Stewartoun, and Mr Connell, wer very keen for us, and said, unles somwhat wer done against this encroachment, Ministers needed not go home to their pulpits. Mr J. Hamilton, Glasgow, Mr M'Dermit, Mr James Dick, [and] Mr J. Rouat, wer for delaying further consideration till the affair came in by the appeal, when the Synod had the full view of it. I said our Presbitry was easy§ when the Synod gave their opinion on the sist; the sist would come in very litle by the appeal, if the appellants could help it; but providing the Synod had time for it, and the generall case, which we took to be [the] main thing, wer not shufled out, we wer easy as to the time. Thus we ended, the Synod time being come.

When the Synod met, the whole papers were read—our procedure, the reasons of appeal, and our answers; then Mr Finlason produced to

* Public.   † Order of procedure.   ‡ Agree at once.   § Indifferent as to the time.

[two] papers never before us—feuars' consent to him whom the Toun was for, and a desire of the Custom-house officers for Mr Moody. Answers wer made to both, though they came not regularly in. The subscribers of the first had all signed Mr Broun's call, and the methods in procuring that paper wer not so much for the honour of the Toun. The Custom-house paper was very idle.

In the afternoon, papers reading being ended, partys wer heard. Mr Finlason read his speech, which was very litle different from the reasons of appeal. He disclaimed any designe to do hurt to the Church by the sist; he said it was a perfect trifle; ther was no record of it, only an interim thing; compleaned of the Presbitry's invading their civill rights, and declared the Toun had no designe to force a person on the people. Mr Grant was imployed by the callers, and we gave way to him. He first called for the Toun's decreit, which they had alleged, and refused again and again to the Presbytry, when called for; because all, indeed, in point of right, depended on that. Mr Finlason said he had brought it with him; and it was not produced to the Presbytery, because papers of that nature wer not easily carryed from place to place, and in hazard of lossing or razing. Mr Grant read it out to the Synod; and, indeed, it made his work easy, and cut the very throat of the Toun's cause. The Lords declare the Toun of Glasgou, and the Magistrates, and the feuars, and tennants of Port-Glasgou, feuars and tennants, (to the Toun, I mean,) presenters and callers of a Minister in time to come. In short, the people who caryed on the process, and wer at the charges, which [were] the feuars and tennants, bore the half of the charges of the persuit,* and the Magistrates their part. This set all in a quite other light. Nou Mr Grant triumphed; he had the Patrons, forty-two or more, against three or four Magistrates, on the side of the call.

Mr Finlason alleged some small evasions, that it was the Toun of Glasgou, and counsell thereof, that wer mo in number; but the words are, Magistrates, feuars, and tennants of the bug† of the Toun of Glasgou; and Mr Finlason's best answer was, that nou all sau hou tender

---

* Process for erecting the parish.

† These three words appear to be superfluous. Probably the author first meant to write " burgh."

the Toun had been of the rights of the Christian people ! The cause
was so strongly pled by Mr Grant, that was litle left to the Presbitry to
say ; and we wer willing to spare time.   Litle was said, only that the
Magistrats had either not knouen their paper, or misrepresented it when
the[y] asserted they wer sole callers, and given us too much trouble ;
but we wer glad to find matters as they wer, and hoped nou all was
plain, and so we wer removed.   The Synod entered on the affair ; and
ther wer many free speeches made on our behalf.   Principal Campbell,
Mr Rouat, Mr Dick, Mr M'Dermit, and some feu others, urged an
amicable comitty to bring in the Magistrates to comply with the setlement, and waved entring on our procedure.   That could not well be
refused, and so they, with Mr Kennedy, Steel, and some others, wer
sent to converse the Magistrates to pass from their appeal, and compromise with the Presbitry.   They did not call us to the Comitty, and we
wer affrayed of delays and amicable proposalls.   Houever, they returned
to the Synod with an answer, that the Magistrates, that is, P[rovost]
Murdoch and Mr Finlason, insisted to have their appeal decided, (which
was strange conduct in so evident a weak cause, as theirs to every body
nou appeared,) and refused to submitt to the Synod's determination till
they heard what it should be : And so the Synod resumed the consideration of the affair.

The bretheren just now named moved, which was the thing that had
been concerted, as we wer told privately, a delay till next Synod ; and
they reconed, in this singular case, it would be best not to be hasty ;
and a Commity to meet at Glasgou, and deal with the Magistrats to
fall from the sist, and go in* with the people and Presbitry.   This was,
at first, like to take in the Synod, till some members opened fully, and
said this was to disapprove the Presbitry, to confirm the sist given to
them, and protract the setlement, and what could not be yeilded ; and
a vote, (and many reasons wer given for it,) craved—" Approve the procedure of the Presbitry" or " Not."   This landed on a vote on the state
of the vote, or " Proceed" or " Delay ;" and ther wer seventeen Delay,
and about seventy-five Proceed.   The next vote was, " Approve the
Presbitry's procedure" or " Not ;" and that was unanimouse ; all the

* Act in accordance.

delayers voted Approve ; only one elder, T. M., was " Go on."• Then
the Synod ordered the Moderator to signify to the Magistrates the Synod's dislike with the sist given the Presbitry, as unusuall, and what
they judged an incroachment on the libertys of the Church. The
Moderator did so, very softly, and hoped, he said, the Magistrates had
no such intention. The Provost declared they never had, and appealed
to the Assembly.

Nixt day, the Synod came to consider the generall case of the sist,
and what [was] proper for them to do upon it. We did not urge things,
being partys in some respects. Some proposed a present Testimony.
A very short Minute was drauen up, and aproven without a vote, declaring that sists from Civil Judicatorys wer an incroachment upon our
constitution, and what the Synod could not but disaprove, as contrary
to our principles, and of very dangerouse tendency ; or to this purpose.
It's recommended to every Presbitry to consider this case, and to prepare ane Overture, to be ripened by the nixt Synod, to be laid before
the Generall Assembly. A meeting of some from each Presbitry was
proposed, to ripen the mater for the Synod ; but that was not gone into,
being the winter season ; and the correspondents from neighbouring Synods wer alloued copys, at their desire, of what we had done ; and our
correspondents to our neighbouring Synods wer ordeaned to lay the
G[enerall] case before the Synods they went to, and desire them to
consider it, and, if they found proper, ripen an Overture upon it to the
next Assembly.

Thus this vexatiouse affair ended for this time. The Presbitry took
Mr Broun's exegesis at Irwine, and appointed him a Presbiterial exercise, and popular sermon, to be delivered at Paslay next week, being
nou resolved to setle him there as soon as the regular time for serving
an edict would allou. Accordingly, that I may give all that concerns
this affair together, we met at Paislay next week, took his discourses
and privat tryalls, wherin he acquitted himself much to our satisfaction.
We had not time to acquaint the Magistrates before we resolved on the
day of ordination, though I proposed that on the Wensday's night be-

---

* i. e. Declined to vote.

fore we appointed the day we should wait on them.   Yet things fell in, that we wer so thin that we could not spare two, and take the tryalls also.   We also agreed upon an act formed by Mr Grant,* with some amendments, (see the papers relative to this process in the MS.,) declaring we meaned not, by going on to setle him, to prejudge the judgment of any Civil Court concerning the stipend, but only to fix a spirituall relation.   This brought Mr Paton in to the ordination, and made us unanimouse in it, and would have been good defence, had the sist been prosecute before the Lords ; at least we hoped it might be so, and without prejudice to the intrant.   The 28th of October was appointed for the ordination.

Next week, Mr R[ouat ?] and Jo. Millar, Mr Paton, and I, went in to the Magistrates to begg them to drop their appeal, and countenance the setlment.   They compleaned of our haste, [and] promised intirely to submitt to the Assembly : They alledged we distrusted the Assembly, and came to them after we had agreed on the setlment.   To the last we told them it was not our choice, but necessity, and that we had made a provision which might pave their way to joyn : That it was not fear of the Assembly, but our being sisted before the Lords, that made us hast ; and reneued our instances that they should joyn, though under a soft protestation.   They told us the sist should not be prosecut till the Assembly ; ther was no designe that way ; and that the[y] could not drop their appeal ; so we parted.

[*October* 28.]—On the twenty-eighth of October, we setled Mr D. Broun.   We wer well† mett ; and, severall Ministers, from Dumbarton, Glasgou, and Irwin, joyning us, twenty-one or twenty-two Ministers. The people were all fond.   We had great numbers from Glasgou.   The Dean of Gild was to be with us, but hindered ; we had the Conveener with us.   Mr Maxwell preached on, " Finish course with joy, and the Ministry," &c.,‡ very well, but long.   Mr Turner preached the people's

---

* Procurator for the Church.   † Fully.

‡ " So that I might finish my course with joy, and the ministry which I have received of the Lord Jesus, to testify the Gospel of the grace of God."—Acts xx. 24.

duty. Thus this affair, I hope, is ended, and happily ended, after a sore
strugle, wherin we have been, I hope, guided of God. Indeed, the
people of P[ort]-Glasgou stuck closs by us, and we by them; and the
Magistrates, or rather Mr Finlason, their Clerk, acted a very poor part,
and did not manage with that wisdome and wit they might have done.
But we are the more in God's debt, and we have the approbation of all
good persons, who have the interest of the Gospell, and the freedom of
this Church from civil encroachments, at heart; and this is our comfort.
I hope the Toun nou will insist no more, and be kind to Mr Broun.

Litle more offers this moneth, save what is in Letters and papers,
save threatning Letters of Incendiarys in the shire of Lanerk, and parish
of Lesmahagou and Straven, which hath very much allarumed that
country; and, indeed, one can scarce knou what to make of them. It's
certain, the end of last moneth, and beginning of this moneth, Mr Aiton,
of Walsely, a Justice of Peace, had threatning letter, to come to the
Corsboat, at Lanerk, and bring fifty guineas, otherwise his house would
be burnt; and assuring him, if he would come and joyn them, he should
double his estate soon. He went to the place, but found none; a second was sent to him, and one within it to Sir James Hamiltoun of
Rosehaugh, for two hundred guineas; and a third to the Laird of Over-
toun. We have many storys of persons seen on the moors of Lesmahagou. The country was raised, and souldiers brought from Hamiltoun,
but nobody found. Indeed, in a country like Scotland, wher strangers
are presently knouen, it's not likely that incendiarys can make a great
hand, and some are of opinion that all this is mere jest of some rakish
young men, to put persons in fear, without any reall designe. The letters to Walsley, who is a grave man, and not very wealthy, looks like
this; but be this as it will, i[t's] a most villanouse thing, and ought
to be punished. The letters are droped at night, or throen in at the
dore.

November, 1731.—This moneth, the Commission of the Assembly
met at their ordinary time. They had nothing remarkable before them,

save our unhappy setlments, and contentiouse heats about them. The West Kirk* has been a long subject of heat in the Presbitry of Edinburgh, and I belive somwhat has been said above on it. The Commission had appointed it to be setled by Mr Witherspoon as soon as might be, and to report. The Presbitry did not go on to setle; and the Synod of Louthian, which met in the beginning of this moneth, censured the Presbitry of Edinburgh for not obeying the Commission's appointment. When the matter came in before the Commission, ther wer some who ordinarly† wer upon the Commission's violent measures sau fit to change hands. Mr Smith, I think, deserted the Commission. Mr Alstoun and Lord Drummore had pretty keen speeches against the setlment, and represented the hazard our generall interests wer in from violenting the people in setlments; and that if we lost the people's inclinations, it would neither be our interest nor that of the goverment. This was a litle surprizing from that quarter! But, indeed, the case of the people is most clamant, as they say, in the W[est] Kirk. They have agreed on a fund for an independent Minister, of 150 lb. a year, and will setle him as soon as ever Mr Witherspoon is setled. Houever, the Commission caryed their point, and ordered Mr Witherspoon to be setled betwixt and the next Commission, and the Presbitry to report. It was moved that a Committy should be named to joyn them, and a day fixed; but that was fallen from. By any thing that appears as yet, the Presbitry will not go on to setle him. The screwing things thus so high, under pretext of preserving the authority of the Commission, will undoubtedly have very ill effects on this Church; and, if mercy prevent not, will rent us in peices!

They had before them the setlement of Kinross with Mr Stark. They keeped not the decency with the Presbitry of Dunfermline, whom they—some of them I mean—recon a rebelliouse Presbitry; and to them they appointed tutors and correspondents, with pouer to enter Mr Stark on tryalls, and setle him. These have since—I think in December—met. Not one of the Presbitry would meet with them, and they could have

---

* St Cuthbert's Church, Edinburgh.   † Usually supported.

no access to the Church ; it was locked and barricadoed against them. They met in a tavern, and began to take tryalls ; see Letters in December.

Mean while, in the end of this moneth, I think, the session of the Old Kirk, and common session,* fixed on Mr P. Cuming, in Lochmaben, for Mr Craiges successor, and collegue to Mr Nisbit. I do not hear ther wer any dispute about it ; and ther will, I suppose, be no difficulty in the matter. It is nou said that this matter will put an end to the long scufle about the West Kirk ; and that if Lord Isla's credite may be salved, and Mr Witherspoon once setled in the West Kirk, he has promised he shall be presently presented to Lochmaben, and transported thither. Thus, in our present unhappy partyes and struggles, and shamefull subjection to great men, Kirkes and Ministers a[re] couped† like horses, and bargains are made to please men and partys, in thir‡ matters, most shamefully. But I doubt much if this project hold, or be gone into ; at least, hitherto, Mr Smith and his party in the Presbitery of Edinburgh sheu no great dispositions that way.

Which brings me to the state of the College at Edinburgh. It seems matters could not be agreed, when [Lord] Isla was doun, who should be Professor when Mr Hamilton is Principall. The Magistrates and Toun, and most of the College, are for Mr Smith, but P[rofessor] Hamiltoun nou sets up pretty openly for Mr Goudie. The matter yet lyes over, and P[rofessor] Ham[ilton] teaches this year. But this matter people recon is at the bottome of the turn in the West Kirk. Mr Smith's side, nou, are turned sour upon Mr Witherspoon, and hagle,§ and are for delayes ; and they certainly can carry the Presbitry's vote as they will. And in choicing the Moderator of the Presbytery—Mr S. Sempill—they have probably balked Mr Goudie of being chosen a member from the Presbitry to the nixt General Assembly.

Towards the end of this moneth, Hugh Earl of Loudon dyed at his

---

* General Session of Edinburgh.   † Bartered, made traffic of.   ‡ These.   § Hesitate.

house of Loudon, pretty suddainly.   He was well and hearty at supper, and went to bed early ; but was suddainly taken with a shortnes of breath, and got up and cast on his night-goun, and dyed in a hour or therby.   See accounts of his offices and posts in the neuse papers.   He got the estate low.*   He has been alwise in some post since the Revolution almost, and yet I doubt his estate is not very much bettered.   He was a well-natured gentlman, favourable enough to our interest, and pleased very well in our Assemblys these severall years.   It's said he lost very much in the South-Sea ;† and that his pension at Court, which was considerable, and much of his one thousand pound for the Assembly, went very much to the Lord Isla, for the money he lent him to answer the South-Sea losses.   His son succeeds.   That family is low. He has but one son, and his brother only another ; and failing these three, it's scarce knouen wher the estate would go if tailzied to heirs-male.

Towards the end of this moneth, Mss [Mrs] Luke's affair with Sir James Stirling of Glorat came in before the Lords.   Sir James questions Mr Luke's setlement, and clames a third of Mr Luke's substance, though his lady gives in a reclaiming bill against him, and refuses to joyn in the prosecution.   Hou far pity to an old family, and to a man miserable enough by his oun choice in a wife, though fairly warned by her parents before marriage, which was irregular, will go in Sir James' favour, I knou not.   Had advice been taken, and Sir James been setled with before Mr Luke's death, two or three hundred guineas might probably have bought a receipt and discharge ; and nou twice that summ will not doe.   My Lord Dun, in the end of this moneth, or beginning of the next, gave a favourable opinion in the Outter-House for Mr Luke's setlment ; but hou that will take in the Inner, no body can well say. Partys in state, and litle emulations between the younger Lords and the elder, make matters in that Bench perfectly uncertain, and nobody can

* In value.   † The South-Sea bubble.

forcast the event and issue. This is a most dangerouse situation of things to the property and liberty, yea, lives of subjects!

The end of this moneth, dyed Mr Henry Hunter, my neighbour, Minister of Merns, of the gravell, at Glasgou. He came in to Glasgou, October 26, with his son, and was designed to be with us at the ordination, but not able. He was seized with the gravell, and languished under it for a moneth. He felt stones come over his hanch, and then no more pain, but constant vomiting and seiknes. He was a faithfull, freindly, usefull man. That parish wer never so happily setled. He was of a good temper, and dyed under comfort as to his soul, and easines as to his family, that God will take care of them, though they are but in lou circumstances. He expressed his fears to me of a young Ministry and corruptions, since the old way of preaching and dealing* was pretty much lost.

Mr Hutcheson hath been in Ireland this summer; and, in conversation, he gives me this hint of Irish matters: That the late Lord Carteret was not favourable to the Presbiterians in Ireland, but struck in, at least in the end of his goverment, with the Torrys and Highflyers there. That when Mr Craighead went over about the *Regium donum*, as has been notticed above, he had free access to Sir Robert Walpool, and fair promises, [that] if Carteret did not doe his bussines, he should; but decency required his† being applyed to. He did apply, and he wearyed him with delayes, and would never do any thing for him. When Dorset was named Lieutenant, this year, and the Instructions a-forming for him, great pains wer taken to get in one to take off the Sacramentall Test, which hes been so heavy to the Dissenters in Ireland, and, as we have seen, was the occasion of the vast run of many thousands to America two years ago. It was given out that he had this Instruction from the King. The Dissenters waited on him, and expected that they should have had a peculiar reception from him, as they would had he been to

---

* Dealing with scandalous persons.   † Lord Carteret's.

take away that burden ; but nothing passed but as usuall. The Archbishop of Armaugh, Primat, who is for removing the Test, and very
freindly, came to the Ministers, and told them he belived they wer disappointed, and so was he himself ; but he had nou seen the Lieutennant's
Instructions, and he was only empoured to take off the Test after the
King's bussines was over in parliament ; and that appeared to be a perfect uncertainty to him and them. Houever, this, at present, keeps
matters among Subs and Nons* quiet and at a hush.

Mr J. Hamiltoun tells me, that he had what folloues from the Dutches
of Hamiltoun's oun mouth—the old Dutches I mean, the heir to the
family ; and so, I think, it may be depended on :—He sayes, Bishop
Guthry's Memoires was published a litle before Clarendon's History,
first printed, 1710, at Oxford : That it was then generally belived that
the edition of Bishop Guthry was much altered from the Bishop's papers,
by the influence of the gentlmen of Oxford who had the publishing of
Clarendon in their hands : That when he was talking of this with the
Dutches, and the approaching edition of Clarendon, her Grace told him
that, when she was at Court, after the Restoration, when the Earl of
Clarendon was writting his History, he came and visited her, and told
her that he kneu her father very well, and took him to be one of the
honestest men of his acquaintance. He added, her father had been
abused and very ill used by the party writters, before and since his
death ; and that, nou he was writing a History of those times, he was
willing to do the Duke all the justice in his pouer, and desired her to
furnish him with any papers which might give light to his actings. Accordingly, when she came doun to Scotland, her Grace called for Dr
Burnet, and implored him to rummage all the papers in Hamiltoun that
related to her father, and to lay out what he reconed might be of use to
the Earle ; and she sent up, by an express, a large bundell of papers,
relative to her father, to England.

That next time she went to Court, a year or two after, the Earl of

* As subscribers and non-subscribers were then nicknamed.

Clarendon came and waited upon her at London, thanked her for the papers she had communicat to him, and returned them all safe : He told her he was nou perfectly satisfyed as to her father's character, and that he was as honnest a man as breathed, and would give it fully and fairly to the world, only ther remained one particular about which he was not yet so clear as he could wish. The Duke's enemies alledged that he brought over ten thousand stand of armes from Holland, and seemed to vouch it : They pretended further that he himself had a designe on the Croun, to accomplish which he got these armes. This, the Dutchess said, touched her very nearly, and she immediatly resolved to send a servant express to Hamiltoun, and ordered a neu search to be made at Hamiltoun, particularly for any thing that related to ten thousand stand of armes ; and very happily the servant brought her [the] originall Commission under the King's oun hand to bring so many stand of armes for his service ! This the Dutches immediatlie sent to the Earle. When he sau and read it, he came back with it to her Grace, and said, " Nou, Madam, I am satisfyed in every point ; and I belive and am assured your father was one of the best, sincerest, and honnestest persons of that time ; and I will give him, as is my duty, a just and fair character to the world."

This passed before Clarendon was published. Expectations wer great enough when the E[arl's] History was a printing. As soon as it came doun, the Dutches got it and read it. When Mr Hamiltoun sau her after she had got the printed Clarendon, he asked hou she liked it ? she answered, with some concern, I have read it, and I and my family am greatly abussed in it, and I apprehend this is the fruit of the Earle's MS. its lying twenty years in the hands of the gentlmen at Oxford ; and she verily belived that the Earle's originall History was grossly vitiated. This passed, my informer tells me, as far as he mind[s,] in the year 1710 ; and that the Dutches was right, is nou apparent to all.

This was, we see, the occasion and begining of Dr Burnet's writing the Memoires of the House of Hamiltoun ; and in that mater, since, I think, in the preface, or somwher, he mentions some papers, which, I remember, by the King's command, through the Duke of York's influence, he was discharged to publish. Ther is room for some impartiall hand, in better times, to glean many things in the Archives of Hamiltoun.

I am told, likewise, by Dougalstoun, who has seen the originall Letter from the M[arquis] of Montrose to the King, at Uxbridge Treaty, 1644, that the copy published by Dr Wellwood, in his Memoires, is a vitiated. copy, and does not, in severall things, agree with the originall in the hands of the Family of Montrose. I incline to enquire further, and to get the particulars, if I can.

December, 1731.—Ther is very litle offers this moneth, save what is in the publick prints and my Letters. My mother, my father's relict, fell suddenly ill of a bleeding at the nose, and bled a great deal for four or five dayes; and it could not be stopped by bandages, or any other way. She is nou seventy-five or [7]4; and, I doubt not, but she bled more then two Scots pints, yet was easy and without pain. It stopped naturally, and she seems recovering, which is a very rare instance. This bleeding uses to be mortall to old people.

On this occasion, [Mrs] Zuil told me a pleasant story of her mother, relict of Mr Antony Shaw, a woman of great piety, and much skill in physick, and long experience. She was in her house, I think, and a good age—seventy or more—and, one morning, she sent one of the bairns for my informer, to come and speak to her. She came to the room, and she gave her out of her hand a napkin-full of clotted blood; and when she sau it, she said, " Mother, what is that ?" " Margaret," said she, " be not surprized; it's the foreruner of death! I have, this [h]our past, been bleeding at the nose. My father dyed of it; Mr Shau dyed of it; and I knou it will be death to me, and I am ready for it! I have no pain nor sicknes!" After some other things, she said, " Margaret, is this a proper room for me to dye in ? or will it not be better in the for-room ?"* She ouned it would. " Well," sayes shee,

* Fore or front room.

" cause make it ready, and make the bed, and I will go thither while I
am able !" This was done, and she went to it, and cast off her cloaths,
and lay doun with much pleasure.   " Nou," said she, " Margaret, this
is the pleasantest bed I ever lay in ! I knou my espousalls with Christ
will be here compleated !" And so it was.   After three or four dayes
moderat bleeding, she got to her rest.

[*December* 24 ?]—In the end of this moneth, my brother, Mr Warner, having been about a bussines of mine, coming home, near [his
house,] his horse fell, all his feet going from him, and he bruised his
breast much.   The Lord support and spare him ; his loss will be great
to many !

December 25.—On the twenty-fifth, just the day after, my daughter,
Martha, came through a very long crisis of a feaver ; and was speechles
and without senses, as far as we could knou, for near ten hours.

This moneth, Bailay Peacock, youngest Bailay, dyed of a high feaver
at Glasgou, much regrated.   He was a sober man, and no drinker ; but
was oblidged to treat the Trades, and with them, it's said, he was the
worse of drinking with them.   O ! that people would take warning !

Mr Andreu Tait tells me, (perhaps it's already set doun,) that, about
the [16]78, or, may be, afterwards, ther was a design laid, and a particular night fixed, by John Nisbit of Hardhill, who was said to [be] the
principal promotter of it, and other violent Cameronians, as they wer
called, to attack all the Indulged Ministers in the shire of Air their
houses, and to murder them.   That one privy to it revealed it to the
Earl of Loudon, the last Earle Hugh['s] father, a very litle before it
was to be execute ; and the Earl immediately wrote letters to them, and
sent expresses with them, requiring them to come to his house at Loudon, wher they should be safe that night ; and that, accordingly, eight
or nine of them came, among whom Mr Heu Campbell of Muirkirk was
one, who told the informer.   This information seems to be very indu-
bitable ; and yet it's strange that, these forty years, I have met with no
hint of this but this one.   One would not wish to belive such a horrid

thing in people who have the name of Christians! I knou sad lenths
wer run to by some at this time, and the coal was blouen by Papists in
disguise ; but one would willingly belive that this may have been a false
alarum, really given to the good Earle, by one who was ane enemie to
the sufferers, with a designe to leave a blott upon them. Houever, I
have set [it] doun as I have it.

END OF VOLUME SIXTH OF MS.

INDEX.

GENERAL INDEX

TO

WODROW'S ANALECTA.

A.

ABBADIE, his knowledge of Scripture prophecies, ii. 239.

Aberdeen, Lord Chancellor; his attempt to ensnare the gentry of the western shires, ii. 365.

    Earl of, iii. 290; loses the representation in 1727, id. 439.

    town of, arming of Jacobites at, in 1714, ii. 276; applies for Mr Chalmers as Professor of Divinity, iii. 485; low salaries of the Professors at Marischal College, id.

Abernethy, Mr, Presbyterian Minister at Antrim, iii. 468; Mr John, iv. 162.

Adair, Mr, Minister at Ayr; his history, by Mr Stirling, iii. 72.

    Mr Patrick, his conversation with Mr Durham on his death-bed, iii. 297.

    Sir Robert, his character, iii. 195.

Adam, Mr, Minister at Howby; refuses to subscribe the Confession of Faith, ii. 256.

Adamson, Mr, a probationer of the Church; his irregular ties, ii. 242; further account of, 263, 295; excommunicated, 377.

Adamson, Bishop; his parentage; the son of Adam Constance, a baker in Perth; is educated for the ministry; travels with the son of Sir James M'Gill; on his return, changes his name, and studies law; returns to the Church, and is promoted by the Regent Morton, iii. 298.

Addison, Mr, coldness between him and Steele; his papers in the Spectator and Tatler; his tragedy of Cato, ii. 213.

Addresses; on the oath of abjuration, and the principles of Presbyterian government, ii. 55; to the Queen, in 1712, from the burghs and shires, 78; from the Lords of Session to the King, on the state of Scotland, in 1727, iii. 404; from the College of Glasgow, 405; numerous from Scotland, on the accession of George II., 439.

Advocate, the; his remarks on Ministers' sons, ii. 51.

Agriculture, remarks on, ii. 368.

Aikman, Mrs, her account of Jerviswood's unburied limbs, ii. 337.

to whom the devil appeared personally, supplying him with a sermon to be preached before the Presbytery, for which he gave a bond signed with blood, 102; anecdote of, by his son, 136; his advice to Messrs Warner and Welsh, ii. 58; his rebuke of the drunkard at St Andrews, 65; reproof of the people for leaving the Church before the blessing was pronounced, 66; reproof of the Earl of Strafford for swearing, *id.*; story of, and the Prince of Orange, 136, 146, *id.*, 331, 363; his peculiar talent, iii. 4; Mr Stirling's history of, 91; his Commentary on the Proverbs, in the possession of his grand-daughter, 484.

Blair, Patrick, a Scotch student of medicine at *Leyden*, who instituted an Atheistical club there, iii. 432.

Mr William, Regent at Glasgow, his death, i. 271.

Blantyre, Lord, i. 15.

Bochell, an Irish Teague, who commanded the troops at Glasgow during Shawfield's mob, and shot the people, iii. 212; his barbarities towards the prisoners, 217; process against, 244, 257; procures letters of remission from the Crown, 260.

Boerhaave, Dr, iii. 433.

Bogle, Baily, of Glasgow, iii. 334, 448.

Bolingbroke, Lord, difference between and Halifax, ii. 109; proposes to bring over the Duke of Brunswick, 281, iii. 232.

Bonnar, Mr James, foretells the deaths of King Charles and King James, ii. 341; account of his birth, death, and resurrection, iii. 135; anecdote of, 150.

Book, Service, the reading of, in the New Kirk at Edinburgh in 1637, interrupted by lads in female attire, i. 64.

Books of the Non-subscribers seized *in transitu*, iii. 184; scarcity of new, in England in 1728, 489; obscene, printed at London and sold in Edinburgh, 515.

Borrowstounness, town of, suffers by the capture of the fleet going to Holland, i. 218.

Boston, Mr, one of the Marrow Brethren, iv. 126.

Bounty, King's, for preachers and catechists in the Highlands, iii. 288.

Royal, how distributed in Ireland, iii. 468; how managed, iv. 57; origin of, 233.

VOL. IV.

Bourbon, Duke of, succeeds the Duke of Orleans as Regent of France in 1723, ii. 388.

Bourignon, Madame, educated at a Jesuit's school, ii. 349; some account of, iii. 472.

Bowes, Mr James, minister at Lochend in Kintyre, i. 20; his account of certain noises and appearances in 1711, ii. 43.

Bowie, Mr, minister at Dolphington, iii. 236.

Boyd, Mr Zachary, his death, i. 167.

William, detects his wife in the act of adultery, ii. 358.

Boyle, John, of Kelburn, plot of the Government against, ii. 365.

Mr, his account of Cujacius' Works, i. 7.

Miss, sees an apparition of her brother; the consequences of, i. 126.

Honourable Robert, appears to his sister after death, i. 126.

Sir Robert, proposes questions to the apparition, i. 126.

Bradbury, Mr, a Dissenting minister of London, taken before the privy council for a sermon reflecting on the Treasurer, ii. 109; hissed at Salters' Hall, 333; his anecdote respecting the Princess of Wales and Dr Waterland, iii. 459-516.

Bradenburgh, Elector of, his piety, his engagement with the Swedes, i. 50; anecdote of, on hearing of the revocation of the Edict of Nantes, ii. 48.

Brand, Mr, of Borrowstounness; his anecdote of Mr John Welsh, iv. 17.

Mrs, iii. 379.

Brandon, Duke of, ii. 1; opposition to his sitting as an English Peer, iii. 292.

Brandt, Mr, character of his History, ii. 334.

Breadalbane, Earl of, tampers with the Governor of Edinburgh Castle, ii. 245.

Breda, conduct of the Scotch Commissioners at, in 1649, ii. 313.

Brethren, clean and unclean, ii. 106, 107; seven, banished, iii. 19, *note*; the Marrow, iv. 126; division among, 135.

Brett, Dr, turns Papist, ii. 300.

Brisbane, Dr, Professor of Anatomy and Botany at Glasgow; not bound by his patent to teach, iii. 332, 429, iv. 2.

Mr Matthew, minister at Erskine, ii. 125; deposed, iii. 22.

Broady, Mr D., minister at Dalserff, his death, iv. 82.

2 R

C.

D.

F.

G.

I.

ginning of the eighteenth century, iv. 64, 137.

Invasion, alarm of, from France, i. 212, 220, 278, 306, 321; threatened by Spain in 1718, ii. 332; the country defenceless, and torn by party divisions, 333.

Ireland, Mr Bruce's prophecy respecting, ii. 60; humours in, about the copper money, iii. 164.

Isla, Earl of, his answer to the English "Tory Duke," i. 262; his pique at Marlborough, 293; his appearance in Scotland in 1713; alleged cause of, ii. 208; his bill for the regulation of the Court of Session, iii. 144; visit to Scotland in 1725, 226, 261, 316, 318, 329; desires to be made Secretary for Scotland; reasons for and against such an appointment,

273; heads the royal visitation of the College of Glasgow, in 1726, 329; his object in visiting Glasgow on that occasion, 333; President and Deputy-Governor of the Royal Bank, 426, 429; his activity at the general election of 1727, 436; anecdote of, 439, 441; recommends moderation in Mr Drummond's case, 444, 485; his great intimacy with Sir Robert Walpole, 489; little intimacy between him and his brother; his great influence at Court, iv. 69; promises his assistance to the magistrates of Glasgow, 75; his influence in Edinburgh, 76; rumour of an intended bill by, on patronage, 205, 260; resolves to determine between parties in the case of the West Kirk of Edinburgh, 278.

J.

Jack, Mr, minister at Carluke; his remarkable success in his parish, ii. 374.

Jacobites, i. 1; strength of their party in England, 257; "very uppish," in 1710, 286; many among Harley's associates, 293; reflections on, 304; Parliamentary, mostly from Scotland, 311; oppose Harley in the October Club, 319, ii. 126; excited, after the accession of King George, and calculate on foreign diversions in their favour, 295; spread of Jacobitism during the last four years of Queen Anne's reign, 300; treatment of the ministers of the North by, in 1715, 302; their growing influence in 1724, iii. 145; impugn the accuracy of the author's History, 146; very busy in spreading disaffection, 153; their opinion of the Advocate's severities in 1725, 226; their condition in France and Holland, 231; Lord Sinclair and Lord George Murray, 232; danger of too extensive pardons to, id.; their hopes from the Emperor and the King of Spain, 340; their intrigues in 1727, 373; some promoted and others pardoned, 374; their allegation against the Duke of Argyle, 375; dissatisfied with the Pretender, 410; many of the Jacobite

Peers did not vote at the election of 1727, 441; adopt the English Service, and pray for King George, iv. 19; consequences of, 20.

Jamieson, Mr Alexander, his election to a regency at St Andrews, i. 140; subsequently minister at Govan; history of, by Mr Stirling, iii. 75.

Mr George, his adultery, i. 302.

Matthew, his account of his mother-in-law, ii. 319.

Mr William, his conversation with Mr Simson in 1728, iv. 11.

Mr William, his death at Glasgow in 1720, ii. 342.

Mr, i. 4.

Jedburgh, Lord, his conversion, i. 11; anecdote of, 23.

Jekyll, Sir Joseph, iii. 208, 234, 260.

Jervey, Mr, Scotch Minister at Campvere, in Holland, iv. 264.

Jerviswood, Laird of, i. 122.

Jesuits, their manner of preaching in France, iii. 267.

Johnston, Dr, Professor of Medicine in the College of Glasgow, iii. 333.

John, an eminent Christian in Paisley, i. 326.

VOL. IV.

L.

N.

O.

VOL. IV.

2 Y

Duncan Forbes, *id.* ; of Mr Patrick Colvin, 126; of Mr William Maitland, *id.* ; of Mr Robert Fleming, *id.* ; of Mr James Naismith, 127; of Mr John English, *id.* ; of Mr William Hamilton, 128; of Mr David Brown, *id.* ; of Mr David Brown of Neilston, 128.

Stirling, Mr James, minister at Paisley; his history by his nephew, iii. 23; wrote the Ecclesiastical Part of Naphthali, *id.* ; died at Bombay in 1671, 24.

Mr James, intercedes with the Presbytery in behalf of his son-in-law, Mr Simson, iv. 20.

Mr John, minister at Kilbarchan, life of by his son, iii. 24; his success as a preacher not immediate, 29; five adulteries in his parish, *id.* ; preached in the heat of harvest, 30; was against popular insurrections, 34; letter of his brother James from India to, 36; his death in 1683, *id.* ; accident to the candles on the day of his burial, 37; noises in the kirk of, on the day that the battle of Bothwell Brig was fought, *id.*

Principal, his anecdote of Mr Robert Blair, i. 84; his communications to the author about the Prince of Orange, iii. 146; states, on the authority of Dr Calamy, that Queen Anne died a Papist, 147; his interview with the Earl of Oxford in 1708, 291; his proposed demission, 332, 429; his death and character, 444; his legacies, 446; recommended the author to write a history of the Church, 447.

Sir James, of Glorat, iii. 524.

town of, third minister proposed for, iv. 198; heats in, respecting, 226.

Walter, Bailie of Glasgow, iii. 448.

Mr William, Baron Bailie of Glasgow, striking circumstances attending his death, ii. 247.

William Alexander, first Earl of, an outline of his history, iii. 298; the Order of Nova Scotia Baronets created in his favour, 310.

St John, Mr Secretary, " one of the lewdest men in England," ii. 67.

Stormont, Lord, issues a presentation to St Martin's in favour of Mr Smith, ii. 69.

Strachan, Colonel, his character, ii. 86; offered the command of the forces in Scotland by Cromwell, but refused it, *id.*

Strang, Dr, his character, i. 260; descended from the House of Balcaskie in Fife, iii. 298.

Strichen, Laird of, made Commissary of Edinburgh, iv. 104.

Succession, Protestant, i. 286.

Succoth, Laird of, iv. 204.

Sumers, Mr Alexander, i. 20.

Sunderland, Earl of, his influence, Secretary to King James, whom he betrayed, i. 17; uses disrespectful language to the Queen, 285; his resignation, 286; refuses a pension, *id.* ; suspected of Jacobitism, iii. 229; strange accusation against, by Lord Ross, 443.

Suspensions threatened against the stipends of the Non-jurant ministers, ii. 257.

Sutherland, Earl of, eminent for his religious zeal, iii. 316.

Sutherlandshire, no charge made for the entertainment of strangers attending communions in, iv. 4.

Sweden, King of, defeated by the Muscovites, i. 209; his death, and its effects on the Reformed interest, ii. 332.

Synod of Glasgow and Ayr, of October, 1710, meets at Irvine; Mr Paisley's case decided; the author requested by, to collect papers anent the late sufferings, i. 303.

of April, 1711, the question of patronage discussed in; petitions against, i. 323.

of October, 1711, i. 353.

of April, 1712, meets at Ayr; prelacy, ceremonies, patronage, toleration, and the oath of abjuration, considered, ii. 133.

of June, 1712, text and sermon on the occasion; the origin of the ministerial power stated; conference about the oath; arguments *pro* and *con* ; appoints a letter of thanks to be written to the Earl of Loudon for his conduct in the matter of toleration and patronage, ii. 56; enjoins a Synodical Fast, which is broken through by the Justices of the Peace, and the Synod's order burnt by the hands of the hangman, 74.

of April, 1713, ii. 188.

of October, 1713, Mr Linning's affair discussed, ii. 251.

of April, 1724, thinly attended, and little done at; Mr Fork's case remitted to the Presbytery, iii. 149.

of October, 1724, collects L.26 for the re-

T.

W.

Y.

Z.

EDINBURGH PRINTING COMPANY, 12, SOUTH ST DAVID STREET.

LaVergne, TN USA
03 November 2009

162830LV00001B/15/A

9 781436 776714